PENGUIN

THE ELECTRON

Dan Jacobson was born in Johannesburg and grew up in Kimberley, South Africa. He is the author of several novels, among them *The Rape of Tamar* and *The God-Fearer*; he also writes short stories, essays and poetry. His work has received many prizes, including the W. Somerset Maugham and J. R. Ackerley awards. He is Professor of English at University College London.

DAN JACOBSON

THE ELECTRONIC ELEPHANT

A SOUTHERN AFRICAN JOURNEY

PENGUIN BOOKS

PENGUIN BOOKS

Published by the Penguin Group
Penguin Books Ltd, 27 Wrights Lane, London W8 5TZ, England
Penguin Books USA Inc., 375 Hudson Street, New York, New York 10014, USA
Penguin Books Australia Ltd, Ringwood, Victoria, Australia
Penguin Books Canada Ltd, 10 Alcorn Avenue, Toronto, Ontario, Canada M4V
3B2
Penguin Books (NZ) Ltd, 182–190 Wairau Road, Auckland 10, New Zealand

Penguin Books Ltd, Registered Offices: Harmondsworth, Middlesex, England

First published by Hamish Hamilton 1994
Published with minor revisions in Penguin Books 1995
1 3 5 7 9 10 8 6 4 2

Printed in England by Clays Ltd, St Ives plc

Contents

PART TWO BOTSWANA

PART THREE ZIMBABWE

Note

☆

The names of places and regions mentioned in this book have undergone many changes over the last two hundred years. In using the different forms of these names I have aimed throughout to be comprehensible rather than historically consistent. Readers should also note that when I speak of 'southern Africa' I mean the entire subcontinent; 'South Africa', on the other hand, refers to the Republic of South Africa, within its internationally recognized borders.

Quotations from the archives of the London Missionary Society are printed with acknowledgements to the Council for World Missions. Acknowledgements are due too to I. Schapera and Chatto & Windus Ltd for quotations from his editions of David Livingstone's letters and journals. Other sources are acknowledged either on the relevant pages of the narrative or in 'Additional References' at the end.

D.J.

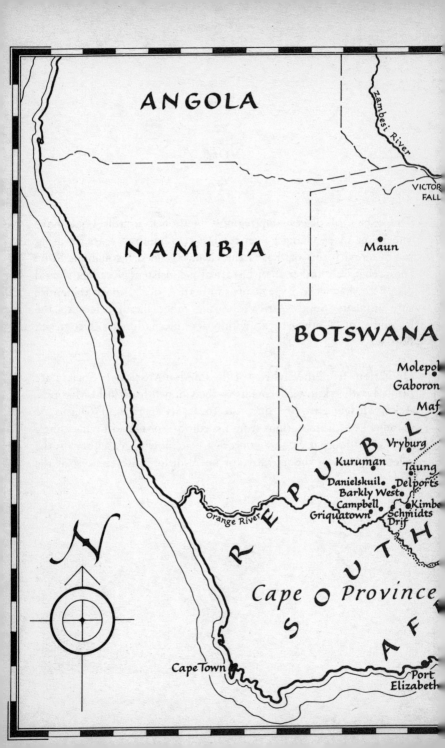

ZAMBIA

ZIMBABWE

ivingstone   Harare

Inyati   •Serima
Bulawayo   Masvingo
     ♠ GREAT ZIMBABWE
•Matopos   •Zvishavani

Francistown

erowe
• Palapye

hoshong

MOZAMBIQUE

Transvaal

C   O   F

Johannesburg

Vaal River

Orange
Free
State   *Natal*

LESOTHO

CA

Limpopo River

• Maputo

SWAZILAND

• Durban

*Southern
Africa*

S · C · A · L · E

0   100   200   300
MILES

Introduction

☆

This book gives an account of my travels along a particular route through parts of southern Africa. The route was known during the nineteenth and early twentieth centuries by a variety of names. It was called the missionary road, the hunters' trail, the traders' road, the road to the north, the great north road, the 'neck of the bottle', and, perhaps most grandiosely of all, the 'Suez Canal of the South'.

Skirting for much of its length the north-western border of the Republic of South Africa, it ran through some of the northern regions of Cape Province and of the 'Republic of Bophuthatswana' (given a nominal form of independence in 1977, which disintegrated shortly before South Africa's first all-race elections in 1994). Then it traversed the length of Botswana and the west-central region of Zimbabwe. The most vociferous projectors of the route declared that it would eventually stretch all the way to Cairo, at the far end of the continent, by which time a single British colony or dominion would straddle the whole of Africa – an ambition never achieved.

For the most part the road passes through some of the driest, most thinly populated, and, in the eyes of almost all who have travelled along any part of it, scenically least attractive regions of the subcontinent. What then is its interest or allure?

To that question my answers have to be partly personal in nature, partly historical.

First, let me deal briefly with some of the historical circumstances which for a century and more gave a peculiar importance to the route I have just traced.

From time immemorial the area it passes through had been inhabited by small groups of hunter-gatherer San (Bushmen) and

equally nomadic sheep- and cattle-herding Khoi (Hottentots). About
a thousand years ago communities of semi-settled Tswana began to
penetrate it from the north. The Tswana were crop-growers as well
as cattle-tenders and metal-smelters; like their predecessors, they
also hunted the game which then abounded in both the bush and
the open veld. The Tswana lived to some extent by trade too: they
dealt with the peoples around them in ivory, cosmetic minerals,
and metal goods.

Penetration from the south began at the Cape, where the first
Dutch settlers had appeared in the middle of the seventeenth
century. Their descendants, known initially as 'free burghers', then
as Boers, and eventually as Afrikaners, fought, subdued, and made
servants of the Khoi they encountered; they also imported slaves
from other Dutch colonial possessions in the East Indies. Sexual
unions between masters and servants duly followed. The offspring
of such contacts remained for the most part in the orbit of white
settlement. Some, however, moved away in small groups from the
colonized areas. Accompanied by white fugitives of various kinds
(deserting sailors and soldiers, criminals, Boers who had lost caste
by entering into permanent unions with dark-skinned women),
these groups associated with the bands of San and Khoi who had
always lived beyond the authority of the Dutch. The result was that
by the middle of the eighteenth century many bands of nomadic
cattle-tenders and shepherds were to be found moving east and
west along the line of the Orange River, well to the north of what
was then the official border of the colony. Their mixed origins
were reflected in the appellations – or epithets – indiscriminately
bestowed on them: 'Griquas', 'Basters' (Bastards), 'Korannas', 'Hottentots', 'Bushmen', 'Coloureds', 'Half-castes'. An appreciable
number of them had Dutch surnames, carried guns, and rode on
horseback.

To these peoples, as to the Tswana further north, the territory I
shall be writing about was never a 'road', never a mere passageway
from one place to another. It was the ground they lived on. The
whites, however, who began to encroach on it from the beginning
of the nineteenth century, were inclined to see it chiefly as the most

direct way of getting from the coast to the unmapped regions further north. That was why missionaries who were to become as famous as Robert Moffat and David Livingstone, as well as others much less well known, took themselves and their wives and their Bibles in that direction. In doing so they were moving away not just from the long-settled regions around the Cape peninsula but also from the eastern frontier, where parties of pastoralist Boers, as well as small contingents of British settlers, were already at war against Xhosa-speaking blacks.

The British took possession of the Cape in 1795, during the Napoleonic Wars: the very year, as it happened, in which the London Missionary Society was founded. Two years later the Society began its work in South Africa; after a further four years the first of the Society's missionaries crossed the Orange River, thus going well beyond the then borders of the Cape Colony. They were not the only whites who chose to strike due north from the Cape at about this time. The route pioneered by the missionaries soon came to be known also as the traders' and the hunters' trail, even as the ivory trail. Many of the early traders and hunters were white and English-speaking; but there were also Boers among them, as well as larger numbers of people of mixed race (Coloureds). All brought guns, wagons, ready-made clothing, axes, Sheffield knives, gold coins, Cape brandy and the like. In exchange they wanted to get their hands on ivory, above all; but they also traded in pelts, ostrich feathers, antlers, grain, and cattle on the hoof.

Inevitably, the distinction between 'hunter' and 'trader', and indeed the distinction between 'missionary' and the two other terms, was often hard for native and newcomer alike to discern or to maintain. Some of the missionaries accused each other of being more interested in trading than in spreading the gospel; what the traders were looking for was in large part the product of the hunters' activities. The effect of all this was that the Tswana, in particular, found themselves confronted not only with the lure of material goods new to them, but also with sophisticated forms of competition for resources on which they themselves had always depended.

Competition for the land itself followed. During the 1830s, the

Boers on the eastern frontier, resentful of British rule, and confronted by the power of the Xhosa-speaking peoples, turned away from the coast and began to move northwards into the central plateau of present-day South Africa. This movement, known to history as the Great Trek, was eventually to result in the establishment of Boer republics in the Orange Free State and the Transvaal. It also helped to produce an ever-widening turmoil among the various black peoples of the subcontinent. The area occupied by the Griquas and by the Tswana (the latter being much the larger and more widely dispersed group) thus began to acquire a different kind of importance from any it had before. It came to be seen, by the whites at least, as a vital strategic asset. This was not because they believed it to be especially valuable in itself (though they appreciated its potential as grazing land), or because either Boers or British felt especially menaced by the relatively unwarlike peoples living there, but because of its *position*.

On the one side of it lay the virtually uninhabitable Kalahari Desert; on the other, the regions which were coming, or had already come, into the possession of the Boers. As they had done on the eastern frontier, the Boers kept trying to expand the territory they controlled; if it helped them do so they were ready to proclaim themselves masters of *ad hoc*, brand-new republics, like 'Stellaland' and 'The Land of Goshen', both of which lay directly across the route which the missionaries and hunters had developed. In order to outflank the Boers, in their turn, politically ambitious British colonists in the Cape (sometimes with the support of the Colonial Office in London, often without it) were determined to keep the route open. Only in this way, they believed, could they maintain some degree of control over the freebooting trekkers and retain access to the uncolonized and 'unpacified' regions lying still further to the north.

With the discovery in 1871 of diamonds in Kimberley, and of gold on the Witwatersrand fifteen years later, the stakes were raised immeasurably for all involved. What was now at issue in southern Africa was not just so many immense tracts of marginally valuable hunting and pasture land, inhabited by a tiny number of whites and by much larger numbers of stubbornly resistant blacks (at war with one another, often enough). The argument now was about wealth greater even than that generated (for some) by what had hitherto been Africa's other greatest item of export: namely, the slaves that had been shipped for centuries to the Americas and the Arabian peninsula. And who could tell how many as-yet-undiscovered Kimberleys or Johannesburgs might not lie further to the north, at the end of the road that ran through places like Kuruman and Mafikeng and Shoshong?

In 1884 Bismarck's Germany claimed sovereignty over what is now Namibia, on the Atlantic coast. Rivalries which would all but destroy Europe in the course of the next century were thus transferred to the foot of the African continent. To British eyes, certainly to the eyes of the British who lived in the Cape Colony, the only 'open' road directly northwards now appeared to be threatened not just by the Boers from the east but also by the Germans from the west, or (most menacingly of all) by Boers and Germans acting in concert. And then there were the Portuguese in Angola and Mozambique to take into account as well. By this time, too, some of the leaders of the Tswana, who were desperately trying to sustain themselves against the pressures of British colonists, Boer pastoralists, and their more powerful black neighbours, were issuing appeals to the imperial authorities in London to come to their assistance. If they judged direct rule from London to be the least of the evils confronting them (the alternatives being rule by the Cape Colonial government, or by the Boers, or by the fierce Ndebele, an offshoot of the Zulu people who had settled on their northern and eastern flanks), this was in part due to the impression made on them by the missionaries of the London Missionary Society.

The missionaries' harvest of souls may have been meagre indeed – after ten years in Kuruman Moffat could boast of about just the same number of converts, *in toto* – but the protection they tried to offer to the people they lived among had nevertheless won for them a degree of trust given to none of the other interlopers in the area.

*

The future must always remain the darkest continent of all. Not the harshest, poorest, most disease-stricken territory is as impenetrable and difficult to understand as the times that are still to come.

Ahead of every one of the parties contesting control of the road to the north – Boers, blacks, Britons, Griquas, Germans, missionaries, miners, concession-seekers, traders – lay vicissitudes as unimaginable to them as the history of the twenty-first century is opaque to us. Among these events were: the seizure by Cecil John Rhodes and his British South African Company of the territories which for about eighty years went by the names of Southern and Northern Rhodesia (now Zimbabwe and Zambia); the war between Boers and British at the turn of the century, which was to end with the humiliation and apparent destruction of the Boer nation; the subsequent formation of the Union of South Africa from two British colonies (Cape Province and Natal) and two former Boer republics (Transvaal and Orange Free State); the First World War and the Second, both of which were marked by extensive military call-ups and campaigns in various parts of Africa; the political triumph at the end of the Second World War of the Afrikaner Nationalists of South Africa, successors to the Boers, and the introduction by them of their grandiose *apartheid* policies, which were intended to ensure their own hegemony for nothing short of forever; the abandonment by the European powers of the colonies which they had once competed for so eagerly – the German possessions being the first to be wiped off the map, the Portuguese the last; the development of industry and of mining (not just for gold and diamonds, but platinum, uranium, coal, iron, manganese, and many other minerals) which was to transform the economy and society of the entire region; the steady growth in numbers and skills of its black population, and their ever-increasing impatience with white rule; the establishment of independent black states all over the continent and the bloody wars that in many cases both preceded and followed their birth; the attempt by the Soviet Union to export its Communist ideology and its arms to many of these states, and the eager adoption by them of policies (like the collectivization of land) which had brought ruin to the relatively developed economies of Central and Eastern Europe, and then did exactly the same to poverty-stricken, debt-burdened, undeveloped tracts of Africa; the sudden, irrevocable abandonment by Moscow of the 'allies' it had so painfully acquired and the concurrent retreat by the Afrikaner Nationalists from their dreams of perpetual and exclusive white supremacy, along with the brutal pieces of social engineering with which they had tried to secure that end.

All that, now behind us, then lay hidden, unbidden, unthought-of.

So much, however sketchily, for some of the historical facts and forces which accounted for the political and strategic significance which the Great North Road was once believed to have.

As for the personal or autobiographical sources of my interest in the subject . . . Well, I have to begin (and perhaps end too) with the fact that I grew up in Kimberley: a town which came into existence only because of the discovery of diamonds in the neighbourhood, and which, within a few months of the first diamond 'rush', had become the second largest centre of population in the country. The missionary road, which had originally run well to the west of the diamond fields, was as a result irrevocably diverted from the course it had previously taken. Kimberley itself became the jumping-off place and source of supply, and eventually the railhead, for almost all movement from the south towards Bechuanaland (now Botswana), Southern and Northern Rhodesia, and the Congo (now Zaire). No less significantly, it became the testing-ground for the migratory labour system which was to dominate southern African economic and social life up to the present day.

Kimberley's pre-eminence, such as it was, did not last long. When gold was discovered on the Witwatersrand in 1886, Johannesburg at once became, as it has remained, the industrial heartland of the entire subcontinent. In the 1920s the diamond trade slumped and Kimberley was left to become something like a ghost-town. That, pretty much, was still its condition when my parents arrived there in 1933. It was only with the outbreak of the Second World

War in 1939 that the city began a process of slow recovery and renewed growth.

In an autobiographical volume, *Time and Time Again*, which was published some years ago, I tried to describe the effect that the appearance of Kimberley, and of the countryside around it, had on me as a child:

The contrast between the feverishness of the past and the lassitude of the present; between the self-assertion of some of the town's buildings and imperial monuments and the vacancy of the earth and sky around them; between the energy and greed which had dug the open holes of the mines and the air of complete uselessness and abandonment they had when I first saw them; between supposed wealth and evident forlornness; between fame and drabness – all these made a profound impression on me as a child. It was impossible to avoid developing a sense of the tenuousness of the human settlement around me, of its dislocation, of the fortuitousness of its birth, early growth, sudden decline.

After my father had bought a cattle ranch about thirty miles out of town, we went there at weekends and swam or fished in the river and clambered about the rocks of its precipitous banks. The only voices we heard were our own. Over intensities of light, odours of heat and drought, glittering horizons, black shadows, the stinging shriek of cicadas, thorn trees caught for ever in gestures of alarm, rose a sky higher and wider than any I have seen since, where giant, theatrical cloudscapes were constantly assembling and dispersing. To this day the first image or form which I would give to the idea of eternity is that of the northern Cape veld: especially perhaps at dawn, when the sun has still to rise and the prostrate earth, already paler than the sky above it, reveals once again how motionless and untenanted are all its spaces . . .

From an early age it was thus clear to me that Kimberley was provincial, done for, on the margins both geographically and histori-cally. If it was remote from what seemed to us sophisticated and go-ahead cities like Johannesburg and Cape Town and Durban, where we went for our holidays, it was incomparably further still from Europe, the mysterious and dangerous continent out of which had come not just our coinage and street-names and many of our teachers, but the language I spoke and the books I read; not to speak of the parents who had engendered me. Yet it was apparent, too, that this forlorn town did have an intense history of its own, the signs of which were visible on its surface and below it. What is more, its history was inextricable from that of its great, semi-desert hinterland lying to the north and west.

All else aside, Kimberley was the city which had seen the beginning, the middle, and in effect the end of the career of Cecil John Rhodes (1853–1902). Founder and chairman of De Beers Consolidated Mines, arch-imperialist and sometime Prime Minister of the Cape Colony, Rhodes had become obsessed at an early stage with the importance of controlling the road to the north. Kimberley's demand for labour and fuel through the northern corridor may have been the germ of his obsession; but it did not end there. None of his obsessions ended anywhere. He was the most passionate of the advocates of a single British dominion stretching all the way to Cairo. He was obsessed by the idea of establishing a 'secret society' which would bring about the domination of the world by 'the Anglo-Saxon race'. 'I contend,' he wrote, 'that we are the finest race in the world and that the more of the world we inhabit the better it is.' 'I would annex the stars if I could,' he also said; since the stars were not available, he did the next best thing by monopolizing the diamond industry, by trying to destroy the Boer republics of the Transvaal and Orange Free State, and by duly conquering and annexing (always on behalf of the British crown, but always on his own terms) the territories farther north which were eventually named after him. In effect, 'his own terms' meant that London should support everything he did; but that he, the man on the spot, should never be trammelled by any opinion or demand emanating from London.

This was the 'immense and brooding spirit', as Rudyard Kipling described him, who still dominated the civic ethos of the town during my childhood. To grow up in Kimberley half a century ago was to see his portrait everywhere. It looked down from the walls of the public library; it looked up from the pages of history textbooks; it hung twenty feet high above an equestrian statue in the Victoria Crescent, a focal point of the town's traffic; it glowered at us among the pictures of forgotten cricket teams and visiting royalty outside the headmaster's office at school; every memoir of 'the good old days' included a picture of the writer lounging with Rhodes under a thorn tree or sitting next to him in a leather chair, at a shining table, under a four-bladed fan. True-blue, jingoistic, English-speaking Kimberley (as it was in those days, for the whites) had almost the air of having been his invention. All its mines and mine dumps, its headgear, its barbed wire, its tramways, even its power station and its sports facilities, belonged then to the De Beers Corporation, which in turn had belonged to Rhodes; sometimes the same seemed to be true even of the heat, the sand, the tin-roofed houses. The convent school, three blocks away from my family home, had been the hotel in which he had lived when the city had been besieged by the Boers during the Anglo-Boer War (1899–1902). A doctor's surgery opposite the polished verandahs and whitewashed, colonial arches of the Kimberley Club had once been his house. The Club itself had been something more than a home-from-home for this woman-hating bachelor. On my way to and from one of the town's few swimming-baths (all then owned by the Corporation) I could peep into what had been his private office, near the original De Beers mine. There too, above stiff-looking pieces of wood and leather furniture, hung yet another elaborately framed portrait of the great man. Down-turned moustache above a small, pouting mouth, also down-turned; penetrating, pale-looking eyes and weary cheeks; something brutal, neurotic, and calculating in the gaze; neatly arranged hair, almost finicking in its oiled exactitude, which did nothing to diminish the overall effect of size, authority, and great age.

He died in fact before his fiftieth birthday. He had been an entrepreneur at eighteen and a millionaire in his early twenties, Prime Minister of the Cape Colony in his thirties. He was the one who spoke of the missionary road as 'the neck of the bottle' and 'the Suez Canal of the South' (to be followed in this by sycophantic newspaper editorialists and parliamentarians both in the Cape and back 'home' in London); the man who, at his own expense, sent troops, prospectors, and concession-hunters through the neck of the bottle and sometimes left them languishing at the far end of it for months on end, in ignorance and danger. The missionaries distrusted him; the Boers hated him; the blacks feared and respected him; the handsome young men he always kept in his entourage revered him; and the Jews (the Rothschilds, the Beits, and others) financed him.

During my youth I made only the briefest of forays into the country which lay behind or beyond the two cattle ranches, one to the north of Kimberley and one to the south of it, which my father eventually came to own. Once or twice I travelled with him to a place called Lohatlha, about one hundred and fifty miles due west of Kimberley, where, improbably enough, he also owned a manganese mine. On another occasion I went by train with a school rugby team to play against a school in the town of Vryburg, which was about the same distance to the north of Kimberley as Lohatlha lay west. We slept in one of the school hostels; in the morning I woke early and walked to the centre of the little town, where I bought a copy of the four-page, weekly news-sheet printed there. It was wholly in Afrikaans, of course, and was called *Die Stellalander*. When I asked about the origin of this title I heard for the first time the story of the short-lived republic after which the paper had been named. Several years later I passed though Vryburg again, on the train journey from Bulawayo to Kimberley (two nights and one day, I think it was): a journey so long that to this day I cannot open Henry James's *Portrait of a Lady*, which I was reading at the time, without seeing the charred-looking bush passing endlessly outside the window, and recalling the tedium of the talk among the five other men with whom I was sharing the compartment. After even more years had passed I visited the 'capital' of yet another no-hope republic, Bophuthatswana in this case, the latest of the statelets established by a fantasizing, apartheid-crazed South African government as a kind of moral cover for its denial of political rights to the blacks everywhere else; and I duly wrote an article for an American magazine about the grim farcicality of some of what I had seen there.

Long after I had come to live in London, however, I used to

dream insistently of a landscape which I always knew, even while I dreamed of it, to lie somewhere to the west of Kimberley. In these dreams I would invariably come (with a sense of both surprise and familiarity) upon elaborate towns, forests, farmlands, beautiful mountains, stately homes and ancient fortresses. A secret territory, altogether: one quite unlike anything actually waiting for me there.

But that it was indeed still waiting for me, the dreams themselves made apparent. It was as if I owed something – though I could not have said what – to that half-known, half-feared region which had lain forbiddingly on the very doorstep of the Africa I had grown up in. In a perverse way, the fanciful inventiveness of my dreams, the complex human and topographical features my unconscious mind bestowed on it, helped to make clearer to me the real nature of the hold the territory still had over my imagination. Ultimately my dreams seemed to express a dread or shame that there might be *nothing there*: nothing to be seen, nothing to be learned, no one to meet, no past to register, no future to care about.

Which would be a source of greater wonder: to go there and discover that this was indeed the case, or to discover that it was not?

Hence the journey I have finally made along *the missionary road, the hunters' trail, the traders' trail, the Suez Canal of the South*, etc. To think of the journey in this way was of course to make a choice of an important kind. Not only would it determine the general direction, physically speaking, in which I would travel, and impose on the journey a particular historical and intellectual context; it was also bound to shape from within how I would see whatever lay before me. From its very beginning 'the road to the north' had been a *concept*, even a slogan; not something given by a neutral, impersonal geography. It had come into existence for specific historical, political, and commercial reasons, as the names by which it was known made manifest. Here – and here – and here – was a route which would open up the continent. Which would bring the word of God to the 'benighted heathen'. Which would 'put Africa on the map' (literally). Which would place in the hands of this group or that the key to the future development of the territory. The advancement of science, of commerce, of true religion, of civilization itself, let alone of the British Empire in Africa, or the independence of the Boers, or the ultimate wellbeing (or otherwise) of the blacks themselves, would depend on it.

The results are evident everywhere in the region today. One can in some sense 'get behind' defunct systems of ideas, but one can never ignore the physical changes they have helped to bring about. The same is true, in even more insidious and tenacious fashion, of their spiritual and psychological consequences. These cannot be wished away or scrubbed out of the experience of those affected by them, or out of their children's experience, or that of their children's children. No degree of intellectual sophistication will ever place us on some kind of supra-historical elevation from which we can look down with an unerring gaze on the place of our birth and the period we live in – let alone those of other peoples – and at last see them revealed to us, as if naked in their truth.

To 'know the place for the first time', as T.S. Eliot puts it in *Little Gidding*, is forever beyond us. All we can do is try to get to know it better. And hence ourselves.

PART ONE

☆

Kimberley and the Northern Cape 'The Republic of Bophuthatswana'

CHAPTER ONE

☆

Kimberley

I had never doubted where this journey should begin. Kimberley was the obvious place. It was where all my journeys had begun.

But there was a difficulty. The missionaries and hunters had pioneered the original road to the north long before Kimberley had come into existence. It had then run through Griquatown and Kuruman, Kanye and Shoshong. It was diverted to go through Kimberley only after the discovery of diamonds.

So what was I to do? Follow the old route to Kuruman, and then come down and start all over again? Or go straight north from Kimberley, pretty much along the line of the later road?

In the end I decided to do something of both. I would start in Kimberley, and go not north but west to Griquatown; then return to Kimberley and make some additional forays from there before turning northwards. To tell the truth, I wanted to see if the journey became more or less plausible after these first excursions.

First I had to get to Kimberley. Sitting next to me on the plane from Johannesburg was a young man of about nineteen years old. He had a head of thick, dark red hair, neatly waved and combed, and an open, snub-nosed face. As with many other red-headed people, his brow and cheeks were covered with pale freckles; the curling hair on his arms was much lighter in colour than that of his head. On his right arm, just below the elbow, was a cruel scar from which no hair grew: not from a break or cut, it seemed, but from a burn. He was wearing navy-blue corduroys, and sat with his jacket folded on his lap – the better, I suspected, to show off his short-sleeved shirt. It was a beautiful shirt. The pattern on it was composed of a profusion of daisies: blue, orange, and red daisies of different sizes, some overlapping, others just touching, all fully open, all turned to the onlooker. The buttons down the front of the shirt matched the red daisies exactly.

He was eager to talk, but shy; he said his English was 'useless'. Still, however haltingly, he preferred to carry on in English rather than put up with my fragmented Afrikaans. (I had once been fairly fluent in the language, but now had difficulty in speaking it.) Just so long, he said, as I didn't *mind* if he spoke slowly. The thing was you hardly ever heard English in Olifantshoek. Yes, that was where he came from. He was on his way to Kimberley to meet his parents, who were driving down from Olifantshoek to pick him up; then they would go home together.

Though I had grown up in the northern Cape I had never heard of Olifantshoek. (Literally translated it means 'Elephants' Corner'.) So he told me about it. It was 'not an important place'. It was about three hundred 'kays' north-west of Kimberley. Three hours' driving, say. Just on the edge of the southern Kalahari. The nearest places were Kuruman on one side, about an hour's drive away, and Upington on the other, which was twice as far. Both Upington and Kuruman were 'well bigger' than Olifantshoek. He'd been born and had gone to school there. 'You can say I've spent my whole life in Olifantshoek. Only now I'm studying in Pretoria.' This was his first vacation; he hadn't been home in three months. He was really looking forward to getting back for a couple of weeks. His father had a farm about thirty kays from the *dorp*. In the 'old days' the whole family used to live there, but now his father just drove out to the *plaas* when he had to. He raised cattle and goats. That was his business.

Goats? For the hair?

'No, no, for the meat. The Moslems, they like goat-meat. They're big buyers, especially in Joh'burg and Durban. My father sends off whole transporter-loads every time there's a Moslem holiday. They go mad for the stuff. They kill them in their own way, you know. Like so.' He drew a forefinger across his throat.

Expanses of dun-coloured veld passed below. From time to time it tilted mildly. Nothing grew down there, apparently, except for countless, distinct black spots, like the stubble of a man's beard. Each one I knew to be a thorn bush.

And he himself – what was he studying in Pretoria? Agriculture?

He shook his head sombrely, yet proudly too, conscious of what was to come next.

'Fashion design.'

It took me a moment to get over my surprise. Then I said: 'Now I know why you're wearing such a beautiful shirt.'

He acknowledged the compliment without discomfort. 'Well, I made it myself.'

'Are you studying at the Pretoria Tech?'

'No, it's a private college. Quite a small place. It's called the Transvaal School of Fashion and Dress Design. The course is two years and at the end of it you get a diploma. That's if you pass the exams.'

By the time the plane landed in Kimberley I had learned that he'd been keen on 'fabrics and fashion' as long as he could remember. Even the shop assistants in the branch of Clicks in Olifantshoek – 'it's just a chain store; and they're just Coloured women' – knew of his interests, and when a nice bit of cloth came in they'd put it aside and his mother would go and buy it for him. There were fifteen other people on the course in the college; all of them were women. But they didn't tease him or anything like that. No, his parents didn't mind that he was doing such a course. Just as long as he was happy in what he was doing: that was what they cared about.

And was he happy?

'I love it there. Except I don't like living away from home.'

We shook hands and wished each other luck after we had got our bags out of the overhead shelf. Before debarking, I asked one more question. What was he going to do when he'd finally got his diploma?

He answered without hesitation:

'I've got plans. I'm going to open a boutique in Olifantshoek.'

*

Back again. Back in Kimberley.

It was not that innumerable memories rushed at me; rather, a forgotten self instantly re-formed within me. Even before the plane had landed it had spoken up clearly if silently. Looking out of the window I had seen the abandoned police post on the Old Boshof Road about six miles out of town. For more than two decades, towards the end of the nineteenth century, that post had marked the border between the Boer Republic of the Orange Free State and the British-ruled Griqualand West Colony. Then it had been dismantled. In my childhood nothing of it remained but a few broken, whitewashed walls and a grove of gum trees. In a town as flat and shadeless as Kimberley, it had the air of being a faintly picturesque place to go to; almost a resort. On Sunday afternoons my father occasionally drove the whole family out there.

That was fifty years ago, more or less. I had not visited the spot since and had never before seen it from the air. The walls were gone. Yet the swerve of the road and the disposition of the trees told me at once what it was.

Not me: the forgotten self inside me, which had forgotten nothing.

And so with all else I saw. The changes out there (new suburbs, new roads, bigger mine dumps), marginal. The changes in myself, abolished.

Yet all those years ago I had never felt surprised by the intimacy I had with this drab landscape; those rusty iron roofs; the sound of African voices; the smell of scuffed dust. That in itself told me how much I had changed. And there was also my present solitude to contend with: the absence of all the people without whom I would never have been here, never have been myself, never have been.

After lunch I went for a two-hour drive around the town: a kind of memory-debauch. From the butter factory my father took over when he arrived in the town to the cattlefeed plant he had subsequently owned, and on to the now-flourishing suburb he had developed on what was then the outskirts of the city (his last and most successful business venture). From the school I attended to the family home on Central Road (with its doors and windows heavily, even penitentially, iron-barred – though as children we had slept night after night on the open porch). From Kenilworth, once a 'model village' designed by Rhodes himself for De Beers employees (now a home for the mentally handicapped), to the former cattle auction pens on the Cape Town Road (since transformed into the Horseshoe Centre, complete with video shop, steakhouse, and liquor store).

The longest halt I made was at the old public lending library, which now houses a specialist collection on the history of Kimberley and the northern Cape. I was curious to get some idea of the published and unpublished documents it stored; but that was not really my reason for going there. I chose to do so because it was the place where I had spent some of the happiest and most peaceful hours of my childhood. The building itself was remarkably little changed, all internal rearrangements notwithstanding: there were the big rooms I remembered; the little rooms; the cast-iron spiral staircase and gallery in the biggest room of all; leather-bound books everywhere and leather armchairs too (some having a tiny wooden balustrade between the seat and the U-shaped roll of leather in which your back was supposed to fit); glassed-in bookcases; open fireplaces; portraits and maps on walls; expanses of shining wood. So unassumingly colonial it looked, and yet so utterly confident of itself as a public, club-like institution set up by civic-minded, Victorian gentlemen for their own kind. Even the smell was unchanged: sweet dust, sour paper, polished lino, leather. It was as if not a breath had been taken in or exhaled since I was last there. The notices on the verandah (about subscriptions, book borrowings, the parking of bicycles) were now displayed as charming mementoes from the past: in my day they had been serious notices; no one had then thought them quaint. The jacaranda trees outside were thicker than they used to be, though no taller; the bronze busts of Sir Alfred Beit and Sir Bernard Klisser – two German-Jewish diamond magnates without whose benefactions the institution would never have come into existence – still looked out severely on Dutoitspan Road.

One of the ladies in the library knew who I was and had read some of what I had written; though I had not met her before, we soon established that we had many connections in common, living and dead. Slight, bespectacled, softly-spoken, of English stock and (it soon became apparent) unillusionedly liberal views, she took me around the building and brought some documentary materials to me. Her superior, a shy and slightly suspicious Afrikaans-speaking lady, yielded the field to her, though not without some misgiving. Among the items shown to me was a selection of my own books in a room given over to special collections. I could not help thinking how much pleasure the sight would have given to the restless, reading, daydreaming youngster who had once haunted the place. But *he*, alas, would never know about it.

In those days the annual subscription to the library was five shillings per year for an adult; half-price for a child under twelve years of age. Whites only were permitted to become members; Coloureds and Asians were allowed to come in to the frontmost of the rooms and read the few newspapers put out for them there – but no further. For this privilege no fee was charged. The question of blacks being permitted to enter in any capacity (other than that of cleaners) simply did not arise. Later, after the Nationalist Government had come to power and had begun to introduce its array of apartheid laws, even that minimal concession to Coloureds and Asians was removed. I can remember feeling somewhat guilty towards the earnest, schoolmasterly Coloured gentlemen, so much older than myself, who occasionally sat in the front room reading the newspapers, while I went into the more richly endowed private rooms behind.

How copiously the town sprawls over its miles of flat space; and to what disdainful heights the sky rises above it! Nowhere is there a hill to climb or descend, a declivity to negotiate, a stream to cross, a wood or lake to circle, a vantage point from which to view it all. Everything looks fortuitous, so flat and featureless is its topography and with such humble readiness does the dun-coloured veld take over where the buildings finally run out. North, south, west, east, it is the same. In the centre of town there are some modest high-rise buildings, the tallest of them, appropriately enough, being the new offices of the De Beers Corporation, with a wall of dark, angled glass in front and an unbroken, curved, concrete wall behind. Scattered in this direction and that lie the suburbs for whites, many of them new and prosperous-looking: street upon street of single-storeyed structures hardly higher than the cars which stand in front of them. Then you come on the vistas of huddled hutment and churned-up sand which make up the Galeshewe township for blacks.

Only the mine dumps (going up) and the open holes of the mines (going down) declare plainly their reason for being exactly where they are. The dumps are the home-made mountains of this landscape, their greenish hue having nothing to do with leafage; the mines are great funnel-shaped chancres on the surface of the earth. On their rims grow a few wisps of dry grass and bush, like the hair on a man's body; then, lower down, layers of brown and orange flesh are revealed, which yield eventually to narrower, harder, hazy cylinders of blue-green stone or bone (Kimberlite), cut sheer and going to depths which make the pigeons flying inside them look hardly bigger than butterflies.

It was simply by digging these open pits that people originally mined for diamonds. When open mining became too hazardous they gained access to the diamondiferous 'pipes' by sinking shafts alongside them, before cutting horizontally across, level by level. Next to the biggest mine of all, the Big Hole, there is now an elaborate museum in which these processes are described and pictured for parties of tourists; the museum also contains two or three 'old-time' streets of shops and public buildings, carefully transported from the sites they had once occupied and then rebuilt and fitted with appropriate furnishings and contents, as well as waxwork figures in paralysed postures. For the accuracy of the interiors of the shops, if not of the waxworks, I myself can vouch. Once upon a time my mother used to take me into those same shops, and others like them, to buy shoes and school uniforms and to have my hair cut. As with the notices put out for display in the old library, we did not know of their quaintness, then; they were just shops.

Blacklaws the shoe-seller; Glasson the optician; Cooper the chemist; Kiddie the baker; Diamond who sold leather suitcases, not diamonds; Blumenthal who sold cutlery and watches; Henderson the draper . . . All Englishmen and Scots, notice, with the occasional Jew. The shops owned by Greeks, Indians, and Chinese were on the outskirts, generally.

It would be easy for me to add the names of a few score more shopkeepers to those just mentioned. At the age of ten or twelve or thereabouts I must have known by name or appearance thousands of people in Kimberley. I mean that quite literally. I knew the name of virtually every one of the six hundred boys at my school, of a good few of their parents, many boys attending the 'rival' Christian Brothers College, some girls at the Girls' High School, almost all the members of the Jewish community (about a hundred and twenty families), innumerable professional people, pigeon fanciers, cricketers, De Beers employees. As well as a few hundred black or Coloured labourers, artisans, servants, delivery 'boys', and suchlike.

This was the consequence of growing up as a curious schoolboy, with two brothers older than myself and a younger sister, in a small, slump-ridden, isolated town. And the consequence of *that*, in turn, was that I often longed to find myself in a place where I knew nobody and was unknown to all.

One thing that never occurred to me, though, was that Kimberley itself, where so many of the buildings I remembered were still standing, with the meagre trees under which I had dawdled my way to and from school just a few feet higher than they had been, with the sand of the unpaved kerbs crunching underfoot with exactly the same sound as before, with the sun and sky looking down on dried-out earth and iron roofs as diminishingly as ever, and the same melancholy whistlings and thuddings and puffings rising by day and night from the railyards in Beaconsfield – that Kimberley itself would one day become a place where I knew nobody and was unknown to all.

But so it was. Or as near as made no difference. During the time I spent there on this visit I met exactly one person I had known before. I did not recognize him; he recognized me. He limped past, paused, turned, came back hesitantly. 'Are you Danny Jacobson?' I admitted I was – though heaven knows how many years it was since I had last heard my name spoken in that way. He said then: 'I'm Bill Carter.'

'Stooge.'

The word came to my lips without thought, without volition. The forgotten self inside me had uttered it. It was the sound of his name only, nothing in his appearance, which had brought the word forth.

How pleased Carter was to be remembered by his schoolboy nickname, I cannot say. How he had managed to recognize me is also a mystery. Perhaps he had seen a photograph somewhere. The Stooge Carter I remembered was a slight boy with glasses and an anxious but merry smile above a sharply pointed chin. This man was bald, swarthy, limping; the belt holding up the trousers of his blue suit was embedded, almost hidden, inside his belly; the point of his chin had disappeared into the several chins behind it; on his forehead was an old, thick, plum-coloured scar possibly acquired in the same accident that had left him with his lurching gait. Also, his glasses were gone.

He knew that I lived in London; I learned that he worked for De Beers. His married daughter lived in Cape Town. Half-proud and half-ashamed, he confessed that he was a grandfather now; his daughter had two 'kiddies' of her own. She and her husband wanted to go to Canada. 'They see no future here.'

Our conversation came to an end. We had no more to say to one another. 'Nice to see you again.' 'Good luck.' Off he stumped. Gone again. The last of those vanished thousands.

Time and absence; nothing else had been needed; then the trick was done. Even those people I knew to be still alive – in Cape Town or Johannesburg, in London or Toronto – were mere ghosts in the forms in which I remembered them. Look at Stooge Carter, who had remained. Look at me, who had left. And the dead? It was they I could now count in their hundreds, if not thousands. Fragments of them, moments of them, remained fugitively in my recollection: this one a look, that one a buttoned waistcoat, him a pair of hands, her a tone of voice, them in paired postures on the front seat of a tan Ford car. No more than that.

Yet I also knew now something about them that had been hidden from us previously. I knew what the world looked like after they were gone. This was how the sunlight fell on the camber of Dutoitspan Road, and the paint peeled in leaflike flakes from the iron roofs of houses, and the trains in Beaconsfield raised their howls to the too-distant sky. *And the place thereof shall know them no more*. Yet they would have recognized it all. My parents too, lying in the sandy, cypress-scented, dark-tableted silence of the Jewish cemetery on the western side of town.

At moments it seemed to me I was the merest breath away, or not even that, from learning just how it would be after I had gone to join them.

As a boy I had taken it for granted that De Beers should own the town's electricity supply, waterworks, and public transport. (These are no longer owned by the Corporation.) I had taken it for granted, too, that all around the town there should be great forbidden stretches of territory fenced off with the characteristic De Beers barbed wire – strands six inches apart, rising to a height of about eight feet, with a large, hooped coil of the stuff running along the top. How much I had taken for granted the right of De Beers to do what it liked with its property came home to me some years ago when I went for the first time behind the barbed wire. I had gone there as a guest of the Corporation, yet I felt an almost eerie and dreamlike sense of guilt as the car drove down a road of whose existence I had not known before. Children sometimes imagine that under the floor or above the ceiling of the house they live in there is another, secret house which they alone know about but can never enter; and it was with something of the wonder and anxiety of that childish fantasy that I stared at the secret settlement I had never before entered. The road ran between old and new

sent on conveyor belts across miles of closely guarded veld; crushed and swirled about in pans; crushed again and swirled about again, and again, and again; and ultimately cast out on the side of ever-growing, mountainous dumps. Yet, before this process is completed, the people responsible for it have managed to find in all that indistinguishable mass of earth the tiny palmful of stones they are looking for.

So much for the wonder. As for the absurdity: just four words can express it. All *that* – for *this*! 'All that', mind you, referring not only to the process just described, but to the whole of Kimberley as it is today and as it has been in the past; to the immeasurable changes in the history of the country which were initiated there; to the political purposes in South Africa itself and elsewhere to which Rhodes devoted the great fortunes he had amassed in the city; to the still-existing multinational corporations (De Beers, Anglo-American, Consolidated Goldfields, the Charter Company) which were fathered there; to the grand Palladian mansions owned by the Beit and Wernher families in Ireland and Hertfordshire, and the artistic treasures housed in them . . .

All *that*, from *this*? One does not know whether to cry or to laugh.

There is a sentence from Anthony Trollope's *Travels in South Africa* (1878) which is invariably quoted in books about the Kimberley diamond fields: 'I can conceive of no occupation on earth more dreary, hardly any more demoralizing than this of perpetually turning over dirt in quest of a peculiar little stone which may turn up once a week or may not.' He also wrote of Kimberley, in a sentence quoted rather less often, that it was one of the 'places to which men are attracted by the desire of gain which seem so repulsive that no gain can compensate the miseries incidental to such a habitation'.

Only on the river-diggings, however, does the 'turning over of dirt' remain anything like so lackadaisical and individual an enterprise as that described by Trollope. I have never been down any of the Kimberley mines – for obvious reasons the Corporation discourages visitors from going underground – but a day spent deep in a Zambian copper mine left me with a vivid impression of what it is like to work at such depths. (The mode of excavation in both operations is the same: it is known as 'block cavity mining'.) The experience also left me with a thoroughgoing scepticism about the power of the written word ever to convey the inward nature of extreme physical experience: of war, say, or polar exploration, or even severe illness. Since boyhood I had been acquainted with George Orwell's account of going down a coal mine in *The Road to Wigan Pier*; a piece of writing which had made a great impact on me and which I still admire. But it took minutes only down the mine to convince me that I was not at all prepared for what was actually confronting me. Nothing could have prepared me for it. The darkness, like a wholly new element; the heat, more familiar at first, but growing fiercer and fiercer as we descended to lower levels; the narrowness of the tunnels through which we crouched and crawled and groped our way; the scaling and descent of moist, vertical, steel ladders – unseen, known only to our hands and feet – that led from level to level; the howitzer-like roar of a six-foot drill hammering at the rock-face inside a tiny cavern, while a dust-allaying jet of water ran from its buried point with another, squealing note and collected about our feet; the surreal abstractness of watching stick after stick of dynamite wrapped in shiny brown paper being rammed home into the drill-holes; the chains and shackles which the miners donned before shovelling the day's loosened output of rock down one particular shaft to the collection point at the very bottom of the mine, from which it would be hauled to the surface. (They are tied to prevent them losing their balance and going down, along with the weights they are shifting.) And then there is the ache in your back; the grit in your mouth; the tremble in your thighs; the battery of your helmet-lamp growing heavier minute by minute; the sweat drenching your underpants and overalls; and always the rough, lightless, inconceivably compacted immobility above and around you – darkness made weight, weight made pressure, pressure made heat.

There: another brief and hopeless attempt to convey an unconveyable experience. But perhaps the most vivid revelation to me of how difficult it is even for the miners themselves to take for granted the nightmarish nature of their job was how suddenly silenced they were when the skip taking us down began its vertical plunge. One moment thirty or forty men had been talking, laughing, swearing; the next, no sound was heard from them. Only after what seemed to be a prolonged, downward lapse into blackness did they find their voices again and begin to swear and fiddle with their tools and lamps and plastic 'skof tins'.

CHAPTER TWO

☆

The Road to Griquatown

Everything in southern Africa is a subject of contention: the land, the laws, the histories, the languages. Every claim that each group makes for itself is a denial of the claims made by the others. There is no neutral ground between them; no neutral time-span either, whether they look back or forward. Nor is there a neutral language or terminology through which they can describe one another. Occasionally what seems truly amazing about the subcontinent is not the ferocity generated by the divisions manifest wherever you turn; it is the regard for order that many people of all races somehow still manage to preserve.

Names like 'Bushmen', 'Hottentots', and 'Coloureds' have long been naturalized in English speech. It must not be imagined that they therefore carry within them no cultural and racial presuppositions, no historical charge or burden. Far from it. To call a man a Bushman was to deny him his full humanity; it was to designate him a creature of the bush, one who dwelt outside any recognizable form of human society. (I was told that 'Sarwa', the Tswana word for Bushmen, translates analogously as 'People Without Cattle'.) Much the same was true of the term Hottentot. To describe someone as a Hottentot was merely to imitate the babble in which he was supposed to speak; it was a way of declaring his speech to be not a language at all, just a kind of stammering. As for the Cape Coloureds (among whom the Griquas of Griquatown and elsewhere are today invariably numbered) – if you call someone of mixed descent a 'Coloured' you are in effect claiming that you yourself are not coloured at all, or that your colour is so much the right one, the natural one, as to be unremarkable. *He* remains the man who carries the burden of differentness; never the speaker. The result is that many Cape Coloureds now simply describe themselves as blacks. They also refer, in ironic fashion, to their own group as 'the so-called Cape Coloureds'. Others have given the whole business yet a further ironic twist by mockingly speaking of themselves as . . . 'the So-Calleds'.

Such contortions are not new. When the first missionaries of the London Missionary Society to cross the Orange River came on 'a mixed breed of Hottentots and other nations', and learned that these people were known as 'Basters' or Bastards, they made haste to change this appellation. (All else aside, it was not a name likely to go down big at fund-raising meetings back in Britain.) Fortunately it appeared that some of these 'mixed breeds' also referred to themselves as the Beriquas; a name which was soon regularly transliterated as 'Griquas'. Nevertheless, writing from what he called 'Beriquas Land' in July 1802, another missionary, Edwards by name, declared that the people actually called themselves 'Moetschoane'. ('They are more peaceable than the Bushmen,' he reported: 'the men have cattle [and] are very lazy [and] hunt with lances and short knob sticks'; the women 'labour in the field and sow a sort of corn which they call Mabaela'.)

What am I to call these peoples, then, in these pages? I could perhaps answer that question more easily if I knew exactly what I should call myself. A South African? An Englishman or Briton by adoption? A secular Jew – who just happens to be following the trail named after the nonconformist missionaries, Scotsmen in large part, of the London Missionary Society?

In the humming, air-conditioned library of the School of Oriental and African Studies of London University, not two hundred yards from the college in which I 'profess' English literature, are the archives of the London Missionary Society. They consist of many files of carefully preserved (and scrupulously catalogued) letters from men like those mentioned above. On cardboard-stiff paper, in ink that is now rust-coloured, they laboriously wrote their reports back home to the officers of the Society; reports which they knew might take six months or more to arrive and to which they would receive no reply for at least a year. In some of these letters they proudly described the effects of their preaching – or lamented its lack of effect:

Numbers hear with tears in their eyes others so distressed that after sitting for some time apparently in great agony faint away and are carried out as dead and so distressing is the place at times that it is impossible to proceed in the Divine Service, My Dear Sir, I do not want you to understand that we think they are all converted, o no, but that so it is, and from the remainder we leave it in the hands of the Lord, for at other times they appear a sort of indifferences, yet with some hearty whoops ... I believe the God of Grace hath charged them with attention and I have often seen a smile on their countenance with a tear falling from their eyes when the name of Jesus and everything relating to his love of poor sinners has been mentioned.

Thus William Anderson, writing to London on 6 December 1801, in the first of the letters he composed from the territory in which he was eventually to spend most of his life. He was then somewhere to the south-west of present-day Griquatown: the settlement itself having come into existence only after he had persuaded some of the 'Beriquas', 'Basters', 'Hottentots', etc. to give up their nomadic way of life. After a further eleven years of devoted labour Anderson was to describe the progress he had made in much more wistful terms (4 August 1812):

The members of our infant church increase but slowly. Since our return [from a visit to the Cape] we have only received three into communion with us, and three have been dismissed on account of their being found guilty of adultry [*sic*] – respecting the others some are aware of their lukewarm state, and complain of it to us ... others appear more indifferent ...

Reading letters such as these, the earliest among them especially, I was puzzled to know the language the missionaries had used in their preaching. English? Dutch? The London Society did employ several Dutchmen from the Netherlands, like J.J. Kircherer, who seems to have been the first of the missionaries to work continuously in the region. But how many of them, immediately on crossing the Orange River, could possibly have spoken any of the San (Bushman) or Khoi (Hottentot) dialects which most of their audience must have retained? Or did they readily find translators among the 'mixed breeds' they were addressing?

They barely discuss the matter. One of them might take up space in his report to London by painstakingly transcribing a list of about a hundred words in one of the local languages and their equivalents in English. (For purely 'scientific' purposes, one wonders? Or to help any future volunteers the Society might send out? Or simply, indeed, to take up space?) But generally they write as if the linguistic problem simply does not exist. Likewise with the historical experience and assumptions they bring in speaking to their audience of such concepts as – let us say – Incarnation, Original Sin, Election, Redemption. Their meanings and intentions appear so plain to them, and so urgent, that the difficulties which arise in the meetings between any two cultures, and in any act of mutual interpretation between them, are never referred to. No 'hermeneutic problem' for them.

One result of this attitude, of course, is their conviction that if the people fail to heed the message brought to them, it is because they are sinful and idle. No other reason could explain it. Their recalcitrance is just another wearying manifestation of the fallen human state.

They for a while . . . came diligent to hear [wrote Mr C. Sass, a missionary of German origin, on 5 February 1814] and some seemed to get serious impressions but they soon looked out again for their old way again which is swimming, drinking, and fiting and to scorn the word of God. There will come ten or twelf of them from more than four hundred of the men, sometimes one or two or even non at all, They make us plain understand that our comming here is a bitterness to them.

For the moment one does not know for whom one should feel more pity: the anguished missionary or the embittered members of his flock.

I return to the question of nomenclature and ideological intent. Am I to write here of Griquatown or Griekwastad? Of Mafeking or Mafikeng? Of the Boer War (as the British still refer to it) or the

Second War of Freedom (as the Afrikaners refer to it)? Of the
chimerenga (the Shona word for uprising) that took place a few
years after Rhodesia had been occupied by the whites, or the
Rebellion, as the settlers called it?'

Every choice one makes is politically loaded. Even setting aside
the offensive terms applied to them, the blacks in South Africa have
been officially known in my lifetime as 'Natives', 'Africans', 'Bantu'
(a speciality of the apartheid legislators, that one), and 'blacks'.
And are the various affiliations among them (Zulu, Xhosa, Tswana,
etc.) to be dubbed 'tribal', 'national', or 'ethnic' – or are we politely
to pretend, as the political left would wish us to, that they are
merely 'cultural'? Why is the term 'Boer' for an Afrikaner an insult
in the mouths of blacks; just as 'Dutchman' is in the mouths of
English-speaking whites?

When I visited Zimbabwe (formerly Rhodesia) a few years after
it had achieved independence, I found that three distinct styles
of address for foreign leaders had been developed by the new
officialdom. Everyone who came from the so-called 'socialist' states
was given the warmly approving title of 'Comrade'. People from
the evil 'capitalist' or 'imperialist' world, on the other hand, were
known merely as 'Mr' or 'Mrs'. As for the apartheid-espousing
whites who then governed South Africa – they were entitled only to
their bald, prefix-less surnames.

It was in Zimbabwe, too, that an aged uncle of my wife's asked
me, in all seriousness, 'Why did they have to change the name of
Salisbury [the capital] to Harare? Salisbury sounds *much nicer.*'

Anyhow, let Griquatown, my first port of call outside Kimberley,
speak in its own terms for itself. Some distance outside the little
town a signboard lists the attractions awaiting the visitor:

WELCOME TO GRIQUATOWN

THE PIONEER TOWN NORTH OF THE ORANGE RIVER WHERE
CHRISTIANITY WAS PIONEERED BY THE LONDON MISSION
SOCIETY IN 1802

Alongside this notice is another, in which the same legend appears in Afrikaans; on it the town is called Griekwastad. Beyond these notices the road, still running dead straight, widens in honour of the *dorp* it is passing through. There are no pavements to be seen, only plenty of whitish, stony soil; some skinny gum trees and thick-girthed pepper trees; a new Dutch Reformed church with a needle-sharp spire – the one structure rising higher than a single storey; a school to the left, also new; cars parked in the shade and in the sun; the American Swop Shop with two or three girls' dresses spreadeagled in its window; a garage; another garage; the Hotel Louis; some general stores and a chemist shop; a modest signboard outside the Mary Moffat Museum.

All this lies in what can hardly be called a hollow: rather, a long, slow, shallow depression. I had passed half-a-dozen such depressions in the hundred miles since leaving Kimberley. These, together with the crossing of the Vaal River fifty miles back, and a handful of lumpish, reddish koppies, had provided the major scenic variations along the route.

The swell of earth on the other side of the *dorp* was the highest yet. On the facing slope, with about a mile of waste ground separating it from the shops and nearest white habitations, was the 'location' or 'township' where the descendants of the eponymous Griquas actually live. Bleak though the centre of the town was, it looked positively haven-like compared with what it confronted. There, across a shadeless flank of earth, rows of brick and iron hutches were ranged not on streets but on so many parallel swathes

of dust. A single open telephone box and some standpipes for water
appeared to be the only public amenities. The main road and a
wire fence skirted it all and curved out of sight. Papers blew about
in the breeze. In every hollow a mulch of plastic and squashed
drink cans had collected. Still more shreds of plastic, fluttering and
muttering incessantly, were caught in the thorns of shrubs that had
somehow managed to survive the tramplings of human feet and the
munchings of goats and donkeys. One of the donkeys wandering
about in preoccupied fashion trailed some rubbish from a hind
hoof. The wind had stuck a plastic bag into the sunken flank of
another.

I had been given the name of someone in the Coloured township,
a schoolmaster, whom I had been told I might find it useful to
meet. My attempt to do so was one of two abortive rendezvous in
Griquatown. (The other came later, when I went looking for the
grave of Mrs Kramer, the first white woman to die north of the
Orange River.) Whether I had got the teacher's name wrong, or
that of his school, or had come to the wrong township altogether, I
do not know. No one there seemed to have heard of him or his
school. Or so they said. All my enquiries were met with a degree of
reserve that shaded steeply into outright suspicion.

Not that I was disrespectfully treated. It was among the Griquas
that for the first time since arriving in South Africa on this visit I
was given the fawning, old-style appellation, 'Baas'. This did not
prevent the people who used it from passing on to me quite a
different message simultaneously. Here was this lone white man,
driving a car endowed mysteriously with a Durban number-plate
(which was what the car-hire firm in Kimberley had given to me),
coming to the township in the early afternoon, on a working day,
asking questions about someone they might or might not have heard
of. Clearly he was up to no good. If he was not a policeman, he
was likely to be a taxman; if he was neither of these, he might be
something perhaps even more sinister: a planning officer, a debt
collector, a man from the water board come to cut off the
standpipes. Men and women, old and young alike, failed to under-

stand my questions (my Afrikaans remains quite adequate when it comes to asking directions to a shop or school), or made a single gesture in answer. They pointed over my left shoulder, back to 'white' Griquatown, which lay in the declivity below. That was where I belonged.

'*Waar is die naaste* [nearest] *skool?*' '*Daar, daaronder, baas,*' – pointing downwards. '*Is daar 'n winkel* [shop] *hierso?*' More pointing. '*Daar, daaronder, basie.*' They stared as my car approached and lost all interest in it the moment I drew up. None of the buildings I had seen had looked remotely like a school, though there must have been one in the neighbourhood. Eventually I gave up and drove away. Some of the children who had eyed me from a distance then began to run alongside the car, shouting for money and food. A man clad in rags crouched by the roadway; one of his feet was bare, the other shod; the shoe missing from his foot was in his hand; he was apparently trying to mend it with some whitish stuff he was squeezing out of a tube. The dust from my tyres rolled over him. Goodbye.

When I got back into town (i.e. the 'white' town), I stopped at the post office and asked another group of Coloureds who were waiting there, apparently for nothing in particular, about the man I was looking for. (Now it was my turn to point – up, back, towards the hillside.) One by one those who could be bothered to make the effort told me, with a submissive, half-insolent caution, that they didn't know him. It was impossible for me to know whether they were telling the truth or not. Belatedly I then thought of going back to the museum and asking for the assistance of its curator. But when I got there I found that it was already closed. So I went instead to a little office and showroom called 'Earth Treasures' where cut and uncut specimens of the extraordinary variety of semi-precious stones to be found in the district were on sale. The most famous among them, as the notice outside the town had indicated, is tiger-eye, which is mined locally in both its blue and brown forms. (The stone is closely related to asbestos: a mineral for which the entire area had once been still more famous, or infamous.) With its brilliant parallel stripes enclosing darker, more mysteriously gleaming depths, the brown variety is generally thought much the handsomer.

The shop was run by an Afrikaner whose thick, greying hair curled over the shafts of his glasses. I made my selection from the goods on offer. When I brought it to him he exclaimed with elephantine, man-of-the-world craftiness: 'Ah! For the *ladies*!' One of the bracelets I bought was made of brown tiger-eye; the other of a heavier and darker stone, the colour of clotted blood. Hence its name: haematite. In the open yard behind the office, under a lean-to shed, several Griqua workmen were going about the noisy job of cutting and polishing more stones for yet more bracelets, brooches, pendants, necklaces, ear-rings, key-rings, paperweights and ashtrays.

A feature of the Hotel Louis in Griquatown, I was to discover during my sojourn in it, is a ceiling-high mantelpiece composed wholly of brown tiger-eye. In Kuruman, a hundred miles to the north, I came on a branch of the Volkskas Bank which had gone even further: its entire frontage, both within and without, was covered with the stuff.

It had taken me something like two and a half hours to get to Griquatown from Kimberley. The drive had been easy enough: it had also given me my first taste of the kind of travelling that lay ahead. My first taste, I call it; yet from beginning to end, like so much of what was to follow, it was a more intense immersion than any since childhood in the combinations of light and shade, mass and vacancy, colour and its absence, through which the world had originally made itself known to me.

The veld was surprisingly well covered, considering the severity of the two-year drought the entire subcontinent had been suffering. From the air the countless thorn bushes may have resembled stubble on an unshaven face; at ground level they swarmed together like flies, so black they were, so numerous, so skinny and feeler-like their branches and trunks. Only when you looked closely could you make out the thorns growing from them; only then did you see, too, that the bushes were by no means as black as they first appeared to be. Each one sported hundreds, even thousands, of thorns: all as long as a man's finger and a pure, merciless white in colour; all caught together in improbable, weightless shapes – balls, pyramids, cubes, icosahedrons. The bushes stood no more than four or five feet high; but now and then another variety of acacia, the camelthorn, also black but adorned with pods as well as thorns, rose ten or fifteen feet above the rest, like a real tree, its branches sparse enough yet spreading widely. Between them stood stiff tussocks of grass, almost knee-high, isolated from one another, without a trace of green in them, not even near the roots. Only the shrubs growing in clumps showed hues of dubious green here and there. I had vague notions of what these shrubs might be called; my father, I remembered, used to refer to them by a variety of names, some of which he possibly invented on the spur of the moment: saltbush, milkbush, vaalbos (greybush), taaibos (toughbush), wild olive.

Carrying all this, and still with plenty of space for loose sand, reddish rock, and nipple-shaped ant-heaps no higher than the tufts of grass, the earth swelled towards the horizon like a wave that would never break. It took ten miles to rise to a height of fifty feet, perhaps, and then as many miles to sink away again. Yet each time the car surmounted the low elevation which had for so long made up the horizon, I was astonished by the space then revealed. Including the next faint rise, now become the new horizon to aim for.

Half-way between it and myself there might be a single farmhouse, complete (I discover in due course) with iron roof and gauzed stoep. Three cypresses and a row of aloes serve as its garden. Behind the house are a steel windpump and a circular water tank, around which some red cattle are listlessly gathered. Another five or more miles: another house, just like the last. Only this one has a child's swing hanging from a branch of one of the trees in front of it, and, sitting in the dust at the gate, a young, bronze-skinned woman with a baby at her bosom. She has a small head, delicate features bunched together, multitudinous wrinkles, the inevitable *doek* covering her head and tied with a knot under her chin. What is she waiting for? Not for me, anyway. She does not even move her head as the car goes past.

A lay-by appears, equipped with concrete benches and rubbish bins. It is planted around with bedraggled poplars. They wear their autumn garb of dead leaves; but look as though they had not much enjoyed the summer either. The sky ahead is thinly freckled with cloud. The gleam which runs along the topmost strand of a wire fence effortlessly keeps pace with the car. Now a dog-sized, black creature emerges and at once sinks back into the grass: a porcupine it could be, to judge from its furtive waddle-scuttle. Not much later a snake-necked, black-plumed ostrich leans over the fence, its head wobbling, its hindquarters balanced awkwardly below, its expression one of indignation rather than alarm. More cattle in the distance, gathered around the flash of another windpump and its circular dam. More sky.

Always more sky than anything else: deeper, wider, shinier than when you last looked at it.

And with what starkness do the solitary people you see walking or waiting by the roadside stand out! Especially as there is usually nothing in sight to which their weary footsteps could be taking them or from which they may have come. Here is a man staggering along with large, flat sheets of cardboard in his arms, like an ant hoisting some giant trophy in its mandibles. No doubt he is going to use the stuff as building material; but where, in all this vacancy, did he get it from and where is he taking it to? Then another man comes shakily into view, also with a gait that seems at first disjointed, even spastic; then you see that he is dancing as he goes along the empty road, actually dancing, to the music coming out of his own pursed lips. There a woman patiently waits for a lift; at her feet are several plastic bags and on her head is a portable television set, of all things. So confident is she of her sense of balance she has not even raised a hand to steady her burden, but stands arms akimbo, fists on hips. Another woman knits domestically out of a plastic bag as she walks along. Yet another stands right in the middle of the veld, scanning with much absorption a single sheet of paper torn from an illustrated magazine. The colours on the page are clearly visible. Now a man emerges from the shimmer of the metalled road with a heavy branch, for firewood presumably, laid in Christ-like fashion across his back and bowed neck. There is no witness of his solitary passion other than myself, for just one instant, from a speeding car.

Soon you begin to long for the relief, even the reassurance, of coming to the next *dorp* marked on the map. This is not because there is so little traffic that you fear being left to languish indefinitely at the roadside should the car break down. (Generally there is more reason to be anxious about just *who* might come along, and with what in mind, than about the prospect of waiting many hours by the road.) No, the tension springs from the apparent sameness and emptiness of the country you are travelling through, and the knowledge that there is nothing but the same to come, to come, to come.

Before setting out on my journey I was repeatedly warned against giving lifts to people on the roadside. So much violent crime takes place every day all over the country – even apart, that is, from the slaughters which claimed to have some kind of political coloration – that people of all races constantly, obsessively, feel themselves to be at risk. Whether at home or in the street, in their cars or on foot, they are always on the *qui vive*. Dogs, guns, private guards, alarms, barbed wire, high walls, steel doors masking outside doors, houses divided internally by yet more steel doors – such things are to be found everywhere. Obviously some districts are more dangerous than others: the black townships and squatter camps, in particular, being supposedly full of menace by day and night for their inhabitants, and simply never approached by the overwhelming majority of whites. However, there is no area anywhere, public or private, white or black, in which people are confident of their safety. A story I heard over and over again – always passed on with a mixture of much fear and a little pride – was that per head of population the murder rate in South Africa was no less than five or six times greater than that of the United States.

But those footsloggers . . .

In the end, in South Africa, Zimbabwe, and Botswana alike, I found myself following some simple rules of thumb when it came to picking up the forlorn walkers or patient bystanders I happened to pass. Women and children, yes; old men, yes; occasionally younger men on their own, provided they carried no bundles and they were dressed in so skimpy a fashion (shirt and shorts) it was impossible for them to be concealing clubs, knives, guns, etc. – yes. Nobody else.

How many people in these categories I gave lifts to, overall, I cannot say. Two score, say; more perhaps. A few of them said interesting things; most were silent, the barriers of language and race and the obligation they were under being too much for them. Too much for me too. I was never threatened or imposed on by any of them. My few narrow escapes from death or severe injury came only from ancient vehicles and reckless drivers, in Zimbabwe especially. The only people who behaved in a directly menacing manner towards me were uniformed members of the Botswana police and customs services.

The Mary Moffat Museum, Griquatown, is a single-storeyed, cottage-sized building. Its thick stone walls and thatched roof have evidently been restored fairly recently. A raised, slate-covered ledge, too narrow to be called a stoep, runs along the front of it. Oblong windows are set into its walls. Notwithstanding the claims it makes for itself (including a reconstruction, complete with earthen floor and pieces of Victorian furniture, of a room called 'The Birth Chamber'), the museum is not the actual birthplace of Mary Moffat Livingstone. Nor was it her residence. She was born in Griquatown, true; but where exactly is not known. Her missionary parents, Robert and Mary Moffat, lived there for about two years, from 1820 to 1822; subsequently, though Griquatown remained a base and place of refuge for them, they moved to Kuruman, about a hundred miles to the north. It was there that their daughter grew up; there that she met and married David Livingstone, later to become the great explorer, and, in places further north still, shared as long a period of cohabitation with him as they were ever to enjoy.

Anyway, the Griquatown building bears Mary's name; on one of its pillars is an ancient photograph of her, together with a typewritten placard bearing an unenthusiastic description by her husband: 'A good but often fearful and dejected Christian.' The building is divided into four or five small rooms containing the usual small-town museum mixture of trifles, trophies, oddities, and genuinely valuable items. Among the things on view are Moffat's yellowwood pulpit, built by Moffat himself; a travelling harmonium which the curator claimed, somewhat implausibly, was a present from Queen Victoria (I have found no mention of this gift in any of the biographies); a fine collection of Bushman stone tools; a photograph of a local Afrikaner worthy by the name of Chris Willers, who died at the age of '103 years, 2 months, and 1 day'; and, built into the rear wall, a massive, walk-in safe. The safe is not there to protect any especially valuable exhibits; it is merely a relic of the decades during which the building had been the Griquatown branch of Barclays Bank Limited.

When I pointed out to the curator that by tracking the dates on the framed title-deeds on display one could trace the successive, post-missionary owners of the property, my acuity astonished her. She had never thought to put the documents together in that way. (From the London Missionary Society it had gone to Percival Ross-Frames, then to Frederick Poirier, then to Johannes van Druten, then to Barclays Bank, and so on, until the Historical Monuments Council had taken it over.) 'I can see,' she said, 'you have the right . . .' At this point her English failed her, and she paused before falling back into her native Afrikaans '. . . *benadering*.' 'Approach,' I suggested. 'Yes, approach,' she agreed – 'the right approach for this kind of work.' A little later, apologizing once more for the deficiencies of her English, she told me, 'Sometimes I get clever – when I don't know the English word I just wait and then the people say it in English, and so I learn something.'

I did not try to cap my archival triumph by telling her that in London I was friendly with a collateral descendant of Frederick Poirier; or that as a boy in Kimberley I had once been a member of a rugby team which had competed for, and won, the Percival Ross-Frames Challenge Cup; or that another member of that same team had been a hostel-boy called van Druten who came from the Griquatown district. All that information was part of another jumbled, museum-like past: my own.

My interlocutor was middle-aged, curly-haired, rather thickset. She wore a cream-coloured linen dress and a dark-blue cardigan; her glasses were also blue-tinted, faintly. I had first seen her in the street outside; though I had not known then who she was or what she did, I had been struck by how staid and correct, how provincial and earnest, was her appearance. How diffident, too. Even her waist and ankles, not to speak of the handbag slung from her arm, had somehow expressed for me her membership of a class of persons which I had once known well. A succession of just such respectable Afrikaner ladies, with names like Miss van Zyl and Mrs Bester and Mrs Visagie, had worked as secretaries and bookkeepers for my father. Narrow in experience and timid in expectation, yet always firmly self-respecting; pillars of the Dutch Reformed Church and the women's societies (*Vrouevereeniging*) associated with it; confirmed spinsters or dutiful wives, as fate had determined; hardworking, neatly dressed, honest in their dealings; given to harmless gossip and intermittent melancholy; unoriginal, unmalicious, undemanding – who could deny that they were women of worth? 'Racist' too, of course, in their attitude to all dark-hued people: not rabidly so; just (in their view) sensibly; just as much as their own self-respect and the conventions of their society demanded of them.

I was not surprised to hear that this lady had been a primary school teacher for many years. Nor was I surprised by the unconvincing note of judiciousness which came into her voice when she spoke of 'the people around here' – meaning not her fellow-whites and fellow-members of the Dutch Reformed Church, but the Griquas – 'They're just not a very developed sort of people, you know.' She added, 'Not here anyhow': thus conceding that there might conceivably be some 'more developed' ones elsewhere, though she plainly doubted it. (This in earshot of a large and silent

Coloured woman, a guard or assistant of some kind, sitting at a table and crocheting a copious white garment. She had responded with a nod to my greeting when I had come in, but for the rest she might as well not have been present.) When the curator told me how pleased she was to have landed her present job, after so many years of teaching, her eyes flickered upwards and a devout hush came into her voice. 'The Lord Itself must have got me this job.'

Later she spoke quite as piously of her hope of becoming a grandmother. 'If God is willing, in a year or five, He will give me a grandchild.' Her hopes for a grandchild were pinned on her only son, who was just twenty years old; hence the latitude she was prepared to allow both him and God to fulfil her wish. She herself had been born in Prieska, still farther to the west on the Orange River, and had grown up there; Griquatown was the only other place she had ever lived in.

Oh, I knew such women; knew them so well, I thought, that nothing she could say would come as a surprise to me. At which point she succeeded in surprising me greatly. It turned out that she, like myself, was a novelist. I had not told her that I wrote novels; all I had admitted to being was a 'university professor' (which was true) interested in the early history of the region (also true). But that had been enough to elicit this unexpected confession from her. I was a professor of *literature*? Really? Then it came out. She had written no fewer than ten novels; all in Afrikaans of course. All had been published and a new one was coming out in two months' time, under the imprint of a firm in Pretoria. Her sister, who actually lived in Pretoria, was also a novelist; a much better novelist than she was. In fact, if it hadn't been for her sister she would never have started writing herself. She would never have had – you know – the 'cheek'. But her sister kept on telling her to have a go. Then one day she gave her an old typewriter – 'and I thought, ach, you don't want to waste a chance like that. So I started.'

What sort of novels did she write? 'Well, I don't aim too high . . . Just novels. Love stories, family stories, that kind of thing . . . My sister's work is much more serious – her writing is more like what *you* would call literature, I suppose.'

Unfortunately she had none of her novels in the museum to show me or sell to me, but she did produce a history she had written, in brochure form, of the local Dutch Reformed church. It contained many illustrations of dark-suited predikants and deacons. She also had some xeroxed sheets, on sale for a few cents each, of schoolboy howlers she had collected during her years as a teacher.

Once I was back in Kimberley I tried to find one of her books in what seemed to be the town's only bookshop. No luck, inevitably. As a novelist, I felt for her.

Before leaving the museum I asked for directions to the cemetery in which lay the remains of the posthumously famous Mrs Kramer. (A lady who had become famous by becoming posthumous, indeed.) I had thought my acquaintance would be glad to help me with so pious an errand. Instead she suddenly became guarded; the enthusiasm with which she had spoken to me about her books and her life left her. There was nothing sinister or spooky about her reticence; it was just that a constraint had entered her manner. 'It's difficult to get to,' she said. Then: 'You'll need permission to go there.' From whom? 'The office.' Which office? 'The town office.' To which she added pre-emptively: 'I think it will be closed now.'

I persisted and in the end she gave me the answers I wanted. She also told me that on the way out of town, on the left, I would see the 'hanging tree' used by Waterboer, the old Griqua chief, for executing felons and enemies. 'It stands in the back garden of a house, so you can't go right up to it,' she said; 'but you can look at it from the road.'

I did see the fatal tree in due course: a tall, brown, leafless object, with branches thick enough to bear the weight of many dangling men. Later I also saw the little monument to Waterboer in another part of the village. This was a crude pylon of stone blocks, flanked by two diminutive cannon given to him by Queen Victoria in acknowledgement of his loyalty. *That* gift is attested to by the historians; but it is hard to believe the cannon could ever have been fired at anyone or anything. Planted at an angle, wearing a coat of pink paint, they look so much like earthenware drainpipes I had to ring my fingernail against them to make sure they were made of metal.

As for the cemetery: no wonder the lady in the museum had tried to turn me from the place. It showed itself first by way of a few tall poplars and pines, well beyond the last of the houses; closer to it, along an oozing water-course, were some willows and a thick growth of bamboo-like reeds. The yells of invisible children at play came from that direction. A broken wall of whitish stones piled on one another surrounded the site. There was also a tilted iron gate which would not open. Barren, neglected, hummocky, vandalized, the graveyard had recently been made yet more desolate by a fire that had evidently begun higher up the slope, rolled across it, and then expired at a bend in the watercourse below.

I climbed over the wall and a cloud of soot at once sprang up at my feet. Every step produced another. After a minute or two my shoes and trousers were blackened; my nose and eyes were smarting. The fierce wind blew burned stuff in all directions. Pines and poplars sighed and groaned and even hooted from time to time, in animal-like fashion, as if their scorched trunks were still in pain from what they had recently been through. The sun shone unblinkingly above the mess, above its silence and tumult.

Scores of shattered and upended gravestones lay about. Some of the graves themselves had subsided, like old mine workings. Elaborate, rectangular, wrought-iron guards which had once protected a few of them had been tossed on their sides, so that they now enclosed nothing but air. Here was a stone, still upright, for Private John Jackson, 2nd Company, Cape Mounted Police, who had died of enteric fever just at the end of the Anglo-Boer War; on its back, cracked in half, was another for a soldier whose name I could not make out, who had been John Jackson's colleague both in the 2nd Company, CMP, and in the manner of his death. There, forever about to fall, was the stone for Joanna Brown, beloved wife of Edmund Brown; and here, safe at last, supine, unable to fall any further, that of George Woodley from Leades, County Cork, Ireland, who had died at the age of twenty-three.

By far the largest number of graves, however, were anonymous,

marked by a swell in the ground and a small piece of the local
flagstone, itself made up of packed, brittle laminae of red and
brown, black and yellow, sticking at most nine inches above the
ground. Book-sized these stones were, but completely wordless.
The sheer number of them, as well as their anonymity, told the
onlooker that they were the graves of Griquas who had been
permitted to lie here higgledy-piggledy alongside whites, just as
they had lived among them when Waterboer and the missionaries
together ruled the town. (The newer cemetery, near the Waterboer
memorial, was strictly whites only.) It was not that time had
rendered illegible the names which these stones had once borne, as
it had done to many of the others; these had never had names
inscribed on them.

And before then? What had been done with the dead? Where had
they gone?

'We think [Mrs Kramer's] death was the result of a miscarriage,'
the missionary William Anderson wrote in a letter dated 26 June
1812. On 4 August of the same year he wrote at greater length on
the subject to William Hardcastle, the secretary of the London
Missionary Society, to whom he was answerable for the work he
and his colleagues were doing in Griquatown:

On 23rd of January it pleased the Lord to take to himself the wife of Bro.
Kramer after a sickness of a few days, we think it was the result of a
miscarriage which she had had a few days before. She was the youngest
among us, so that it calls loudly to us, to be active in our work and be ready
waiting for the coming of our Lord, it is also the first trophy of Death's
victory among us Missionaries therefore I hope it will have a more lasting
effect upon our Minds, quicken us to more diligence in our work, and make
us more faithful in dealing with our own and the Souls committed in our
care.

As it happened, another writer put pen to paper about Mrs
Kramer's demise. William Burchell, the most urbane of the earlier
writers and artists who went about this region, arrived in
Griquatown shortly before the event. In his *Travels in the Interior*

of Southern Africa (Volume 1, 1822-4), he refers genteelly to her illness as 'an inflammatory attack', which had afflicted her about eleven days before. Then he continues:

In the alarm and distress which the missionaries and Mrs Anderson, her only female companion, felt at the too evident prospect of a fatal result, they flew to me for advice, as well as medicine, and, would that I possessed the knowledge and the power to save my poor fellow-traveller! I interpreted to them the opinions of the medical books which I had by me, and added all that my own judgement could suggest. This they hastened to adopt; and, at my representation, cleared the room of a crowd of sorrowful, but useless Hottentots, who, distressed and anxious for her whom they appeared much to esteem, created a suffocating heat, which considerably increased the danger. To mitigate this, I recommended a small opening, or window, to be cut through the reeds and plastering to admit fresh air: this also was immediately done; but, alas! all was in vain; and her pain and delirium left her only to make way for the last symptoms of dissolution.

She was buried two days later.

All the preparations and arrangements were managed with greater propriety than could have been expected. A sufficient quantity of black linen was found for a pall, with which the coffin was covered, and black crape hat-bands were worn by the missionaries. The corpse was born [*sic*] by six Hottentots, was preceded by the same number of people, and followed by the four Europeans and her son; after whom walked the two captains [chiefs], Kok and Berends. A long train of people, about fifty in number, then succeeded two by two, all cleanly and decently dressed, the greater part in European clothes. Every one conducted himself with a degree of decorum which was truly gratifying, from a tribe of people who in many other respects had made but little progress in civilization.

On arriving at the burying ground . . . an extempore discourse or address was pronounced by the missionary; after which the body was deposited in a *grave* [italics in original] seven feet deep, and covered in a mould to thickness of a foot; then, experience having taught them the necessity, the Hottentots covered it over with large, broad, flat pieces of rock, to secure it against the depredations of wild beasts, which, otherwise, would scratch it out of the earth during the night . . .

We had now witnessed, most probably, the first burial of a white woman which had ever taken place beyond the Gariep [Orange], and a knowledge of this fact rendered the ceremonies and transactions of the day doubly impressive and mournful. The Hottentots themselves were not insensible to that impression, and many of them noticed the circumstance.

The noise of the wind came and went; I could hear also the cries of the children in the reeds and the sound of my own stumbling footsteps on the blackened grass-tufts. The roof of my car, an improbably gaudy red, stuck out above the wall. It had never occurred to me that I would have any difficulty in finding Mrs Kramer's grave, one so honoured above all the rest, advertised as you approached the town, memorializing the real death of a real woman, attested to by an elaborate historical record. (As against all those wraith-like creatures of another hue, and of a letterless culture, whose deaths had had to go unrecorded for countless centuries before Mrs Kramer's arrival.) Surely it would be marked out unmistakably from among the others.

Perhaps it is. I could not find it, however, in the sad squalor of the place. Beyond the broken wall the veld rose up again, at once threateningly dark and gleamingly pale, revealing nothing but more and more of itself as far as the eye could see. Untouched, it looked, and untouchable. Stumbling about the graveyard, I did not know which was the more desolate view: the one in the distance or the one immediately around me. I remember thinking too that no fire had been needed to put the cemetery to the torch: the sun itself was strong enough to do the job.

My clothes and hands growing blacker by the moment, and the feeling of futility within me ever stronger, I suddenly became aware that I was no longer alone. A man, a Griqua from his appearance, was regarding me from a corner of the graveyard. He was on the other side of the wall. How long he had been there, I did not know. I could see little of him but his eyes and the stained felt hat on the back of his head. We stared at one another in silence; then I started to go over to him, to ask if he knew where Mrs Kramer's grave was. At my approach he turned, mounted a bicycle which had been hidden from me, and began pedalling in the direction of the *dorp*.

His lack of hurry made his departure seem all the more disobliging, somehow.

At that point I gave up the search. Some minutes afterwards, driving into town, I passed him on the road. The jagged sweat-markings going all the way around his hat, just above its brim, were like a map of ancient effort, of past fatigues. Neither of us acknowledged the brief moment of the other's parallel, journeying presence.

What if, *per impossibile*, he had chosen to wait for me and had then challenged me about my reasons for wanting to find that particular gravestone? What would I have said? How would I have explained myself? What was I looking for? What was the meaning to me of the mission that had brought her to this desolate spot? What was I doing there?

Not for the last time on this journey, but never more acutely than in that cemetery (with the possible exception of my arrival in a closed-down, boarded-up Mafikeng on a Sunday afternoon), I felt acutely depressed.

CHAPTER THREE

☆

Campbell – Schmidts Drif – Hunting the Wild Boshies-Men – A Farm Called Still Waters

Monuments, hanging trees, museums, and graveyards notwithstanding, you would never have thought Griquatown to be nearly two hundred years old. Even in what was now its 'white' and more prosperous quarter it was dusty and bedraggled, scratched up, knocked down. Stony, limey roads petered out at the first opportunity. Wire fences ran this way and that. Sun-tormented fruit trees were stuck unconvincingly into the sand, like theatre props. Nor had the Great Designer, as the missionaries would no doubt have called him, forgotten to litter the scene with gutted cars.

It could be worse. Campbell, an 'out-station' of the original Griquatown mission, which I had passed through previously, but visited only on my way back to Kimberley, is smaller and even barer in appearance. It too has a historical monument in the shape of a tiny stone church known variously as the Bartlett church or the Livingstone church, depending on which map you look at. Both Griquatown and Campbell came into existence because of the conviction of the missionaries that they had to get the local people to abandon nomadism. In this way they would acquire the habits – of labour, of steadfastness, of sobriety, of wearing clothes – which were necessary adjuncts to the faith. So the missionaries looked for places with natural sources of water (springs), and then tried to persuade a chief to settle there with his clan and to set about the tasks of irrigation and the cultivation of crops. When there was a falling-out within the clan, or between clans, another settlement would be proposed. Hence Griquatown, then Campbell, then Danielskuil, and various other places.

The Livingstone (or Bartlett) church is a small but sturdy stone box, no more than fifteen paces long and half-a-dozen paces wide, decorated inside with coloured prints of the Virgin and Child and of a bound, thorn-crowned Jesus, as well as several old photographs of various members of the Kok family. The photographs are all of small, old, wrinkled males, in ill-fitting suits. The Koks, like the Waterboers, were prominent in the annals of the Griquas; Campbell itself had once been the particular fiefdom of one branch of the line. A few oil-lamps hang from the roof of the church; half-a-dozen backless benches and a pair of wooden kitchen chairs serve as pews; the pulpit, made of packing-case wood, stands about waist-high and is evidently collapsible. Near the door is a wooden chest; inside it, jumbled together, are a jug of Sta-Soft Fabric Softener (empty), a plastic bowl (also empty), some dusty cloths, and a couple of battered *Diensboeke* (prayer books). The secretary to the Anglican Bishop of Kimberley had told me earlier that the vicar of Douglas, some twenty miles off, came to hold a service in the church once a month. He said also that though it had been founded by 'the nonconformists' (a distinctly unecumenical note of disapproval coming into his voice as he said the word), the Anglicans were formally to take over responsibility for it from the end of the year.

Outside, the wind that had been blowing across Griquatown the previous day was still at its work. The sun gazed through it in the same distracted manner as before. It hissed in the big pine trees planted around the church, drove to madness the vanes and wagging tail of a steel windpump some distance away, raised scurries of dust across the sloping, uneven piece of ground in which the church stands. Around this lumpy 'close' are small houses of plastered mud-brick and patched iron roofs. Next to the church is a memorial to the missionary Bartlett and a marble plaque affixed to a tree stump celebrating Livingstone, 'the great African explorer and missionary who held divine service under this tree and who

preached in this historic church'. Rather oddly, the words 'who
preached in' are incised into the marble on a deeper level than all
the others, as if some erroneous claim or 'misprint' had been
discovered, gouged out, and then rectified. The biggest of the
monuments is a brick cube surmounted by a cream-coloured twist
or coil of plaster (like a Softee Ice Cream sticking out of a cone) –
simulating a candle-flame, presumably. Set into the brick, a bronze
plaque informs the visitor that the church was opened in 1831 and
was the 'outspan' of 'such early travellers as William Burchell, John
Campbell, George Thompson, Dr Andrew Smith and Dr David
Livingstone'.

The few remaining spars of a broken ornamental gate mark the
entrance to the whole area. Bits of laundry flap and dance wildly
from a line behind one of the houses, as if there is something to
celebrate here which I cannot see. Another of the houses has been
abandoned – its windows are boarded up, its little stoep is full of
rubbish, an upended advertising sign, itself something of a memorial
to Livingstone, is nailed in its doorway. Half the sign is taken up
by the Coca-Cola logo; the other announces vertically: THE
LIVINGSTONE LIQUOR STORE. In the gap between two
scrub-covered ridges the northern Cape veld shows itself – shows
more and more of itself with every step you take in that direction.
There is not a sign of human or animal life out there, only a kind
of twilight (though it is midday) produced by the dust in the air
and the thickness of the thorn scrub.

How is it that a landscape so pale always has so much darkness
in it?

The whites of Campbell, like those in Griquatown, appear to be
wholly Afrikaans-speaking. When I asked in one of the shops (there
were only two) whether there was still a missionary centre of any
kind nearby, I was told no, there wasn't, nothing like that. 'Not
any more,' the shopkeeper said uneasily, even guiltily, from behind
his counter, with its iron-barred kiosk for desk and safe to one side.
'You know, they' (with a by-now familiar gesture, as if in the
direction of some other, remote country) '– they have their own

churches over there. And sometimes – *sometimes* – I think they still also use this Livingstone church. I don't really know.'

On the main road six Griqua women, descendants presumably of the Kok family and its followers, are squatting in the dust. There are no children among them, rather surprisingly. Perhaps they are waiting to be taken to some invisible and unimaginable workplace. One woman sits by herself, several paces from the others, head down, face in hands, in an attitude of despair or illness. The others gaze at me as I walk by. Farther down the road is the police station, much the smartest and biggest building in Campbell, ringed about with razor wire and bristling with radio antennae and floodlights. About a mile off, just out of sight of the salubrities of the white settlement, is the area where the habitations of the Griquas litter the open veld. There is a fence around them and a double-track leading to them through churned-up red sand; in the space between fence and houses graze the usual sand-inspecting, sand-snuffling, sand-devouring goats and donkeys. With a long-tailed dog or two, also forever nose-down.

It is impossible to say how many such settlements I was to see in the course of my journey. Nor can I separate them from the miniature versions of the same sort of thing lying behind roadside stores or isolated farmhouses. Usually some huts, or sections of huts, are composed of a building material quite conventional for these parts: burnt brick, mud brick, compressed mud-and- dung (*dagga*), breeze-block, planks, corrugated iron, corrugated asbestos, reeds. But the rest? A kind of incredulity seizes one, here in Campbell and everywhere else, at what will be made to serve for shelter. Heavy-duty paper bags which had once contained cement or lime, plain plastic sheeting, bubbled plastic sheeting, upright cardboard cartons (for rooms), collapsed cardboard cartons (for walls), wooden packing-cases, patches of linoleum, plywood, boulders put on top of everything else, to stop it blowing away – in the circumstances all these, too, one might expect to see being used. After all, they are sometimes used by the homeless in major cities in Britain and other prosperous countries. But a galvanized bath-tub? An old traveller's trunk with wooden ribs, as

if from the great days of steamer travel? Thorn-bush branches? A
car bonnet? Rags? Grass? Newspaper? Bits of foam rubber? The
side-panel of a refrigerator? Parallel sheets of chicken wire with
little stones stuffed between them? Advertising signs? House doors
– never used as *doors* but as walls only, the 'doors' themselves
being hessian bags hung over apertures? Chunks of expanded
polystyrene? Old tyres and inner tubing?

MITSUBISHI and SIEMENS says the lettering on some of the
cartons and packing-cases; and THIS WAY UP; and HANDLE
WITH CARE; and PROTECT YOUR ENVIRONMENT.

All over the northern Cape, all over 'Bophuthatswana', all over
Zimbabwe, many hundreds of thousands of people were doing their
best to protect their own personal environments from rain, wind,
dust, heat and cold, in just this fashion, with just such materials. As
were millions of others across the continent.

There was more traffic on the road as I drove back to Kimberley
late that afternoon. Passing again the few koppies that rose up
from the veld and at long intervals the name-boards announcing
the entrance to this or that farmhouse, I realized that one reason
why the veld was so little grazed was that much of the ground
belonged to the De Beers Corporation. It was De Beers that had put
up all the formidable fencing alongside the road; De Beers that had
left so many tens of square miles of the veld houseless, cattleless,
sheepless (even by the meagre standards of the northern Cape). But
De Beers was not the only organization to whom credit for the
relatively good condition of the veld was to be given. The other
great landholder in the district was the South African Defence
Force.

I was alerted to this possibility simply by the number of army
trucks travelling back and forth along the road, now that evening
was approaching. Many of them had groups of uniformed young
men, blacks and whites, sitting together in the back. Sure enough,
when I stopped to inspect one of the signs hanging on the fence
along the road, I found that it was in the name of the SADF that I
was being warned to keep off the property. And when, a couple of

miles from where Schmidts Drif was marked on my map, I passed a sign proffering BUSHMAN CRAFT AND CURIOS, I noticed that a double-track leading off the road at that point had a painted barrier across it, and that an army truck which had been ahead of me had come to a halt there. Two armed black guards then appeared from the tent alongside, one of whom exchanged words with the driver before giving a formal military salute and instructing his companion to lift the barrier. The truck passed through, and proceeded to make its careful, jolting way along the double-track, towards some destination hidden behind an upward swell of the veld.

So I also turned off the road. Two things struck me when I came to the barrier. The first was the stature of one of the soldiers: he was small, yellow-skinned, round-faced, big-bottomed, with a strong arch to the small of his back. Of course I had read the sign on the road and had been primed by it; still, I was surprised at the word which at once came to my mind. It was: 'Bushman!' Secondly, I registered that both of them, the Bushman and his companion, who was much the taller, darker, and more strongly built of the two, belonging apparently to quite a different racial type, had difficulty in understanding what I was saying, though I tried in both English and Afrikaans. Eventually my elaborate enquiries about where exactly the Bushman craft and curios were to be found and how I could get there were reduced to dumb pointings back towards the sign at the roadside and generous gesticulations ahead of me. At this they consulted briefly with one another. Again the boom was raised.

Some minutes later I parked my car in the middle of a collection of prefabricated huts and tents, some sheds, the cement floors and foundations of a few abandoned houses, and a double row of thick-trunked pepper trees, positively a little avenue, with several army cars and trucks parked between them. There was a dusty parade ground in the distance, and, much nearer, two brand-new rondavels with thatched, pointed roofs. Through the window of one of them I could see a multitude of entirely predictable Bushman curios on display. Some were in glass cases, some on shelves. There were bows, arrows in quivers made of animal skins, *karosses*, gourds, hand xylophones, clay figurines of people and animals, pokerwork pictures on wood or bark. A sign on the window read: *Mrs A. Fourie: Prop.*

Three or four soldiers, who had evidently debarked from the truck that had been travelling ahead of me, were walking towards the prefabricated huts; they must have heard the car arrive but took no notice of my arrival. No one else was about. It was late afternoon. In the distance the sun was going down with a surprising lack of ostentation, for that part of the world. No blood, no molten metals, no silent explosions. All the boulders and dry stalks of grass starting out of the earth had the self-conscious air of items giving you your last chance to look at them.

The footsteps of the soldiers receded. My knocking on the locked doors and windows of the rondavels went unanswered. Then I noticed two small buildings, huts really, which looked as though they had been there much longer than anything else in the vicinity, aside from the little avenue of pepper trees. Both were solidly built of uncut stone. Their doors were open. Across the lintel of the nearer of the two was a crudely daubed sign, in black letters. TEACHER'S PALACE, it said. To the left of these words was an equally crude picture of a rolled-up diploma of the kind that graduates traditionally receive. This was painted in red. To the right, also in red, was a picture of an old-fashioned academic mortar-board, complete with tassel.

Naturally I made my way there. Inside the hut two young white men were seated, each at his own desk. One was staring into a computer screen and tapping on its keyboard. The other, nearer to me, was filling out what looked like an elaborate schedule.

He got to his feet when I appeared in the doorway: a small man in neatly pressed uniform. On one of his rolled-up sleeves were a corporal's stripes. On his upper lip was what was intended to be a stripe of an even more intimidating kind: a thick, flattish, black moustache. However, the soft nose and brown eyes above it were eager, almost puppy-like, and he had a boy's fresh complexion.

'*Kan ek u help?*' he asked.

I told him, in English, that I had been hoping to buy some of the Bushman curios which I understood to be on sale here.

'Are you sure the place is closed?' he asked, ready to oblige. 'Let's go and have a look.'

As we walked back to the rondavels he took a bunch of keys out of his pocket; when we got there he tried some of them on the padlocks hanging from the doors. No luck. He pushed at the windows, also without success. Giving up, he told me that he didn't know when Mrs Fourie would be back. She didn't come every day, only sometimes. Maybe it would be best if I phoned before I came, next time.

He spoke in the effortful, breathy, mimingly emphatic manner many Afrikaners adopt when speaking English. (An object is not heavy but *hevvy*; a place isn't far but *fa-a-r*; and so forth.) Seeing he was so eager to be helpful, I asked him about the camp itself. What was it? Why were Bushman curios on sale here? Why did the sign on that hut say TEACHER'S PALACE?

'It's for the Bushmen,' he said, as if answering all my questions at once. Also as if nothing could have been more self-evident.

'Bushmen? What Bushmen?'

'The Bushmen we brought back with us from Angola.' Then, seeing I still did not understand: 'They were our trackers, in the bush – you know, during the war, when we were fighting up the-e-e-re in Angola. Against the MPLA and the Cubans and all that lot. The Communists, man. We couldn't leave them there after the war – hell no, it would have been too dangerous for them, because they'd helped us. So we brought them back with us. Other lots of people also, not just Bushmen. But this place – here – is for the Bushmen.'

'Where are they?'

'Some live just here, but most of them over there, in another camp, about two miles away' (pointing to the west, where nothing but sun and silhouetted thorn scrub could be seen).

'Can I go there?'

He shook his head emphatically. 'No.'

'How many of them are there?'

'About five thousand.'

'Five thousand! All men?'

'No – men, women, children, families, the lot.'

'What do they do with themselves?'

'They do handwork. They go to school. The young men are still in the army.'

'And you teach them?'

'Me and others.'

'What do you teach them? Basic literacy?'

This made him indignant. 'No, man. We teach them everything. Junior Certificate. Matric. Whatever they want, we teach them. We're all qualified here. The days when the army used untrained people for *anything* is long past. I got my teacher's certificate in PE [Port Elizabeth]. I'm a PE boy myself. PE!' he exclaimed enthusiastically, bringing himself upright, like a man about to take an oath: 'The Friendly City!'

'And how do the Bushmen like it here?

'Not much. They're getting bloody homesick. And I don't blame them either. This place!' And he gestured in contemptuous fashion not just at the camp, dedicated in improbable fashion to the education and, by way of those wretched curios, the economic advancement of some five thousand Bushmen transplanted from Angola, but to the veld beyond. 'Look at it! Flat!' he said with disgust. 'Dead! Dry! You tell me tomorrow morning I can go back to Port Elizabeth and I'll be packing my bags all night. And first thing when I get home, I jump into the sea!'

His brown eyes shone at the thought. We stood on the little porch between the rondavels and looked around us. No one else was to be seen. A radio was playing somewhere. I asked him what the place had been before the army had taken it over, and he said that he had heard it had been a hotel, a *he-e-ll-offf-a lo-o-ng* time ago. At first it seemed to me impossible that there could ever have been a hotel in so isolated, even desolate a place; but the soldier-teacher told me that though you couldn't see the river, the Vaal, from where we were standing, it was just down there, behind those

sheds. Then I remembered from my childhood that there had been
more than one hotel in or near Schmidts Drif. In those days, when
people were more modest in their expectations than they are now,
the 'drif', or river-crossing, had been regarded as near enough to
Kimberley for people to visit in order to enjoy briefly some version
of rural life: to recuperate after an operation, say, or to do some
fishing. I even had a notion that there had once been talk of my
mother going there with one or more of her children, when she or
they had been feeling poorly. Modder River, further to the east,
barely any bigger or more 'scenic' than Schmidts Drif, had also
been touted as just such a resort.

After I had left the camp and returned to the main road which
led to Schmidts Drif and Kimberley, I remembered too that as a
boy I had driven along this road with my father. (I could not recall
the reason for the journey; perhaps we had been going to or coming
back from his manganese mine near Postmasburg.) On the way we
had stopped at Schmidts Drif and had a cup of tea in the hotel. It
was owned, inevitably enough, by an elderly Lithuanian Jew who
had also kept the little general dealer's shop. So I decided to turn
off the road to explore.

Soon enough I discovered that there was nothing left of Schmidts
Drif for me to explore. It had been done away with. Just a shell of
it was left. One could hardly call it a ghost-town now, since the
settlement had never remotely resembled a town. But whatever
there had been – the hotel with its long stoep, the store nearby, the
filling-station, some houses – had been reduced to cement squares
and oblongs on the ground that marked out vanished rooms; or
walls here and there holding up no roofs above, with gaps for long-
gone windows. Through these gaps I could see all the way down to
the Vaal River and the tarmac-coloured water between its banks.
Not a soul was to be seen, neither at the river, nor among the ruins
of what had been Schmidts Drif. As for the 'location', where the
blacks had lived: that consisted of a few wind-eroded stumps of
mud only. Amid all these signs of abandonment only the tangled,
straw-coloured bundles of the weaver-birds' nests, hanging in the

thorn bushes like the heads of giant dried flowers, suggested life, busyness, constructive endeavour.

The desolation was so complete and so unexpected – why should this place be a ghost-settlement, while Campbell was still alive, in its own fashion? – I felt compelled to see if I could find any clues to what had happened. An answer of a kind was not far to seek. Some distance behind the ruins was another army camp: a much bigger and more imposing one than the odd affair I had found myself in a few miles back. It was nothing less than a cantonment, complete with guardhouse, sentries, lawns caressed by busy water-sprinklers, rows of brick barracks, officers' houses, a parade ground, armoured cars and half-tracks in rows, and South African and regimental flags fluttering from tall wooden staffs.

The guards, three of them, tall black men, smartly turned out, looked enquiringly at me. I told them that I was looking for Schmidts Drif and had found that there was nothing left of it. Where had the people gone? They continued to look enquiringly at me, like dumb men; or like the two I had spoken to a few miles back. Then an open vehicle came through the gate. About half-a-dozen men were sitting in the back of it. The guards saluted. The man at the wheel, an officer, a white, said something to them and they responded to it. After my previous experience I was better attuned to this slightly uncanny neighbourhood than before. Surely the language they were speaking was Portuguese?

So: these men too were refugees, in a sense. Or perhaps the idea had originally been to send them back into Angola should the need arise. Or they had been intended for other purposes. I had read reports in the papers, both in England and here, that some Angolan troops had been maintained by elements in the S A D F for 'special operations' within South Africa itself. Having no local political or tribal-ethnic loyalties, it had been hoped they would turn on anyone whom their officers ordered them to attack. And now?

The vehicle budged forward until the driver's window and mine were no more than a foot or two apart.

The man addressed me curtly. '*Ja?*'

'I'm looking for Schmidts Drif.'

A bleak movement, hardly a smile, affected his lower lip. 'Schmidts Drif is finished.'

We stared at one another a moment longer. He said, '*This* is Schmidts Drif. There's nothing else. And this is army property, and you better go now.'

In the light of history, there is an almost surreal quality to the idea of a South African government bringing Bushmen into the country in order to secure their safety. The pages of southern African history are full of bloodshed; they abound with massacres, some elaborate and protracted, some as swift and random as thunderstorms, inflicted by different groups and tribes and races on each other: blacks on whites, whites on blacks, blacks on blacks, whites on whites. (The two Boer republics lost something like fifteen per cent of their entire population in the course of the Anglo-Boer War; most of them dying of disease in the concentration camps set up by the British.) During my visit dozens of people were being done to death, day after day, week after week, month after month, in the course of a quasi-political, quasi-tribal, quasi-gangster warfare going on in various parts of the Republic, especially in the black townships near the major cities.

It is impossible not to feel both terror and weariness at the thought of it: what is happening now, what happened then, what may yet happen, whether the prizes at stake be the land and bony cattle for which people once warred, or today's forms of economic and political power, or the mere illusions of these, or the cameras and credit cards and pay-packets for which so many are ready to kill now.

Yet of all the beastly episodes in this history, few are comparable with those involving the indigenous San, the Bushmen, who almost certainly were the first occupants of the subcontinent. In effect they came to be seen as vermin by Boer and Xhosa, Zulu and Griqua alike: marked out for destruction as a people, more or less as the Aborigines were by the white settlers in Tasmania, later in the nineteenth century. True, attempts were made to enslave some rather than kill all.

The capture of slaves from among this race of men is by no means difficult and is effected in the following manner. Several farmers, that are in want of servants, join together and take a journey to that part of the country where the *Boshies-men* live. They themselves, as well as their *Lego-Hottentots*, or else such Boshies-men as have been caught some time before, and have been trained up in fidelity to their service, endeavour to spy out where the wild Boshies-men have their haunts. This is best discovered by the smoke of their fires. They are found in societies of from ten to fifty and a hundred, reckoning great and small together. Notwithstanding this, the farmers will venture on a dark night to set upon them with six or eight people, which they contrive to do by previously stationing themselves at some distance round about the *kraal*. They then give the alarm by firing a gun or two. By this means there is such consternation spread over the whole body of these savages, that it is only the most bold and intelligent among them, that have the courage to break through the circle and steal off. These the captors are glad enough to get rid of at so easy a rate, being better pleased with those that are stupid, timorous and struck with amazement, and who consequently allow themselves to be taken and carried into bondage.

Thus Andrew Sparrman in his *Voyage to the Cape of Good Hope* (1785). The trouble, however, as Sparrman himself goes on to note, was that even the stupid and timorous among the Bushmen failed to become satisfactory slaves. As he puts it: 'Detesting all manner of labour, and . . . having been used to a wandering life, subject to no control, he most sensibly feels the want of liberty. No wonder then, that he generally endeavours to regain it by making his escape.' Since they proved to be such unprofitable slaves, fewer and fewer attempts were made to capture the Bushmen in the manner described above. This seems to have been especially the case in the northern and north-western Cape. There the Boers and others developed the practice of organizing Bushman shooting-parties. Even in talking to government officials they boasted of their 'bag'. Witness a report written almost a century after Sparrman's account by the Civil Commissioner of Namaqualand – 'a terrible document,' according to the historian from whom I have taken it, 'tell[ing] the last phase of the tragic history of the Cape Bushmen'.

[T]wo commandos ... entered Bushmanland from the Roggeveld side, one consisting of Boers, the other of Bastards. The Europeans went in the direction of the present village of Kenhardt and killed 200 Bushmen, women, and children – almost all they came across. The Bastard commando which went to the Karee mountains killed an even larger number after luring the Bushmen to their wagons with professions of peace. On another occasion, according to one of the witnesses ... '[The Boers] surrounded the place during the night, spying the Bushmen's fires. At daybreak firing commenced and it lasted until the sun was up a little way. The commando party loaded and fired and reloaded many times before they had finished. A great many people – women and children – were killed that day. The men were absent. Only a few little children escaped and they were distributed among the people composing the commando.'

Kenhardt is some three hundred miles to the west of Kimberley. The 'rescued' Bushmen, late allies of the South African troops in Angola, must have flown over it on their way to safe haven near Schmidts Drif.

About six weeks before leaving for South Africa, my wife and I had been to a dinner-party in London. Our hosts, the Poiriers, lived in a South Kensington square: all cream-coloured stucco, fluted pillars, tall windows, and wrought-iron balconies opening on to giant plane trees. I had known Nigel Poirier for many years. His grandparents had once been prominent figures in Kimberley and the owners of land in the district; he himself had been born and brought up in Cape Town. You would not think it, though, when you hear him speak. My ear has no difficulty in picking up South African vowels and stresses in the elocution of some famous West End actors and actresses; let alone in the voices of other socially ambitious South Africans resident in Britain. But not in Poirier's case. 'Oh, him?' a friend once said: 'He's always sounded like a Tory cabinet minister!'

And looked like one, he might have added. And lived like one. Everything in the flat – carpeting, wallpapers, silver trophies in glass cases, nineteenth-century prints – spoke of a peculiarly English, metropolitan, upper-middle-class prosperity. No stranger looking around the flat could have guessed that more than two decades before, in the most granite-like years of the apartheid regime, our host had been a member of a small revolutionary sect engaged in blowing up installations of various kinds in the Cape peninsula; and that when the police had finally closed in on the group, he had made a hair's-breadth escape from the country by stowing away in the belly of a Canadian merchant vessel.

Subsequently he had worked as a businessman in London, and had also taken part in émigré politics and publishing. When the great turnaround took place in 1989, and the South African government formally abjured its apartheid policies, unbanned the organizations which had been proscribed for decades, and pardoned political offenders, Poirier went back to the country on an extended visit. He re-established contact with the friends he had left behind, some of whom had spent long terms in jail; he also paid a visit to Kimberley, and to a cousin, the sole remaining member of his family, who still farmed in the district.

Now it was my turn. This was after I had returned to Kimberley from Griquatown. Something I had seen there had made the visit seem worthwhile, no matter how brief it might turn out to be. The directions I had been given were not difficult to follow. A painted sign at the side of the road said *Stiltespruit* ('Still Waters';'Quiet Stream'); beneath it was inscribed the name of the owner: *M. Poirier*, my friend's cousin. I turned off towards the wide, low farmstead. It had the inevitable tin roof above, a stoep in front, and a garden of raised, sandy beds in which aloes chiefly seemed to prosper. Their fleshy, pointed leaves, some four or five feet long, keeled over in the middle, as if out of fatigue. Behind the house was an oil-soaked, vehicle-littered yard.

I had not phoned in advance and was doubtful of finding the man I was looking for. But he was there, all right. He was doing something in the garden, together with two or three black labourers. They looked up as my car halted in the sandy track to the side of the house. Then Poirier slowly, suspiciously, walked over to me.

Though he was about the same age as his cousin in London, he did not at all resemble him. His face was cramped, lined, sun-dried;

his shoulders were slightly bowed; he wore a farmer's hat, an old sweater, work-trousers, scuffed shoes. He greeted me from a few paces away.

Yes, what could he do for me?

His accent was not remotely like that of a Tory minister. But there was a dry self-confidence, not at all diminished by wariness and reticence, in his manner.

Through the open window of the car I explained who I was and my connection with his relative in London. He listened carefully, standing half turned away, glancing intermittently at me from under a tight, creased brow

Yes, he remembered my family in Kimberley. They had owned that cattle-feed plant. I had two brothers, wasn't that right? Yes, he was glad to hear that all was well with his cousin Nigel. Yes, it had been interesting to meet him again, when he came out, after all this time.

A wintry irony came into his eyes; for a moment it even unsettled the cautious lines of his brow.

'I never thought I'd see him again. I never thought the day would come when he'd be able to show his face around here, I can tell you.'

He said nothing more about his cousin's political views and adventures. He had spoken as he might have of a marital misfortune, or an undischarged gambling debt, or an alcoholic disgrace of some kind.

I then told him that when I had visited the Moffat Museum in Griquatown two days before, I had seen the name Poirier on one of several deeds of transfer showing how the former mission house had passed into private hands, more than a hundred years ago, and then out of them again. He listened intently, nodding from time to time.

Then a final, rapid nod. 'That Poirier was my grandfather. Nigel's great-uncle. And you know what he did with the money he got from that property?' For the first time since he had come to the window of the car he made a gesture. He pointed directly at the ground, at the dry, scuffed sand under his shoes. 'He bought this place.'

The black men in the garden waited, looking in our direction. We were both silent. It was a strange moment. There had been no vainglory in his voice; if anything, a kind of resignation, along with a great firmness. I wanted to ask, 'Have you got children? Will they be taking it over?' but there was something in his manner which forbade me from doing so.

He'd been in Griquatown several times, he went on, but had never gone into the museum and had no idea that an item from his family history was hanging on its walls. Next time, if there ever was a next time, he would make a point of looking it up.

I saw in his eye that he was wondering whether or not he should invite me to come into the house, to have a cup of tea. But I could see also that he wanted to get back to the work he had been doing. So I pre-empted him by starting the engine of the car.

'I'm glad you called.' He leaned a little closer. 'Give Nigel my regards when you get back to London.'

'I will.'

He nodded. We exchanged an awkward handshake through the window. He watched me do a reverse turn in the narrow lane, between a line of pepper trees and a wire fence. Then I regained the road.

In London, many weeks later, Nigel said to me, 'No, he's not the *jolliest* man you can meet, my cousin Michael.'

CHAPTER FOUR

☆

Kimberley Again – Stone-Age and Modern Moments – Barkly West

By the time my wife arrived in Kimberley, to join me in some of the travelling that lay ahead, I was more than ready to leave. This was not because of the ghosts I encountered wherever I turned; it was my own ghostliness I had begun to find so burdensome. I remember talking to a young Tswana woman outside the new Kimberley Hospital, when I was trying to see what remained of the old building in which my mother had died, my father had almost died, and into which my brother and I had been carried after a serious motor accident. When I gave her the date of that accident (1947), she looked at me with incredulity and amusement; it was if I had said I was a survivor of the Anglo-Boer War or had dug for diamonds with Cecil Rhodes. She herself, dressed in a floral overall, with a pencil stuck jauntily into the back of her tight-packed head of hair, was neat, small, curious, self-possessed, ready to humour this old humbug. On hearing that I now lived in England, she said with more intensity than hope, 'One day I wish to see such places.' After a thoughtful pause: 'In England the summer is just beginning and here it is autumn. Strange.' Then: 'How much is the ticket to England actually?' The figure I gave in response shocked her even more than the date of my accident. She worked as a clerk in the hospital, she told me; she had one sister who was a nurse and another who was in the police farther north, near Mafikeng. Her mother was disabled – in a wheel-chair ('also from a road accident') – and her father was at home – 'no job'.

Across the road was a brand-new 'Medi-City': a private hospital for those in flight from the largely desegregated services now on offer in the state institution. The Medi-City, too, was desegregated of course; but the prices it charged would put it as far out of reach to most blacks and Coloureds as an air-ticket to England. My sister had been born in a ramshackle colonial-style house which had once occupied the Medi-City site. It had then borne the title of 'Sister Tyre's Nursing Home'. I could even remember the eponymous Sister Tyre, a large-bodied, noisy maiden lady from England, who had seemed to me more frightening than anything that went on inside her nursing home. The first time I was taken to see the baby, Sister Tyre held a small bundle of wrappings aloft and said (presumably because the baby's mouth was open) – 'Look, she's catching flies!' Why should she be doing such a thing? Later my mother had some kind of post-partum collapse, to which no doubt the heat contributed its share: the baby had been born in the middle of a particularly hot summer, with the temperatures in the upper nineties and low hundreds for week after week. One of the terrors that possessed her, I learned decades later, after her death, was that she would accidentally drop the baby down the Big Hole . . .

No, it was definitely time to be gone. At night, I drove alone around the deserted streets. Occasionally a car passed; never a pedestrian. People were frightened to walk about after nightfall, whether in the town centre or the suburbs. Uniformed black men with walkie-talkies patrolled the precincts of the hotel. Private houses were floodlit and barred like penitentiaries. It used to be one of our great pleasures during the summer, when it was too hot to be out of doors by day, to go for walks in the evenings; but nobody did it any more. In the local newspaper one morning I read of two armed holdups that had taken place the previous night: a truck and its contents had been hijacked three miles out of town, and the driver left shot by the side of the road; an Indian storekeeper had had his day's takings snatched from him by two masked bandits. The one lot had used AK-47 rifles; the other pistols. In Kimberley? Of course, there used to be stabbings and shootings in the old days – family and neighbourhood affairs, invariably, among black and white alike – and occasional burglaries. But this? The next day yet another hijacking was recorded: another driver injured (beaten about the head this time); a lorry-load of butter (*butter*?) taken.

The people I knew had vanished; so had their language. That contributed too to my ghostlike state. In my earliest years the whites of Kimberley spoke English only; Afrikaans was the tongue of the Cape Coloured people. In those days the town did not have a single Afrikaans-medium school. I could remember the introduction of a small shelf of books in Afrikaans in the Kimberley Public Library; and how those lucky enough to have Anglo-Saxon noses had looked down them at this intrusion. Now I was addressed in Afrikaans everywhere I went, by white, black, and Coloured alike. It had become the *lingua franca* of the city.

Not that it will hold that position for long. Passing the old building which still housed the headquarters of the De Beers Corporation, I saw that a section of it was occupied by an outfit called 'Operation Uplift'. *Each One Teach One*, said the brave notice above the door. Through it, at 5 p.m., as the rest of the central area was closing down, there trooped a crowd of eager black adolescents, talking animatedly, some in English, some in Tswana and Xhosa. All were girls. All the notices and classes advertised were in English.

A mere half-an-hour after sunset, the night already as black as it would get, I went across the road to a Portuguese-owned 'café' – i.e. a place at which you could not eat or drink but which sold just about everything: magazines, sweets, milk, bread, cooked foods, canned items, tobacco, fruit, soft drinks, toys, condoms, patent medicines (only alcohol and clothing excluded). Sitting in a huddle on the pavement outside the café, but well away from its entrance, was a group of black children. They were all boys, the oldest about thirteen years, the youngest six or seven. They were barefoot and dressed in rags which hung from them in loops. As much of their backs, ribs, and bums showed through as was hidden. Too timid to approach the customers coming out of the shop, they merely called out from time to time – '*Baas! Basie! Soek kos!*' ('*Baas*, little *baas*, want food'). A thickset white man in open-necked shirt and khaki shorts came out of the café and carried various parcels to his car, where his wife and two fair, straight-haired daughters waited for him. He handed the bags to them, through the open window at the back, before turning towards the crouching boys. They sat or lay a half-dozen paces from him. With an expressionless face, uttering not a sound, he drew back his arm to its full length and hurled a handful of change straight at them. The ferocity of the gesture was extraordinary to see. The boys burst to their feet, shouting in pain and fear, and started to flee down the road; then the noise made by the coins as they hit the paving jerked them to a halt. As abruptly as they had begun running they doubled back and started to scrabble around in the gutter. The man and his family were already driving off. No one in the car – not him, not his wife, not his daughters – made any comment on what they had just seen. Their lips had not moved.

The largest area of habitation for blacks in Kimberley used to be known as No. 2 Location; then it was dignified by the name of Galeshewe Township; subsequently it was dignified yet further by being designated the City of Galeshewe. This last dignity was, however, of a highly suspect kind. The intention of the apartheid government in conferring it was to make it clear to the inhabitants of the place that they had nothing whatever to do with the city of Kimberley proper – their contiguity to it notwithstanding. They were to understand that they lived in different cities, they belonged to different polities, had different histories, looked forward to different futures. That 'Kimberley' and 'Galeshewe' had always been parts of a single economy without which neither could have come into existence; that ninety per cent of those living in Galeshewe who were lucky enough to have jobs were employed in Kimberley; and that Kimberley's commercial and industrial activity would have come to a halt without them – none of this was to be permitted to interfere with the fantasy of a hermetic social and political separation between the two communities.

The inauguration of 'Galeshewe City' was in fact yet another instance of Grand Apartheid: which amounted, in effect, to a grandiose, ideologized version of the policies followed in a more haphazard manner by all preceding South African governments. The entrenchment of racial separation and white economic privilege had been the prime aims of government since the founding of the Union in 1910. The Afrikaner Nationalists, however, made it a matter of quasi-biological theory and quasi-Stalinist practice, especially when it came to the moving of unwanted populations to the desolate corners of the country chosen for them by their rulers. (The so-called 'homeland republics'.) On a humbler level, Grand Apartheid was both reinforced and symbolized by what was called Petty Apartheid: the fiercely policed exclusion of blacks, Coloureds, and Asians from all civic amenities – public halls, parks, post offices, railway platforms, etc. – used by whites.

Hence the apparent generosity of a white government in choosing to call a black township a 'city'; and, what is more, in conferring on it the name of a Tswana chieftain, Galeshewe, who, in 1878 and 1896, had led his people in unsuccessful wars against the annexation of their territory by the Cape Colonial government. (Subsequently he was given sentences of twelve years' and ten years' imprisonment, respectively, for the part he had played in these 'rebellions'.) Hence, also, the triumphant notice M. and I saw as we left Kimberley on one of the main roads going west: CITY OF GALESHEWE: ADDITIONAL SERVICES.

These additional services consisted of pairs of small, single-seater brick latrines, each pair set apart from the next at a distance of perhaps fifty yards. They looked like vertical coffins, two by two, put down on the barren veld for a distance of a couple of miles. No trenches connected them with one another, so it seemed that no pipes for sewerage were in the process of being laid. Presumably the 'night-soil' would eventually be collected by hand. Between the latrines there was only stone and dust and a relatively small number of squatters' hovels, the first of innumerable others to come.

Somebody had evidently been looking ahead. One could only wonder if his plans had taken account of the fact that the so-called

City of Galeshewe will have ceased to exist by the time those latrines are in daily or hourly use. Barely a week after passing the place, I read a newspaper report which stated that the cities of Kimberley and Galeshewe had just begun the process of being 're-united'. Why? Because apartheid, in both its Grand and Petty versions, was even then being rapidly dismantled. It had (since 1989) been officially declared 'unworkable' and 'morally indefensible'.

So at last the chance had come for those who had always opposed the mad dream of apartheid to replace that discredited fantasy with their own visions of the future. This some of them were doing by speaking of bringing into being a 'non-racial' South Africa, with a 'non-racial culture'.

Putting into effect the new constitution and a system of personal law which make no distinctions on grounds of race is going to be task enough. But a 'non-racial' South Africa? One might as well talk of breeding a kosher pig. Or of staging a non-competitive prize fight.

About half-way between Kimberley and Barkly West there is a turn-off to the glacial striations and ancient rock-carvings on the farm Nooitgedacht. (Meaning: Never thought-of; never imagined.) The veld appears to be changeless all the way to the horizon, but after some miles it suddenly cracks open, with a conjuror-like flourish, to reveal a broken, hidden landscape. (This effect was one we were to see repeated over and over again during the days to come.) Below the road there was a wide, gleaming bend in the Vaal River, of which not a glimpse had been given before. The line of the river meandered away to the north; southwards it disappeared under a reddish, rocky bluff. On the far bank, seemingly tucked into its very elbow, was a tree-surrounded farmhouse, built of stone, with irrigated fields and an orchard behind it. On this side of the river stood another farmhouse also built of roughly hewn stone. Its windows were holes merely and its iron roof was in shreds; bales of hay were stacked in what had once been its rooms.

The glacial striations and 'Bushman carvings' we had come to see lay immediately below the abandoned farmhouse. Under a shelter put up by the Historical Monuments Council there was also a display of maps and pictures which directed visitors to important features of the site and explained the way of life of the vanished San people. Notices warning visitors against vandalizing the site were also posted in several places. To make sure that the notices themselves would not in their turn be vandalized, they had been made of the toughest material possible: namely, sheets of thick, stainless steel which bore their warning messages not in some painted or stuck-on form, but stamped deeply right into them.

With what result? All else having been unavailing, the notices were riddled with bullet-holes. Fat ones: ·45 calibre, I would guess. On one notice alone I counted no fewer than fourteen of them.

The marksmen were not the only ones to have left the scars of their visits behind. Alongside the carvings of the Bushman artists, sometimes intertwined with them, was a litter of names, initials, and dates. Some were recent; some might almost have themselves been called historic. For instance, here was a name, Joe or Joz Rohan, with the date 1889 next to it – a mere twenty years after the discovery of diamonds along the river. There was another name which for personal reasons interested me even more. It was that of Wieland Dold, who had painstakingly made his bid for immortality in 1904. In my childhood the Dolds had been a prominent family in Kimberley. There had been a succession of boys of that name ahead of me at school, all of them great sprinters and athletes: so much so that one after the other they had triumphantly assumed the nickname 'Zippy'. This Wieland had perhaps been the very first Zippy of them all.

The site was associated with one other item of modern history which was not mentioned on the posters of the Historical Monuments Council. In 1869 thousands of diamond-diggers arrived in the district, then pretty much a no-man's land, and began scrabbling for treasure up and down both banks of the Vaal River. So a conference was called at Nooitgedacht. The participants were a chief or 'Captain' of the Griqua people by the name of Nicolaas Waterboer and the presidents of the Boer Republics in the Transvaal and Orange Free State. The republics were still the most shaky of political entities, to put it politely. Waterboer – son of the 'Hanging

Tree' Waterboer of Griquatown – was accompanied throughout by his legal representative, David Arnot.

Arnot was a Cape Coloured by origin, a British imperialist by conviction, and a lawyer by training. The four of them met ostensibly to settle the question of who the river-diggings rightly belonged to. (Mining had already begun on the 'dry diggings' twenty miles to the east, which were to become the city of Kimberley; but no one then knew that that was where the true wealth of the region lay.) The meeting at Nooitgedacht went on for several days. No agreement was reached between the participants. Waterboer and Arnot walked out. A few days later President Brand of the Orange Free State, with the support of his Transvaal colleague, unilaterally proclaimed the area to be Free State territory.

As things turned out, this proclamation helped him not at all. After further argument and correspondence, much of it initiated by Arnot, the British administration in the Cape solemnly declared that it supported Waterboer's claims. In response Waterboer made haste to cede the territory to the Governor of the Cape Colony – and thus to the British crown. This was to be of no help to him, either. Governor Barkly (after whom the town of Barkly West was to be named) graciously accepted Waterboer's concession. He and his officials then proceeded to make sure that just about every inch of the territory Waterboer had ceded – diamond lands and grazing lands alike – duly passed into the possession of the white miners and farmers who were pouring into it. The Griquas were utterly dispossessed. An embittered Arnot, whose own motives in defending the rights of Waterboer had by no means been as pure as he pretended, later said that had he known 'the nature of British justice', he would 'ten times sooner have gone in for the Free State'.

It would have made no difference had he done so. There was no hope for the Griquas once diamonds had been discovered on the territory they claimed. (The same was true of some other groups of blacks, like the Korannas and the Tlhaping branch of the Tswana, who also tried to claim the lands as their own.) Arnot's retrospective bitterness was almost as idle as my own curiosity, more than a hundred and twenty years later, as to which of the two farmhouses had been the site of the meeting. Both the abandoned one just a few yards from the glacial rocks, and the inhabited one across the river, looked old enough. They were built of a sombre granite, black and rust-coloured in its raw state, dark grey and sharp-edged when cut open. This had been the material used throughout the northern Cape in constructing most of the buildings of the period which still survive. Then, for reasons unknown to me (the development of local brickfields, perhaps?), builders simply ceased to use it, at about the end of the Anglo-Boer War (1902).

The sloping extrusions of rock on which the Bushmen did their engravings are rather like scabs in colour and shape: swollen yet flattish, ruddy, brown, black, with protruding or flaking edges. In scablike fashion, again, they look stuck on to the rough skin of the veld, like the detritus of ancient eruptions and acnes – dislodgeable from it, you would think, by ruthless scratching.

Anthropologists and archaeologists now believe that the art of the Bushmen was connected with their ritualistic feasts and celebrations (the hunt prominent among them) and the states of trance and ecstasy which accompanied these. Such assertions I have to take on trust – or not – like any other layman. Certainly you cannot look at the delicate, passionate engravings scattered about the sheets of rock at Nooitgedacht and doubt the intensity of the endeavour that went into them. Or the skill. Nor can you doubt that the artists had felt there to be something magical about the site itself. It was not just that so many stone 'canvases' were at their disposal here. More than that: so many of them already bore elaborate, quasi-geometrical markings, long, parallel scratches which must surely have looked to them like the work of a vanished race preceding their own.

The engravings appear both in clusters and as single items. Most of the figures are representations of animals and birds; some could be of humans; a few are abstract – a circle with a hole in the middle, or a pattern like that for the game of noughts and crosses. The smallest are no more than a few inches in length and breadth; the largest about a foot. I was particularly struck by a group of buck pictured running so closely together as to mask one other; and an elegant giraffe, head turned back at the end of its long neck, as if looking to see if it were still being pursued. Here was a serpent apparently begun and then abandoned, there another creature weathering so badly as to be almost indecipherable. Unlike the later carvers of initials (JJTV, for instance, in big bold capitals, the freshest of them all, exactly like the logo of a new television company) – unlike these latecomers, the Bushmen artists had no spray-paint canisters or tempered steel and jewel-bladed tools at their disposal; they had to achieve their most delicate and dramatic effects by striking the head of one stone with yet another, while holding the point of the first against the outcrop on which they worked. You could see exactly how each picture had been made, blow by blow; it was as if not only each line was still visible, but also the repeated physical acts through which it had come into existence. The effect was that of a kind of *pointillisme*: a form discovered and deployed over undated years by a host of anonymous artists. (Not a single initial among them.)

As for the infinitely older markings which the artists had found waiting for them, the notices of the Historical Monuments Council inform the visitor that they are the result of glacial action: disordered, tumbled weights of ice and rock scraping with unimaginable slowness over one another, between mountains long since vanished. At least, remembering my one visit to a glacier, at a place called Fjaerland in Norway, that is what I must assume this landscape then looked like.

Impossible! As impossible to believe, in fact, that the open holes of the diamond mines twenty miles away – the De Beers mine and Kimberley mine, Dutoitspan, Wesselton, Otto's Koppie, Bultfontein – had once been so many volcanoes, spewing their lava abroad and sealing within themselves, at pressures never again to be equalled, those small crystals of carbon to which human beings would one day ascribe an incomprehensible value.

If 'sincerity' is the state of actually feeling what we know, while also knowing what we feel, then we are all hypocrites. Glaciers? Volcanoes? Scrub and rock stretched away in all directions to the distant horizon, interrupted by nothing but their own small, ever-repeated irregularities. The half-coil of the river lay motionless, with a bluish light reflected from it. A silent breeze tugged at the upright stalks of grass and fluttered the tiny yellow flowers growing here and there. They looked like buttercups, but we hesitated to give so juicy, so cosy, so English a name to them. No one had passed the place since we had come, and we met no one on our return to the main road.

'*Lunch?*' said the man I accosted outside a government building. 'Lunch in Barkly West? Now that *is* a problem!'

He was heavily built and neatly dressed, wearing jacket, tie, and white shirt. He spoke with a strong Afrikaans accent. For all the excess flesh that besieged them, his lips and eyes looked innocent. Especially as he was so bewildered by my question.

'The best thing for you,' he said, shaking his head, 'is to go back to Kimberley. It's only thirty-two kays down the main road.'

'What about the hotel?' I asked.

'You won't get anything there. Here –' he gestured all around him – 'just takeaways, that's all. The best one is the Yellow Coco Pan.'

I had seen the Yellow Coco Pan, as well as one or two of its seedier rivals, before approaching him. 'Nothing else?'

'Nothing else.'

He got into his car and belted himself behind the steering-wheel. Then he took a last look at me – the man who had come to Barkly West for lunch – before driving off.

I had remembered Barkly West as a rather 'quaint' little town (by local standards, of course) – unusually cramped for a South African *dorp*, with the road taking a sharp turn uphill into it and a sharp turn out of it at the other end, and many small stone buildings between. And some fine views over the river. But it had changed for the worse since then. The road was three times as wide as it had been, and the sharp turns had been done away with. All but one of the old stone buildings had disappeared. In their place was a multitude of flat-fronted shops with fascias of corrugated aluminium – selling agricultural equipment, groceries, liquor, Mohammed's Groceries, Mohammed's Shoes for the Family – as well as several garages. Painted, plastic, and metal signs in hideous colours abounded. On one side of the town was a depot for government or police vehicles: an expanse of tarmac on which were ranged rows of cars, pick-up vans, fuel tanks, and tin huts of various shapes; the whole surrounded by a girdle of razor wire. The river was nowhere to be seen. A score or two of Coloured men – and a handful of women – sat on the kerbs and in the shade of doorways; some reclined in the capacious gutters, others were gathered in a group outside the liquor store. Lunch-time for everybody. They ate out of bags, drank out of tin cans and wax cartons, shouted at one another, stared at nothing in particular.

So we went to the hotel. Like the Hotel Louis in Griquatown, and the Commercial Hotel in Danielskuil, and the Mahalypye Hotel in Botswana, it was another of what I was to discover was a rapidly vanishing species: the old-fashioned southern African country hotel. For the most part such places have either given way to up-market hotels belonging to chains, or have been turned into bars merely, with perhaps a couple of rooms attached: all this being not so much a consequence of ordinary commercial pressures as of the abandonment of racial segregation. The chain hotels, behind their impressive security fencing, are patronized largely by whites; the ex-hotels, by blacks; in between remain an ever-diminishing number of survivals – single-storeyed for the most part; musty; verandahed; be-gauzed; with desolate dining-rooms and lightless, linoleum-floored corridors.

The one in Barkly West, which stood sideways-on to the main road, was pleasantly shaded by some substantial trees. Its verandah was the usual affair of polished, red-dyed cement and white pillars, with a low parapet in front, a few pot-plants, and an iron roof above. The 'lounge' was equipped with a tired-smelling couch, at once over-stuffed and broken-backed, and a picture of snow-topped mountains and waterfalls in what could have been Norway – or perhaps the northern Cape in its long-gone glacial days. The dining-room was veiled in mosquito netting to a degree of whiteness and stillness that put me in mind of Miss Havisham in Dickens's *Great Expectations*. In the bar I came on young, thin, sullen Raymond, the Coloured barman, who was playing a game of pool with his sole customer, a white man of about the same age and disposition, only fatter. When I asked Raymond – his name was on a plastic tag on his shirtfront – if there was any food to be had, he swore briefly; then disappeared somewhere beyond the white hush of the dining-room. Minutes passed. We waited in the lounge. In addition to the snow-and-mountain picture there was a dead television set to look at. Connected to nothing, it sat on a shelf eight or nine feet above ground level.

Raymond reappeared and leaned contemptuously against the door jamb. '*Kok het niks gemaak,*' he announced with savage pleasure. ('Cook has made nothing.') His return to the bar was celebrated a moment later with a racket of balls striking against balls.

Back on the stoep I found two Coloured women dressed in domestic overalls, sitting on the parapet. They were eating hamburgers from plastic containers. They too advised me, in Afrikaans, to go to the Yellow Coco Pan and buy my lunch there. But they added kindly, as if they owned the hotel – I was to learn later that they did not even work in it – 'You can come back here to eat it.'

Which is what we did. On the pavement outside the Yellow Coco Pan there was indeed a yellow-painted coco pan, as an advertising device. It was set on a short stretch of rails. When I was a boy these coco pans – heavy, wheeled, cast-iron, tip-up bins – were the only means available for conveying the diamondiferous 'blue-ground' and the subsequent 'tailings' (waste) from one place to another. One used to see whole chains of them, pushed or pulled by small electric tram-cars, trundling about the De Beers properties; on the small river-diggings gangs of weary blacks did the pushing and pulling. Now everyone uses conveyor-belts: the longest, belonging to De Beers needless to say, stretches around one side of Kimberley for several miles; the shortest to be seen on the diggings are like grain-mill elevators. Either way, coco pans were finished. As a result they have become 'picturesque'; to be painted in bright colours and used as garden and commercial ornaments.*

*

* The word 'coco' has nothing to do with the manufacture of chocolate. An entry in Beeton and Dorner's *Dictionary of English Usage in South Africa* states that the term is of Nguni origin: 'possibly derived fr. Hott. ghoeko/ghoughou = hedgehog, porcupine'.

Barkly West was the scene of the country's first great diamond rush in 1869. Subsequently, for hundreds of miles to the north and south, the banks of the Vaal River were dug over, sifted, riddled with shafts, turned into smaller and larger heaps which were themselves later sifted and turned over yet again. In many places the digging still goes on. Some of the abandoned workings are covered with a thin growth of grass and thorn; others remain bare. Perhaps the most startling thing about one especially worked-over area called Canteen Koppie, just outside Barkly West, is not the number or depth of the shafts with which it is pitted, but simply the amounts of beautiful, light-filled pebbles that can be picked up in handfuls there. Tiny garnets and amethysts are freely speckled among them. They too, presumably, like the alluvial diamonds, were seeded by the original volcanic eruptions in the Kimberley district, and then washed down to the river over the aeons of which geologists speak.

Once the diamonds had been discovered in and around Barkly West, bitter contention arose between the white diggers and the many blacks who were also drawn to the district to try their hand at this new mode of suddenly amassing wealth. (I am not speaking here of such hifalutin' matters as territorial sovereignty; merely of the right to work individual claims, holes, heaps, bits of riverside.) The white diggers were as motley a group as could be found anywhere on earth; on one issue, however, they were united here, as they were to be in Kimberley later. That was that 'niggers' should never be 'diggers'. Only as employees were they to be allowed on the fields. To enforce this point the Barkly West diggers elected a 'Diggers Committee' which was subsequently elevated by some excitable writers into a 'Diggers Republic', under the presidency of an adventurer named Stafford Parker. Later, Barkly West became the constituency of Cecil Rhodes for the Cape Colonial parliament, and remained his seat until his death. Rather surprisingly, there is no monument to him there. Perhaps it was felt that the imposing equestrian statue in Kimberley would do. Not until Mafikeng was I to come on another.

CHAPTER FIVE

☆

Along the River-Diggings to 'the Most Charming Spot on Earth', with Castles in the Air, a Stately Home, and a Barmitzvah on the Way

Travelling across the expanses of the northern Cape is like being in mid-ocean. The veld is hard, waterless, indefeasibly earthy; yet the analogy remains hard to resist. You are always conscious of the horizon and of the emptiness that lies between yourself and it. You are surrounded by a sameness that is also constantly changing. Just as the sea heaps itself into crests and sinks into hollows, in a movement that always threatens to form a pattern but never quite does so, here too your sense of order is provoked and defeated by the irregularities of the earth's surface, its changing colours and textures, its scattered boulders and antheaps, its varieties of grudging and begrudged vegetation – white-spined thorn, brittle grass, flat-leaved bushes, tiny, fugitive, earth-hugging flowers.

Only one thing can never be questioned: the authority of the sky over everything below it. Often the veld appears to be nothing more than a foil to the real drama taking place overhead. Clouds gather in a tumultuous silence; they reveal depths and heights which they themselves have brought into existence; distant rainstorms hang down from them like strands of a girl's hair after she has washed it; they unfurl their sails (black and blue, white and purple) and embark on destinationless journeys across darkening or glittering vacancies they alone can intrude on.

The metalled road points west or north in so straight a line the eye aches to look at it. Alongside run docile telegraph wires, forever sagging from and rising to meet the poles that carry them. Elsewhere power pylons stride off at angles, and meet in strange congresses or conventions in the middle of nothing, before going their different ways. As the hours go by you begin to long for new words with which to describe the landscape; the obvious ones, like wide, endless, scorched, flat, desolate, boring, empty, soon begin to lose their meaning.

How about: pointless?

Or: a waste of time (and of space)?

For a considerable distance the Vaal River, with all its tumuli of dead diamond workings, runs parallel to the road out of Barkly West; then it swings south and is lost to view. At regular intervals signs point to the places where the diggers still cluster, as well as to others which have been largely abandoned. Romantic names they have; romantic at least to those who have never had to live and work in any of them: Waldeck's Plant ('plant' here referring to machinery, not to growing things); Gong-Gong (an onomatopoeic word, describing the sound of water passing over rocks); Winter's Rush (which speaks for itself). There used also to be a whole series of Hopes, most of which are no longer signposted or marked on maps: Delports Hope; Cawoods Hope; Good Hope; Bad Hope; Bluejackets Hope; Forlorn Hope.

Gong-Gong I had last visited something like a half-a-century before. In my class at school there had been a Jewish boy by the name of Rosenberg whose stepfather had kept a store at Gong-Gong and who had also been a diamond-digger in his own right. On the occasion of Johnny Rosenberg's barmitzvah two open lorries transported a group of young people from Kimberley to a party at the house. There we consumed the usual amounts of food and listened to the usual speeches; later we trooped down to the river and clambered about the breakwater which Mr Rosenberg had constructed. (These are built by the better-funded diggers in order to divert the course of the water and thus make available to them the sediments of the river-bed.) On the bank were piles of gravel waiting to be put through horizontal sieves of different sizes, as well as piles that had already gone through the sieves and been thrown aside. There was also a single sorting table under a shelter, where the final, heaviest residues would be combed through by hand.

The river was low; the workings were idle (it was Sunday); the light of the setting sun came even more glaringly off the rocks on the river bank than from the sky. Naturally we scratched about in the gravel with our bare hands and failed to find any diamonds. Then we got on the lorries and began the journey back to Kimberley. I was on the second one to leave. By now it was dark; it had started to rain; we huddled under the blankets provided for us. At some point between Barkly West and Kimberley we overtook the vehicle which had gone ahead. It had been in a collision with a cyclist – a 'native', as people used to say in those days. Everyone said also, with much conviction, that he had been 'drunk', though it was a mystery how this could have been known, given the dark and the rain and the instantaneity of such an accident. The dead man was not to be seen; presumably he had been laid out somewhere on the side of the road. One of the lorry's headlights had been shattered in the collision, but the light itself was still shining. Shafts of rain gleamed in front of it and vanished. On fragments of glass sticking to the rim of the headlight were impaled small, red pieces of meat.

We then had to squash up so that all the people who had been in the front lorry could climb on to ours.

Revisiting Gong-Gong, I recognized nothing other than the river itself: not the house, not the shop, not the remains of the breakwater. So on to Delports Hope, which I had never been to before, and which stands at the confluence of the Vaal and the Harts Rivers. Partly because it is off the main road, Delports Hope looked quite unlike Barkly West: it was quiet, neat, shady, free of traffic, virtually without advertisements. Some government offices were grouped together in a row of single-storeyed buildings with an open space in front of them, like a school yard. I stopped there to ask the way to the meeting-point of the rivers. The office I happened to go into was a Tax and Revenue establishment. Behind a ferocious set of vertical security-bars reaching from counter to ceiling sat a middle-aged Afrikaner lady. For all the mildness of her demeanour, and the especial mildness of her spectacles, she had been made to look like a caged animal or a madwoman in a seventeenth-century bedlam. On the public side of the counter another lady of the same sort sat on an office chair, calmly knitting. In her lap was a pink garment-in-the-making. I soon learned that this lady ran the clinic, two doors down. It was a quiet afternoon in both offices: that much was obvious.

My attempt to speak Afrikaans to them both was brushed aside. No sooner had I said 'Goeiemiddag' than they responded with 'Good afternoon'. 'How do you know I'm English-speaking?' I asked. 'Because of the way you said Goeiemiddag,' they answered, amused at my imagining that I could pass myself off as one of them.

Eventually the Tax and Revenue lady was kind enough to come from behind her counter to walk with me to my car, the better to point out the way. To do this she had to undo from within various locks, bolts, and bars. Clang, clang, clang. Now I could see that her body, like her face, was long and thin. Her glasses had oval lenses and freckled frames; behind them was a pair of light, lively, ingenuous eyes. On her forehead, though, were many weary lines. By this time we were positively friends, so I introduced her to M. and we stood under a pepper tree and talked for a while. She was from Pretoria, she told us; she and her husband had come to the neighbourhood because he had always had 'this *thing* in his life': he just *had* to try his luck at prospecting. Was it because he'd come originally from the Kimberley district? 'No, no. It was something inside him. It just wouldn't leave him in peace. So I said OK. Then after a few years here the Lord took him away from me. I lost him last October. He was still young.'

And the prospecting? 'It was up and down,' she answered, making a wavelike, horizontal motion with her hand. 'Always up and down. In the end we never saw our investment again. It all went.' Didn't she want to go back to Johannesburg, now that she was on her own? 'Well, you know how it is. I have a son at school here, he's nearly in Matric already, I don't want to make another big change for him now. And my other son is in the post office, in Kimberley. So here I must stay. It's all right. It's quite peaceful really.'

She shook hands with us both, and she made us promise that if we had difficulty in finding the *samelooping* (that was the one word for which she fell back into Afrikaans), we would return to the office, and then she would get in her car to show us the way. But her instructions led to the confluence all right, over about a mile or two of rather dusty road, most of it parallel to the river.

The meeting of the rivers was described by the Reverend John Campbell, on 17 July 1813, as 'one of the most charming spots on earth, the river and its elevated banks being covered with trees' (*sic*). Campbell had been sent out by the directors of the London Missionary Society to inspect the work of their outposts in South Africa, and to report on how well they were going about 'the conversion of the heathen, keeping in view at the same time the promotion of their civilization'. (A peculiarly ambiguous phrase, that last one. Could it possibly refer to the promotion of *their* – the blacks' – civilization? Or should it, more plausibly, be read in context as their promotion to civilization?) Campbell travelled to Griquatown, among other places, and further north to Lattakoo, near Kuruman; in due course he produced an artless volume entitled *Travels in South Africa*; this was followed in 1820, after yet another inspectorial trip, by *Travels in South Africa: a Second Journey*.

One of the striking features of both volumes is the positively Adamic confidence with which the author went around naming the places he visited after people for whom he had a high regard:

At eleven a.m., we passed a pool of water, which we named Newton Fountain, in memory of the late valuable rector of St Mary Woolnoth . . .

[At] this junction a considerable stream was produced, which we named Arrowsmith River, in reference to that gentleman's laudable attention to the improvement of maps ... About a mile from what we named Wilberforce Pass [a tribute to the leader of the anti-slavery movement], we found near a hundred Lattakoo people ...

And so he goes on, scattering his memorials broadside: a mode of appropriating the territories different from that of the Boers or of the English colonists who were to follow him, but effective enough in its own terms. Philip and Vanderkemp (two of the earliest missionaries in the eastern Cape); Hardcastle (the secretary of the London Missionary Society); Steinkopff, Bogue, and Alers (whose achievements remain unknown to me) all were remembered. One can hardly begrudge him the evident satisfaction with which he finally reports his arrival at a village 'connected with Klaar Water' (Griquatown). 'When I asked the name of it, I was told that it was *Campbell*' (italics in the original).

Strangely enough, he did not choose to give a name to the confluence of the two rivers, in spite of the rapturous description of it quoted above; a description which goes on:

A Bushman with his two wives visited us. They witnessed our worship, but seemed to take very little notice of it. After our worship, I went to a retired eminence on the banks of the river. The views to the north-east and south-east were very extensive. The reflection that no European eye had ever surveyed these plains, and mountains, and rivers, and that I was ten thousand miles from home made a solemn impression on my mind, which was deepened by the stillness which at that time prevailed.

Notwithstanding all the changes that have taken place since then, the stillness Campbell noted a hundred and sixty years before, almost to the day, was still evident. Upstream along the Vaal some prospecting was going on in lackadaisical fashion: scattered among gravel heaps were various idle items of machinery; in the shade of a van sat two or three Coloured workmen, with a white man squatting above them, talking earnestly. Below the meeting of the two rivers was a concrete pumping station for the Ulco limeworks; it may have been doing its pumping, for all I could tell, but no sound came from it. The Vaal was quite wide above the point where the two rivers joined, but evidently shallow: the branch of a fallen tree stuck out of the water about a third of the way across. On it perched a solemn row of four cormorant-like birds who kept a cautious eye on us. The movement of the water in the Vaal could just be made out, chiefly because the much narrower and apparently motionless Harts was choked from bank to bank and as far upstream as the eye could see with a trailing, finger-thick weed. Some of it had spilled out, as it were, into the conjoined river; and there, against the dead weight of the weed, the ripples of the Vaal could clearly be seen.

The banks of both rivers were covered not with Campbell's 'trees', but with reeds and thorn bushes, growing out of an apparently hard clay which broke into grey sand when you stepped on it. Leaving M. with the car, I made my way on foot up the bank of the Harts for some distance, before being halted by an impenetrable thicket of reeds.

I had been hoping to see, somewhere on the opposite bank, the remains of the mission station Dikgatlhong, which I knew to have stood for many decades on that side of the river. It had been established in 1829 by the missionary Holloway Helmore, who persuaded a group of the Tlhaping branch of the Tswana to settle there with him. (Twenty years later, eight hundred miles to the north, in pursuit of one of David Livingstone's wilder schemes, Helmore was to meet his death. His wife and two of his children died with him. They are believed to have died of malaria, though rumour had it that they had been poisoned by the tribesmen he had been trying to convert.) The settlement he had founded at Dikgatlhong remained in existence until 1908; then it was destroyed in the course of the Cape Colonial government's programme of 're-locating' the blacks of the northern Cape.

There is a peculiar irony to Dikgatlhong's having come to an end in this fashion. In 1853 it had been the site of a meeting of missionaries under the chairmanship of Robert Moffat. They had gathered there to compose a 'memorial' protesting against the

British government's decision to relinquish claims to sovereignty over all territories north of the Orange River; and thus, in effect, setting the Boers free to do as they pleased there. (Throughout the nineteenth century the policy of the imperial government seems to have been to take one step forward, three-quarters of a step back.) The missionaries were convinced that the 'aborigines' were being surrendered to what they called 'the lure of plunder and lust of power and the desire of obtaining constrained and not paid labour on the part of the Boers'. However, the Cape Colonial government which destroyed Dikgatlhong and expelled its people seventy years later *was* directly answerable to London – which of course did nothing about it.

Anyway, I saw no sign, as far as I was able to go, of the remains of the settlement. On returning to Delports Hope I stopped to let our friend in the Tax and Revenue office know that I had found some, if not all, of what I had been looking for.

The dreams I used to have about the country I was travelling through were invariably furnished with castles, bridges, cathedrals, and other such improbabilities. Now I found that these did have their analogues in the territory. Also, if the mountainous landscapes my unconscious mind had also invented were nowhere to be seen, it did contain some quite imposing ranges of hills (for example the sombre-looking Asbestos Mountains to the north of Griquatown; and the more serene and shapely Kuruman Hills); as well as some dramatic ascents and descents to and from the Ghaap Plateau, which the outsider would never have suspected to be there until he had passed through them.

As for the 'castles': they were in fact mines. All but one of those we saw were mining and processing lime. Even if you had known of their existence before, you would hardly have thought the industry to be such a mighty one. From twenty miles away or more their smokestacks and headframes were visible, reared up and fuming into the empty sky. The Union Lime Company mine was battlemented in true castle fashion (or so it seemed); the PPA mine with its fangs and spikes was like some medieval instrument of torture, grown to space-fiction size; the Anglo-Alpha mine at Danielskuil could have been a ship at sea, forever trailing its smoke and steam to leeward; the Finsch diamond mine resembled from a distance a medieval walled city. In each case the mine seemed to stand alone, in an uninhabited place, though the PPA and Finsch mines were at opposite ends of a single valley. The reason was that the purpose-built villages like Ulco and Limeacres, where most of the workers lived, could hardly be seen until you were right on top of them.

And all this was without even visiting Postmasburg and the manganese and iron mines which run for many miles to the north of it. All this, too, without any activity around the many asbestos mines which had once studded the area and had since been guiltily closed down.

We also discovered a kind of 'stately home' out there. To get to it (not by the best route, we learned later) we went forty miles along a dirt road, the entire length of which yielded not one other vehicle travelling in either direction. All we passed was the occasional farmhouse with its iron roof pulled well over its eyes, as if in a sulk, and a few abandoned-looking huts. No one at home, apparently. Then we dropped down a well-hidden escarpment, overlooked by red-toothed bluffs. At the foot of it was an entrance that had been carefully described to us beforehand: not because it was anything special but, on the contrary, because we would otherwise have gone by without noticing it. It was an ordinary, sagging farm-gate of tube iron and wire, dignified by not so much as a name plate. It opened on as rough a double-track as I have driven over.*

On and on it ran, for several miles, or what felt like several miles. At longish intervals it was interrupted by gates which M. at first patiently and later disconsolately opened and closed in turn. Not a single living creature was to be seen, other than the birds which we ourselves startled from the thorn trees. We had been told to count the gates as far as the eighth; then turn right and go

---

* The Afrikaans language has a charming word for the strip of growth and stone that lies between the two tracks. It is called the *middelmannetjie* – 'little man in the middle'.

through two more. And there, at last, when we had all but given up hope of finding the place, and had begun to think we had turned off the public road too soon or too late, or had miscounted the gates – there, on a slope, behind its trees, stood the house.

Its central portions were built of stone; the more recent additions were of brick and glass; its roof was of corrugated iron. (In the old days you would begin to upgrade an old house by replacing its iron roof with slate or tile; now, even in the smartest suburbs of Johannesburg, such roofs are jealously maintained. 'Preserving the local vernacular', the architects call it.) The front looked over the broken countryside, all ruddy rock, pale grass, black scrub, and purple God knows what – sheer distance, I suppose – stretching down towards the Vaal River fifteen miles away. No other habitations were visible in the whole semi-circular expanse. Immediately in front and to the side were well-tended lawns on terraces, flower-beds, and giant jacarandas; lower down, other flower-beds were in the process of preparation.

A fine setting: no question. But what made the house extraordinary was that its many rooms were full of beautifully arranged, lovingly tended museum pieces, a lifetime's collection of treasures. These were of differing origins: some Cape Dutch, some English, others German, Venetian, Turkish, Chinese. There were antique chests, cabinets, rugs, tables, four-poster beds, cupboards, mirrors, book-cases, embroideries, pictures, copperware, vases, china bowls and plates. There was a Victorian 'English bedroom' and an eighteenth-century 'Cape Dutch bedroom'; the biggest room of all, in which were kept most of the continental pieces, had a hushed, demurely self-conscious air, like that of a beautiful woman content to let strangers look their fill at her. The floors were exquisite, let alone the rugs (chiefly Turkoman – these being a speciality of the house) which covered them. I would guess that the most valuable items on display were those of Cape Dutch origin. Made of yellowwood, stinkwood, and ironwood, they were gravely proportioned and embellished with brass and wooden mouldings. The cabinets in particular had something in their lines that unmistakably echoed the ancient gabled homes in the Cape peninsula they were originally intended to furnish.

Tall, bald, bespectacled, stiff-gaited, rusty-voiced, the owner of the house was dressed in a cotton shirt with a delicate yellow stripe, and immaculate cream flannels. He was full of stories of how he had come by this piece in Cape Town, or that one in London, or Istanbul, or wherever. An Afrikaner by origin and upbringing, his English was not merely fluent but commanding; that too was evidently a source of pride to him. His wife was small and jumpy; given to quick smiles, the occasional wink, and frequent little flutters of disagreement with him over minor matters – disagreements voiced so timidly as to be even more flattering, I suspected, than outright subservience might have been. They were most hospitable to us, complete strangers though we were, who had come to them simply by way of a friend of a friend of a friend. They were also, I felt, essentially indifferent to us; so self-contained they were, so devoted to the possessions which few people other than themselves would ever see, so wrapped up in the life they had created for themselves in the midst of the thousands of hectares they owned and on which their flocks of cattle and sheep were raised.

On one of the Cape Dutch chests, its brass fittings agleam and its woodwork as full of reflections as the mind of a daydreaming child, there rested an incongruously cheap-looking pile of magazines issued by the Rosicrucian movement. The Rosicrucians did not come up in our conversation. But I learned a great deal about our host's views on many other topics. On South Africa (not optimistic); on the blacks (not high); on the Jews (ostensibly admiring, even to the point of claiming that he wanted to convert to Judaism, and yet full of resentment at their cleverness and money-making proclivities); on the English (snobs); on Eastern wisdom (they've forgotten more in the East than we in the West ever knew); on God (all the great religions worship the same God, only they call on him by different names); on man's responsibility to Nature (to hand on the earth to future generations in the condition we received it); and on man's responsibility to his fellow-man (to 'have respect', regardless of whether he's white or black, Jew or Christian, English or Afrikaans, rich or poor, and so forth). This last sentiment notwithstanding, it was from his lips that I heard for the first time a formula which was to dog me all the way north: 'I'm no racist; but ...' – the *but* being invariably followed by some fierce animadversion on the blacks. ('I'm no racist,' one man said to me in all earnestness; 'but I can tell you that ninety-nine point nine-nine per cent of them haven't the beginnings of morals or manners or a sense of human decency.')

We ate the food they offered (with silver cutlery, off bone china) and admired both their collection and the pertinacity they had shown in accumulating and maintaining it in so isolated a place. I did not have the heart to reveal to them that I was there under a misapprehension. It was not in search of Turkoman carpets and antique furniture that I had arranged this visit. Somewhere in the passing of information from friend to friend to friend there had been a misunderstanding. I had been told that I would find in my host an expert on the history of the northern Cape. But on that topic, or on anything like it, we exchanged hardly a word. At the beginning of our visit I had described to him the journey I was making and why I was making it. He showed no interest in the subject. He appeared to be no more knowledgeable about the route I planned to follow than anyone else I had met so far. The stately home aspect of the visit was a complete surprise to me. It was not for that that I had come.

Still, I was glad we had made the journey. Not least because in a country where even the lady in the Delports Hope tax office had to be guarded like a gorilla in a cage; where the hotel-visiting traveller can sometimes feel as if he is moving from one be-sentried encampment to another; and where, when I went out for a short walk early one evening with a high official in the government of the so-called independent Republic of Bophuthatswana, we were accompanied by no less than two rottweilers – in such a country, this house, packed with portable, saleable treasures of great value, did not have a single barred window or security gate anywhere about it. True, the huts of the farm labourers, who were presumably known and trusted by the owners, were close by, and there were several labrador dogs roaming about the garden; but even so, its apparent openness and vulnerability were astonishing. I could only assume that its remoteness, anonymity, and difficulty of access – or, to put it another way, its sheer implausibility – were considered sufficient protection by the owners and their insurers.

CHAPTER SIX

☆

The Old Prospector – A Multi-Media Academy – Three Danielskuil Ladies

The original 'strike' at the Finsch diamond mine, the largest to be developed in the northern Cape after the major nineteenth-century discoveries, was made by a prospector named Allister Fincham. His grandson attended my school and was intermittently my 'best friend'. As a result I knew his grandfather slightly. I used to see the old man when I went to my friend's house; I also met him at least twice in my father's office. This was when my father was involved in his manganese-mining operation near Postmasburg. Fincham was always looking for partners in his own never-ending, ever-urgent searchings for mineral deposits all over the northern Cape. My father did once put up some money for an option on a piece of ground which Fincham had high hopes for. I cannot remember what industrial mineral or semi-precious stone was supposedly at stake. Nothing came of it anyway. When Fincham finally did make the strike that transformed his fortunes his backer was someone named Schwabel; hence the portmanteau name 'Finsch' given to the mine.

I remember Fincham as a thickset man of middle height, with stooped neck and shoulders, as if from the habit of constantly scanning the earth for what it might conceal. His skin was roughened by the sun; his manner was doggedly cheerful, though there were times when I saw him looking downcast and withdrawn. I had the impression that my friend disapproved of his grandfather's irregular, obsessive way of life, with all its solitary journeying and endlessly unfulfilled anticipations. My father spoke of 'old Fincham' and his schemes with a kind of amused pity; but he did not begrudge him the success he eventually achieved. By then I had left Kimberley and was no longer in touch with my old schoolfriend. When I bumped into him by chance in Johannesburg one day, I congratulated him on his grandfather's discovery and added, crassly enough I suppose, 'It must have made a great difference to your expectations.' He answered me curtly, with a gloomy frown, 'It's not like that *at all*' – which left me wondering.

Well, there, a mere hundred miles north-west of Kimberley, was the Finsch mine and its headgear, its sorting and extraction plant, and its man-made mountains of tailings. At the foot of them was the company town of Limeacres. The mine is now owned, inevitably, by the De Beers Corporation; and so is Limeacres. It has elaborate traffic schemes to prevent cars driving through it, a shopping-centre, green lawns and playing-fields, and streets of brand-new homes of varying sizes, each with its own well-watered garden. What also struck me about it was that it was by far the most visibly integrated town, racially speaking, of all those I visited anywhere in South Africa. Only in one respect was it deficient from the casual visitor's point of view. The hotel we had been expecting to find there no longer existed. Or rather, it had been turned into a company guest-house. You couldn't get in without a 'chit'. Money and credit cards were of no use.

This depressing news was given to us by a broad-faced, wide-bodied Coloured lady behind the reception desk. She was of sympathetic disposition and was sorry to disappoint us. Especially as we had turned up late in the afternoon; she knew, as I did, that it would be dark within thirty minutes. Helpfully but hopelessly she said, 'I'm sure that if you could just find the mine administrator he'd make out a chit for you. But he leaves his office at five o'clock and I don't know where he is now. Maybe he's playing golf. He likes to play golf after work.'

There was not much appeal in the picture of M. and me wandering about the Limeacres golf-course in search of the mine administrator, hoping to talk him into making out the magic chit for us.

Would he carry spare chits in the pocket of his golfing trousers? In his bag?

'Is there anywhere else we can go?'

'Not here, no. There's nothing. Maybe you could try Postmasburg.'

I did not feel like trying Postmasburg, though (or because) I knew it to be the biggest town in the region. Also I remembered it from all those years ago as an exceptionally ugly place. No doubt it was bigger now, and even uglier.

'What about Papkuil?'

'No,' the woman said, 'you don't want to go there. The hotel in Papkuil is finished. The blacks have taken it over.'

A bizarre remark to hear from the lips of a Coloured woman? Not really. Years of propaganda about 'the unity of the oppressed' from black and white radicals, as well as centuries of abusive treatment from the generality of whites, have not diminished the desire of many Coloureds to preserve the distinction between themselves and the blacks. (The same could be said of those blacks who are as contemptuous of 'mixed breeds' as any diehard, apartheid-loving white.) Secondly, I had learned that the phrase 'the blacks have taken it over' did not mean that they owned it, but that no amenities or facilities were to be found there. Only liquor.

'If you don't want to go back to Kimberley –' (again! I thought) – 'you'd be better off in Danielskuil,' the woman advised us. 'There's a proper hotel there.'

So to Danielskuil we went. That evening I made a couple of phone calls to Kuruman and to Johannesburg, and got much the same response in both cases. 'Danielskuil!' said my acquaintance in Johannesburg. 'What the *hell* are you doing there?' And the Kuruman contact asked anxiously: 'Danielskuil? What's the matter? Has your car broken down?' 'Danielskuil?' the lady of the 'stately home' said to me when I phoned her too – 'It's the kind of place where you used to find only poor Coloureds and poor whites.' (The phrase 'poor white' referring here to a distinctive caste, the equivalent of 'white trash' in the American South.)

After all of which I found it to be rather an agreeable place, as northern Cape *dorps* go. For one thing it was unlike all the others in having a wide stretch of water to the side of it; positively a lake. (From which, it must be admitted, squadrons of mosquitoes took off after dark, like World War Two bombers, to torment us through the nights we stayed there.) It had some well-tended open spaces, with rough lawns and beds of cannas, as well as several prosperous-looking homes. Some of them were in terraces of neat brick 'town houses', Johannesburg-style, with smart gardens in front. The biggest of the shops were off the main road: the most striking of them as handsome specimens of nineteenth-century stone buildings as we were to see anywhere. (The village was founded in the 1830s by a group of Griquas who had fallen out both with the missionaries and the ruling Kok and Waterboer clans of Griquatown.) These particular shops were shaded with immensely thick pepper trees and had, like historical monuments, been most carefully kept free of advertisements. To the side of one of them was a single painted sign, separate from the building itself: A. GERS (PTY) LTD SUPERMARKET – *Weapons, Ammunition, Gifts, Jewellery, Fashion, Clothes, Shoes.*

Apart from the usual garages and a chemist, the town also contained Polene's Dress Shop, another called A Bit of Everything, and an old Dutch Reformed church transformed into a woebegone *Kulturele Klub* (Cultural Club). And of course the Anglo-Alpha limeworks about two miles down the road, the fumes of which blew straight over the Coloured and black quarters of town. (Their siting could hardly have been an accident.) In the usual fashion these areas began quite promisingly with small, four-square, brick-built houses, standing on clearly demarcated though unpaved roads; behind them were smaller houses of breeze-block construction, some whitewashed, some not, which were more crowded together; behind these, again, where the roads failed and mere tracks took over, were tottering shanties cast down anyhow. The children hanging around them had fleshless limbs; their feet were shod in dust only.

The hotel itself was a pretty Spartan affair (iron bedsteads, an airless dining-room, the briefest of menus). But it had a certain appeal. It was indeed a 'proper' country hotel, as the lady had promised me in Limeacres: more alive than the one in Barkly West; smaller, less forlornly echoing, than the one in Griquatown. I especially liked the garden at the back, a bewilderment of little concrete courtyards planted with Barberton daisies, everlastings, marigolds, and the inevitable cannas, as well as dark green, leathery-leaved orange and kumquat trees. (All of which could not wholly suppress the smell of drains.) At the end of the garden was a roofless, cemented square for dancing – ominous sight – with red and blue light bulbs strung over it and a concrete bar at the side for serving drinks. It suggested we would be well advised to be elsewhere by Saturday night. On the other side of the hotel, at the far end of a gravelled yard where cars were parked, were a couple of cypress trees and a steel windpump which clanged and creaked whenever a breeze blew.

One of the items on the hotel menu was 'Rump Steak'. Beneath it, at a somewhat reduced price, was another offering: 'Ladies Rump'.

The only blacks and Coloureds to set foot inside the hotel were members of staff. The two public bars which faced the road appeared to be thoroughly segregated, though there were no signs explicitly saying so. One of them was equipped with windows overlooking the stoep, ornamental plates on a dado, linoleum on the floor, a range of bottles on shelves behind the counter, pictures and advertisements on the walls, and a pool table. None of these amenities were to be found in the other bar, which was a small, cement-floored box, with a single barred window high up in the wall. Chalked up on a metal sheet was the barest statement of tariff I have ever seen: Beer – R2.00; Brandy – R4.50; Gin – R4.50; Rum – R4.50. No brand-names; no nonsense. No bottles on display either.

There were four customers inside that bar when I went into it, on my first evening. All were Coloureds. Each was sitting in a more or less comatose state by himself. A black bartender was reading a newspaper he had spread over the counter. Utter silence. The bartender looked up at my entrance and slowly shook his head.

❖

So I went on with my after-dinner walk. No one else was in the road outside. Behind the hotel, at the end of a lane that ran towards the lakeside, I saw to my surprise a large, brightly illuminated sign: the only one in town, apparently. Its colours were orange, white, and blue. It dominated the inauspicious tin hut on which it stood. It said MULTI-MEDIA AKADEMIE.

Multi-Media? Academy? Here? It was as startling a proclamation as TEACHER'S PALACE had been in that army camp near Schmidts Drif. Even more so, indeed, since this sign, aglow with neon, was so much bigger, smarter, more professional in every way.

I drew closer. The hut, inside a small fenced yard, seemed to consist of just one room. It was lit with fluorescent tubes and was quite crowded; there must have been about fifteen people in it. They were sitting around a long table on which there was an array of computer terminals. The people were attending to a speaker who stood at the end of the table.

In order to see all this I had had to come inside the fence; I was now standing among a half-dozen parked cars. The windows of the hut were open, but I could hear nothing of what was being said.

There: I had been seen. A man detached himself from the group in the hut, opened the door, letting out two large and noisy dogs, and came towards me, the dogs bounding ahead of him. I greeted him (and the dogs) propitiatingly from several yards away. He responded not impolitely yet with a distinct air of challenge. '*Ja? Wat soek meneer?*'

Several heads inside the hut were now turned in our direction. The dogs were no longer barking; instead they were growling and sniffing at my feet. I said, in English, that the sign above the hut had made me curious. I added (it seemed a good idea) that I was a visitor from London and that I taught at one of the colleges of the University of London.

The man shouted at the dogs and they retreated a few paces. 'We mustn't disturb the people inside,' he said, and gestured me to go back into the road, where we would not be so easily visible from inside. Then he introduced himself to me; his name was Steenkamp.

I gave him my name and we shook hands. At these signs of amity the dogs grew bored and went back towards the hut. By the light that came from it, and with the help of a deep ruddiness still reflected from the lake, though the sun had long since gone and the air had suddenly grown quite chilly, I could see that Mr Steenkamp wore a yellow shirt; that he had thick grey hair and a thick but neat moustache; that his forehead was lined; that his face somehow looked younger than the tense, defiant, and strangely apologetic expression it wore.

'Some people say we are rebels,' he told me. 'They call us all kinds of things. But we say we stand for the old order. We stand for the old Afrikaner way of doing things. We want our Afrikaner children to have a true Afrikaner education. That means they must be educated with their own kind. There is no other way.'

So here it was. Ever since I had returned to South Africa I had been asking myself: What has happened to Afrikaner nationalism? I meant the nationalism so familiar to me from my childhood and youth: narrow, provincial, racist, defensive, full of fear and hence full of aggression too, clinging fiercely to a sense of profound historical grievance – an ethos and an attitude that amply vindicated Isaiah Berlin's remark that all nationalisms spring ultimately from 'wounded pride'. Out of defeat in the Anglo-Boer War and continuing economic disadvantage *vis-à-vis* the local English-speaking whites; out of memories of innumerable wars against 'the kaffirs' and the sense of a constant threat yet remaining from them; out of the pain of knowing their language to be regarded by others, even their former kinsmen in the Netherlands, let alone the haughty English, as a mere patois; out of the never-to-be-acknowledged consciousness that it was also the native tongue and perhaps the very invention of the despised and rejected Cape Coloureds, in whom their own blood ran freely – out of all this, a section of the Afrikaners had struggled for half a century to create a political party, the Nationalist Party, which would do for them what the Risorgimento or Sinn Fein or the Pan-Hellenic or Zionist movements had tried to do for their peoples. (With a good dose of Nazi racial theory, in the Afrikaner case, thrown in from the 1930s onwards.) The Dutch Reformed Church had become the Nationalist Party at prayer; the Afrikaner youth movements the Nationalist Party at play; the schools and universities the Nationalist Party at its studies; and so on, through cultural clubs, literary magazines, burial societies, eventually the machinery of government and the economy itself – which, after the Nationalists had arrived in office in 1948, they had succeeded in turning into a vast system of handout and uplift for their own people.*

And now, where had all that passion and effort gone? From probably the last man of their race ever to serve as the country's president the Afrikaners had learned that the era of their mastery was over; that the blacks were as much citizens of South Africa as they were and would henceforth be dominating the government of the country; that their repugnance against those with a darker complexion than their own, given to them as if by God and history, was a sin; that the immense experiment in apartheid, to which they had committed themselves with such fervour and from which they had drawn so many benefits, had been nothing more than a 'mistake'. What were they to do?

I knew from the newspapers and television how bitterly unreconciled many of them were to this turn their history had taken; I knew also of the assassinations and casual murders that some had committed recently, by way of warning of their intentions for the future. It was said too that a handful had already been trying to set up territories of their own, some lying even further to the west than my own route would take me. But the rest? Where were they? When would I come on their traces?

Evidently some of them had made it to Danielskuil. The Multi-Media Akademie was proof of it. It was the project of Mr Steenkamp and his partner. 'It's one of our introductory evenings

---

* The population of South Africa stands today at about thirty-seven million. Of these, twenty-six million are black and six million white. Four million of the latter, approximately, are Afrikaans-speaking. There are four million Cape Coloureds and over a million Asians. It is said that Durban is the largest Indian city outside the Indian subcontinent.

tonight,' he explained to me. 'We're meeting people and explaining our plans to them. There are lots of people in the district who are very sympathetic. They don't want their children mixing with –' there was a perceptible pause before he chose his phrase – 'all sorts.'

In one sense I knew clearly enough what he was talking about; in another not at all. 'Is it a night school, then?' I asked, pointing at the hut.

'No, no, it's for the children. If there's a demand maybe we'll start evening classes later for people who were ill or had accidents with their education, and want a second chance now. But we must begin with the children. They're the ones who count most of all, because they're the coming generation.'

'From what age do you take them?'

'All ages. We already got twenty-one pupils, from Sub-A [infants] to matric. Three of them you could really call adults – they're in their twenties.'

'You teach them all in the same room?'

'Yes, but that's not such a problem. We're using modern technology. Our teaching is all done via computers – interactive computers,' he said, using this piece of jargon with pride. 'That's how we manage it. Each pupil will be able to follow his own course on the screen.'

Hence the terminals I had seen; not to speak of the 'Multi-Media' boasted of in the illuminated sign behind him. Now I knew how 'the old Afrikaner way of doing things' was being preserved in this tin hut, in this small *dorp*, in the emptiness of this bleak countryside.

I was a passer-by, a non-Afrikaner, nobody, yet Mr Steenkamp was eager to persuade me not just of the desirability but also of the potential profitability of the enterprise. They had been holding such meetings, he told me, every Monday evening since the start of the term in January. There was much, much interest locally in what they were doing. More than that: enthusiasm. People were very anxious about all these . . . changes . . . that were being forced on them from on top. Yes, forced on them against their will. He and his colleague had applied for 'recognition' to the Cape Province Education Department, and once they got it then things would be much easier. And their overheads were low; there was only him and his colleague to run the school; they were both qualified teachers so they could help the pupils with their work. The two of them did everything, the secretarial work also. He had taken his diploma at the Transvaal College of Education in Pretoria; then he'd worked in the gold mines in Welkom for ten years, mostly in education and training.

'That's when I really became aware of the problems,' he said, somewhat obscurely. Was this a complaint about some measure of racial integration enforced by the mine-owners? I simply could not tell. 'It's going to be difficult financially until we're properly established,' he went on. 'You know, we're pioneering! And things are always hard for a pioneer. But it will work in the end. It has to. The way this country's going, people who feel like we do, our people, have got no choice.'

The lake behind him had lost its last vestiges of colour and light. It had simply disappeared; it was gone, done away with. The first stars were out. The man's expression was more difficult to read than before. The strain in his voice – the strain of speaking English; of presenting his case; of persuading himself that he would 'see his investment again', as the lady in Delports Hope had put it – had not diminished. But he had yet more to say to me.

'You must come in tomorrow morning,' he said. 'I don't want to disturb the people inside now. But I'll be glad to show you around when the pupils are here, and you can see our procedures.'

The last word was brought out almost as proudly as 'interactive' had been. I promised him that I would take up his invitation. We shook hands again and I returned to the hotel.

That night I woke at about three and went to the open window to look out across the yard. The stars were so bright, so profuse, and hung so low over the windpump and the black spires of the cypress trees, I wanted to reach out and pluck them in handfuls. There was the familiar clank of vanes and a hiss of water into an open tank, as the windpump turned slowly. It was not those noises, though, which had woken me up; on the contrary, I had fallen asleep to them. Out in the street, at this improbable hour, someone was trying to start a car, and failing over and over again. Even worse than its catarrhal garglings and scratchings was the low whine with which the motor gave up, each time. Finally it got going, leaving a poisonous stink behind it.

I did return to the Multi-Media Akademie after breakfast that morning, but I did not go into it. Mr Steenkamp was nowhere to be seen. In the yard, seated on benches in a circle, were the twenty-one pupils he had spoken of, from the smallest to the largest. Mr Steenkamp's colleague stood in the middle of them. Some kind of ceremony was taking place – that much was clear – and I found that I was as little keen on having it explained to me as I was on having to explain myself to the man conducting it. Above the children there floated an outsize, old-Boer-style flag, with modern fascistic flourishes. It had a border in orange, white and blue (the colours of the old Orange Free State Republic), and an expanse of white in the middle (guess why); in the centre was a thick dark blue arrow pointing resolutely upwards: half-aspiration, half-weapon. Mr Steenkamp's colleague was reading something to the children, looking up at them, waving a finger; then waiting while they all, even the couple of six-year-olds, chanted out an answer in chorus.

When I had lived in South Africa I always thought of myself as someone more sympathetic to the Afrikaners as a people, and (at one time) more knowledgeable about their literature, their poetry in particular, than any other English-speaker I knew. But what was going on in the Multi-Media Akademie, under that flag, in the light of day, brought back all the old fear and distaste which this brand of nationalism had aroused in me, the sense of its fundamental hostility to everything I was and wanted to be. I was glad to turn my back on the place.

The woman in charge of the kitchen was tall, shy, sharp-featured, small-voiced; she wore the wraparound overall and cloth dustcap which was virtually the uniform of the non-white staff in the hotel;

she stood in the middle of the dining-room, holding a dishcloth with one hand in front of her stomach. She answered my questions about her education and about schools in Danielskuil out of politeness, it seemed; not because she had any special interest in talking about herself. Initially I had asked if she understood English, and she answered deprecatingly, bringing her free hand to her ear, 'I *hear* it.' So we spoke Afrikaans.

It turned out that she had actually been educated in an English-medium school in Kimberley, the William Pescod School.* But she had gone only as far as Standard Three before coming back to Danielskuil. They had always spoken Afrikaans at home. There was a Coloured primary school in Danielskuil, she told me; also one for the blacks. Her two little girls went to the Coloured school. The medium of instruction there was Afrikaans. And was there a school for the whites? She smiled: 'Oh yes, they've always had a school here. Just primary, I think.' Afrikaans-medium? 'Of course.' Was there any mixing in the schools – did any Coloured or black children go to the white school, nowadays? She answered with a toss of her head, as if to say, 'That'll be the day!' Did she know of any plans to mix the children in the schools? She shook her head again. Had any Coloured or black people bought houses in the white parts of the *dorp*? '*Nooit nie.*' Never. What did she think of the Multi-Media Akademie? A sharp look at me; a silent shake of her head.

'Are you a Griqua?' I asked towards the end of our conversation. She met the question with one of her own.

'*Wat is Griekwa?*'

'Coloured, then?' I suggested.

Her answer this time was even more grim than before.

'*Kleurling is niks.*' ('Coloured is nothing.')

*

* William Pescod had been a public figure of sorts in Kimberley when I was in junior school. He was an aged Methodist minister, always clad in black, who used to appear at school functions like prizegivings and sports days, when he would stand on the platform and be given a clap for being so old and reverend. Then he went senile, and it was gleefully reported in the school quad that someone had seen him peeing against a tree in Dutoitspan Road. Then he died.

We encountered each other in the chemist shop; the mere novelty of my face seemed to draw her towards me. We exchanged various commonplaces; then, finding out that she was employed in the office of the Anglo limeworks, I turned the conversation (as innocently as I could) to the asbestos mining which used to be so important to the economy of the region. By then we were standing on the pavement outside the shop. Behind her I could see the miserly stalks of grass and dusty spaces that lay between the shops and the Coloured area of the town.

'The mines are all closed now – gone, finished,' she said. 'Every last one of them. Nobody wants to buy the stuff because of all these health problems. When I was a little girl there were lots of mines around here – some big ones, many small ones too. My father and his partner owned one of the small mines, and me and my brother and sister used to go there and help him. We would even jump into the sacks to make the asbestos fibres go down, so that they could sew up the bags afterwards. Nobody knew anything in those days.'

She was dressed in navy blue with red dots; her pale, soft face was elaborately made up; her hair was tormented into a multitude of curls; its colour could best be called anodized bronze. Her fingernails, painted precisely to match the spots on her dress, were now spread across her capacious bosom. Her expression had changed. 'My mother was the one who suffered,' she said. 'She got it in her lungs and died. It didn't take long: a few months and she was gone.'

Then, contradicting what she had just told me about all the mines in the region having been closed down, she added: 'In Kuruman there's one mine still working. I know they're digging the asbestos up, even though they're not selling it. They're stockpiling it in case the market picks up again. You never can tell what is going to happen in the world. We never dreamt the mines would have to close. Maybe one day they'll find a way of making the asbestos safe again.'

'Again?' I asked.

She smiled, picking up my point. 'Well, we thought it was safe in those days.'

Smiling still, she told me she had no fears about working in the office of the limeworks. 'Lime is safe, hey.' She had to be getting back now, otherwise they'd be wondering what had happened to her.

Some days later, in Kuruman, I was told that its last asbestos mine had in fact closed down just two years earlier. My informant also told me that in the end the asbestos was being sold to just two countries – to Iran and Yugoslavia. He had made himself unpopular in some quarters, he said, by objecting to the mining itself and to the passage through town of lorries loaded with the material. These objections had been voiced in the local paper and also in an interview with a British television crew. Some of the locals had been furious at his 'interfering', as jobs had been lost as a result.

Oddly enough, the maker of that television programme had come to see me in London – about quite another topic – just a few days before I had set out on my journey. He had told me then about his television investigation of what he called 'all the asbestos dust flying about the northern Cape'. But my interest in the topic was of much longer standing than that. Again quite by chance, I can honestly claim to be one of the first people anywhere in the world to have heard about the deadly connection between asbestos and certain kinds of cancer. Early in 1960 I paid a visit to Kimberley which coincided with one by a cousin of mine, a physiologist who worked for the Medical Research Council in Johannesburg. He told me that over the previous few years a startling number of 'freakish' and 'florid' carcinomas had been reported from 'all over the northern Cape'; now he and a colleague had come down to examine the possibility that these were a consequence of the vast increase in the mining of asbestos locally.

(I have just looked up the lengthy article on asbestos in the 1962 edition of the *Encyclopaedia Britannica*. It contains not a word about the mineral presenting any danger to those mining it or using it.)

'Are you from overseas?'
'Yes. From England.'

'From *England*? What's it like there? Is it different?'

'Very.'

'Do you live in London?'

'Yes.'

A long silence. Then, hopefully, 'Have you seen Princess Di?'

My questioner was a not-so-young Afrikaner woman working in an office in the little town and living with her mother in the hotel.

This was her story. She came from Pietersburg in the Northern Transvaal, originally; then her father had been transferred to the Anglo limeworks in Danielskuil. Then he 'passed away'. She and her mother went back to the Transvaal, to Johannesburg, where she'd been working for the past eight years. But the two of them had returned here for the funeral after her sister's baby died. Her sister had married a local man and had remained in Danielskuil.

'They were visiting her mother-in-law in Bloemfontein, and she was cutting her older boy's hair – he's four – and she asked her mother-in-law to look after the baby. It was just five minutes and they found her floating in the swimming-pool. She was such a pretty little thing. Then when the funeral was over my mother and I thought we might as well stay on. But you know, I'm more used to the big city life, after all that time in Joh'burg. There's not a lot going on in Danielskuil. There are some days, I can tell you, when I just sit behind the desk and I ask myself: How long can I handle this?'

After another long silence: 'That's why I'm always so interested in hearing about other countries.'

She had gold in her teeth, many silver rings on her fingers, a variety of bracelets on her wrists, and some curiously roughened patches in the whites of her melancholy eyes. When I made as if to go she detained me a little longer by digging in her handbag and offering me a peppermint from the packet she found there.

CHAPTER SEVEN

☆

Kuruman: 1

Towards the end of 1801 the authorities in the Cape sent two commissioners, Somerville and Truter, to travel to the north on a cattle-buying mission. Some distance to the north-east of where Kuruman now stands, they came on the Tswana settlement of Lattakoo (Dithakong). This is how John Barrow, who wrote up the commissioners' journey, described what they saw:

The sight of so great an assemblage of human habitations, after so long and dreary a journey, was equally as unexpected as it was agreeable. In a country so desolate as Southern Africa, where so few human beings are met with, and those few in the last stage of misery, the pleasure must be doubly felt of encountering a large society of mankind whose condition has something like comfort . . . The town, in its circumference, was estimated to be fully as large as Cape Town, including all the gardens of Table Valley; but from the irregularity of the streets, and the lowness of the buildings, it was impossible to ascertain, with any degree of accuracy, the number of houses; it was concluded, however, that they could not be less than two or more than three thousand . . .

Barrow goes on the describe the 'cottages or huts' ('the ground plan of every house was a complete circle . . . the floor of hard beaten clay . . . the whole covered with a tent-shaped roof, supported on poles built into the wall and carefully and compactly thatched with reeds . . . each hut enclosed within a sort of palisade') and sums up the travellers' impressions thus:

The dwelling of a *Booshuana* is not ill calculated for the climate. In elegance and solidity it may probably be as good as the *Casae* or first houses that were built in imperial Rome, and may be considered in every respect superior in

construction and comfort to most of the Irish cabins into which the miserable
peasantry are off-times obliged to crawl through puddles of water . . .

The Booshuanas may, in every respect, be considered to have passed the
boundary which divides the savage from the civilized state of society, and to
have arrived at that stage of moral refinement which is not incompetent to
the reception of the sublime yet simple precepts of the Christian religion. It is
here the missionary might employ his zeal to some advantage; here a plentiful
harvest is offered to the first reapers who may present themselves.

At the beginning of the eighteenth century the most southerly of
the 'Booshuana' (also 'Moetschouane', later 'Bechuana', now
Tswana) peoples had begun to meet, mingle, and compete with the
Griqua, Koranna, and Hottentot clans who moved with their flocks
along the Orange River. Much larger groups of Tswana occupied
the country along what later became the border regions of the Boer
republics of the Transvaal and the Orange Free State. The women
did the sowing and hoeing of their crops (sorghum and melons in
particular); the men hunted; some groups among them specialized
in smelting iron and copper and traded the implements they
produced over considerable distances; subject tribes (like the
Kgalagadi) tended the herds. Gathered together in semi-permanent
villages or wards, which in turn were gathered into four or five
large conglomerations, the Tswana were governed by a complicated
system of local headmen, district chiefs, and the members of several
royal families.

These were the people whom Somerville and Truter had
encountered at Lattakoo; a people whom Thomas Campbell was to
describe, in his *Travels* of 1813, as 'sprightly and ingenious . . .
superior to any of the African nations we had seen'. As a missionary
he was especially struck, as Burrow had been a decade earlier, by
the sheer numbers of them. So many souls awaiting salvation! So
many, as things stood, destined for perdition! In the course of his
visit Campbell tried to get the chief in Lattakoo to accept the
presence of a missionary and left believing that he had succeeded in
doing so. On returning to London he sought four new recruits to
go to this promising field of endeavour, as he imagined it to be.
Only two of them, Hamilton and Read, actually got as far as

Griquatown. From there, two years after Campbell's visit, they and the resident missionary gloomily reported that the 'door to Lattakoo' remained 'closed'. (Letters to London, 19 and 28 April 1815.) After the lapse of another eighteen months Hamilton was in Lattakoo again, this time with a companion named Evans. Again they were rebuffed. They returned to Griquatown. Then, at the beginning of 1817 Hamilton and Read tried yet once more and gained the permission they were seeking.

They were joined in 1820 by Robert Moffat, who two years later established the missionary settlement of Kuruman, a few miles from an unfailing source of underground water, and persuaded the chief and people of Lattakoo to follow him there. His work in Kuruman and elsewhere was to win for him a degree of fame as a pioneer in Africa that would eventually be surpassed only by that of his son-in-law, David Livingstone.

If it were not for the great-great-grandfather of the novelist Evelyn Waugh, Robert Moffat would never have gone out to Africa. He would have gone to the South Sea Islands instead. And if, as the author of *Missionary Labours and Scenes in Southern Africa* and a successful lecturer to evangelical audiences, Moffat had not become a national figure in Britain, the young David Livingstone would probably not have met him and have been inspired to follow him to southern Africa, where he married Moffat's daughter and eventually embarked on his own legendary career as an explorer.

Witness the following extract from *The Lives of Robert and Mary Moffat* by their son, John Scott Moffat (1886):

During the discussions in the missionary committee as to how this band of men was to be distributed, it had first been proposed that John Williams and Moffat should go to Polynesia; but this was overruled at the suggestion of Dr Waugh who deemed 'thae twa lads ower young to gang togeither', so they were separated. On these small links hang our lives.*

---

* John Williams was later to win fame for himself as 'the martyr of Erromanga' in the South Seas.

And then this from Evelyn Waugh's autobiography, *A Little Learning* (1964):

My great-great-grandfather was educated for the Ministry at Edinburgh and Aberdeen. In 1782, at the age of twenty-eight, he was sent to London to the chapel, now demolished, in Wells Street, off Oxford Street, which he served until his death. He became one of the most prominent Nonconformist preachers of his day and, among other public activities, helped found the London Missionary Society and the Dissenters' Grammar School at Mill Hill.

Finally, lest it be thought that J.S. Moffat, in quoting Dr Waugh, was laying on too strongly the Scottish accent, here is another sentence about him from *A Little Learning*: 'His sermons and lectures were all in pure English, but in private he delighted to resume the dialect of his youth, remaining fervently Scottish throughout his long exile.'

Moffat was a market gardener by training. He became an ordained minister of the Congregationalist Church; a builder (most notably of the great stone church in the Kuruman mission); a teacher; a linguist (the first man to reduce the Tswana language to written form); a translator of the Bible (into Tswana); a printer (who produced in Kuruman his own translation of the Bible, among other things); an indefatigable traveller across difficult parts of the subcontinent; a friend of the leading Tswana chiefs and a confidant of Mzilikaze (Moselikatse), who was the founder and leader of the Ndebele people.

Like many of the missionaries sent to South Africa by the London Missionary Society, Moffat was a Scot. His wife, Mary, was also of Scottish descent, and the daughter of a market gardener. In fact Moffat met his wife-to-be when he was working for his future father-in-law. By then he already intended to become a missionary. In due course he set out for South Africa; Mary followed him three years later. She was to have ten children, three of whom died in infancy. Of those who reached adulthood, two more predeceased her. She too taught in Kuruman (needlework, among other things), kept house, corresponded voluminously, and, in times of adversity, succoured to the best of her ability both the local Tswana as well as the missionaries and traders who passed through her door. Her letters suggest that she was a livelier writer than her husband, at any rate in the informal mode: she was more intemperate in expression and had a sharper turn of phrase than he.

What is one to make of them – Moffat with his great beard half-way down his chest; Mary with her bonnet; both of them toiling for so long, in such arduous circumstances, for negligible material reward and for so few converts? (Even in the last decade of the Moffats' fifty years in Kuruman their church had no more than about seventy communicants.) An earlier generation of historians and biographers had little doubt how to answer the question I have just asked: almost as little doubt, one might say, as Robert and Mary Moffat themselves had about their life's work. They were bringers of light in a great darkness, carriers of the word of God to a miserably heathen race, 'great and successful African missionaries who had, with so much Christian fortitude and heroism, faced a thousand dangers and surmounted a thousand difficulties, during the half-century in which they had toiled on behalf of their swarthy children in the faith' – to quote just one encomium written after Robert Moffat's death.

To a later generation of radical white and black historians, on the other hand, they were the forerunners and more or less conscious agents of a predatory imperialism, the fanatical disrupters of traditions about which they knew nothing, the deliberate destroyers of a culture for which they had absolutely no regard. (Polygamy, for instance, was never seen by the Moffats as anything but a gross sin, at once sign of and reason for eternal damnation. If it had occurred to them that in attacking it they were attacking a practice essential to the maintenance of the structure of Tswana society, with its family groups, wards, and clans, they would have seen this as a source of satisfaction rather than regret.) Whatever the achievements of the Moffats and their colleagues in introducing the Tswana nation to the culture of writing and reading, and in making available to them new forms of agriculture, medical care, and technology (guns not least – to the fury of the Boers); however strenuously they may have tried to defend the people they had come to live among from the depredations of Boers, of British colonials, of other blacks, and at times of the British government itself – nevertheless in the eyes of today's radicals they remain guilty as charged. The fact that they sought no material gain for themselves is in this view ('objectively speaking', as its proponents would say) neither here nor there.

Consider this, though. The missionaries may have had nothing but contempt for the way of life which the indigenous peoples had developed and which they tried to preserve from disruption – as any people would when confronted by strangers more powerful than themselves. Yet had the Moffats and countless others like them not brought the written word into Africa, and not made such efforts to pass it on to the peoples they met, then a historiography which tries to look at the past from a specifically African point of view might still be waiting to come into existence.

Let the Moffats now speak for themselves, for better or worse. Better and worse.

Mary Moffat to her parents, February 1822:

The people, instead of desiring that their children should be instructed, are afraid of their becoming 'Dutchmen', so tenacious are they of their old customs and habits ... As to some of these people having correct notions of God and of heaven, death and hell, as has been asserted, you must not believe it; for daily conversations convince us that the wisest of them have most corrupt notions on these subjects. We are astonished at their dreadful stupidity about such things ...

Mary Moffat to her parents, 29 July 1822:

The Bootsuanas seem more careless than ever, and seldom enter the church ... Five years have rolled on since the missionaries [Hamilton and Read] came, and not one soul converted, nor does anyone seem to lend an ear. All treat with ridicule and contempt the truths which are delivered.

Mary Moffat to her parents, July 1824:

It is not conferring with flesh and blood to live among these people. In the natives of South Africa there is nothing naturally engaging: their extreme selfishness, filthiness, obstinate stupidity, and want of sensibility, have a tendency to disgust, and sometimes cause the mind to shrink from the idea of spending the whole life amongst them, far from every tender and endearing circle. But when we recollect the Saviour of men has said, 'Deny thyself, take up thy cross and follow me,' we blush for harbouring such a feeling. Oh how imperfectly do we follow him!

Robert Moffat to his brother, 'end of 1822':

Alas! We still hang our harps on the willows, and mourn over the destiny of thousands hastening with heedless but impetuous strides to the regions of woe.

Robert Moffat in *Missionary Labours and Scenes in Southern Africa* (1842):

To tell them, the gravest of them, that there was a Creator, the governor of the heavens and earth, of the fall of man, or the redemption of the world, the resurrection of the dead, and immortality beyond the grave, was to tell them what appeared to be more fabulous, extravagant and ludicrous than their own stories about lions, hyenas and jackals.

Mary Moffat, April 1826:

By an especial providence a very young child was committed to my care . . . One Sabbath morning . . . some of our children brought in a report that a child was heard crying among the stones on the side of the hill . . . We immediately set off for the spot . . . At length [it was] discovered literally buried alive and covered with stones. At this moment I arrived, and, as you will easily conceive, was dreadfully shocked. The inhuman mother had pulled out stones to make a hole sufficient for its little body, and then put it in and laid upon it one huge stone, the corner of which rested on its little nose and made a severe wound. Its limbs were sadly bruised with kicking about, and its eyes all bleared with cold. I took it up and brought it home, fed and washed it and dressed its wounds, to the great astonishment of the natives. They viewed it with indifference; said the mother was a rascal, but wondered much that we should love so poor an object.

And how about this from *The Matabele Journals of Robert Moffat: 1829–1860*?

About half a dozen of children, chiefly girls, poor things, appeared quite cheerful and familiar, with animated countenances, as if we were friends come to visit them. I gave each of them a few beads, which made them look as if they felt rich for once in their lives. How my heart did yearn over them! If they had been born in a Christian country or even a missionary station such as the Kuruman, what a difference of ideas and impressions would pervade their minds, compared to those arising from the monotony of their present life ... Their houses are the merest shadows of huts and their fences of the most fragile description. They are in the deepest ignorance, their dress ragged skins. How hardy that they do not perish with the cold, for though the days are agreeable, the nights are very cold ... As we had meat enough a quantity was given to these people, which made them look blithe.

What First World (or 'North') traveller in a Third World (or 'South') country is not familiar with such waifs, such gifts, and such emotions on both sides? But who today, on either side, has anything of Moffat's confidence about how matters can be put to rights?

The great attraction of the Kuruman valley to Moffat was that it had an exceptionally generous and reliable supply of water from an underground spring known as the 'Eye'. Having chosen the site of the mission station, he set about leading the water into a canal to irrigate the crops he intended growing, and intended to encourage others to grow. The course of the canal he and his fellow-missionaries dug in those first years can still be seen at the bottom of the mission garden, running alongside the concrete 'sloot' which carries the water today.

Unlike the underground sources in Griquatown and Campbell, which have all but dried up, the Eye of Kuruman still gushes out of the earth as copiously as ever. It now forms the centrepiece of a park in the middle of town. The spring is also adorned – or desecrated, Moffat would have thought – by a series of bombastic monumental plaques to the Boer Voortrekkers, whose expansion into the southern African hinterland he had opposed so bitterly. The whites of the town, which lies at a distance of about three miles from the mission station, are almost entirely Afrikaans-speaking.

Like all the more substantial of the small towns I passed through,

Kuruman contains a few 'old-style' streets of low, whitewashed cottages with iron roofs, each standing in the middle of a wire-fenced garden, where shrubs (oleanders, hibiscus) and fruit trees (peaches, figs) do their best. Like the others, Kuruman also has a supply of brick-built, ranch-style houses, with lawns and driveways and double-garages, standing in brief suburbs of their own. In the centre of town are branches of the Standard Bank, OK Bazaars, Clicks, the local agricultural co-operative, and garages selling Volkswagens and Toyotas. Over one of the garages there floats at the height of a hundred feet a tethered, zeppelin-like balloon, forever advertising CALTEX. There is also the branch of the Volkskas Bank I mentioned earlier which has its entire front wall spectacularly sheathed in varnished tiger-eye stone. In Kuruman, as elsewhere, the Dutch Reformed churches seem to be in competition as to which can boast the highest and thinnest of steeples. The municipal buildings, set in immaculate gardens, are brand-new; the public monuments celebrate the struggles of the Afrikaner people, the worth of the Afrikaans language, the reliability of the Afrikaner God, and the achievements of the Afrikaner government which (among other things) swept away the districts inhabited by Kuruman's blacks many miles to the north and east of the town.

At all times, one is conscious of the empty spaces around towns like these, and of the even bigger spaces above: at night too, when bands of stars hang directly overhead, or a moon strong enough to cast not just light but black shadows too, a moon to read by, gazes down on the only Greek or Portuguese takeaway still open for business.

What is more poignant about such places – their forlornness or their spruceness? The human and aesthetic thinness that is somehow revealed in their every line, or the pertinacity with which those lines have been drawn? And in what form will they survive a movement into them of the penurious throngs who dwell in the tatter-towns around them?

The disparities of wealth and poverty in South Africa can produce in resident and visitor alike a kind of vertigo, a disbelief in the evidence of their own eyes. The wealthier groups are not a thin layer of expatriates and a yet thinner, positively molecular, layer of middle-class locals, as they are in many Third World countries. They can be seen almost everywhere, in town and country alike, and so can their possessions – houses, cars, swimming-pools, furnishings, electronic goods. Yet the poor, a category which includes the overwhelming majority of unskilled or semi-skilled blacks lucky enough to be employed and housed after a fashion, are incomparably more numerous; while beside them, beyond them, beneath them, are the armies of the truly poor – hungry, houseless, uneducated, unemployed, half-clothed; at once disregarded, even 'transparent', and yet never forgotten.

Now, to such disparities add the following. The rich are usually, indeed almost invariably, of a different colour from the poor, though there is some degree of overlap. Rich and poor speak different languages from one another, and it is in the languages of the rich (in English, above all) that the important, skills-giving books are written. Rich and poor have different histories and national identities (or so most of them believe, and belief in these matters is more important than any question of 'fact'). Their cultural habits and expectations are different. The gulfs in education and training between them, above all in the technological, mathematical, and accounting disciplines which more and more determine who has power over whom – these gulfs may be somewhat narrower than they once were, but they remain huge nevertheless.

Add the angers engendered by an embedded conviction of racial superiority on the one side, and a centuries-old experience of displacement and contempt on the other. Add too the fears arising from a consciousness of the disasters (political, economic, social, medical) which have overtaken so many African countries to the north – fears felt not only by whites in South Africa but by many blacks too, and almost all Asians and Coloureds.

The strange thing is that in such circumstances, under such pressures, it is possible that some of the dispossessed may actually find it easier not to attack those of a different colour who own everything they lack, but to pursue instead ancient, internecine enmities among themselves. Or to turn only on the most vulnerable of the wealthier groups, the Indians especially, many of whom today feel themselves to be even more threatened than they were by the manias and humiliations of the apartheid era.

Not that I would wish to suggest that all the whites in South Africa are prosperous. Far from it.

For instance. M. and I are sitting on the porch of a tea-room – or rather a house which sells teas from its front door – on one of the streets near the town centre. Across the road is a big garage, doing brisk business, and next to it a grocery-cum-takeaway which is positively besieged by young white soldiers who have just climbed off a halted army truck. They wear maroon berets and fancily pugnacious insignia on their sleeves; they emerge clutching chicken parts, hot dogs, sandwiches, soft drinks, apples. In the midst of them there suddenly appears a man in a wheelchair who, using one stiff, thrust-out leg as a means of propulsion as well as a rudder, is pushing himself *backwards* along the pavement. With every thrust the wheelchair sways from side to side – almost a half-circle each time. His hands rest in his lap, clutching a brown cardboard box. Obviously he cannot see what is behind him, but this seems to deter him not at all. A car about to turn into the garage forecourt has to brake suddenly to avoid him. He does not even acknowledge its presence. The garage crossover or ramp gives him a chance to manoeuvre his chair from the pavement into the street without encountering the awkward edge of the kerb. So, still going backwards, still lurching from side to side, he unhesitatingly sets out into the busy street. Cars come to a halt on both sides of him; passing Africans and the crowd of soldiers pause to watch him go. No one offers to help him across; in any case he has the obsessed, preoccupied air of someone who neither expects help nor would welcome it.

Now he has almost made it to our side of the street. He is a white man, possibly in his twenties, dressed in some kind of safari outfit. On his head is a broad-brimmed khaki hat; on his feet a soiled pair of *veldskoen*; on his chin and sunken cheeks, a scraggly beard. His non-working leg, bent at the knee, rests on a special little platform. With jab and thrust, sway and lurch, he manages to crash his chair over the kerb on this side and on to the pavement. Suddenly something about him, some movement of his head or shoulders, tells me what the objective of this worse-than-crablike journey has been. It is ourselves.

Should we clear off? Help him? Wait for him? In the end he manages to get up the slope of the little garden and to park himself next to us. In the cardboard box on his lap are some metal spoons bearing the badge of the Kuruman Municipality. His speech is thick and difficult to follow, but he manages to get out the price of the spoons. ''n Paar! 'n Paar!' he says over and over again, insisting that we buy two of them. We bend to his will. The transaction completed, he demands that we satisfy his curiosity. Having spotted – at such a distance! – our newness to the place, he wants to know what we are doing in Kuruman. What is my *besigheid* (business) here? 'Buying spoons,' I answer. The joke does not amuse him. He thrusts violently at the ground with his leg; the wheelchair swings away and begins to roll backwards down the path. It goes off at such a rate that his stuck-out leg has hastily to be put into service as a brake.

Only then do I see that on the side of the chair is a bright sticker, in black, red and white. It says: I ♡ KURUMAN.

Not long afterwards, about to drop an empty mineral-water bottle into a litter-bin, I am stayed by a cry of 'Master!' from a small, middle-aged African woman. She is dressed in a pair of cracked shoes and lengthy layers of cotton and nylon. Her head is wrapped in a *doek* and on her cheekbones are dark, almost purplish patches. They are like bruises, yet they look also as though they have always been there: a part of her. She carries a shapeless bundle containing God knows what in her arms, but it does not prevent her from clapping her hands – around the bundle – in a gesture of appeal.

'Can I have the bottle, master?'

'If you want it.'

It vanishes at once into the bundle. 'And the top?' – with a screwing movement of her fingers.

The top? Where is it? I look through the window of the car, and there it is, lying on the front seat. 'What do you want it for?'

'I get extra five cents for the top, master. For the bottle – seventy-five cents.'

I pass her the bottle top and a one-rand coin. Again she claps her hands, for joy this time. 'Master, now I'm very happy. Now I can buy bread for my children.'

'How many have you got?'

'Six. Three are still small.'

'How small?'

'Fifteen years the one, she is still in school. The other two are very small. They are my daughter's children.'

'Where is your daughter?'

'In Mothibistad, with her husband. But she has to work. I must work also. My husband –' As if uttering of the word 'husband' is too much for her, she suddenly collapses, sinking right down to the tarmac. Her long skirts are spread out around her; her head waggles from side to side to express extreme weakness. From below she tells me, 'It costs too much money for the children to go to school – we must buy the clothes, pay for the bus, pay for the books, pay the government.'

'Where are your other children?'

'One in Joh'burg, one in Upington, one here. But they're like their father, all of them.' By this time she has somehow come upright again – bundle, skirts, and all – and is performing another rapid piece of mime: her head thrown back, she brings a clenched hand to her lips in bottle-like fashion, and makes exaggerated swallowing movements with her lips and the muscles of her wrinkled neck. 'I've not been lucky with my children, master. They're just like their father, with this drinking, drinking, drinking. But when the youngest one is finished school, and the little ones can go back to my daughter, then maybe I can take it more easy . . . Even the son who's a mason – a good job, master – he's also the same.'

More mimed drinking; followed this time by a fling of the arm into the air behind her, as of one discarding an object – her son, it seems, rather than an empty beer-can.

For fifty years, from 1820 to 1870, Moffat's Kuruman was 'the gateway to the north'. Then diamonds were discovered in the Kimberley area and Kuruman at once lost its strategic and commercial importance. There is an almost uncanny appositeness in the fact that Robert and Mary Moffat retired from Kuruman and went back to Britain in 1870; precisely the year which inaugurated an entirely new industrial and urban phase in the history of the country.

The little town was left to wither on the vine. The road to the north now ran through Kimberley and Mafikeng, well to the east, instead of following its previous route through Griquatown, Danielskuil, and Kuruman. The coming of the railway (it arrived in Kimberley in 1885; in Mafikeng nine years later) settled the matter. Kuruman would never be anything more than another northern Cape *dorp* – admittedly better watered and therefore larger and more oasis-like than most; endowed, also, with a remarkable historical monument in the buildings and gardens of the Moffat Mission.

That this should have been the fate of his mission – that it should become a kind of museum instead of a great centre of Christian worship – would have seemed to Moffat a travesty of his ambitions for himself and the church he served. It would also have seemed to him highly unlikely. He may well have found the conversion of the thousands who were 'hastening with heedless but impetuous strides to the regions of woe' a heartbreakingly sluggish business; but, as the years passed, as other missionaries went further north and west from Kuruman, as trade with the interior expanded and permanent trading posts were established, as Kuruman's fame as a missionary and educational centre spread more and more widely in South Africa and back 'home' in Britain, so Moffat's stature grew among Tswana, Ndebele, Griqua, Boer, and British colonial alike. In the bloody raids, skirmishes, land-grabs, cattle rustlings, the trading expeditions and treaty-makings which together constitute so much of the territory's history, Moffat again and again makes a crucial appearance: as friend and mediator to many, as determined foe to some.

By 'some' I mean the Boers, chiefly. The missionaries detested them as enslavers and killers of blacks; the Boers heartily reciprocated this detestation, accusing the missionaries of a variety of crimes – gun-running to the blacks being probably the most heinous of them. Indeed, the Great Trek into the interior, on which the Boers embarked from 1834 onwards, was in large measure precipitated by their hatred of the 'philanthropic' and 'humanitarian' activities of the missionaries in the eastern Cape. The proclamations the trekkers issued were explicit about it. 'Interested and dishonest persons' acting 'under the cloak of religion', they said, had made life in the Cape Colony intolerable for them.

But once they had succeeded in penetrating the interior, what did the trekkers find? Missionaries again: even here among the Tswana, on the very rim of the land that was worth holding, where thorn and grassveld finally began to give way to immitigable desert. Furthermore both the missionaries and the Boers knew exactly what the former were doing there. They were evangelizing the blacks, yes. But they were also there to thwart the Boers, and they made no bones about it. They were keeping open for themselves and for their sponsors back in Britain a route to all the territories lying still further to the north.

Or, as David Livingstone put it, in 1852, in a letter to the Colonial Secretary in London:

Now, the path to this distant region has been discovered in its entire course by Englishmen, and no portion of it runs through the territory occupied or claimed by the Trans-Vaal Boers. The mission stations of Kuruman and Kolobeng [his own station] are situated on this path, but both are about 100 miles west of the boer territory. In addition to the traffic carried on by Englishmen in the region beyond Kolobeng, many English gentlemen availed themselves of our route in order to enjoy sport among the large game with which the country abounds . . .

I beg that it may be particularly observed that the above referred *English path* is the only route open to the interior of the continent.

CHAPTER EIGHT

☆

Kuruman: 2

The only congregation left to the Moffat Mission is that of the trees. Or so you feel when you enter the mission grounds. There are giant Australian gums with their usual litter of dried leaf and bark lying about them, syringas, pomegranates, pines, walnuts, apricots, acacias, African others to which I cannot give a name: all growing in an interpenetrating profusion of branches and leafage, sunlight and shadow. It is a beautifully quiet and secluded place, carefully tended and yet imbued with an air of abandonment and desuetude. When I remarked on its peacefulness to Father Alan Butler, the present director of the mission, he said, 'It's strange to think that this was once the violent frontier. We're all fascinated by things that have been violently in motion and have now come to rest ... Even if it's just an old wagon.' And he pointed at an ox-wagon which now, like so much else on the site, was undergoing restoration. It stood in the wagon-house – which was itself also under repair. A little later he spoke of the mission's future as probably being that of an 'Educational Enrichment Centre': another melancholy phrase, in my view.

The T-shaped church is built of large stones mortared together, with rough-cut timbers and thatch above. It has a mud-and-dung floor, in the traditional African style: a surface which feels strangely, even insidiously, soft underfoot. Further along, on the same 'street' (an unpaved roadway), is Moffat's house and another house built originally for the missionary Hamilton. These too are of stone, timber, and thatch. Not far behind the church is a mud-walled schoolhouse. Set still further back is a flimsy, modern, disheartened-looking 'Conference Centre'. No conferences appear

to have taken place in it for a long time. The rest of the site is
occupied by trees, boulders, tufts of grass, well-trodden pathways,
unseen Namaqua doves in the branches. They are forever uttering
their sweet, grinding call, as if tiny melodious mills are constantly
at work up there. All the older buildings have been restored (or in
the case of the schoolhouse totally reconstructed) recently. Father
Butler has done much of the labour himself. The buildings make an
impression of both solidity and modesty: even the church, which
was built originally to seat up to a thousand people.

Yes, a thousand. At that time (1831–1838) Moffat's congregation
could be counted on the fingers of one hand. The dimensions he
gave to the church were clearly a proclamation of confidence in
what the future would bring. In later years he himself walled off
the unused nave so that he could use it as his printing shop; in
years later still, long after his death, a dismayed visitor reported
that chickens were roosting on the press on which he had printed
his Tswana Bible and other devotional works. The machine – a
cumbersome cast-iron affair, with wheels and plates and an improbably long operating handle, like some kind of antiquated rudder –
was then transferred for safekeeping to the Kimberley Public
Library, and stuck in a corner in one of its back rooms. As a boy, I
used to play with the machine when I found myself alone with it.
There was no sign to say what it was, but somehow I knew it to be
'Moffat's press', on which a translation of the Bible had been
printed.

'In those days you'd find chickens everywhere!' Father Butler
protested indignantly about the misappropriation (as he sees it) of
the press by the Kimberley Public Library. The subject came up
within minutes of our arrival; it is obviously one on which he feels
strongly. He was not mollified by my assurance that the library
now prominently displays the press in a small, well-labelled room
of its own.

Butler has a beard which reaches half-way down his chest, in
luxurious and Moffat-like fashion. (Not accidentally, one is sure.)
He is a tall, sharp-featured man with a boisterous laugh and

generous gestures; his talk darts off in many directions at once. The other clergyman living there, Reverend Joe Wing, the secretary of the mission, is small, stocky, round-faced, close-shaven. His speech is soft and orderly; the movements of his hands are carefully controlled. In every respect the two men might have been chosen to illustrate two different ways of being missionaries, or two ways of being human. Butler was dressed in an informal, pale-blue safari suit; Wing in a long-sleeved white shirt, its stiff cuffs secured by gold cuff-links with a black cross embossed on them, and a black and red tie. Wing has a head of thick white hair; Butler an expanse of naked scalp. While both men are originally from England, Butler speaks with a distinctly West Country burr while Wing's pronunciation is what is known as 'received'. Wing is a Congregationalist; Butler an Anglican.

In the morning we had tea with Butler in the closed-in porch of his house; in the afternoon we sat with Wing in Mary Moffat's *voorhuis*, the front room of the mission house, which is now used for the sale of books, postcards and (in little plastic bags) pieces of the tree under which Livingstone proposed to Mary Moffat. Behind our host was an imposing Spanish mahogany bookcase with glass doors; behind me hung an oil portrait of the missionary John Philip and two blacks who were taken to London – presumably as real-life illustrations of the work the Society was doing in Africa. They are both shown in court dress. In another cabinet was displayed the silver communion set which arrived providentially at the mission just as Moffat was about to baptize his first communicants, eight years after his arrival in Kuruman.

The only other people we saw in the mission on our first day were the lady behind the counter in the bookshop, a man who had come to speak to Butler about a plumbing problem, and a caretaker/watchman figure whom we passed near the gate as we were leaving. He was sitting on his haunches, feeding a fire with pieces of wood. Flames and sparks leapt and flapped like a wild pennantry into the darkening air, higher by far than the iron and brick hutment behind him. Nearby was a trash can, an old oil drum actually, on which he had painstakingly painted the legend:

DUST BEAN. Earlier we had also encountered a lean, almost haggard, shabby-smart clergyman from the indigenous Ethiopian Church of Christ, in tie, flannels and sports jacket, with briefcase and dusty leather shoes below, who had come in hope of getting a donation to his church from Butler. (Who gave him, I saw, pretty short shrift.) Later, looking even hotter and more disconsolate than before, he asked me for a donation too. He was from Soweto, near Johannesburg, he said. He had come to Kuruman to see his mother who was 'not very well'. He wished he was back in Johannesburg. For that I could hardly blame him.

I had told the missionaries that our interest in the station and in those who had founded it had many roots, but a common religious belief was not among them. I was a secular Jew; my wife a secular Gentile. If they were disappointed on hearing this (and I have no doubt they were), it did not affect the courtesy they showed us. As it happened we had arrived just two days before Easter; and it transpired that in preparation for the festival they would be conducting the service of Tenebrae in the church the following evening. When I asked if we might join the congregation, they very kindly (and yet, I thought, rather puzzlingly) said that they would begin the service an hour later than planned, to make it easier for us to come.

Neither the quietude of the place nor this postponement had prepared us for what we found when we returned for the service the following night. I drove down the track from the gate, through the deserted-seeming grounds, and parked near the church. A stark moon was shining overhead. No light came from any other source. The shapes of trees, of the church, of the schoolhouse, were as sharp in outline as their own moon-shadows. Random boulders rested as if in pools of blackness. Then the gleam of a flashlight appeared from the direction of the Hamilton house. Picking his way carefully across the rough ground, Wing came towards us. A moment later, from the other direction, another swinging beam of light announced the approach of the Butlers. Then a third beam appeared. It was in the hands of Mrs Wing. Handshakings took place. I still found it impossible to believe something that had been staring me in the face for several minutes past. M. and I were going to make up the entire congregation, aside from the two clergymen and their wives. The puzzle about their ready postponing of the starting time for the service was a puzzle no longer.

Despite the afternoon silence of the place, I had imagined the two of us as a sceptical, unnoticed twosome in the midst of a congregation of a couple of dozen at least. But *this*? Me? My vehemently atheistical wife? Why had nobody from the town come out? Where was the DUST BEAN chap?

Wing disappeared into the church, the lights came on, and we entered. From then on I avoided M.'s gaze; and she mine. Some bats emerged from the thatch and began to fly about in excited fashion. Butler was dressed in a high-necked sweater with the points of his shirt-collar sticking over it, and a pair of jeans; Wing, as might have been expected, was dark-suited. By the light of the few electric bulbs now burning we could see that the altar was covered by a white cloth on which a cross was embroidered. Five lit candles were standing on square wooden blocks ('to save wax dripping on Marge's nice cloth,' Wing explained). Another large candle, in the middle of them, was set in a too-small silver holder. Wing went behind the altar; the rest of us sat in the front row of the seats in the nave. He poured some wine into a goblet which he had taken out of a briefcase and started making a blessing over it. At this point the big candle fell out of its holder, knocking over the goblet and spilling wax as well as wine on Marge's nice cloth. Wing righted the candle, mopped up as much of the wine as he could with a napkin, took a bottle out of the briefcase, refilled the goblet, and started the blessing again. This time it was completed without mishap. He covered the goblet with another white napkin.

We were then asked if we would be willing to read a passage from the Bible in the course of the service. I agreed to do so; M. declined. I was given a Bible with a marker in it. Wing, who conducted the service throughout, put on a black gown, something like an academic gown, which in that dim light made him appear extraordinarily – and yet with complete appropriateness – like the portrait of a Congregationalist divine in early Puritan America: silver-haired, pale-faced, severe, turned inward. Embarrassed by our presence, or perhaps embarrassed by our witnessing how many others were absent from the rows of benches behind and around us, yet engrossed in what was to come, he explained some features of the service. He hoped we were in good singing voice; if not we were welcome to 'growl along' as best we could. He led the singing into the first hymn; Butler joined in with much earnestness, though with less command of melody; then the ladies followed. After the hymn, a reading. After the reading, a prayer. Another hymn. The unaccompanied voices rang out poignantly in the empty church. The bats flew about.

Invited to come forward, we took our places in a semi-circle directly in front of the altar. A prayer for the unity of the Christian church, with special mention of the Roman and Orthodox churches. A prayer for the welfare of 'thy ancient people Israel' (in my honour, I assumed). Another hymn. A period of silent prayer: Wing's face hooded, frowning, sorrowful; Butler, eyes closed, uttering small murmurs and groans of what sounded like assent; Jacobson, head lowered, teeth clenched, wondering what further unlikelihood this unlikely evening was still to bring forth. Making sense of my presence there was impossible; impossible also not to feel the strangest mixture of wonder, embarrassment, mirth, fraudulence, compassion for our hosts, even a kind of protectiveness towards them.

But something else was at work. Sitting in that empty church of thatch and stone and mud, listening to the sounds the celebrants made and the words they uttered, I could not doubt that for them the entire universe had been created and ordered by a personhood which, in some ineffable fashion, resembled their own and felt as they did. It followed, then, that their universe was an attentive one; addressable and responsive; interested in them, in me, in my wife.

To me, it was not. It would never be so. Not in church; not in synagogue; not in Kuruman; not anywhere. Whatever the world was, it was irremediably the same all the way through. There was nothing behind it. Its surfaces were its depths; and vice-versa. Here too. Always.

Not surprisingly perhaps, given the conditions, this thought cheered me up.

Butler rose and switched off the lights; now only candles illumined the scene. Wing blessed the wine and wafers (in a small silver box) and these were passed around. It had been indicated to us that we would be welcome to partake, if we so wished. We both declined. Then each read the passage that had been marked in the Bibles we had been given; mine was from the Gospel of Mark. 'Not what I will but as thou wilt.' At the end of each reading, the reader put out the candle in front of him, either by blowing at it or by pinching it between tongue-moistened fingers. The last, big candle was quenched by Wing. All gone now. We sat in the darkness for some time. The only sound I heard was a sigh from Butler. Then Wing lit the big candle, once again after some fumbling with the box of matches in his hand. Still in silence we got up and left the church.

Outside I expressed some anxiety at the thought of a candle which had already once fallen over being left alight in a church with so inflammable a roof; but Butler assured me that it would shortly be put out. Mrs Butler departed into the darkness without a word. Mrs Wing invited us to her home (the Hamilton house), where she set about preparing and presenting a delicious tea of scones, cake, and hot cross buns. The room, under its lofty, shadowy, thatched roof, was well lit and comfortable; equipped with large armchairs, a music centre, a television set, and many books. After the intensity and awkwardness of what had gone before, the conversation was sociable and relaxed, slightly melancholy. We learned that both our host families had grown-up children living in England; the Wings also had a daughter in Australia. Later we talked about politics, the drought, about whether there were any Jews left in Kuruman. (The answer was no: the last one, an old widower living on his own, had died a decade before.) Wing and I reminisced about Kimberley, where he had spent some time as chaplain to the De Beers 'compound' for black labourers. It was a period in his life about which he obviously felt a certain uneasiness, for reasons to do with the nature of the compound system. He also gave us some useful advice on what to look for on the road ahead.

The next morning, as if to sustain the feeling of melancholy with which the evening had left us, we paid a visit to the mission cemetery. It is no more than about fifty yards from the nearest of the houses. You come to it by a path marked out with boulders on both sides. It is surrounded by an exceptionally thick growth of acacia; surrounded and penetrated also by the doves' eternal, intense cooing. The sound is so incessant you wait for fatigue, or perhaps a climax of some kind, to supervene. But it never does.

Some of the old gravestones encroach on one another; the sand encroaches on them all. Two of Moffat's infant children are buried there; one under a stone with an inscription in Tswana on it – the first stone ever, I had been told, to have had words of that language incised in it. The Moffats' grown son, who predeceased them after having become a trader in Kuruman (much to their disappointment, for they had wished him to become a missionary), is also buried there. Nearby is the grave of Sarah Dixon Ashton, described as the 'beloved wife of Wm. Ashton', who had served earlier in Dikgatlhong (Delports Hope). 'Also of their children William aged 2 years and 7 months; William Dixon aged 3 years; James who died in Cape Town aged 11 months; Catherine aged 3 days; Sarah Elizabeth aged 9 years and 3 months ... "For of such is the Kingdom of Heaven".'

The Moffat Mission may today be silent, even deserted; but it would be quite wrong for the reader to assume, therefore, that Moffat and Ashton and Hamilton and the many others like them ultimately failed in their endeavours. Nothing could be further from the truth. The number of converts Moffat made over the decades he was in Kuruman might have been tiny; but his total was much higher than that of David Livingstone in his time, or that of the first missionaries at Inyati, near the present-day city of Bulawayo, Zimbabwe. But no one can doubt that the Christianization of southern Africa was achieved.

As I went from Kimberley to Griquatown, from Griquatown to
Kuruman, from there to 'Bophuthatswana' and to Botswana, and
then on to Zimbabwe, I began to see the route I had chosen to
follow as one littered with the wreckage of successive ideologies. It
was littered with the wrecks of old cars too; but since my car
escaped joining them, it was the ideologies that interested me more.
There they were: the imperialism of the European nations (the
British variety in particular, but those of the Portuguese and
Germans too), Boer nationalism, the Darwinian modes of Victorian
racialism, once-potent notions of economic autarchy, apartheid,
African nationalism, Marxism. The upholders of all these had
vaunted themselves, declared the power and necessity of their
beliefs, set up polities and institutions, or tried to do so, killed
people, changed irrevocably the direction of peoples' lives and the
lives of following generations too – and then each of the systems of
ideas they upheld had failed, been turned awry, become the opposite
of itself, or become merely irrelevant, implausible, even risible.

But not Christianity. True, many of the forms it has assumed are
remote from those which Moffat would have wished to see taking
root; some he might not even have been able to recognize. The
independent African churches, in particular, with their rites and
uniforms and the hierarchies special to them, their dancing and
marching, their 'Zionist' and 'Ethiopian' mythologies, would have
filled him with dismay. But all over the territories he had made his
own he would have seen also the establishment of denominations
more familiar to him; he would have rejoiced to see how their
buildings are still likely to dominate the clusters of humble dwellings
around them, just as medieval churches once dominated the villages
of Europe.

On Easter Sunday, as we drove about Mothibistad – a sprawl of
barrack-like houses and buildings ten miles out of town, to which
Kuruman's black population was moved by the apartheid government – we saw whole armies of churchwomen on the march.
Across the sandy spaces of the township they went: some in scarlet
tunics and black skirts, some in turquoise blouses with big white
sailor collars, some in white hats and long sky-blue robes. (An

infant niece of mine, who knew black women as domestic servants only, used to speak of such worshippers as 'Soldier-Nannies'.) Only a relatively small number of men accompanied them. Assiduous church-going has always been a female speciality in South Africa, as elsewhere; in any case most of the men would have been away in distant cities, trying to earn a living.

On the outskirts of the township I picked up a mother and daughter wearing the uniform of their sect, who were patiently waiting by the roadside for a lift. They told me that they were going to Tsaelangwe, yet another township fifteen miles on.

'What would you have done,' I asked, 'if I hadn't picked you up?'

The mother had no difficulty in answering. 'The Lord would have sent us another lift, because He knows we are going to church.'

When she got out of the car at the Tsaelangwe turn-off, she offered me twenty cents for the ride.

Here is a sampling of the names of indigenous 'Zionist' churches, taken from the various countries I passed through. The list could be extended by a few score.

First Born Church. The Brotherhood Church. Pentecostal Holiness Church. International Pentecostal Church. The Zion Church of Christ. Church of the Risen Christ. Brothers in Christ Church. Beth-El Temple Service (this one with a sign that looked suspiciously like a Star of David). Miracle Crusade. True Church of God. Full Gospel Church of God. Church of the Saints of the Lord. Church of the Nazarene. Ethiopian Apostolic Church. Church of the Beloved Apostles. The Old Apostolic Church of Africa. Judgement Day Church. First Church in Galilee. Andrew Wutawunshe World Witness and Family of God Church.

It must not be supposed that these are all tin-shack affairs. The Zion Church of Christ, much the biggest of them, is able to draw up to two million people from every quarter of the subcontinent to its Easter pilgrimages. These take place at its own 'Mount Moriah', situated in a dry but populous valley north of Pietersburg in the Transvaal.

All this activity flourishes, of course, alongside that of the 'regular' Christian denominations: Catholic, Methodist, Anglican, Congregational, and the rest. Many American apostolic and adventist churches are also active in these parts, as well as a variety of more exotic sects and cults. When I was in Harare, the capital of Zimbabwe, I noticed that the centre of the city was liberally placarded with the announcements of a group called *ECKANKAR – RELIGION OF LIGHT AND SOUND OF GOD* (*How to Open Your Inner Door and Discover How Dreams Divine Love and Spiritual Exercises Can Help You*). At the foot of each of these placards was the following warning: *The terms Eckankar Eck Ek Soul Travel and Vairagis among others are the trademarks of Eckankar, PO Box 27300, Minneapolis MN, USA.*

All of which struck me as hardly more mysterious than the notice outside an exceptionally large general store on the roadside between Vryburg and Taung. MISH & SONS, it says, all over the roof and canopy of the shop; and then, on the roof of another building alongside, in letters almost as large: *Mish Because of Jesus.*

The surprising thing about Islam, by contrast, is that up to now it has made virtually no impact on the black population of southern Africa: this despite the fact that the local mosque is a prominent building in virtually every town above a certain size. (And I don't mean a large size either: I mean places like Mafikeng in South Africa and Lobatse in Botswana and Masvingo in Zimbabwe.) The reason must surely lie in the fact that in southern Africa the followers of Islam are almost invariably the descendants of Malay slaves and of indentured Moslem labourers from the Indian subcontinent: groups which have been held in disesteem by the whites, to put it mildly, and (hence?) wholeheartedly despised by the blacks. So their religion has remained without status, without any relationship to power, and hence without appeal.

Perhaps that situation is about to change.

CHAPTER NINE

☆

Taung – The High Life in Bophuthatswana – Vaal–Harts – Boipelo

When we left Kuruman and entered Mothibistad, some ten or fifteen miles away, we had also left the Republic of South Africa and entered the then supposedly independent Republic of Bophuthatswana: a country which owed its existence to the fanaticism with which the policy of Grand Apartheid was once applied. That policy has since been officially abandoned, of course; but while we were there Bophuthatswana – the 'homeland' for the Tswanas – survived, after a fashion. So too, awaiting a new constitution for the entire country to be put into effect, did several other such statelets scattered over various more or less remote areas of South Africa.

Even after the new constitutional order comes into effect, however, their legacy will remain. Over the last thirty years major institutions and vested interests of many kinds have been created in the homelands; and I suspect that these will prove to be more enduring than the ideological fixations which brought them about.

The chief problem, as the Afrikaner Nationalist government saw it when it came to power in 1948, was that there were so *many* blacks in South Africa: poverty-stricken, uneducated, unwanted, full of menace, racially and historically repugnant; yet also indispensable to the economic wellbeing of the whites and the future development of the country. In the euphoria of victory, of at last finding themselves its political masters, things seemed clear to the Nationalists; even easy. All you had to do with the blacks ('kaffirs') was keep them in their place: *kaffer op sy plek*, as their brutally simple election slogan went. So the 'Pass Laws' were applied more savagely than ever before; 'black spots' in the white cities were bulldozed into the ground and their inhabitants driven into the tribal reserves or into townships sited just within commuting distance of the industrial and commercial centres; their leaders were put in jail; wherever possible, and in many places where you would not have thought it possible, their comings and goings, even their buying of such items as stamps and train tickets, were physically screened from those of their white masters.

Later the inadequacy of these methods became more and more apparent. Something had to be done to moderate the increasing restiveness of the blacks about the *plek* assigned to them. Especially as, contrary to what was intended, they kept on coming into the cities – which kept on needing them to do so. Also, the white rulers of other territories on the continent were disappearing one by one, and world opinion was growing more and more hostile to the naked and initially unashamed racialism on which the policy was based.

Well then ... what about ... what about – setting up a whole lot of independent states in the fourteen per cent of the country that had hitherto been the tribal reserves; paying large sums of money to secure the co-operation of certain important blacks who lived in them; and then informing the rest, whether in the reserves or in the big cities, that they had just been granted citizenship of these newly-created political entities? Most of them would remain where they were of course; they would continue to work in Johannesburg or Cape Town or wherever. Nevertheless, depending on their original tribal affiliations, they would have become citizens of the independent republics of Bophuthatswana, Transkei, Ciskei, Venda, Kwazulu and the rest. As citizens of those new countries they would be unable to make political claims on the Republic of South Africa; and then everybody would be happy.

Brilliant, no? If they wanted a vote, let them vote in whatever tribal territory was assigned to them. If they wanted to acquire freehold property, let them do it there. If they wanted to become presidents or ministers of public works or generals, likewise. And if it turned out (as it soon did) that some of them wanted to become presidents *and* generals *and* ministers of public works *and* directors of large corporations *and* representatives of international corporations *at the same time* – then by all means, let them do it there. What is more, thousands of Afrikaner civil servants could be seconded to help in administering these new republics; thus jobs and opportunities for instant self-enrichment would be created for them as well as for some of the eager local blacks. And then just think of the companies, South African and overseas, that would be constructing all the new parliaments, courts of justice, cabinet ministers' houses, luxury hotels, convention centres, universities . . .

And who would pay for all of this? Oh, the government of the Republic of South Africa. And how would the government pay? Oh, by soaking its mining and manufacturing industries. And if that proved insufficient? Oh, by the ancient, infallible means of printing money.

And then?

What do you mean 'and then'? This would go on for ever.

Oh.

Hence 'Bophuthatswana'. There were no frontier posts to mark the numerous entries into it and exits from it which we had to make, for it actually consisted of about a dozen disjunct pieces of territory isolated from one another by distances of up to several hundred miles. (Had it tried to maintain customs and passport offices at every crossing point, the entire population of the country would have been employed in them.) Still, in all its patches and pieces, Bophuthatswana had its flag and anthem, army and police force, judiciary and civil servants. The last especially. It even had its own nickname by then: Bop. It had an airline too, with the jaunty name of Bop Air – which made it sound like some kind of song. (My wife later flew Bop Air, and very comfortable she found it too.) When we drove past the prison in Mothibistad and saw prisoners sitting with their legs through the bars of the windows and shouting out their Sunday greetings to visitors and passers-by in the dusty square below, these were the prisoners of Bop; the local clinic was run by the Bop Ministry of Health, and the local schools by the Bop Ministry of Education; the armoured cars parked in rows behind the police station, identical to those used by the South African Police, were Bop, Bop, Bop all the way through.

Politics is like life in this respect, at least: our ends never know our beginnings. The 'independent homelands' policy was intended to make more secure the future of the whites; actually it helped to do the reverse, though this has been for reasons radicals on the left have never been willing to acknowledge. Here, in these supposedly independent statelets, within reach of the major South African cities, Grand Apartheid had created areas in which all the systematized restrictions of Petty Apartheid were done away with. (How could even a nominally independent black country forbid blacks and whites from eating in a common dining-room or swimming in a common swimming-pool – or sleeping in a common bed?) And that was not all. A multitude of other activities which the influence of the Dutch Reformed Church had long made illegal in South Africa itself were suddenly on offer to visitors of all races. You could gamble, drink at all hours, get hold of dope with little effort and of whores with even less, watch pornographic films and floorshows – and you could do all these things *on a Sunday too*!

Suddenly the problem of how to fill in a weekend in Johannesburg or Pretoria or Port Elizabeth was solved. If the price of these new pleasures for whites was that of eating alongside blacks, and having to defer to them in a queue, and rubbing shoulders (and other parts of their anatomy) with them – well, it was cheap enough. Not to say exciting enough.

In other words, the existence of the statelets, and the activities that went on in them, did much to corrode the whole mystico-ideologico-pollutio-politico dread among whites of encountering blacks on any terms other than those of master and servant. If it was possible to eat, swim, sit in a cinema, go to the lavatory and go to bed alongside blacks in Transkei or Bop – then why not in Johannesburg too? If blacks were to be treated like 'citizens' rather than 'lepers' there – why not here? (It was a Nationalist president who used the word 'leper' to describe how blacks had been treated under his own government's policy.) With all this came a corrosion too of the old puritan ethic which had for so long fortified and stultified the Afrikaner people.

The truth of the matter is that blacks and whites in South Africa, from the first days of white settlement onwards, have always been like cats in a bag. The more desperately they have tried to get away from each other, or to get rid of each other, the more hopelessly entangled they have become.

Many years ago three or four Coloured men came to my father's office to discuss a business project with him. In the course of their conversation he asked his secretary, a highly respectable Afrikaner lady, a pillar of the Dutch Reformed church, to bring tea and biscuits for himself and his visitors. This she did. The next day she brought to the office a brand-new cup, around the handle of which she had tied a special piece of string, so that everyone in the office would know that this was *her* cup, and that no portion of its rim had ever touched or would ever touch a dark lip. When my father remonstrated with her, saying among other things that she had seen for herself that his visitors had been perfectly clean and respectable persons, she did not deny it. She merely snapped out, 'That's apartheid!' and the discussion ended there.

Twenty years pass. Long after my father's death my brother makes a visit to Kimberley and arranges to meet this lady for lunch. In the course of the meal she tells him that she and a group of her friends, all widows like herself, have just come back from a long weekend in the Mmbatho Sun Hotel, in Bophuthatswana. They had gone there to do some gambling. 'You won't believe how crowded it was,' she told him. 'You could hardly get to the tables for the crush. And around the machines – !' 'There must have been a lot of blacks among them,' my brother says mischievously, recollecting the episode recounted above. 'Mister Jock,' she gleefully replies, still on a high from the experience, 'there were *hundreds* of them!'

In effect, on leaving Kuruman we had done what every other traveller to the north had done once diamonds were discovered in and around Kimberley. We had abandoned the old road to the north – Moffat's road, that is – and rejoined the route developed subsequently. This involved crossing the fictitious border between Bop and South Africa at Mothibistad and elsewhere a few times, back and forth, until we finally wound up a mere seventy miles north of Kimberley in a place called Taung (pronounced Ta-oong).

When I was a boy the settlement was called Taungs (pronounced Tongs by all self-respecting whites). It was nothing, in their eyes: just another forlorn halt on the interminable railway journey to the Bechuanaland Protectorate and the Rhodesias. Try to imagine such places: all of them; any one of them. The single line, with a loop in acknowledgement of the halt, comes straight in from the south and goes straight out to the north. (Or vice-versa.) Next to it is a sandy platform and two iron-roofed houses with gauzed verandahs, in which live the stationmaster and his assistant. A signboard announces the name of the station in block capitals and its height above sea-level. Water drips from the tank and hose at which steam locomotives refresh themselves. A cattle-pen made of tubular iron stands empty. So do several goods wagons that look no less permanently stuck there than the cattle-pen. A black woman sits in the shade of a pepper tree. A few bluegums and several 'native trading stores' ('kaffir stores') straggle along the main road some distance away, along with a bar and two petrol pumps. The veld nearby is diversified only by heaps of ballast for the railway and some tatterdemalion huts. And a donkey cart, complete with drooping donkey in harness.

Further off – the usual. It is formless, unpeopled, seasonless. Black bushes like scorch marks. Rock outcrops like scabs. A bare paleness that is the very skin and scale of the countryside. And sun. And sky.

I do not want to be misunderstood. I am not being contemptuous about such places. All the romance and desolation of the innumerable train journeys of my childhood were compressed in them. The sway and clatter of the train halted, the steam engine's many voices silenced, a murmur coming from a neighbouring compartment, a day or a night's travel still ahead: now stare your fill at this new place, so well known already from those you have passed and those still to come. Look away; find something triflingly different for your gaze to rest on; look back and there it still is, just as it always has been; as intimate as the lines on your hand (on which your fate is supposedly written); as speechless as the semi-circle of the horizon.

And at night? To describe that experience I turn to the American poet, Yvor Winters.

> Small stations by the way,
> Sunk far past midnight! Nothing one can say
> Names the compassion they stir in the heart.
> Obscure men shift and cry, and we depart.

Then fame came to Taungs. Nearby there is a quarry which produces marble with exactly the look and colour of nougat. (The word itself, I now see, looks suspiciously like an anagram of Taungs.) For some reason this quarry attracted the attention of an anthropologist at the University of the Witwatersrand, and lo and behold, in Taungs lay buried the first skull to be discovered of creatures now known as the *Australopithecae*. The remains of many more have since been found in other parts of southern and eastern Africa; and it is to them that we are now believed to be indebted, no matter what part of the world we come from, for having the heads and hands, brains and posture, that we do.

Let me say it straight. For someone like myself, whose parents and grandparents came *to* Africa; whose language came *to* Africa; who has always known that letters, industry, science came *to* Africa (south of the Sahara, at least), as did most of the political orders and concepts which now supposedly govern the continent – for such a person, there is something especially strange and touching in the thought of the entire human species emerging *from* Africa. Africa the passive? The backward? The awaiting one?

But so it is. Here in the chalky, marbley soil of Taungs lay the first-found evidence of it.

Anyhow, the next big thing to happen to Taung (as it had by

now become) was the invention of the Republic of Bophuthatswana and the subsequent arrival of the Taung Sun Hotel and Casino. In front of it flew the flags of Great Britain, the United States, France, the Netherlands, Greece, Portugal, Israel, and Bop. Not the flag of the Republic of South Africa, notice. For we were now in a free and independent country, and there was going to be no unseemly kowtowing and truckling to our mighty neighbour here. True, South Africa began about three miles to the south of the hotel (maximum) and about the same distance to the north of it; the railway line and the road itself belonged to South Africa; behind the hotel, to the west, you had to cross just another few miles of tribal land – all of it grazed to extinction – before this tract of Bop expired yet again. (You knew you had crossed the 'border' out of white-owned lands because the condition of the veld at once deteriorated spectacularly.) Still, there we were and duly grateful to the South African government for bringing Bop into existence, and to 'His Excellency Lucas Mangope, President of Bophuthatswana' (always so described) for governing it. Had it not been for them, no one would ever have thought of putting up a marble-fronted and marble-floored hotel just here, complete with parking lots, security fencing, lawns and flower-beds, swimming-pool, private game park, miniature golf course, tennis court, children's entertainments centre, indoor and outdoor dining areas, air conditioning, casino, porno movies, and several large, coloured, besashed photographs of His Excellency President Lucas Mangope.

The place could also have done with a few large photographs of Mr Sol Kerzner, the Jewish entrepreneur whose casinos in Bop and in the other 'independent' statelets had not only made him a very wealthy man, but had provided them with a large portion of their national budgets. The most famous of his resorts is Sun City, in another chunk of Bop about fifty miles north of Pretoria, which is renowned for its hotels, theme parks, lavish floorshows and international sporting events (golf tournaments, prize fights, Miss World competitions). Down here in Taung we could not expect anything like that, since we are so much more local, cheapskate a crowd, coming as we do from no further afield than Kimberley to the south and Vryburg to the north, and from the *dorps*, mines, and farms all around.

Yet what we lack in money and sophistication we make up in enthusiasm and numbers. We avoid the 'expensive' roulette and blackjack tables (five-rand minimum stake); on the whole we avoid the cheaper tables too, because of the complicated rules governing the games played on them. But the machines! Man, we're mad for them! Crazy! How can we not be, what with the disco lights and music going at us all the time, the bells, handles, buttons, the spinning wheels that carry our fortunes, the magic machine-gun rattle when-ever someone makes a hit and the coins fusillade into the cup below and continue doing it like a demented firing-squad for longer than we can believe, and come to a stop, finally, in a holy hush that can be heard, even with the racket unabated all around, just there, at that machine, where one of us stands gazing at the handfuls of silver-nickel that a cut-rate god has poured into his or her Danaean lap?

You should have seen us: every shade of pigmentation, hair, feature, build; agog, half-dazed, half-drunk, loud-voiced, exhausted; speaking in Afrikaans, Tswana, Urdu, Portuguese, Italian, guttural English; Boer women with legs and bodies and even necks like bags of flour; excitable Indians and their sari-clad wives; bejeaned, sweat-shirted youths in trainers so fancy they look as if they could bite you or run off on their own; elderly blacks whose decaying sports jackets and frayed shirts show how little they can afford to be there; 'poor whites' to match; rich blacks with such stiffly starched shirt-cuffs they could commit suicide with them, if the need arose; grim Greek shopkeepers; diggers with pitted, pig-leather skins; dirty weekenders from Kimberley, all perfume, after-shave, and bodies slotted together even while they gamble or wait to gamble; truncheon-wielding, walkie-talkie-carrying security guards in brisk military caps. While just outside, another guard makes sure that no one under eighteen years of age goes into the movie house next door, where there is a continuous showing of *Mobile Home Girls*, *Outlaw Girls*, *Pleasure Maze*, and *Sweet'n Short*.

'Suddenly,' M. said, gazing around in astonishment, 'suddenly – it's Brazil!'

It made quite a change from the previous night in the Moffat church, Kuruman, I had to admit.

'Last night you looked very cross. I think you had bad luck with the machines.'

I assured the security guard who said this to me that was not why I had looked cross. I had not been cross at all; merely put out because my wife had been afflicted by a stomach ailment. He expressed his sympathy and asked if there was anything he could do to help.

The two of us were standing near the swimming-pool, at midday, watching still photographs and a video being taken of a wedding group.

It was a big and elaborate party, and I found several things about it puzzling. Most of the guests, about thirty of them, were dressed in identical tie-dyed garments of pale brown and white – the women in long dresses of this material; the men in loose shirts hanging over their khaki trousers. The bride, wearing a green suit and white hat, looked remarkably mature; the groom, in suit and bow tie, a little less so. He was much darker in complexion than she; his skin was truly black, with a west African rather than southern African hue. In the strong sunlight the paradoxical effect was that his face shone more brightly than hers. Their retinue was a large one: three older bridesmaids and four little ones dressed in identical frilly cream dresses and white bows; the same number of pageboys in miniature versions of the groom's attire. Everyone, adult and child alike, wore white gloves. They lined up at the edge of the pool in different combinations for the camera – bride and groom holding hands, embracing, blowing kisses; now in-laws, apparently; now retinue ranked in size; now all females; now all males. The men were sweltering in the heat of the sun, which was made more fierce still by the glitter from the swimming-pool. The trousers of one of the pageboys kept slipping down, much to the mirth of everyone else. The guests in their tie-dyed uniforms looked on, smiled, commented on the scene; then they too were summoned forward for video purposes.

At this point my curiosity got the better of me, and I sidled over to the (stills) cameraman and asked him if the guests all belonged to one church. Was that why they were wearing the same clothes? He lifted his head from the howitzer-like barrel of his machine, through which he had lately been taking dummy shots, and looked pityingly at me.

'They not guests. They not church people. They musicians. They a group. They sing and play for the people.'

'And the wedding? Was that in a church somewhere?'

'Wedding? This isn't the wedding. The wedding was ten years ago.'

'I don't understand.'

He was amused by this confession; so amused I could see he was tempted to leave me bewildered. But his good nature got the better of him. 'This –' and he pointed – 'is a tenth anniversary. That why they having a party. They re-living the past. Everything exactly like it was then. The whole lot. The works, man.'

He took another couple of dummy shots, then added scrupulously, 'Except they have no children in those days.'

After that he began snapping away in earnest. For all the abundance of light from the sun and glittering water, he kept the camera's flash going for some reason; its sparks flickered about the guests like a kind of visual squeak. Presently the entire group made its chattering way towards the hotel entrance, where several beribboned cars were waiting to carry them off.

To the east of the hotel and railway line lies another half-hidden Taung. This one has been a main centre of the Tlhaping branch of the Tswana people for something like a hundred and fifty years. It has also been a missionary centre for about the same length of time. But the visitor to the hotel would know nothing of it unless he went in search of it. It begins with a police station, an army camp, a sign announcing Taung Light Industries, with no light industry visible other than the Spick-Span dry cleaners, a modest agricultural and technical college, a dire café. Then come the missions (Catholic and Adventist), a hospital spread out over a wide area, new brick houses – and everything else, sprawling across great distances of trodden dust and hardened litter. Shacks of every description, and beyond description, totter up every faint rise, slide into every hollow, crouch behind each clump of rocks, stagger along the line of every *donga*. There are no roads, only trails across the reddish soil; a few pale dogs; copious amounts of black stones; some clapped-out cars (how did they ever get to the places where they finally expired?). Finally the landscape begins to rise more steeply towards the horizon, where the boulders cluster together in natural cairns; there the huts peter out and a pale sky takes over.

Winding through all this, now down, now up, ran the narrow, single-lane road I was on. Eventually I stopped by the roadside and got into conversation with an elderly man seated on a rock. He was wearing a threadbare linen suit, a straw hat, and partly dismembered shoes; on his lap he had a leather briefcase. Its stitching was coming out too. When he heard that I came from Kimberley he told me that he had been educated there a long, long time ago, at the St Boniface Mission School. 'Brother Dundon's school,' I said. He was so delighted at hearing this name fall from my lips that his face produced an entirely new array of wrinkles; several stumps of teeth also appeared. 'You knew him? You knew Brother Dundon? What a wonderful man! He was first my teacher, then my headmaster, then my friend.' He himself had become a teacher afterwards, not in Kimberley, but here in Taung, at the St Paul's Mission. Now he was retired, but he worked also 'in insurance'. At this point, by way of evidence, he lofted his briefcase, briefly. Insurance? Here? In those sad shoes? To which unasked questions he said, a little reluctantly, 'Burial insurance.'

He gladly accepted my offer of a lift and we drove back towards St Paul's Mission, which he said he was heading for. It was the tallest and most imposing set of the buildings I had passed since leaving the main road. At the centre of it was a church in brown and cream stucco of a distinctly Germanic cast, together with a matching residence for the monks or brothers who ran the place. From what he had said I thought he would go into the mission grounds, but after thanking me for the lift, and remarking again on the amazing fact that I had known Brother Dundon, he struck off towards some shacks a few hundred yards away. Two boys of about sixteen, in shorts and the inevitable trainers, then approached me. They had been standing at the entrance to the mission. Did they want a lift too? No, just some chat. It turned out, rather strangely given the conversation I just had, that they too were currently at the St Boniface School in Kimberley; they had previously been going to the school here at St Paul's, but now that they'd started their matriculation course they had been sent to Kimberley. I asked them if they had they ever heard of Brother Dundon? They thought for a long time, hoping for politeness' sake to dredge the name from their memories. But eventually it had to come out – no, they'd never heard of him. So they offered me instead the names of two other Brothers, also from Ireland. Here at St Paul's there were three Fathers, from Austria. I asked if they ever went to the Christian Brothers School in Kimberley, which used to be the city's white Catholic school, and which I knew since to have been desegregated: did they play games there, or go there for lessons? No, it was 'too expensive', one of the boys answered, rubbing thumb and forefinger next to his ear. 'For rich boys,' the other added, 'with rich fathers.' And once they had taken their matric – what then? 'Then we look for work.' What kind of work? 'Any work. So long as we make some money.' (Pronounced with a long-drawn-out plaintiveness, as of a prospect unutterably distant: ma-a-ane-ey.)

They watched me leave. My thoughts reverted at once to Brother Dundon, who was surely long since at rest in some cemetery back in Ireland, to which he had returned for his retirement. He and my father had worked together in a charity known in the language of that time as the Native Relief Fund. (The lady who had been so kind to me in the Kimberley Library had acted as its secretary.) The money raised by the fund each winter was spent on blankets and food parcels for indigent blacks, the old and the young especially. Sometimes Brother Dundon would come back to the house for a drink with my father after meetings; at his invitation I went at least twice to the school. Bare walls. Bare corridors. A smell of unwashedness. An office with a wooden crucifix on a wall as bare and as bitterly unpainted as all the rest. Flat spaces all around where nothing grew but two posts with rings attached, nets long since gone, for the girls to play netball. Dust.*

When I got back to the Taung Sun Hotel and Casino from this long drive, the security guard who had been so matey with me at the mock-wedding, and who had commiserated with me over my supposed losses the previous evening, now chose to forbid me from going into the hotel until I produced my pass to show that I was a *bona fide* guest. Inevitably I had left the card in the room. 'But you know me!' I exclaimed. 'My wife's in bed. She's not well. What are you playing at, for God's sake?' 'It's my duty,' he answered, half-proud, half-abashed. 'Good for you,' I said and walked past him. I expected him to put out an arm to detain me, but he merely wailed at my back, in suddenly reproachful tones, 'Don't be so like that, sir.'

While I waited for M. to recover I gambled a bit, not profitably; I drove about the Vaal–Harts irrigation scheme – another of Cecil Rhodes's schemes or dreams; one which he did not live to carry out. I also walked several times within a large area of open veld attached to the hotel and known grandly as the Boipelo Nature and Game Reserve.

South of Taung the valley of the Harts River is lower than the course of the Vaal River, some fifty miles away. In the 1930s they brought water from the one to the other. The result? Between barren, parallel crests of rock you find fields of maize, lucerne, potatoes, groundnuts, cotton; poplar-lined roads; water running fast in wide, shallow streams; cattle standing in fields of green grass; frequent farmhouses; a few *dorps* with many ostentatiously modern and prosperous houses. A place called Hartswater was particularly well endowed with these: it could boast of one grossly

---

* Since writing the above I have heard from Kimberley that arsonists ('radical' blacks, it is assumed) have burned down St Boniface School. Perhaps the paragraph above should end with the word: Ashes.

Hollywood-Spanish affair of arches and patios, tiled verandahs and stone-faced external stairways curling like vines, the whole thing several storeys high and set above a lofty terraced garden. With swimming-pool, of course. It was like a mirage. Where the local blacks lived it was impossible for me to find out. Even Vincent, a thin, embittered miner on his annual leave from Virginia, in the Orange Free State goldfields, was of no help to me, since he was just visiting his girlfriend here who lived in the servants' quarters of one of the big houses. When I asked him what he thought of 'the new South Africa' he answered, 'What new South Africa?' When, as evidence of the new South Africa, I pointed to some black children swinging on the swings in a park in the middle of Hartswater, he said, 'That means nothing to me.' When I asked him what it was like in the mines he said, 'Terrible.'

On the outskirts of the town I came across a multicoloured shrine, chapel-like in shape, Papist in architectural inspiration, overwhelmingly Nationalist in intention. It was dedicated to the 'Pioneering Afrikaner Mother', and came with virulent stained-glass windows, an altar at one end which wasn't quite an altar, poems incised in stone to the pioneering Afrikaner mother ('I see you win because you are wife and mother'), idealized murals of ditto, and a visitors' book full of reverent inscriptions. 'Here we see what we owe to the generations who have gone before.' 'Afrikaners, forget not your heritage!' 'May this building stand for ever like a prayer of thanksgiving to the mothers of our people.' And so forth. Nearby, shaped exactly like a rocket, only in concrete, was a monument to the Afrikaans language. Such monuments may be described as a speciality of the Afrikaners: this was not the first or last such object I saw on my travels.

No one shared with me either the memorial to mother or the monument to the language. The same was true of the several visits I made to the Boipelo Nature and Game Reserve. You could get to it only on foot and through the hotel grounds. Ringed all the way round by a fence of mesh and razor wire, it was surrounded also by the voices of nearby, unseen Africans, citizens of Bop, whom the fence was designed as much to keep out as it was to keep in the animals. What the Africans' land looked like I knew well: all trodden sand marked with knots the size of infants' shoelaces, which showed where tufts of grass had once grown. And the melancholy debris of huts scattered far and wide. Here, however, in the many acres of the reserve of which I was a temporary Crusoe (for it wasn't to go walking in the veld that people came to the Taung Sun Hotel and Casino), shrubs and grass grew to a respectable height, and the acacias were alive with birds: doves and wild pigeons especially, but also a couple of indignant korhaans whose nesting place was among some reeds, and a flock of scurrying guinea fowl who could be relied on to appear agitatedly in front of me wherever I walked.

It all looked and smelled exactly like the veld I had known in my boyhood. There was not a tint of colour, not a scrap of herbage, not a small, glittering cloud in the sky, not even an intonation of those debarred African voices, that was not as familiar to me as the sound of my own breathing. On the crustiest stretches of soil the red ants of my childhood had marked out their trails, some as much as fifty or sixty yards long and as busy as motorways. Every pair of minute, fern-shaped leaves that started from the thorn bushes was accompanied by a pair of bodyguards in the shape of matching spur-like thorns. They would still be growing when the leaves had gone: some remaining spurs merely; others extending into long white needles angled like a pair of compasses. Not a finger's length of twig and branch would be left unprotected. No wonder that the Namaqua doves, their colours all pearl and ink-smudge, their bodies no bigger than a girl's fist, settled themselves down on the bushes with such careful beatings of their wings, anxious not to impale their tiny feet. All but invisible unless you looked for them down below were innumerable wild flowers, even in autumn and after a two-year drought: scarlet trumpets; veld violets; pansies no bigger than the head of a tack; yellow balls like the head of a hatpin; bigger yellow tufts of a space-age, geodesic structure; fingernail irises. When I got back to the room in the evenings I would try to identify them in a handsomely illustrated book called *Wild Flowers of the Northern Cape* (which for some reason was printed upside down).

There were bigger living things in the reserve too. On a couple of occasions I saw a dozen or more impala at a distance of about a hundred yards. Also a group of smaller antelope I never got close enough to identify, making an orientally fluttering performance of their grazing: tails, heads, ears, and delicate hoofs always on the go; unpredictable, white-bottomed scurries as they competed for a particular place; elaborate startles over something, anything, nothing, the shadow of a bird, a cry carried in the evening air, the scent of a visitor on the wind.

Once, too, with a barrage of hooves and a rending of branches, a hartebeest burst out of some bushes not five paces ahead of me. Head down, huge-eyed, he was running for his life, his close-packed pelt gleaming. It was tan and black from end to end. When I had got over my own fright I felt like grieving for his. I wanted to have seen more of him. It was as if the fear we had felt was somehow shaming to us both.

CHAPTER TEN

☆

'The Chace of the Elephant' – Hunting for Litvaks – In Praise of the Railway – Finding Tiger Kloof

Later, in Zimbabwe, when I was visiting an incomparably larger and more spectacular nature reserve, a woman said to me about the blacks on the other side of the fence, 'Of course if you let these people in, there'd be nothing left after twelve months.'

'These people' I knew to be an ominously coded phrase, like 'I'm no racist' or (another favourite, always said in a tone of amused contempt) 'This is Africa, you know.' But the speaker's hostility to the people she was speaking of did not make her statement untrue. The proof of it lay in their semi-starving condition, in the gauntness of their cattle, in the dusty wastes of their grazing-lands. Let the fence around the reserve come down and its game would indeed be wiped out in short order, its grasslands trampled flat by hungry herds, its trees felled for fuel and building material.

The whites, though, are hardly in a position to point fingers or throw stones on this subject. It is not just that black land-hunger in southern Africa is largely a consequence of the appropriation by whites of all the best lands available. There is also the question of what the whites themselves did to the flora and fauna of the region as they took it over.

The road to the north earned its titles as the 'hunters' trail' or the 'ivory road' in the bloodiest manner possible: through the killing of vast herds of wild animals. It was never called the 'timber trail', so far as I am aware; but that too would have been a suitable name for it. Along it travelled nearly all the timber used for domestic and industrial purposes during the first fifteen years of Kimberley's existence. Until the arrival of the railway in 1885, after which coal was brought in from Britain, no other fuel was available for the pumping and haulage machinery used on the mines.

The results were exactly what might have been expected: the steady northward retreat of the 'ivory frontier' and the effective denudation of the veld of its timber for hundreds of miles to the north of Kimberley. In 1891 the traveller J. Theodore Bent, who was to become most famous for his confidently 'scientific' pronouncements about the builders of Great Zimbabwe ('By diligent research . . . we were able to re-people this country with a race highly civilized in far distant ages, a race far advanced in the art of building and decorating, a gold-seeking race who occupied it like a garrison in the midst of an enemy country') – this same Theodore Bent remarked that even beyond Kanye, in what is now Botswana, more than two hundred and fifty miles north of Kimberley, 'the road is treeless, until the area is reached where terminates the cutting down of timber for the support of the diamond fields of Kimberley'.

In other words, the near-universality in the region of what people call 'thorn veld' or 'thorn scrub' is largely a man-made affair. The scrub looks as if it has been there since the dawn of creation, but that is an illusion. The acacias most worth chopping down – the genuine trees, that is: camelthorns, umbrella thorns, sweet thorns – were felled wholesale and then sent on the long journey south in wagonload after wagonload.* Indeed, the last of these wagons were still to be seen trundling through the streets of Kimberley in my boyhood: hauled not by oxen, as in the old days, but by spans of a dozen or more dejected donkeys. By that time the trade was in domestic firewood only and was carried on wholly by blacks for blacks.

---

* In *The Colonization of the Southern Tswana 1870–1900*, by Kevin Shillingford (1985), we are told that by 1882 the four major mines of Kimberley were using two hundred wagonloads of wood each week. To this figure must be added the diamond fields' domestic consumption of fuel.

As for the wild animals . . . From the 1840s onwards, professional and 'gentlemen' hunters abounded in the regions stretching north from the Orange to the Zambesi and Chobe Rivers. F.C. Selous, who hunted in the most northerly part of these territories, reported a modest bag in a typical month (September 1879) as follows: eight buffalo, five elephants (brought down in a single day), five zebra, one lioness, one lechwe, one wildebeest, and one reedbuck. Comparable single-handed feats of slaughter, all logged with the same care, were carried out by him for about nine years. So you can imagine the grand total. After the publication of his book, *A Hunter's Wanderings in Africa* (1881), Selous became the most famous of southern African hunters; but there were hundreds of others like him, some of whom could boast of higher scores than his. Henry Hartley (later to win his share of fame by uncovering workable reserves of gold ore in Mashonaland) claimed a lifetime bag of about twelve hundred elephant bulls. Fourteen of them he killed in one day. This last figure was easily surpassed by two Boers named Viljoen and Jacobs who shot a record *forty-seven* elephants in their best day. In his *Missionary Travels and Researches in Africa* (1850), David Livingstone describes without apparent disapproval the activities of another hunter, David Cummings, as 'five years of warfare with wild animals'; and vouches for the accuracy of Cummings's own account of his prosecution of this 'warfare':

The statement of Mr Cummings as to the number of animals he killed is by no means improbable . . . Two other gentlemen in the same region destroyed no fewer than seventy-eight rhinoceroses in a single season.

To understand such figures we have to think of the whites coming on herds of game so extensive that at first they probably believed them to be inexhaustible: as endless as the African continent itself, as infinitely reproducible as mosquitoes or flies or wild bees. Naturally enough, the response of the blacks to competition of this kind (which was on a scale previously unimaginable to them) was to try to get firearms into their own hands. Soon the white professionals were remarking on how much further into the interior they had to go in order to find their prey, and how much

more difficult it was becoming for them to make a profit from their
ventures. Yet the allure of the chase and the romantic glamour of
the hunters' way of life were sufficient inducement for them to
carry on; and there were also many wealthy sportsmen from
Europe who were not looking for profit at all – merely for excitement. On this subject the Livingstone of *Missionary Travels* can
again be brought in as a witness; and all the more tellingly since he
was a sensitive observer of most aspects of the natural history of
the territories he travelled through:

The chace of the elephant is the best test of courage the country affords, and
the number killed by Bechuanas, Griquas, Boers, and Englishmen, will give
some idea of the prowess of the respective races. The average for the natives
was less then one a man, for the Griquas one, for the Boers two, and for the
English officers twenty each ... The reason for the superiority of our
countrymen was that they had the coolness to approach within thirty yards of
the animal before firing.*

The Portuguese did not do too badly for themselves either. Of
this I once saw the physical evidence. Many years ago a major

* In private Livingstone could be much more contemptuous of the activities of the
hunters than he evidently thought it wise to be in public. In a letter to his sister Janet
[21 July 1843] he writes:

We are in company with a party of hunters. Two are gentlemen from India, & one a son of
a planter from the West Indies. As he is the greatest fool of the three, I shall tell you of his
adventures first. [There follows a delighted account of the swindles perpetrated on this man
by 'Boors' and others.] ... Well, the next in our list is a Mr Pringle, a Scotchman ... the
next, Capt. Steele of the Coldstream Gaurds [*sic*] & aidecamp to the Governor of Madras
... He & Pringle have spent one thousand pounds in the journey up, by purchasing horses,
waggons, provisions, &c &c., & all they will take away will be a few skins and the heads
of animals ... Their object in coming up to this part of the country is simply to kill
animals. They frequently do so, & then leave their carcasses to be destroyed by the
vultures. They are enthusiastic hunters. We have a nobler subject on which to be enthusiastic. We shall part with them in a day or two.

Sardonic scorn was always one of the special notes of Livingstone's private correspondence. Of the hunter Cummings, for instance, whose veracity he was publicly to vouch
for in his *Missionary Travels*, he wrote at various points in his letters that he was 'a
miserably poor thing', 'cowardly', and a great stealer of sheep. Still, Livingstone could
not have made his first major journey of exploration – to Ngamiland, north-west of
the Kalahari Desert, in 1848 – had he not been accompanied by the hunter, William
Oswell.

avenue leading into Lourenço Marques (now Maputo), in Mozambique, was lined with flowering trees, conventionally enough. Less conventionally, it was lined also with rows of elephant skulls stuck on pillars. This by way of striking an extra note of welcome to the arriving traveller.

Not surprisingly, then, outside the reserves I saw very little game; nothing more than some ostriches, the porcupine that had scuttled across the road to Griquatown, and a mother kudu and her calf on a cattle ranch I visited. And a snake which came sliding out of the rondavel assigned to us in a 'rest camp' near the Victoria Falls. However, I did come across several of the present-day, would-be successors to those nineteenth-century English officers whose prowess won Livingstone's praise. Slouch-hatted Americans and Germans they were, chiefly – brandishers of hunting licences; exchangers of itineraries; bearers of weapons gleaming like brown and black jewels in the elongated metal cases in which they were nested; retailers of stories and information about this or that private game farm and its owners.

Here, for instance, is a fair-haired, plump-cheeked, spread-breasted girl of seventeen from Texas, artlessly chewing gum and swinging one booted, khaki-trousered leg to and fro while telling me how 'great' it had been at Johnny Smit's place in the Tuli Block and how 'great' he had been to her.

'It was our last morning and we were all packed up and everything and just when we were going he said hang on, he had a goodbye present for me. You know what it was? Screw the licence – he'd let me take out an extra zebra! So we got in the jeep and ten minutes later –'

She jerks her head to one side, makes a loud click in the roof of her mouth, and winks an eye, all in one movement. End of zebra. 'Great!'

She also told me that her brother had stayed behind at Johnny Smit's – 'He's a bow-hunter, you know, and Johnny really likes that.'

A bow-hunter? A licensed, post-modern Bushman from Texas?

After two or three such encounters I discovered that it was not really their killing of beasts that put me off these people. It was their self-love; the heroic light, so carefully and expensively arranged, in which they choose to see themselves.

Animals aside, there was another declining species for which I had decided to keep my eyes open *en route*: that of the backveld and small-town South African Jew.

When people think of the Jews in South African history, the names most likely to come to mind are those of mining magnates like Barnato and Beit, Joel and Oppenheimer. (So prominent were Jews among the early 'Randlords' that *echt*-Gentile millionaires like Wernher and Robinson were universally assumed to be Jewish, their denials notwithstanding.) Almost without exception, however, the Jewish gold and diamond magnates hailed from Germany and England; for that reason they were not typical of the larger community which was then coming into being. That community, like its counterparts in the United States, Canada, the Argentine, and indeed Great Britain, was effectively a creation of Jews who were fleeing from the Russian Pale of Settlement at the end of the nineteenth century and the beginning of the twentieth.

Two things, though, did distinguish the community in South Africa from the others just mentioned. First, it was remarkably homogeneous in origin, some eighty-five per cent of it being of Lithuanian (Litvak) stock. Secondly, though most of the immigrants went to the bigger cities – to Johannesburg above all – they also scattered themselves across the length and breadth of the country in a fashion unparalleled elsewhere. In the early decades of the twentieth century there was not the smallest *dorp* in South Africa that did not have its Jewish general dealer and hotel-keeper; places hardly more conspicuous could boast of communities big enough to set up their own synagogues. There were remote railway sidings too, nothing more, graced with just two buildings: the store and the house of the Jewish storekeeper. (My father spent some of his earlier, unmarried years in South Africa in just such a situation. Both my mother and father, as well as their parents and siblings, belonged in every respect to the immigration of which I am speaking.) A small but significant number of Jewish immigrants also farmed in sheep or cattle, maize or potatoes, depending on the district in which they found themselves.

The Litvaks arrived penniless; within a generation the community had become prominent in every aspect of the country's commercial, professional, and intellectual life. It took hardly longer before it ceased to be so widely dispersed. More and more of the younger generation from the *platteland* went to the cities and remained there; eventually their parents followed them. A contraction of a different and more radical kind has since been taking place: a low birth-rate and a higher than average rate of emigration have resulted in rapidly shrinking numbers in the big cities too.

The consequences were apparent to me everywhere. In Kimberley I learned that between twenty and thirty Jewish families now live there (as against the hundred-odd families of my childhood). In Kuruman I was told by Father Butler that when the last Jew in the town, an old, solitary widower, had died some ten years before, a difficult problem had been set for the local townsfolk. They felt it would not be fitting to consign him to the grave without a prayer of some sort being said over his body. But who would be the one to say it? After some of the clergy in town had declined the privilege, the then head of the Moffat Mission finally agreed to do it. In Mafikeng, which boasts a firmly constructed, red-brick synagogue, complete with optimistic memorial stone recording its rebuilding and rededication in 1963, I was told that it is rare for there to be enough people to make up a *minyan*, or quorum, for prayers. (This in spite of the fact that various Israeli technicians and entrepreneurs have turned up to help in the grotesquely lavish construction of Mmbatho, the neighbouring 'capital' of the Republic of Bophuthatswana.) In places like Griquatown, Barkly West, Pokwani, Boetsap, Taung, which I knew to have once had their representative Jews – nobody. (Many years ago there was a Jewish lady of surpassing plainness in a place called Espach's Drift, near Taung, with whom my mother used to exchange novels and other books.) Only in Danielskuil did the Gers Brothers, grandsons or great-grandsons of the original founders of the stone-built store, apparently still live in the *dorp* – though they were away when we were there. And further afield, in Botswana and Zimbabwe, I came across some quasi-archaeological traces, in the form of shop-signs, of a vanished tribe: the Mazeltov Furniture Stores, say, or Cohen's Skins and Hides. Even a biggish city like Bulawayo, I was told, now had a community of no more than about a hundred and twenty souls in all; and of those, my informant said gloomily, almost all were 'old'. He himself had two sons and a daughter in New York and another daughter in Cape Town.

On the other hand, it should be recorded that the Lemba people, most of whom live in the north-east corner of Zimbabwe, and have done so for centuries, firmly declare themselves to be Jews. They make this claim on the basis of some of their dietary habits and Sabbath-day practices. The Israelis, who rescued the black Falashas of Ethiopia from war and famine, have so far shown no interest in the Lemba.

Some miles outside Vryburg, M. and I had tea with a Jewish lady who was running a large cattle ranch with the help of her twenty-year-old son. She was an impressive person – calm, steady-eyed, alert, hospitable – who had lived through the loss of an older son in one car accident and the loss of her husband in another. She had a daughter at boarding-school (now home for the Passover holiday, together with visiting cousins from Johannesburg) and another daughter studying in Israel. The farmhouse was a comfortable, squareish affair built of stone; it overlooked a rough defile which, in the manner characteristic of this countryside, was hidden until you came on it. I had seen a sign carrying her name – not a common one – by the roadside, and had turned on to the dirt-track, hoping to find there a member of a clan of butchers and cattle-dealers who had once dominated the meat business in Kimberley. It transpired that she was no relation of theirs, though she knew that a family with the same name as her late husband's used to live there.

My mistake did not make her any the less welcoming. She was in fact one of the few people I met on the journey whom I had not known before, or corresponded with, who recognized me immediately by name. 'Oh, the writer,' she said with neither surprise nor inquisitiveness when I introduced myself. 'Why don't you come in?'

Not only did she give us tea; she also gave us *taiglach*, a baked confection, at once sticky and crumbly, a speciality at Passover-time, which appears to be peculiar to South African Jewry. From her I learned that there were now four Jews in Vryburg, though that little town too had once supported a synagogue and community centre which I later inspected. (The Alfred Liebenthal Memorial Hall, it was called: quite a handsome beige box, steadfastly locked and unused, with pillars in front and a peach tree at the side.) She also told me that on one occasion when her husband had been alive they had made a great effort and had managed to get together no fewer than forty people, adults and children, from all around the district for the *seder*, the celebratory Passover meal. The guests had come from as far afield as Mafikeng in the north; and, yes, the Gers family of Danielskuil had come too.

While we were talking in this way, and the youngsters were playing in the courtyard outside, there was a knock on the door and two more people came in. They were both men. The one was her neighbour, a handsome, reserved, blue-eyed Afrikaner, upright in bearing and courteous in manner, who lived in a house about a half-mile nearer the main road. The other was his newly-arrived farm manager, who turned out to have been brought over specially from Denver, Colorado, to take up this position. Tea was poured for them and they were introduced to *taiglach*. '*Dis vir ons pasfees*' – it's for our Easter – our hostess explained in a quick aside to her neighbour. A kindly mutual respect between them was evident. I sensed too that he felt a degree of chivalrous protectiveness towards her. When he heard that I taught at a university in London he asked me if I knew anything about American university entrance requirements. Why? Because his son had just taken the SAT tests at the American consulate in Pretoria. With what in mind? A course in agricultural economics at Texas Agricultural and Mechanical University.

Later our hostess saw us to the door, and then came further to have a final chat with us on her drought-bitten lawn. I learned then that in addition to his farm up the road, her neighbour had a beef feeding station near Bloemhof, in the Transvaal, where he would fatten fifty thousand bullocks at a time. Fifty thousand! No wonder he could afford to bring an animal husbandry expert from Colorado to help him, let alone send his son to Texas.

Once we were back on the main road it was not long before Vryburg appeared in the distance: a scatter of tin roofs winking in the sun, a grain elevator or two, and a telecommunications mast, all on a dry, stony, tilted flank of land. Two girls were resolutely walking towards this distant and unenticing spectacle. I stopped and picked them up. One was silent; the other quite talkative, though her English was limited. She said that she went to school 'in Bophuthatswana'; that she was 'a citizen of Bophuthatswana'; and that at school she studied History, Geography, Maths ('too hard'), Civics, Religion, General Science, and Singing. There were thirty pupils in her class and they had to sit 'boy-girl-boy-girl-boy-girl' to keep them out of mischief. Her English reader was called *Old Mali and the Boy*; the history lessons were about 'our people and white people' in South Africa, Swaziland, Mozambique, and Zimbabwe. After a pause, and perhaps out of politeness, she added, 'In England, also.'

'But school is no good now,' she went on. 'We have no teacher. My teacher has a bad car accident on this road next week.'

Her bizarrely mistaken turns of phrase made the announcement more shocking, if anything, in the light of what we had heard from our hostess earlier. Again? Another?

'Not old – a young woman with two children. Now she is killed.'

It took many years for the members of the London Missionary Society to resign themselves to the fact that the route Moffat had helped to pioneer through Kuruman had been irrevocably superseded by the road and railway line due north from Kimberley. Even today, when rail traffic has in its turn been largely superseded by motor and air transport, the territory alongside the line remains much more thickly populated than any of the areas west of it.

It could hardly be otherwise. For decades crucial to the development of South Africa itself, of Bechuanaland (present-day Botswana), of the Rhodesias (Zimbabwe and Zambia), and of the southern reaches of the former Belgian Congo (Zaire), everything and everyone moving north and south between the Cape and the Congo depended on a single-track, narrow-gauge line stretching from the coast for a distance of some two and a half thousand miles – through Kimberley and Mafikeng, skirting the borders of the Transvaal, running the full length of Botswana, crossing the Limpopo, swinging north-west to bridge the great gorge of the Zambesi at the Victoria Falls, and then continuing northwards still, though never far enough to fulfil Rhodes's dream of reaching Cairo at last. It is strange and affecting to stand astride the railway anywhere along its length and to think of the transformation wrought on the huge continental mass by the two steel strands below. There they are, embedded in ballast and a miserly three feet six inches apart: vital once for generations of people of all races; used today for little but certain kinds of freight.

As with ideologies, technologies too are discarded, one after the other. Yet their traces and consequences can never be erased.

Not that the missionaries surrendered without a fight their hard-won wagon-road to the north. During the 1870s and 1880s money was collected in Britain and elsewhere to set up the Moffat Institution in Kuruman as a memorial to Robert and Mary. It was thought that the Institution would revive the mission and serve as a school and seminary for black pastors.* Once the Institution had been built it soon became apparent that the cause was a doomed one. Kuruman simply could not attract the pupils it needed. So after a mere twenty years the Institution's activities were transferred to new premises at Tiger Kloof, right on the railway line and some distance south of Vryburg. A large collection of stone buildings – a seminary, a trade school, an agricultural college, a church, teachers'

---

* In a speech to the Cape Colonial parliament at around this time, Rhodes graciously referred to black clergymen as 'a peculiar class of human beings – the Kafir parson'. It was a class, he said, which 'could easily be overdone'.

quarters and much else – was built there on a campus-like stretch of ground owned by the London Missionary Society.

The buildings and the campus are still in existence. I drove back from Vryburg to see them. All are in a ruinous condition. This has come about not because Tiger Kloof failed to attract sufficient numbers of pupils, but because in the 1960s the apartheid government declared it illegal for a black school (officially designated 'a black spot') to remain in what had been declared to be a white area. So the school and its grounds were expropriated and its inhabitants scattered.

It looks today like a place that has been fought over, occupied by two contending armies, and then abandoned by both. (Which in a sense is what has happened.) Each army has left written signs of its period of occupation. The Scottish and English churchmen scattered marble plaques bearing legends like *The London Missionary Society: To the Glory of God (For other foundation can no man lay than that which is laid which is Jesus Christ – 1 Corinthians 3:11)*, or *Here let the true faith, the fear of God, and brotherly love remain forever*. There are also inscriptions like *Masonry Department, Domestic Science, Technical School*, neatly incised in stone above the doorways to a series of long, stone-walled buildings. The Dutch Reformed churchmen who then took the site over, and intermittently used it as a kind of holiday camp for boys, before selling it to a local farmer, seem to have confined themselves to wooden name-boards with large gold Gothic lettering on a black background: *Tierkloof Jeug Oord, Huis Kobus Keuter, Bennie Venter Swembad ... Godsdiens, Rolprent, Liggaamlike Opvoeding** and so on. Evidently some religious compunction, and doubtless a guilty conscience, had prevented them from taking down the previous owners' piously engraved exhortations.

Between the buildings are empty spaces thinly covered by blue gravel chippings; a broken bench or two; gum trees and self-sown

---

* Youth Centre, Kobus Keuter Residence, Bennie Venter Swimming-Pool ... Religious Service, Film, Physical Education.

acacias; an overturned bathtub; the remains of a cactus rockery. The iron roofs of the buildings are mosaics of rust-coloured oblongs. Inside one building is a mound of disintegrating mattresses; inside another several dozen school desks are rammed together; in a third the same has been done to a collection of metal bedsteads; in a fourth cement tables stand in rows (a dining-room? a chemistry lab?). The doors hang open and broken glass accumulates on the floors. Only the stone walls are as strong and fresh-looking as ever. The biggest building on the site is the church, which is in a particularly poor state, a home for birds and wasps. The only brick building there, which must have served as the Institution's headquarters, boasts a gable and a separate clock-tower. Someone seemed to have made a dead-set at the clock faces, for they have been badly holed. Yet on one of them a pair of clock-hands still hang on grimly, pointing to 5.35.

A.m. or p.m.?

While I was wandering around, a woman came towards me across the open spaces. She seemed to emerge from the railway line and drift vaguely but unmistakably in my direction. Young and thick-bodied, she was dressed in a filthy blouse too small for her. It hung straight down from her large bosom, failing to reach the belt of her skirt. That too was filthy. It had once been brown in colour. On her back, not tied on by a shawl in the usual African manner, but simply clinging there as best he could, was an infant – quite large; about eighteen months old, I would say – in a singlet as dirty as anything his mother was wearing. His bum, legs, and feet were bare. On her feet were soiled bedroom slippers, edged with what had once been pink fluffy stuff. Her expression was vacant; her head was uncovered; in the white of her left eye was a blood-spot.

I greeted her and she responded, '*Middag baas*.' I asked if she knew about this place. '*Nee baas*.' Where did she live? '*Daar baas*.' She pointed to some hovels in the distance, well away from the school buildings and in the opposite direction from which she had come. '*Dan moet jy iets van die plek ken*,' I said – then you must know something about this place. '*Nee baas, ek weet niks*.' No, she knew nothing.

After a long silence she repeated the phrase, as if she had said it many times before; as if it was the one thing in the world of which she could be sure. She knew nothing. Nothing, she said again. *Niks. Weet niks.*

Only then, while we stood at this impasse, did I realize why her words were so slow and were emitted with such gurgling intensity from somewhere within her throat; why her expression was so empty, her eyes so ready to slide in different directions. Poor thing. And poor child too, who gazed at me around the buttress of his mother's shoulder in steady, silent alarm. I am not superstitious by temperament; but I could not help thinking of her as a kind of *genius loci*, the very spirit and guardian of the place: vacant, solitary, humiliated.

Clearly she had been drawn to my company though she had nothing to say and did not know what she wanted of me. She did not even ask for money, which, given her appearance, might have been expected. She continued to gaze at me, and I at her; then, silently, in the same drifting manner in which she had approached me, she retreated a few paces. Sitting down on a boulder in the shade of one of the gum trees, she lifted her skimpy blouse, brought the baby round with a swing of her shoulder and a scoop of her hand, and placed it on her breast.

They sat in silence together. She crossed her legs and one of her slippers fell to the ground. When I started to go back to the car the infant's eyes moved to watch me, and he desisted from sucking. His mother too was moved to incomprehensible expression.

'*Huis*,' she said. After a pause she repeated the word twice more, with that throttled intensity of hers. '*Huis. Huis.*'

House. House. House.

Did she mean that this was her house? Or that she had no house? Or was she merely announcing that she was going home? Or I? It was hard to believe that the word was just one that had come into her mind and out of her mouth with no meaning at all.

She said no more. She put the baby in her lap and sat there unmoving. I had just crossed the railway line on my way out when I was approached by an old man carrying an empty cloth bag in his hand. He seemed to have been busy with some task though I could not see what. With the air of a man doing his duty, yet anxious not to give offence, he told me that he was in charge of the place while his *baas* was in Pretoria. His *baas*, he said, did not want people on the property.

This *baas*, presumably, was the farmer who had bought the place from the Dutch Reformed Church. Now that the Group Areas Act and other apartheid laws had been revoked, I knew he was negotiating to sell it to the United Congregational Church of South Africa. The story had been told to me in Kuruman. The Congregationalists were the successors in law to the London Missionary Society; they planned to restore the site and put it once again to its original use. However, negotiations were at a standstill because the farmer was asking an exorbitant price. He was entitled to this, he said, because of the 'historical associations'. Naturally the claim enraged those who felt that both the site and its 'historical associations' were rightfully theirs anyway.

Well, I could hardly ask this old man about the present state of negotiations. Something about the cast of his features made me think of the woman I had met. So I asked him, with a backward nod of my head, if she was his daughter. Bringing a significant forefinger to his temple, he told me that she was. With resigned sadness he added a single word:

'*Bedondered*.'

Which could be translated as: Messed up.

CHAPTER ELEVEN

☆

*Stellaland – The Land of Goshen – The
City of Free Burghers – Mafikeng Besieged
and Memorialized – Palaces Galore*

During the second half of the nineteenth century, the struggle for
sovereignty in the areas I was now travelling through took the form
of a three-way tug-of-war. Briton, Boer, and Tswana pulled as hard
as they could against each other. Sometimes two of them would
unite briefly to pull against the third. Occasionally one would let
go, sending the other two tumbling.

For example: when in 1852 the British unexpectedly renounced
all claims to territory beyond the Orange River, and granted 'the
fullest right of the emigrant farmers ... to manage their own
affairs and govern themselves according to their own laws',* the
Boers promptly celebrated by attacking and destroying Kolobeng,
David Livingstone's mission station, where an important group of
Tswana had been living under his protection. The Boers made no
bones about their reasons for doing this: they wanted to teach the
Tswana a lesson and to make secure their control over the route to
the north. Similarly, when British policy went through yet another
of its spasms exactly twenty-five years later, and the Boer republic
in the Transvaal was (after all) briefly annexed and declared to be a
British colony, the Tlhaping branch of the Tswana felt relieved of
the pressure the Boers had put them under. So they seized the
opportunity to turn on the imperial forces. The result was a series
of sharp skirmishes in the territory between Taung and Kuruman,

* See page 92 above.

which ended, as might have been predicted, with the defeat of the natives.

Complicated enough. But the triangular conflict just described was not the only one played out in the area. The interests of the British colonists in the Cape and those of the imperial government in London seldom coincided. (Essentially, the Cape Colonial government was all in favour of expanding its influence in the north – as long as London would meet the costs. London was usually ready to oblige – as long as the colonists footed the bill.) The Tswana groups north and east of Kuruman fought among themselves and also came under attack from other marauding tribes. Inevitably some of them sought the help of white mercenaries. The only mercenaries (or 'freebooters') available were Boers. What happened next can be readily imagined. Once the fighting was over, they snatched all the land they could from the people they had ostensibly been fighting for.

It was at this stage that the Boer Republics of Stellaland and the Land of Goshen were proclaimed.* A delighted Transvaal republic, now self-governing again, announced its intention of annexing them both. The Germans were in the process of seizing Namibia, on the other side of the Kalahari Desert; the Portuguese to the east, in Mozambique, raised the stakes by ostentatiously befriending the Transvaal. After even more than the usual amounts of hesitation, buck-passing, and double-dealing, the British decided they had to step in yet again. All the territory immediately west of the Transvaal border was placed under British protection. The Tswana in what had been the Land of Goshen (the area around Mafikeng) drew some benefit from this move. They were so numerous, and the Goshenites so few, that the British had no choice but to 'reserve' most of the land for tribal use. The blacks who lived further south, in what had been the Republic of Stellaland (roughly the area around Vryburg), were less lucky. After solemn consideration the

---

* 'And thou shalt dwell in the land of Goshen, and thou shalt be near unto me, thou, and thy children, and thy children's children, and thy flocks and thy herds, and all thou hast. And there I will nourish thee' (Genesis 45:10–11).

territory's new rulers confirmed the rights of the white mercenaries to almost all the ground they had already seized and distributed among themselves.

So there Vryburg, the former capital of Stellaland, stands today, still clutching to itself the name it took as the city of 'free burghers'. Towards the end of its main street, after you have passed the usual row of chain stores, as well as the local Karate Club, you come on the bust of President Gerrit Jakobus van Niekerk. He is described on the plinth as 'the first and only president of the Republic of Stellaland'. The bust is sheltered by a whitish plastered segment of wall, hollow in shape and rough in texture, like a large fragment of eggshell embedded vertically in the ground. Affixed to it is an embossed bronze plaque, giving van Niekerk's dates (1819–1896) and a noncommittal word of explanation, in Afrikaans only: 'The Republic was proclaimed in 1882 but was incorporated in 1884 into what was then the Protectorate of Bechuanaland.'

The whole arrangement has been erected in front of the town hall. Above the entrance to the building is the coat of arms of the short-lived republic. Like any good coat of arms, it also has a story to tell. The black chieftain who had originally called in the help of Gerrit van Niekerk and his commando of six hundred Boers was one David Mosweu, the head of a tribe known as the Koranna. Their symbol, predictably enough, was the korhaan, a local variety of bustard. Mosweu had summoned the Boer mercenaries to his assistance because he was at war with the Tlhaping. The totem of the Tlhaping was the fish. One quarter of the republic's coat of arms therefore shows the Tlhaping fish skewered on a sabre all the way through, as if for a barbecue. Fair enough, one might say: they were the enemy whom van Niekerk's men defeated. However, the opposing quarter of the shield shows a korhaan, the bird of the Korannas, the supposed allies of the Boers, firmly entrapped and tethered by the feet.

Just to let everybody knew who was really to be the boss henceforth.

The remaining quarters of the shield are occupied by a solitary star and a set of scales. The star represents a comet seen by van Niekerk's commando when it was out on campaign – from which spectacle they derived the name they gave to their republic. (I am convinced they had the Lone Star State of Texas in mind as well.) As for the scales of justice – well, what with the prominence of the sabred fish and the tethered bird, it was probably felt that a bit of justice might come in handy too.

Something of the same sort can be sensed in the motto inscribed beneath the whole affair. *Gewapened en Regtvaardig*, it says. Armed and Righteous.

Armed first, then Righteous.

From the look of him, President Gerrit Jacobus van Niekerk is still grieving over the disappearance of his republic. The bust is the most lachrymose I have seen. Something bad – a virus, a chemical, perhaps a vengeful lump of bird-mess from a passing korhaan – has bitten into the metal. As a result a trail of greenish stuff runs in tear-like fashion from one of the president's eyes and down his cheek. The other eye has a sympathetic stye on its lower lid and will probably soon be weeping too. Further down the road is a bust of another local boy, Sir Arnold Theiler (1867–1936), described on his plaque as the discoverer of a vaccine against botulism, 'whereby productive cattle farming in South Africa was made possible'. Strangely enough, Theiler also has an ocular problem, though of a different kind. Just above his left eye is a large wart of red mud which could have been thrown there by an urchin or is perhaps the early stage of a wasps' nest. Fearing the latter, I forbore to investigate.

After inspecting the monuments, we went looking for the school hostel in which I had spent a night in Vryburg so many years ago, before playing a game of rugby against the local school. (We were beaten – an unusual experience for us – chiefly because the Vryburg team possessed a thick-thighed, moustached wing-threequarter, with the improbable name of Piet Mack, who burst through our lines again and again. I do not know which demoralized us more: his name, his thighs, or his moustache.) My recollection was that the hostel was on the slope of a hill; not only did I fail to find it,

more disturbingly still I failed to find anything remotely resembling
a hill.

So we drove on to Mafikeng: a distance of about a hundred
miles, with just one tiny *dorp*, Stella, between the two centres.
Almost all the land we passed through is owned by white ranchers
and maize-growers. The maize-fields stretched into the distance:
stalks dry and dwarfish, a dirty white in colour; leaves that broke
into pieces if you touched them; cobs the size of your thumb. The
only sound to be heard from the fields was a spectral crackling.
That was what the drought had done to them. It was a pitiful, even
a macabre, sight. Everything is relative, however. Somewhere south
of Mafikeng we came once more into 'Bophuthatswana'. No
crackling here. Only earth grazed and trodden to extinction: turned
into something other than itself, like the waste product from an
industrial process. Then, on the eastern side of the road, there
appeared the largest, poorest, dirtiest area of peri-urban habitation
since we had left Kimberley. Montshiwastadt, it was called, in
honour of the chieftain who had been defeated by the sturdy Boer
Goshenites. It could not be distinguished from the squatter-camp
attached to it. It went on for miles. There were some handkerchief-
sized houses with asbestos roofs; a few bare brick schools with iron
roofs; one-room shops barred like little forts. The rest was litter.
There was the litter people lived in; there was the litter they had
thrown away. You could hardly tell the one sort from the other,
except that there were hollows in some of the heaps, for the people
to come in and out of. A dead dog lay by the side of the road, its
mouth open in a jubilant grin. About a mile further on, in a more
advanced state of decomposition, a dead horse or mule lay in the
middle of the road.

Then we came to Mafikeng. By the time we arrived there it was
late afternoon. Everything was locked up in honour of Sunday: not
just locked but blockaded, encaged, fixed, rigid: like the Man in the
Iron Mask. Of the white owners of the stores nothing was to be
seen. Small groups of blacks squatted on street corners; others
walked in slow threes and fours down the middle of the road. In
the Tswana language Mafikeng means 'The Place of Stones'. It was

now also The Place of Plastic Cartons. The Place of Orange Peel. The Place of Fish and Chips Bags. The central area looked like a parody version of all that is most unbeautiful, unadorned, imaginatively penurious, about the standard South African *dorp*, where people buy, sell, and huddle apart from one another. And flat, flat, flat. The boredom of it! The vacuity! It made me feel as if South Africa's deepest secret was being laid bare before me. For all the old hatreds and new gadgets, the guns and constitutions, it is not the physical spaces of the veld that remain unfilled, but the hearts of the people. And their minds. And the place where some common notion of themselves should reside. Concrete porticoes stuck out over the pavements, names like tattoos on their foreheads, corrugated iron above, unswept gutters below, parked cars here and there. While the sun leaned down to have a closer, more contemptuous look at it all, its heat relenting not one whit.

But what ultimately made the place unendurable to me was that even in the finest vibration of red-yellow light, the faintest tang of dust and tar, the last fringe of dispirited leaf hanging from the gnarled branch of this or that karreeboom, in the very shapes and colours of the block capitals painted on the shop-fronts, I recognized everything I had been born into, had first opened my eyes to see; in scaled-down fashion it represented everything that had compelled me to get away, to go elsewhere, to find another country, as soon as I could.

To no avail, apparently. For here I was still, seeking it out, hankering after it, hugging it to me.

We kept going northwards along roads torn up for widening; through a residential area which could have been taken brick by brick from the Kimberley of fifty years ago; past a cemetery decorated with lugubrious stone angels around whom bluegum trees shed strips of bark, in lieu of flowers; through an industrial area about which I refuse to say anything at all – and then, hardly a mile further, scattered haphazardly across stretches of the kind of threadbare veld we had been seeing for so long, what did we come on?

Call it a mirage that did not disperse, as mirages are supposed to do, the closer we drew to it. It was a parade of newly completed or half-completed buildings in marble and slate, blue glass and tile, red glass and pale wood, face-brick and aluminium, concrete and anodized bronze, steel and plastic: all as big, all as modern and post-modern, as money and architectural ingenuity could make them. In front, elaborate railings, tentative gardens, cobbled yards; behind, large tarmac parking terrains. A Convention Centre, an Energy Centre, an Agri-Centre, a Broadcast Centre, a Tennis Centre, a Civic Centre, a Manpower Training Centre, a Cultural Centre, a Parliament, a Court of Justice, a shopping mall called Mega-City, a Presidential Palace, a University, an International School in raw-beef brick, a National Stadium tilted like a spaceship, a water tower like a memorial for the dead of all the wars ever fought. Then a luxury hotel disposed around a central courtyard, where piped music incessantly came out of holes in the lawn.

We had arrived in Mmbatho, the capital of 'Bophuthatswana'.

In Mafikeng M. left me and returned to Johannesburg. She had planned to go back by rail, but was discouraged from doing so by everyone she spoke to, not excluding the man who was supposed to be selling tickets in the booking-office at the railway station. A policeman patrolling the deserted platform was also unenthusiastic. 'Oh, you'll be safe on this side, in Bop; but near Johannesburg – ?' At which dread name he pursed his lips and shook his head.

Outside the station, in a littered crescent of what was supposed to be grass, stood a statue of Cecil Rhodes. Rising above it were two bedraggled palms and a broken street-lamp. A few loungers and a woman with a baby sat with their backs against its stone plinth. Rhodes himself was on foot and (inevitably) facing north. He looked plump but uncomfortable: almost rheumatic somehow. In need of a wash too, and of a word of consolation. In one hand he held his hat; the other gestured ahead. I wanted to greet him and tell him that I knew him well; that we had our memories of Kimberley in common. If I had guessed the condition in which I would find him in Bulawayo and Harare, further north, I might have tried harder to bring him comfort. Across the road were the Madeira Cash Stores, Portuguese-owned presumably, and the Rooigrond Butcher Shop, ornamented with a corrugated iron canopy and a Coca-Cola sign. (The Goshenites had initially called themselves the Rooigronders, after the farm Rooigrond – Red Ground – on which they had gathered to go to war. Later they had decided that something biblical would do better.) The Rhodes statue was much disfigured by pigeon-dung; indeed, a pigeon was standing on his head when we came out of the station. It too was solemnly facing north, as if trained to do so.

The following day M. flew to Johannesburg on Bop Air. I stayed on with some people I had barely known before. They could not have been kinder to me; but since my host then occupied a senior position in the Bop administration, and since so much of what I have said about Bop has been hostile, or at any rate derisive, and is going to continue to be so, I think it would be better if I did not write about him and his wife in any way which would make them identifiable.

Their house was in Mafikeng, which hung on grimly to Mmbatho, like an elderly relative afraid of being discarded, who had an incomparably poorer relative hanging on to him in turn (Montshiwastadt). To complicate matters further, there was a quasi-middle class suburb for blacks called Montshiwa, *tout court*, between Mafikeng and Mmbatho. Mafikeng may have looked rundown when I first saw it, but the house I was now living in was a large-roomed, luxury affair, immaculate inside and out, equipped with two full-time servants, a handsome garden, every conceivable domestic utility, a swimming-pool, and no fewer than six dogs, two of which were full-grown rottweilers. It was surrounded by high walls and there were fancy steel bars (all whorls and flower-like patterns) across every door and window. The other houses in the suburb were of the same kind: big, new, luxurious, set in gardens which you could only glimpse through the security fencing, defended by dogs which went into a chain-reaction of frenzied barking and fence-clawing whenever you walked down the block.

On my first evening, my host and I went out for a walk; we had gone hardly a block or two, amid a turbulence of our dogs and other peoples', when a uniformed man emerged from one of the houses to inspect us. A Kalashnikov rifle was slung over his shoulder. 'Hmm,' said my host to me. 'Someone new must have moved in.' He shouted at the silent, dusk-silhouetted figure opposite, 'Who you working for?' From a face without features came the sombre answer: 'De Min'ster o' T'ansport.'

My hosts lived in a ministerial or ambassadorial style; and so did I, briefly. There were two Mercedes in the garage and a third on call, together with uniformed driver, whenever they wanted it. The husband had a grand office in one of the palaces in Mmbatho, with an ante-chamber in front and a space for flunkeys to one side. Smartly uniformed soldiers saluted with much zeal whenever he entered or left the building. On one occasion a pair of soldiers actually escorted him and me from one building to another, and then formally passed us on to the next lot with more saluting. These splendours notwithstanding, he and his wife left for what they called 'the Republic' (i.e. South Africa 'proper') whenever they could get away: almost every weekend, so far as I could make out, with not infrequent long weekends and vacations thrown in as well. They seemed to have few friends locally, and of these none were black; not even among his fellow-officials in the Bop government. Their whole way of life was like a game, really; only more lonely than games generally are. The state in which he held his position was not a state; the honours it bestowed on him were not real honours, since they were recognized nowhere else; the sociabilities it was able to offer him he did not want. Even his salary was actually paid by the South African government; and, he told me, he had made damn sure that his pension rights were registered in South Africa, not Bop.

It was hollow, then; anchored in nothing. And no wonder, since the same was true of the so-called republic itself. The more grandiose the buildings, the more implausible they seemed, parked in the withered veld on the far side of Mafikeng. Of course I enjoyed (after a fashion) being shown around them by my host, plus stamping, shining-booted soldiers. Here was the Supreme Court, smelling still of fresh plaster, full of panelled chambers in which, amid much bowing and bobbing, black-gowned people were saying 'May it please the court' and 'As the court pleases' and 'Yes my lord'. (Uttered in a variety of accents, but always in English.) Here at the far end of a courtyard as big as a parade ground was a lofty parliament chamber in greenish leather and Taung marble. Across the way, look, an aluminium-columned, rubber-floortiled Convention Centre with seating for four thousand people. Here was the Cultural Centre where you could do any of the following: art, graphics, dressmaking, physical training, music, quilting, pottery, drama, traditional dancing, aerobics, ballet, and social welfare. And here was the Tennis Centre with something like twenty courts on which I did not see a single ball being struck during any of the time I was in Mmbatho. And here . . .

In the evenings my hosts followed their respective hi-tech hobbies; and watched videos, or the South African TV channels, or CNN, or BOP TV. The last of these specialized in footage of His Excellency Mr Lucas Mangope, President of the Republic of Bophuthatswana, opening something: a primary school, a police station, a conference.

Thinly disguised behind its two recently transposed vowels, Mafikeng is of course identical with the much better-known town of Mafeking. Under the latter name it was for a brief period as celebrated a spot as any in the British Empire. During the Anglo-Boer War it was besieged by the Boers for two hundred and twenty days. The Relief was the occasion for scenes of wild rejoicing in London and elsewhere, when orgies of drunken near-rioting went on from a Saturday (19 May 1900) to the following Thursday. It is difficult now to understand why the raising of the siege of a place so small and inconsequential, guarded by inconsiderable numbers of British and colonial troops, was greeted with such a degree of hysteria. But some reasons can be guessed at. A surprising number of English grandees and blue-bloods – a Cecil (the son of the then

British Prime Minister), a Cavendish-Bentinck, a Courtenay, a Sudeley, a Fitzclarence, a (female) Churchill – had contrived to get themselves locked up in the besieged town. This meant that many influential people at 'home' were especially interested in its fate. The siege had gone on for longer than the war's two other major sieges (Ladysmith and Kimberley). Above all, the commander of the town's garrison, Colonel R.S. Baden-Powell, the future founder of the Boy Scout movement, had an unparalleled flair for publicity. By way of the dispatches he managed to smuggle out of the town he had succeeded in making a hero and a national figure of himself.

Not surprisingly, photographs, memorials, and mementoes of the siege abound in and around the museum, which is housed in one of a smallish group of attractive Victorian and Edwardian public buildings still standing. Among the latter is a convent, now transformed into offices for lawyers and suchlike, and a hospital behind an ornamental wrought-iron gate with the following message thickly embossed in the middle of it: THIS GATE WAS PRESENTED BY THE INDIAN COMMUNITY OF MAFEKING IN COMMEMORATION OF THE CORONATION OF HIS MAJESTY KING EDWARD VII EMPEROR OF INDIA AUG 9TH 1902. Similar (but less sycophantic?) patriotic-imperial messages are also to be found on the monuments outside the museum. On one of them the names of the white soldiers of the garrison who died during the siege are engraved in marble; around the corner is a small, belated bronze tablet 'to the memory of the members of the Cape Boy Contingent, the Native Fingo Contingent, "the Black Watch", and the many hundreds of Coloured and Native non-combatants who died by shot, shell, and starvation'. None of the names of the 'Coloured and Native' soldiers and non-combatants are listed; but great care has been taken with the indispensable quotation marks around 'the Black Watch'.*

In fact, much the greatest number of deaths during the siege took

* The Black Watch is of course the name of a famous Scottish Highland regiment. In Mafikeng it was given by way of a joke to a scratch force of blacks armed, according to a historian of the siege, 'with obsolete rifles and elephant guns'.

place among the blacks: hardly surprisingly, since they outnumbered the whites, lived in more exposed positions, and were generally kept on thinner rations. It is also relatively little known that after Mafikeng had been relieved, the British set up one of their concentration camps for Boer women and children near the town. (These camps were established in order to deny the Boer guerillas shelter and food they might otherwise have got from their kinsfolk.) According to Thomas Pakenham's *The Boer War* (1979), the death-rate in the Mafikeng concentration camp eventually reached the figure of four hundred deaths per month. Today, well away from the British memorials, there stands a modest, highly polished granite arch with yet another kind of inscription on it. *Vir vryheid en vaderland*, the lettering declares: *in liefde gewy aan die nagedagtenis van die vrouens en kinders wat gedurende die Anglo-Boere Oorlog in die plaaslike konsentrasiekamp gesterf het* ('For freedom and fatherland: dedicated in love to the memory of the women and children who died in the local concentration camp during the Anglo-Boer War'). It is surmounted by the white marble figures of a Boer woman in traditional long garb and bonnet, with her hand on the head of a boy.

That the Anglo-Boer War was the result of the deliberately aggressive policy adopted by Britain towards the Boers of the Transvaal and Orange Free State is no longer disputed by historians, British or other. By the end of the nineteenth century, imperial and financial circles in London and Cape Town had decided that the time had come to settle the hash of the Boers once for all. The major prize on offer, needless to say, was control of the Rand goldfields. In fact, four years before the war broke out Rhodes had already tried, by way of the Jameson Raid, to launch his own takeover of the goldfields. Following his direct instructions, Dr Jameson and a few hundred irregular troopers rode into the Transvaal, where they were supposed to be greeted by an uprising of discontented Britons in Johannesburg. The uprising did not take place; Jameson and his men surrendered ignominiously after a few hours; Rhodes was disgraced (temporarily) and had to give up his premiership of the Cape Colony.

The war itself, which broke out in 1899, also turned out to be not at all the quick dust-up many British volunteers had assumed it would be. At first the Boers held the upper hand; then they frittered away their advantage in stupid and useless sieges of the Mafikeng type; then the British drove them back, broke their armies and occupied the two capital cities of Bloemfontein and Pretoria. That, as far as the British were concerned, should have been the end of it. In fact the struggle went on for another two years. By the time a peace treaty was signed, the Boers of the two republics had lost fifteen per cent or more of their entire population. (I know that this figure was mentioned in an earlier chapter. It bears repeating.) Twenty-five thousand British and imperial troops were dead, most of them by disease rather than enemy fire. Eight years later the independent, wholly self-governing Union of South Africa (consisting of the British colonies of Cape Province and Natal, and the former Boer republics of the Orange Free State and Transvaal) was summoned into existence.*

In effect a deal had been cut. Economically, the supremacy of the goldmining interests had been acknowledged. Politically, the Boers were given equal rights with the English-speaking element. Racially, the whites of both language groups were set free to do with the blacks whatever seemed to them fit.

The curator of the museum in Mafikeng was a small, balding, softly-spoken, light-eyed man in his late forties or early fifties, dressed in a blue sweater and grey flannels. He had the appearance of an enthusiastic monk in civvies: bald area at the back of his head included. There was something priestlike too in the softness of his voice, the gentleness of his gestures, the directness of his gaze, the lack of self-consciousness with which he launched on his story when I asked him how he had come by his job. He spoke like a man with a vocation – which he unquestionably was.

He had been born and had grown up in Llandrindod Wells in Wales, near the border with England. The town had once been a

---

* The country became the Republic of South Africa in 1961.

spa, as its name suggests; and not far from it was a Roman site, Castel Collen. So it was a place with an interesting history. He went to the local grammar school and among other subjects studied Latin, which he greatly enjoyed. ('In those days a boy was allowed to enjoy a subject like Latin.') As a result, and because a Roman site was nearby, he made something of a hobby of the Roman occupation of the area. One day he had the luck to find a blue glass bead worn as an insignia of rank by non-commissioned officers (or their equivalent) in the Roman legions. The local museum had a similar bead on display; but the one he had found was a much finer specimen. He was asked to give it to the museum; instead it became the first item of his own collection. ('I still have it.') He used to go on his own little digs ('dragging my poor father through the mud with me'). Soon he had established a 'museum' in his bedroom – a couple of shelves with various items which he had found and had thought worth preserving. ('Not all of them Roman, by any means. I was interested in anything old.') Neighbours and others heard of the collection and brought him things to identify, and date, and sometimes keep. He began to charge people a penny a time to see his collection. ('A lot of money it seemed to me, in those days. I was rather nervous about doing it, at first.') Eventually an item about his bedroom-museum appeared in the local paper. ('I've still got that cutting.')

Later he went to St Albans College of Art; he studied also in Leicester, before returning to St Albans to teach in the abbey school. Then he decided it was time for a change, and came out to South Africa. Landing in Cape Town without a job, he soon found work in Johannesburg, again as an art teacher, and did a stint too in Swaziland. After four years he went back to Britain; by that time he was married, having met someone who came 'from another part of Bophuthatswana'. They lived in England for some time before deciding to return to South Africa. He got a job as a teacher in Mmbatho and began to give a hand to the elderly curatrix who then ran the museum. When she retired he applied for her post – 'and here I am,' he said, with a gesture of understandable pride, which took in everything around him; not least the extensive redevelopment of the museum taking place under his supervision.

There were new glass cases on all sides and a traditional Tswana *kgotla* (or meeting-place) was under construction at the end of the central room. As with all other museums in the country, a new emphasis was being placed on the history of the local black communities – not, as they had been presented in earlier years, merely as a form of ethnography (at best) or of general freakishness (at worst); but as nearly as possible on equal terms with the history of the whites.*

Anyway, that was the curator's story, from the time of his finding a Roman soldier's bead to his guardianship of an 'old ship's gun' which stood among many other items in one of the rooms devoted to the history of the siege of Mafikeng. The gun, its placard told me,

was sold to Chief Sechele by German traders 1852/54 and ... later used by Bechuanas against Transvaal and Free State freebooters in 1884. Acquired by Mr Brownland and used as a garden ornament at his farm 'The Homestead' until well into the siege, when it was fitted up and proved one of the town's most effective pieces of artillery. The cannonballs used were manufactured in the railway workshops.

A hundred years after their defeat in the Anglo-Boer War the resurgent Boers had created an empire of their own. The Nationalist Afrikaners' plan had been to surround themselves with a host of manufactured satrapies like Bophuthatswana, which would keep them safe and which they would keep subservient. To help them achieve this end they would use money, advisers, technology, guns. Further afield, in Mozambique and Angola, they also put into the

---

* One room in the museum was being prepared to honour Sol Plaatje (1876–1932), for many years a resident of both Kimberley and Mafikeng. Newspaperman, founder of the African National Congress, translator of Shakespeare into Tswana, author of the first novel by a black South African to be written in English (*Mhudi*), Plaatje is probably best known today for the jaunty diary he kept during the siege of Mafikeng. Reading Brian Willans's account of his life (*Sol Plaatje: A Biography*, 1984) is both depressing and inspiriting: depressing because almost all his initiatives were met with patronage, indifference or contempt by the white authorities; inspiriting because he never allowed his personal and political ambitions to be entirely crushed by them.

field either their own armies or shadowy 'national movements' to achieve the same end. The blundering Marxist regimes that once ruled those two countries are no longer in power; but the wars between them and the South African surrogates plunged them both into a state of strife and famine hardly equalled elsewhere in Africa.

Back home, though, things had begun to run away with the Afrikaner Nationalists themselves. Softened by success and *embourgeoisement*, many of their own people ceased to believe in the exhausting historical mission they had assumed. The economy of the country could not stand the strain of their policies – 'homeland republics', foreign adventures, inflated bureaucracy, military expenditures, and all. The Afrikaners' birth-rate dropped sharply, as bourgeois birth-rates have a habit of doing. By contrast, the numbers of blacks within 'white South Africa' never ceased to grow; nor could they be prevented from acquiring skills they had not had before. The hostility of the world outside was unremitting. The whole vast enterprise had become impossible to sustain. Even the dreaded communists in Angola and elsewhere threw in the towel.

Mmbatho remains: a memorial to a particular moment in South African history. Luck also played a part in the form it took. The chunks of land bestowed on Bophuthatswana consisted of some of the most poverty-stricken of all the tribal reserves in South Africa – which is saying something. To the chagrin of the South African government, platinum was promptly found in some of those lands, after Bop had been given its 'independence'. So there followed a rush to Mmbatho by various international mining corporations, with South African, British, German, French, and Israeli construction companies close behind. Hence the extra-ordinary lavishness of Mmbatho's public buildings. At the time of my visit, my host told me, only twenty-five per cent of the exchequer was still being supplied directly by the South African government. The rest came from platinum and gambling.

The thought of the deals and the deals-within-deals that must have taken place in the process of constructing Mmbatho was enough to make one feel faint. So was the contrast between its palaces and the inhabited heaps of litter to be seen in the squatter-camps of Montshiwastadt.

Since my visit to it, Bop's existence as a supposedly independent republic has formally been brought to an end. The Republic of Bophuthatswana is now one with Nineveh and Tyre; or, if not with them, then at least one with the Republics of Stellaland and the Land of Goshen: a historical might-have-been, never-was, not-a-hope.

Mmbatho, now officially reunited with Mafikeng, has become the capital of the newly designated North-West Province of post-apartheid South Africa. Its purpose-built palaces have been taken over by the provincial administration. His Excellency President Lucas Mangope has apparently retired to console himself with the farms and other properties he acquired during his period in office. Among those properties, it is said, are two large houses in London.

Now it remains to be seen what his successors, under a different racial and political dispensation, will make of their inheritance – palaces, cabinet ministers' expensive homes and all.

Montshiwastadt is not going to go away either.

PART TWO

☆

Botswana

CHAPTER TWELVE

☆

*Botswana Past and Present – Crossing the
Frontier – Time Out in Palapye,
Mahalapye, and Serowe – Encounters with
Men (and One Woman) of Power*

Of the countries I visited in the course of this journey Botswana
was the one least known to me. I was born in South Africa and
grew up there; Zimbabwe I had visited twice before under its old
name of Southern Rhodesia and once under its new one; even
Zambia – to which my wife and I eventually made a courtesy visit,
by crossing the bridge at the Victoria Falls on foot and then getting
a lift to the town of Livingstone – I had spent time in before. But
Botswana? My sole acquaintance with it was the train journey
along its eastern rim mentioned in the introduction to this book.
Boredom, the laborious trundling past the window of bush thicker
than I had expected it to be, the crowded compartment I shared
with five other men – that was my experience of Botswana (or the
Bechuanaland Protectorate, as the territory was then called). The
most talkative of the men in the compartment was a small, gnarled,
parrot-nosed figure, Cape Town-bound, who had joined the train
in Bulawayo. He began by regaling us with stories of his just-
completed visit to his 'ranches' in Northern Rhodesia, and of the
hunting he had done there – 'No roads out there, I can tell you, we
had to be carried on litters by a crowd of blacks.' By the time we
got to Kimberley, about thirty-six hours later, he was reduced to
complaining that a recent increase in the taxi-fare from Cape Town
to Muizenberg had helped him not at all. 'When the fare was

fifteen shillings they'd give me a pound note and tell me to keep the change. Now it's seventeen shillings and sixpence, and they still give me a pound and tell me to keep the change!' So much for the fantasies of a more-than-imperial glory he had proffered us earlier: himself prone on a litter, blacks in attendance, nose reaching skyward.

Another feature of that journey I remember was that in places like Palapye and Mahalapye, where the train halted to take water, local entrepreneurs had set up small bars on the platform, to tempt the passengers who got out to stretch their legs. (Which we all did, of course.) In Palapye some enterprising soul had gone further still. He had cemented over a small area of the platform, put a canvas awning above it as a shelter from the sun, and hired three black musicians (sax, drums, guitar) to strike up as the train arrived and to play non-stop until it departed: the idea being to lure us on to the 'dance-floor', for a small fee. Since the rest of the platform consisted of so much trodden Kalahari sand, the only people who dared to dance without paying were the handful of barefoot urchins who turned up to share in the excitement.

I must have passed through Gaborone, but remember it not at all.

On just such a journey a few years later, a friend of mine was on a train that was delayed for a couple of hours in Mahalapye. Having exhausted the possibilities of the station platform, he wandered into the little tin-roofed town itself. Soon enough he found himself in yet another bar. It was mid-morning and the place was empty, apart from the barman and a sunburnt local in shorts and shirt. Both were white, inevitably, for in those days it was illegal to sell liquor to blacks. 'No,' the customer was saying to the bartender, as he drained his glass and put it emphatically down on the counter, with the drinker's air of having given the matter much thought, 'No, Mahalapye's never going to be another Joh'burg, you know. It's never really going to *boom*.'

He was a true prophet. Mahalapye has not boomed. That good fortune has arrived in some degree to Palapye, forty miles to the north, which now serves as a source of supply for a coal mine nearby and for the more distant diamond mines at Orapa and Selebe-Phikwe. Mahalapye, on the other hand, can boast today of being the home of a Marxist quarterly entitled *Clarion Call – Botswana's Socialist Journal for Labour and Youth*. I bought a copy of it during my visit there. On the cover is a picture in black and red of the globe, clasped between a pair of hands which have just broken the chains encircling their wrists; below them is the misspelt slogan: 'Workers of all countries unite, you have nothing to loose but your chains.' Inside are articles discussing (and denying) 'the failure of socialism' and complaining about 'the plethora of Marxisms: orthodox Marxism, structural Marxism (*à la* Althusser and Poyiantzans), neo-Marxism (*à la* Gunder Frank and other dependency theorists) ... the "post-Marxism" of Ernesto Laclau and Chantal Mouffe'.

As for Gaborone, then hardly more than a siding, it is now the country's capital, and in some ways, or looked at in a certain light, quite a handsome one, as towns in southern Africa go. It has a government quarter, the modesty of which is especially attractive after the extravagances of Mmbatho; two or three truncated shopping malls; a university; an excellent museum and art gallery; a couple of luxury hotels. To the south-west rough hills rise perhaps two hundred feet above the plain – almost as high as any in the country, I would guess – and seem to draw closer to the town at sunset.

When it gained independence, in 1966, Botswana was one of the poorest countries in black Africa; indeed one of the twenty poorest countries in the world. Today it is *per capita* one of the better-off on the continent. In 1966 the British government had no qualms in getting rid of its responsibilities for the territory. The Empire was finished; there was no resident white population of any consequence to make a nuisance of itself (as there was in Rhodesia); though serious exploration for minerals had been under way for some years, nothing much had been found and there were no investments to protect. Time to go. The Botswanans could be left to look after the few miles of tarred road and the many miles of veterinarian fencing the colonial administration was bequeathing to them, and to come to whatever terms they could with the Nationalist Afrikaners of South Africa, the English-speaking whites of Rhodesia (who by then had in effect become the Afrikaners' allies), and with the rivals or successors of both groups.

So off they went. Whereupon, rather after the fashion of what was to happen with the platinum found under the trodden-out lands of Bop, exploitable resources of diamonds, coal, nickel, soda-ash, and copper were soon discovered. The Botswana government did not hesitate to strike advantageous deals with the De Beers Company and others (no damn Marxist nonsense here, whatever the true believers in Mahalapye might have been hoping) – and Botswana, overall, and in its own modest fashion, proceeded to boom.

The ironies abound. The essential point of securing the road to the north, as far as Rhodes in the Cape and some of his allies in London were concerned, was to outmanoeuvre the Boers and to set up a white-inhabited, English-speaking country in the territory farther north, between the Limpopo and Zambesi Rivers. To Rhodes, Bechuanaland (Botswana) itself was of relatively little interest. It was what lay beyond it that really mattered to him. In speeches, letters and telegrams composed during and after the Stellaland and Goshen crises he hammered the point home:

If we get Mashonaland [the eastern province of present-day Zimbabwe] we shall get the balance of Africa.

The Boers resolved to shut up the interior, I to open it. We shall see who succeeds, they or I.

Part with the interior road and you are driven into the desert.

I do not agree with you as to your plan of a chartered company for this district. [Bechuanaland] is a poor country and no company could cope with the intrigues of the Transvaal. It must either remain under the Imperial Protectorate or else be annexed to the Cape Colony.

If you part with the road you part with everything.

What we want is to annex land, not natives.

Bechuanaland is the neck of the bottle and commands the route to the Zambesi. We must secure it unless we are prepared to see the whole of the North pass out of our hands.

[Bechuanaland] is suitable for cattle ranching but not for British settlement. *Its real value is as the link which may join our settlements to the richer districts beyond* [my italics].

And so on. Yet a mere seventy years after Rhodes's death what would he have found, could he have returned to the area? The descendants of the Boers predominant in South Africa and the whites of Rhodesia wholly dependent on them for whatever hope they still had of surviving as the country's ruling group. And ninety years after? White-ruled Rhodesia gone for ever and the country's legendary mineral wealth revealed to be worth relatively little, while despised Botswana is more and more recognized as a treasure-house of minerals – of diamonds, Rhodes's diamonds, above all, just to rub the irony in.

Not that the present-day De Beers Corporation is complaining. In any case, no matter how slightingly Rhodes may have spoken of Bechuanaland, he certainly wished to prise it from the grip of the imperial authorities in London and from the missionaries on the spot, and to put it under his own wing. Prising the land from the Tswana themselves he never thought of as a serious problem.

He scored some notable successes and suffered some defeats in this campaign – or sideshow. ('It is humiliating,' Rhodes said to one of his cronies, after three Tswana chiefs had successfully appealed to London against the cession of their territory to his British South Africa Company, 'it is humiliating to be beaten by these niggers. They think more of one native, at home, than of the whole of South Africa.') Then his plans for the territory were irreparably damaged by the fiasco of the Jameson Raid. The borders of Bechuanaland were defined by proclamation to include all the regions 'not within the jurisdiction of any civilized power' which lay north of Mafikeng, west of the Transvaal, and south of the Zambesi. The bland qualification about 'any civilized power' was made in order to avoid encroaching on the neighbouring German and Portuguese holdings, and on those which Rhodes had already staked out for himself further north. Bechuanaland's status as a Protectorate was confirmed: within it the interests of the indigenous inhabitants were to remain 'paramount'.

A strip of territory was made over to the British South Africa Company (the Charter Company), to enable it to build its railway to the north. Another area, the Tuli block, was given to the Company for distribution to white ranchers. Their descendants and successors own much of it still. As for Mafikeng and the regions south of it (Stellaland, Goshen, etc.) – they had already, at Rhodes's urging, been successfully incorporated into the Cape Colony.

Which explains why you have to go through border posts about ten miles north of Mafikeng, where you leave South African territory and enter Botswana. The people on both sides of the border are Tswana-speaking; in fact they belong to the same tribal grouping among the Tswana – the Rolong. As far as the border is concerned that makes not a damn of difference. A border is a border. How can you know it to be a border unless there are huts, gates, flags, and soldiers here, and more of the same over there, with a strip of no-man's land between? What is the good of it unless you have to fill in several forms and show them to a plethora of officials, all armed with rubber stamps for stamping with and bottles of Coke for drinking from? (Above those on the Botswana side hung a sign: *Tough Guys Wear Condoms*.) Essential also is that you should queue up in the heat to go through these procedures; and that you should not expect any continuity of transport between the two sides. Can you arrange to hire a car on the other side of the border? No. Get a taxi? No. Catch a bus? No. This is a serious border. Only if you take the train, or come in your own car, or travel with a taxi-driver whom you know to have posted a bond for his vehicle on the other side, can you continue your journey directly.

Fortunately I had been warned of all this by my hosts in

Mafikeng, so I kept the car I had hired in Kimberley (and paid through the nose for the privilege of taking it across). Even then my troubles were not ended. Half-an-hour after entering Botswana I came to a road-block. First a warning (with soldiers in attendance) that a road-block was ahead; then a large Stop sign; then about fifteen yards further down the road a barrier and more armed soldiers checking cars before allowing them to proceed. There was a small queue of cars ahead, but not more than five or six minutes passed before I arrived at the Stop sign. There I waited until the car in front of me was cleared before beginning to move slowly forward. At the barrier I halted again. A head was stuck into the open window of the car. The muzzle of the rifle in the man's hand was prominent alongside – upright, not pointing at me. His greeting was as follows: 'You don't read? You don't know what "Stop" means? You want me to shoot you dead?' 'No,' I answered. 'Then why do you not stop?' 'I did stop.' 'No, you don't do it. You must do what I tell you. Stop means *Stop*! It means you stop there until I go like this –' and with a finger extended two or three inches from my face he made a beckoning gesture. 'Then you come to me. Otherwise I shoot you dead.' 'Oh.' 'Now you understand?' 'Yes.' Satisfied with this performance, he stared about the interior of the car, glared at me again until he tired of doing it, and waved me on.

I have no recollection of his face; only of its expression, engrossed not so much by anger as in the pleasure of expressing anger. Still, I preferred him to the police lieutenant I was to encounter later in Serowe, the capital town of the Ngwato branch of the Tswana. He uttered no direct threats and kept his revolver in its holster throughout. But he possessed a more developed style of being unpleasant.

I had turned off the main road through Serowe in order to see the *kgotla*, the traditional meeting-place of the tribe. A sign with an arrow on the roadside had invited me to do so. On this journey I was accompanied by a driver, Njo, whom I had hired both because I was tired of driving and because I was sleeping so poorly it seemed wiser not to spend long periods behind the wheel. The *kgotla* turned out to be a flat, trodden, circular piece of earth, about thirty yards wide, almost entirely surrounded by a heavy fence of ancient-looking, rough-cut tree-trunks driven perpendicularly into the ground. Below it was a cattle kraal of much the same size and shape, also surrounded by palings. As I arrived, a cloud of dust hiding an indeterminate number of oxen was being driven into the kraal by a solitary herder.

No one else was visible. Nearby were a few buildings – a modern council chamber, a low, whitewashed police station facing the *kgotla*, its back to the road, and other offices. Above them rose a group of trees and a ruddy, rock-littered hillside. This hill I knew to be the burial site of the heroes of the Ngwato: most notable among them Khama III, dubbed 'Khama the Good' and 'Khama the Great' by the members of the London Missionary Society, in recognition of the alacrity and puritanical severity with which he had accepted Christianity (in 1860) and imposed it on his people. Tshekedi and Seretse Khama, his son and grandson respectively, are also buried there. All three of them had done their best to manage the difficult trick of opposing the wishes of their British overlords while also working with them. Khama III had been the leader of the delegation whose success in London Rhodes had found so 'humiliating'; his grandson Seretse had become the first president of the Republic of Botswana. Indeed, on the day I visited the *kgotla* a statue of Seretse, wrapped all over in bright blue plastic, as if in a kind of body-bag, stood upright on the hillside. Presumably it was awaiting a ceremonial unwrapping.

Well, I inspected the municipal-style council chamber, which was empty but for large photographs of Khamas and other worthies staring at each other. As it happened I was carrying a camera that day, something I rarely did; I had not used it, but it was in my hand when I came out of the building. It was then that I encountered the policeman. He too was on foot, having apparently come from the direction of the cattle kraal. Tall, slender, smooth-skinned, dressed in a dapper pale-blue uniform, he had a high forehead, an unusually high bridge to his nose, and long, forward-sloping planes to his cheekbones. He carried his head in a manner which was literally self-regarding: his gaze travelled admiringly down his own cheekbones before it reached the world beyond.

He took offence at my camera rather than the fact that I had gone into the building without asking his permission. He gestured to me to go with him to the police station; once there he demanded that I produce my passport (which I was able to do); that I produce a permit for my camera from customs (which I did not have because no such permit had been given to me); and that I produce my 'certificate for photographing' from 'the Travel Authority' (which I did not have because no such body exists in Botswana).

My passport was stared at, turned over at length, put down on a table, picked up again. Then followed a variety of questions and insulting repetitions of my answers. They were delivered in tones that made the little office echo. What is your name? Jacobson? (Check in passport.) Where are you from? From London? (Check in passport.) When did you come here? (Check in passport.) What are you doing in Botswana? Just visiting? You come from London for visiting? Who are you visiting in Botswana? Nobody? How can you visit nobody? What are you looking for in Serowe? What museum? Who tells you about such a thing? Where do you go now? Palapye? What do you want in Palapye? Why?

Interspersed with this were repetitions of another kind: 'You can't go where you like . . . For cameras you must have permission from the Travel Authority . . . We have a law in Botswana . . . There is no such place in Serowe as this museum you talk about . . . The Travel Authority . . .'

I stood in the doorway of his one-roomed police station, in the sunlight, unwilling to go further into it. He too stood throughout, in front of his desk, a pace or two away. Below and just behind me, on the step of the little cement stoep to the building, sat a couple of women, their heads turned, looking on; inside, a junior policeman sat behind a desk and typewriter – he too looking on, learning his trade. The officer was proudly conscious of the figure he was cutting; I was humiliated by his questions, by the presence of the onlookers, by his idiotically repeated invocation of that non-existent Travel Authority. And alarmed too, of course; all too well aware of my isolation here in Serowe, everywhere in Botswana. Especially as his questions came home with a self-echoing force of a kind he could hardly have imagined. What was I looking for in Botswana, indeed? Who in his right mind would ever choose to come 'touring' in shabby, dusty, messy, thorny, rocky, straggly Serowe, creeping among its mingy hills, at the end of so many utterly flat, empty miles?

And all that apart from the other questions that inevitably rose in my mind. How long would he keep me? How far would he go?

Looking back, I think that last question puzzled him too. His repetitions of what I said were not intended to be merely insulting and incredulous (which they were); they also gave him time to think. Perhaps to think of the trouble he might get himself into if he pushed his luck, if he tried too hard, if he went too far.

Quite unexpectedly, with no change in expression, in a sudden silence, he held out my passport. I took it and made my way back to the car, which was behind the building. Whether the policeman had spotted Njo at the wheel of the car I do not know; what was certain was that Njo had seen the policeman summon me, and, in the unpeopled silence of the place, had heard the cross-examination I had been put through. He could have understood little of it, for his English was painfully limited. But the tone and volume of the policeman's voice had been unmistakable. It had put the fear of God into him. He could not wait to get out of the place. I had found the incident scarey, if grotesque; but it was an eye-opener to see how it had terrified Njo. I had positively to compel him to drive around from the one hill to the next, so that I could look my full at whatever else was on offer in Serowe: its assemblage of rundown shops, some of them looking this way, some that, in what I suppose was the middle of town; the unpaved, gulley-riven spaces across which the car lurched and wallowed from the shops towards an enormous Congregational church, complete with spire, on top of a hill which almost matched in height the one above the *kgotla*; a telecommunications mast rising out of rocks and thorn trees; many huts and bungalow-type houses; some sprawling public building; the Serowe Coffin Co-operative. The museum I had been in search of, about whose existence the policeman had been so scornful, I could not find. Yet I knew it to be there. I must have missed it. Perhaps Njo, whom I tried to use as an interpreter with some uncomprehending passers-by, did not know what a museum was. (A building with old things to look at: that was one version I suggested.) Perhaps he deliberately did not tell his interlocutors what I was looking for.

About an hour and a half later, anyway, we were back in the Cumberland Hotel, Palapye. The lounge was crowded with two distinct groups of men. One consisted of white ranchers – skins of leather; shirts and shorts of cotton – who were discussing the cheapest way of buying a BMW. The consensus was that it was best to fly to Schiphol Airport, Amsterdam, and pick it up there. (This with reference to an exhibition of the latest BMW models currently on display at the Gaborone Sheraton, which I had seen the day before; each vehicle standing safely behind red ropes, as remote and cosseted as a visiting film star.) The other group was made up of deputy head-teachers from all over Botswana who were holding a conference in one of the hotel's public rooms, and for whom a festive table was already being prepared in the dining-room. They were all men; even plumper, if anything, than the ranchers, and more genial in manner; smartly dressed in suits, ties, white shirts.

Then there was me, and Njo, and a solitary white traveller in the stiffest and most implausibly golden wig I have ever seen.

My last brush with authority in Botswana came when I was just about to leave the country. I had already been through customs and passport control, and had collected the necessary two pieces of paper to show the man at the final gate. Unfortunately when I reached him I passed only one of the papers to him; the other had fallen without my noticing it from the passenger's seat on to the floor of the car. I am sure that if I had handed both to him I would have been gone in a second; as it was, he had to ask for the other paper; I had to look for it on the floor; he had been given his opportunity. He was an undersized nobody, the lowest in the official hierarchy, without cap or even boots to boast of. But he and I had met, so to speak; I had been found wanting, momentarily; he had the power to open or not to open the gate for me.

So: what had I been doing in Botswana? for how long? how many bags did I have? where were they? how much currency did I have? And more. He made me open my case and zip-up bag and the boot of the car, all of which he peered into and from which he selected items to prod; he made me present my modest (to me) wallet of travellers' cheques, which he unzipped, looked into, and turned over and over again in his hands. I could see how painful it was for him to have so much money in his hands and to own none of it; more painful still was that he did not have the nerve simply to pocket it. The cheques represented (to him) an unimaginable sum; but *how* they represented it, what you did with them in order to translate them into the kind of money he was familiar with – these were mysteries too daunting, in the end, for him to meddle with. A ten-pula note, I was pretty sure, would have satisfied him; but I was determined not to give it to him. In the end he had nothing else to ask of me. No other corner of the car was left for him to poke his fingers into. As with my passport in a different place, the cheques were returned to me wordlessly. This time, though, it was done with a perceptible tremble of his hand and a prolonged gaze, directly into my eyes, of grief and hatred.*

Finally, while on the subject of my dealings with officialdom, let me mention a meeting with an accredited diplomatic representative of Her Britannic Majesty in Gaborone. I had written to him from London at the suggestion of a former student, who had thought he might be of some assistance. In spite of the perfunctoriness and belatedness of the reply I received, I went to see him soon after my arrival. What I found was a plump-handed, neatly combed,

---

* Someone who knows Botswana, and to whom I later mentioned these misadventures, suggested that the South African number-plate on my car may have had a provocative effect on the officials involved. I do not know whether there is anything in this suggestion; but pass it on nevertheless.

clean-shaven man of early middle age, dressed in striped shirt and
tie, whose suit-jacket was suspended from a hanger behind his door
and whose shiny cuff-links were prominently on display. His chair
was filled by his backside: his desk was empty. The sunlight came
in through slatted plastic blinds and fell on a handful of official-
looking volumes in the bookshelf behind him. It took me fully three
minutes to gather that he was ignorant of and blankly indifferent to
the history of Botswana, and determined to remain so. It followed
that my errand there roused no curiosity whatever in him. The only
expression I could discern in his round blue eyes was one of alarm,
even panic, at the thought that I might ask something of him which
would compel him to exert himself on my behalf.

After another two or three minutes I got up to go. Making what
he plainly regarded as a gesture well beyond the call of duty, he
summoned a skinny, floral-frocked secretary to guide me to a
government office nearby, which I had said I would be visiting.
There I met his Botswanan equivalent: also round-eyed and round-
cheeked, as it happened; but of the female sex. Her desk was also
strikingly empty. She made haste to pass me on to her assistant, a
tall, bearded, upright expatriate. From him I did at last get some
assistance. He knew what was available in the department and
might be relevant to my purposes, enjoyed showing me around,
answered my questions with alacrity, and was clearly the one who
actually did whatever serious work was being done there.

Such an arrangement – between idle boss and hardworking
assistant – is to be found all over the world and in every kind of
institution. One unexpected thing about this instance of it, however,
was that the enthusiastic yet somewhat melancholy expatriate who
helped me in Gaborone was not a displaced European, as most
readers may have assumed, but a Tanzanian.

CHAPTER THIRTEEN

☆

*Roads Northward – Rivers of Sand –
Botswana and Its Big Brother – Neville the
Trader – Styles of Shopping Here, There
and Elsewhere*

The original road to the north led from Kuruman through such places as Kanye, Molepolole, and Shoshong. It could not have done otherwise. The sites of the major Tswana settlements had been chosen for a good reason: they ran along a line offering relatively secure sources of water. Because they were tucked among such hills as were available, they also provided a measure of defence against attacks from the east. To this day the overwhelming majority of Botswana's tiny population lives on that same narrow strip of territory. At Shoshong the old road divided: one arm went north-west across the desert in the direction of Lake Ngami and the Okavango swamps, the other north-east towards the areas where the borders of Botswana, Zimbabwe, and South Africa now meet.

The second major route through the territory came into existence after the British occupation and the setting-up of the Protectorate. In this case it was the arrival of the railway line, and the direction it took towards Rhodesia (Zimbabwe), that proved decisive. As had happened further south, the railway, together with the road alongside it, rapidly superseded the older route. Circumstances here were different, though, from what they had been in the Cape Colony. There the original road and its replacement ran parallel at a distance of about a hundred miles apart. In the Protectorate the exigencies of geography and politics demanded that they be much

closer to each other. Go east and you were in the Boer domain of
the Transvaal: something, in the eyes of the developers of the
railway, to be avoided at all costs. Go further west and there was
no water to be had; certainly no permanent water. As a result the
older and newer roadways were never at a distance of more than
about twenty or thirty miles from one another.

The older route was rapidly marginalized, nevertheless.
Nowadays it can hardly be said to exist, as I discovered when I set
out on it from Molepolole southwards towards a place called
Masopa, and found myself on a dirt road which was quite populous
by Botswana standards, but vilely corrugated and potholed. I had
gone to Masopa in search of a woman who worked for my brother
and his wife for many years, first in Kimberley and then in
Johannesburg, and who had later taken over the task of nursing my
father in his last enfeebled years. She then retired on a pension to
her home in Botswana. To my regret, I did not succeed in seeing
her.

Subsequently when I visited places along the old route I did it by
travelling up or down the modern main south–north road,
Botswana's one major axis, and then striking west, as everybody
else did.

There must be literally hundreds of references to the presence or
absence of water in the diaries and memoirs of nineteenth-century
travellers through the territory. This was true even of those who
travelled along the old, intermittently inhabited route, let alone of
those who struck out across the desert. Here, chosen not for their
specialness or literary merit but precisely for their humdrum typical-
ity, are some observations from *The Recollections of an Elephant
Hunter 1864–1875* by William Finaughty (1916), describing a
journey along the main route to the north.

We stopped at Kuruman about a fortnight and then started on a long, dreary
journey, skirting the Kalahari desert and passing through the Bechuana
villages ... Before us was a stretch of 140 miles, with very doubtful water,
but we were very lucky and got water about 20 miles from Shechillies. The

roads were very heavy with sand and quite 18 inches deep. We were very lucky again in getting a little muddy water at a place called Beatlanamie . . .

We started again and hearing that the Pan Selinya, about 20 miles ahead, had plenty of water, we got there all right, only to be confronted with another stretch of over 40 miles, with no water and a very heavy road. We arrived at Shoshong, a very large Bechuana village of about 80,000 inhabitants . . .

Even today, after decades of borehole-drilling first by the British and then by the Botswanan authorities, travellers who venture across the desert are warned severely about the kind of vehicles they should use and the supplies of water they should take with them. In such a country it is hardly to be wondered at that the formal, loyal greeting to a chieftan has immemorially been 'Pula! Pula!' – which means, simply, 'Rain! Rain!'. (The same word has since been adapted to serve as the name of the currency.) In fact, the precipitation along the eastern edge of Botswana is not that much less than it is further south; but the Kalahari sand, which covers so much of the terrain, swallows with great rapidity whatever rain does fall, and the summer temperatures are higher. In the months immediately before my visit the daytime temperature had stood at or above 40° C for many weeks and had barely sunk below it at night.

Hence (among many other triumphs of desiccation) the river-beds you find in Botswana. Step from the powdery soil of the bank into the river itself and you sink more than ankle-deep into thick, coarse, yellow sand, which pours over your trouser-ends and into your shoes, as if it really were water. Wading across one such river, near Mahalapye, I was assured by the person accompanying me that in the last two months it had twice had water in it. 'Then it's gone. But sometimes the water will run for as much as a week at a time.'

Not a sign of moisture was now to be seen. Starting directly out of the sand in mid-'stream' were several substantial trees, competing in size with those that lined the river-banks – which suggested that under the thirsty sand, if only one could get there, water was still to be found. That night, as it happened, there was a thunderstorm: a bright, boisterous, rapidly moving affair which lasted for a few minutes only and left behind the smell of hot, suddenly drenched earth and elaborate drippings and garglings in every corner. But the river-bed showed no sign of anything having happened to it when I went to inspect it the next day.

All this, mind you, in a country which until very recently had no indigenous source of wealth other than the raising of cattle; no substance to export other than beef.* So let the reader not be under a misunderstanding. Botswana may now be counted among the better-off countries of black Africa, *per capita*, and a small number of its inhabitants may have amassed real wealth in recent years. (Mostly by holding key posts in government; or by taking appointments in local branches of the mining corporations and other multinationals; or by doing first the one and then the other.) But it remains a poor, poor place; one in which everything is being built up virtually from scratch. As late as the 1940s, for example, twenty years before independence, there was no suitable institution at which the adolescent Seretse Khama, chief-to-be of the Ngwato and future president of Botswana, could receive his secondary schooling. For that purpose he had to be sent away to South Africa – to Tiger Kloof, in fact.

Generations of less notable Tswana went in much the same direction for other reasons. 'Protected' or not, 'paramount' or not, they were driven by drought, hunger, and taxes to seek employment in South Africa's cities. As much as any of the 'tribal reserves' or 'homelands' in South Africa itself, the country's economic role was essentially that of a provider of cheap black labour for South Africa's mines, industries, and middle-class white households. (The woman who looked after my brother's family and my father in his last years being very much a case in point.) The first road across the north of Botswana, from Francistown to the Okavango swamps,

---

* Strangely enough, in drought-stricken Botswana I met quite by chance no fewer than two *duck farmers*, of all things: one living to the south of Gaborone; the other outside Maun. Both were ex-South Africans; the one was an elderly man, the other a young woman; both were of exceptionally cheerful disposition; both said quite spontaneously 'I love it here!' about their country of adoption.

was scraped out of the sand in the 1920s expressly to bring black labourers from the north-west region of the country, and from still further afield in Angola, to the railway line at Francistown – from where they were despatched by train to the gold mines of the Witwatersrand.

The people who developed that road were putting into effect, in different political circumstances from any he had envisaged, Rhodes's own determination to keep access to the north open. He could say what he liked about wishing to 'annex land, not natives'; but it was not only for the sake of empire, territory, glory, undiscovered riches beyond, that he valued the northern route so greatly. It was also because it brought down the cheapest, humblest, most despised and indispensable of all the items needed by his enterprises: the labourers who from the earliest years of the diamond field had begun streaming south to Kimberley, and who were soon to be diverted to mines bigger and more profitable than those.

Botswana, in short, has always lived in the pocket of its giant neighbour. A striking symbol of the nature of the relationship between the two countries was provided by the British government itself. The Resident Commissioner, the highest official in the colonial administration of the Protectorate, actually ruled it from his offices in Mafikeng – which from 1910 onwards was inside sovereign South African territory. Just as the South African labour market governed its economic life, so too did South African traditions of racial segregation govern the Protectorate's social life. When Tshekedi Khama, Regent of the Ngwato, dared to order the flogging (in 1933) of a young white reprobate named Phinehas McIntosh, who had been repeatedly found guilty of drunkenness, brawling, and impregnating the girls of Serowe, the British government responded to this act of *lèse majesté* by summoning a squadron of marines and several pieces of field artillery from a naval base near Cape Town, sending them a thousand miles north, and, after a summary trial, expelling Tshekedi from the lands of the Ngwato. In the hectic words of the Resident Commissioner it was impossible to exaggerate the effect in the Protectorate and in South Africa generally of the public flogging of a European by natives in a native court . . . The effect on public opinion in South Africa – of all parts of the world – of an action of this kind is too serious to contemplate . . .

Similarly, in 1948, when Seretse Khama, Tshekedi's nephew, returned from London with a white wife, the Colonial Office in London declared him 'unfit to become chief of the Ngwato'. The reason given was that 'a friendly and co-operative South Africa and Southern Rhodesia is [*sic*] essential to the wellbeing of the tribe and indeed the whole of the Bechuanaland Protectorate'. Later the official White Paper on the case stated that His Majesty's Government were

fully aware of the very strong feelings aroused on the subject of the merits or demerits of mixed marriages, but that is not the issue which is here raised . . . [N]o representations on this matter have been received from the Government of the Union of South Africa or Southern Rhodesia

– all of which was a lie. The issue raised was that of the propriety of mixed marriages, as the use of the word 'unfit' about Seretse clearly suggests; so far from 'no representations having been received', the British government had been officially informed that the South African Prime Minister was 'desperately worried' by the affair, and that his Rhodesian counterpart considered the marriage to be 'disastrous'.

After independence, considerations of *realpolitik* weighed as heavily on the government of Botswana as they ever had on the imperial authorities. It would have been suicidal for Botswana to have tried to impose economic sanctions against the apartheid government in South Africa. The same applied to granting permission for anti-South African guerilla bases to be established in the country. So the government of Botswana gave the usual amounts of mouth-honour to the necessity of 'an unremitting struggle against the forces of apartheid' – and did its best to keep well out of it.

Neville, a white South African, spoke as directly to me about the present state of relations between South Africa and Botswana as anyone I met. He described himself simply as 'a trader', without, so far as I could see, knowing that in this part of the world the word had once had a particular connotation: it had referred to those who brought goods in wagons up from the Cape to barter directly with the Tswana. He had been a trader for the last ten years, he said; he'd been trying his luck since leaving high school. He'd had just one year at university and then dropped out. 'I had no money. I couldn't afford to hang about. I had to get going.' What did he trade in? 'Anything I can make a profit out of. Anything legal, that is.'

He had intense grey eyes and cropped fair hair that started from low on his forehead and bristled up in all directions, with no sign of a parting anywhere. Neat and clean in appearance nevertheless, his shirt, tie, and lightweight suit were immaculate and his skin was surprisingly soft and pale for someone who spent as much time on the road as he did. He was amazed at the progress Botswana had made over the past few years. For this he believed the campaign of international economic sanctions against South Africa deserved much of the credit. 'Sanctions couldn't have suited Botswana better. Any South African firm that wanted to operate in Africa, all it had to do was to open a little company here or an office or a packing-plant or something – and bingo! they were a *bona fide* Botswanan outfit. No questions, no problems. You could flog your stuff in Nigeria, Kenya, anywhere you liked. Of course the Botswana government knew all about it, but they weren't going to interfere. They must be mad?

'Things have been so bad in South Africa I don't know what I would have done if I hadn't been able to do business here. I mean, there's money here nowadays, real money. In Botswana of all places! It isn't just diamonds and stuff like that. Plenty of South African manufacturers are here. And there's been a flow of capital from the US, Germany, Holland, Taiwan . . . Some of the money they didn't dare to send to South Africa has come here. I bet Botswana is secretly weeping and wailing now that apartheid's over and sanctions are finished. The Indians have also been investing. Would you believe that India exports capital? Well, it does. And the Botswana army has Indian military advisers.

'I find the people here very friendly. It's different at home. Getting back is a real downer, as far as that's concerned. You feel it all the time. Look at my home in Randburg [near Johannesburg] – bars, alarms, floodlights, Dobermann pinschers – the bloody lot. Especially with me out on the road half the time and my wife on her own with the kids . . .

'I started with perfumeries and powders – cosmetics, you know – made up for me by the wholesalers in Joh'burg. But there just wasn't enough in it. So now I'm into chemicals, industrial and household chemicals. What I do is, I look for a niche, establish the product, package it, and go out and sell it. I *like* selling. I'm in partnership with one of the biggest private companies in South Africa [giving me his card to prove it] – they provide the capital, I must do the business. But I'm still independent, it's still my show. Like I've just established a Botswana agency to handle these products. I've done it off my own bat. I didn't have to ask anybody's permission. Yesterday I was interviewing applicants for jobs as salesmen. I'm just going to see a few more people and then I'm off, back home. Three-and-a-half hours, that's all it takes, sometimes even less. It depends on how much hassle they give you at the border. Those guys! But sometimes you're through like magic. I gave one of them a lift into Gaborone once; next time I went through, he was on duty. So – magic!

'We're *praying* for investment back home, things have been so bad for so long. In the end that whole apartheid business really screwed us. The thing that people abroad never realized is that there've always been ethnic wars in southern Africa. Not just black–white either; plenty black–black ones too. Nobody ever gave apartheid credit for actually trying to do something about it.'

I said: 'Well, it was just a way of continuing the wars by other means.'

He gave me a sharp look, followed by a sharp laugh. 'That's good. I'll remember that.'

Later I had to answer his questions about what I was doing in Botswana. He listened with the same intensity as when he had spoken earlier. He was a fierce, independent soul, though also edgy, naive, a little apologetic in the face of my writer's credentials and knowledge of the region's past. He had heard of Moffat and Livingstone, of Rhodes and Tshekedi Khama, but knew little about them and nothing of the struggle over the road to the north. Or indeed that there once had been such thing. The brief existence of the Boer republics of Stellaland and Goshen also came as news to him. While I was telling him about them he became excited by the continuity he perceived between the past I had been describing and current developments. 'It's still going on today! The same thing! Those Afrikaner right-wingers – Conservatives, AWB, *Boerestaat** – what do they want now? – some of them anyway? They want to set up their own little Boer republic somewhere in the northern Cape! A kind of Afrikanerstan, a Bophuthatswana for the Boers, where they'll be nice and safe, they think. I read about it. Some of them have already gone out to Prieska or Upington or somewhere and bought a couple of farms – you know [gesturing with a single finger at his temple] – small beginnings and all that ... I wonder what's so special about the northern Cape that makes people think it's just the place to start your own republic. There's bugger-all there.'

Pause: 'Maybe that's what they like about it. It's so damn empty.'

Another pause and a gesture taking in the whole of Botswana: 'Mind you, we used to think there was bugger-all here. And it wasn't true. Not really.'

A few hundred miles to the north, near Francistown, I met another white South African, resident in Botswana, who also gave me her view of how she saw relations between the two countries.

'When I can't stand it here any longer,' she said, 'I just jump into my car and drive back to the Republic *to remind myself what shopping is really like*!'

She was thin and ironic. Her dyed hair was teased into ringlets in

---

* AWB – *Afrikaanse Weerstand Beweging* – the Afrikaner Resistance Movement; *Boerestaat* – Boer State Party.

front and brandy-snap shapes on top. She wore a scarlet blouse with a button or two undone to reveal hints of lace beneath. Her husband, stockily built, unshaven, round of face and feature, looked at us both with an air of gratification, as of a man who knows what women are for and is always ready to indulge their whims. Like shopping, for instance. He told me that he had gone to the UK to do his apprenticeship as an engine-fitter. When his mother couldn't manage on her own any more she'd asked him to come back and help in the business. While we talked his wife went back to striking intermittently at her typewriter – how old-fashioned the clack of it sounded! – with the door of her office open to the garage forecourt and the road beyond. Invoices and order-forms were scattered about her small desk.

They had been there just six months, the man said. They were going to make a go of it, I needn't worry.

'It's all right for *him*,' his wife darted in, ironic as ever, 'he was *born* here. I'm used to something better.' Then she commiserated with me over the drive I had just done. 'It's so *flat* . . . Whenever I drive up from the south I just *long* for the sight of those first hills. You know, by Shoshong. They tell me it's not *so* far to go.'

Before I could say anything, she got in another shaft at her husband; and at herself too. 'Not so far to where? *Here!*'

By the time my travels were over the following sequence of things said, things read, things seen, had become indissolubly linked in my mind.

(a) In northern Botswana, near Francistown, a woman tells me that whenever she can't stand it there any longer, she climbs into her car and goes back to South Africa, to remind herself *what shopping is really like*.

(b) A hundred miles further north, in Bulawayo, M.'s cousin says that she and her husband sometimes get into their car and drive across the border to Francistown. There they stock up with the luxuries – tins of biscuits, soft toilet paper, Scotch whisky – which have disappeared from the shops in Zimbabwe because of the country's perennial economic crisis.

(c) Another two hundred and fifty miles further north we come upon scores of women from Zambia, their infants tied to their backs by fringed blankets, walking great distances to cross the border in order to buy a couple of loaves of bread in hungry, drought-stricken Zimbabwe. Then, carrying their booty, they set out to walk back home.

(d) In the crowded passport office on the Zimbabwean side of this border there hangs a notice tied by twine to a pillar. It is written in felt-tip pen on a piece of brown cardboard.

It is FORBIDDEN to take out of Zimbabwe more than 2 loaves of bread, 2 kilo of flour, 750 mg of butter or margarine, and 1 litre of cooking oil. Zimbabwe residents visiting Zambia may take out not more than 2 kilo of sugar *for their own use*.

Just to remind everyone what shopping is really like.

CHAPTER FOURTEEN

☆

The Scottish Livingstone Hospital – A Mother of Three – A Father of Seven – The Long Road

The people in banks, post offices, and government bureaux in Botswana have a style of their own: one of graceful lethargy, of a physical litheness that somehow manages to express delay rather than action. There is always time for inward reflection after a request is made of them; for a slow duck or stretch to produce whatever book or register may be required; for a movement of the whole arm, from wrist to shoulder, to turn a single page; for an interval of stillness in which to gaze at the page just revealed; for a blink to acknowledge that its contents have been taken in; and then, just when it seems that no further delay can supervene, for yet another page to be turned, and another period of perusal to begin. Only then are you instructed how to go about getting what you have asked for; or requested to show your I D; or passed a form to sign; or, best of all, told that you have been waiting in the wrong queue for the past twenty-five minutes.

A queue which I managed to jump, unintentionally, was the one in the family medicine section of the Scottish Livingstone Hospital in Molepolole, about twenty miles to the north-east of Gaborone. A pregnant woman, chewing languidly on the remains of a leg of lamb, opened a gate for me and soon I found myself at the family medicine section. (It was simply the first building I came to.) Soon too I was being taken by a blue-uniformed nurse through a cement-floored corridor full of people sitting on benches against the walls: men, women, children, all ages. They were silent, except for one crying infant. Their eyes turned to watch me go past. A woman stood upright with her infant clasped against her bosom; she was swinging at the hips from left to right, right to left: an immemorial movement, perhaps as soothing for herself as for the child.

The sister in charge, dressed in white, sat in a room bare but for the inevitable desk, couch, screen, poster or two. At first suspicious of me, justifiably enough, she softened when I mentioned the name of the doctor I had arranged to visit; and even more so when I went on to say that I was visiting Botswana because I was collecting material for a book. At that she abandoned the people waiting in the corridor and insisted on showing me around the hospital. We made our way through the throng, who responded with their eyes only to this indication that their wait was going to be even longer than they had expected it to be.

It was only when we came into the sunlight that I realized the sister's white outfit was not a uniform, as I had assumed it to be, but an ankle-length wedding dress. It was decorated with bits of lace and a multitude of tiny satin bows; it also had some see-through panels at the waist and bust. An extra touch of freakishness was given to it by the fact that, like the lady at the gate, she was heavily pregnant. Presumably she was obliged to wear white to distinguish her from the nurses of lower rank, and, sensibly enough, had thought it a waste to leave this dress hanging in a wardrobe until the time came for a younger sister or daughter to get married. On her head, instead of a nurse's starched cap, she wore a small, vertical cylinder of lace, of the same kind as that decorating her dress. It was kept upright by an elaborate array of hairpins. Beneath this was a fine, bony, clear-complexioned face, retreating above a prominent mouth and wide eyes to a naked brow and raked-back hair.

She was very thorough. She took me from one barrack-like building to the next, all single-storeyed and iron-roofed. Between them were unpaved, sandy areas of different sizes. The courtyard at the main entrance, which carried a plaque commemorating the opening of that section of the hospital by Sir Seretse Khama, President of Botswana, in 1970, was paved; some of the wards had their own tiny cemented forecourts with scraggly hedges around them and windows looking over them. Patients were leaning over the sills for a breath of air or simply to see what might be going on elsewhere. Coming out of the fierce sunlight into the wards, I could make out rows of beds, and seated or recumbent shapes on them, and a gleam of something unidentifiable here and there; nothing else.

The subdued, timeless, suspended air that all hospitals have (when no crisis is taking place) – as if suffering and boredom have a routine of their own which has to be learned – had an additional African element of exhaustion and inertia to it. Especially now, at midday, with the sun staring down from its seemingly permanent vertical posting overhead. Shadows clung like underlinings to the base of the buildings; the trees growing here and there provided fragments of shadow only, in which dappled people sat or lay. Some ate mealie meal from tin plates, others talked in desultory fashion, the sound of their conversations interrupted by sharper utterances from birds overhead. I noticed that the throb and roll of doves' voices which had accompanied me for so long was missing here: perhaps because of the heat, perhaps because the vegetation in Molepolole did not suit them. Or perhaps they had all been shot and eaten.

By now I had learned that the sister had come from the north of Botswana; that she had been trained in Gaborone; that her husband ('not a medical man') worked in the Ministry of Health as a Resources Officer. (He had taken a degree in medical statistics, she said, at Lancaster University in England.) The word 'resources' recurred in different contexts a half-dozen times during our conversation; obviously she liked the impersonal, professional sound of it, even while mourning at every turn the paucity of the resources available to the hospital. It had been founded, she said, by the London Missionary Society; now it belonged to the government. There were four doctors on the staff; none of them were expatriate.

She said proudly: 'We used to depend on people from abroad here, but Dr Merriwether was the last one. One day it might be like that all over Botswana.' Of Livingstone she knew little, other than that he was a doctor and a missionary who had worked 'near here – a long, long time ago, I think'.*

We came to a halt at the building from which we had set out on our tour. Two women, their hands over their eyes, their bare ankles crossed, lay fast asleep on the cement of one of the vestibule-like places mentioned above. Near them two boys of about four or five years old were playing in the sand. Each pushed a wheel-less, oblong, plastic object, perhaps four inches long and an inch deep, in which some piece of equipment had presumably been packed. Now they had been carefully filled with sand, cigarette ends, and, right on top, a scattering of the metal pull-rings from cans of Coke or beer. 'Br-r-r-r!' they said, as little boys playing with toy cars always do, 'Br-r-r-r!' – pushing their pretend-trucks through the dust, making roadways with the vehicles themselves and carefully steering around each other.

The sister wrote out her husband's name and office number on a piece of paper which she folded and gave to me; she was more confident than I was that I would use it. We shook hands and I thanked her for showing me around. No sooner had she left than I was accosted by a tall man in a dusty boiler suit, with a yellow, too-small industrial helmet perched on top of his head. On his chin were the tufts of a tiny beard. He was so prompt in getting to me that I guessed he must have been keeping his eye on us for some time; perhaps even following us around. He was about thirty years old, but he walked and spoke like an old man, his hand clutching

* About a visit to Molepolole Livingstone wrote in *Missionary Travels*: 'Near the village there exists a cave . . . which no one dared to enter, for it was the common belief that it was the habitation of the Deity. I proposed to explore it. The old men said that everyone who went in remained there for ever, and added, "If the teacher is so mad as to kill himself, let him do so alone, we will not be to blame." There was little enough to reward the curiosity. An entrance about ten foot square became narrowed into two water-worn branches, ending in round orifices through which the water once flowed. The only inhabitants it ever seems to have had were baboons.'

the small of his back. Little groans interrupted his words from time to time. My own words were not allowed this privilege; he simply talked, in a rather distant, formal manner, through everything I said.

'I am very sick,' he informed or instructed me. 'You must give me a lift. I have a pain in my back. I have been waiting three hours and now they tell me to come tomorrow. They are stupid. How can I do my work with this back? It is such a heavy work. Also I have nothing to eat. I need some money or else I am hungry.' When I asked him where he worked he pointed vaguely into the distance, northwards, and said, 'Over there. They are building a dam.' Who was building it? 'The Italians,' he answered.

He took no notice when I told him I was going only as far as the former mission house, just a couple of hundred yards away, so it was hardly worth his while getting into the car. He accompanied me to it and groaningly lowered himself into the passenger seat. When I stopped the car at the gate to the mission house he sat where he was, immobile, quite incredulous at the thought that I really was going to turn him out so soon. Finally he produced one indignant utterance. 'And my lunch?'

I put three pula coins in the palm of his dusty hand. He inspected them in silence for some time before opening the door of the car and sliding out. The vehicle was only a yard or two from the closed gate to the driveway; but unlike the woman who had opened it for me earlier of her own accord, and passed on with no more than a cheerful wave of the lamb-bone in her hand, he just shuffled off in his heavy boots, giving me not a backward glance.

Pepper trees and yellow-flowering tacoma alternated with hot, pale, dusty space on both sides of the drive. Inside the former mission house it was cool and quiet. The thatched roof over the living-room was as steeply pitched as a bell-tent, and came to a point perhaps twenty feet above. Supported by a trellis of naked rafters, the thatch looked like close-packed fur. On the walls were several bronze bits of Afro-kitsch and many family photographs. The most prominent item in china cabinet was a cream-coloured statuette of the Queen Mother wearing the blue sash of the Garter, with her head tilted in ingratiating fashion. On the couch lay a book, face downward: *The Birds of Southern Africa*. Nothing else in the reading line, other than a large pile of *Woman* magazine. Windows opened on the well-watered garden, which was protected by a hedge of aloes and hung about with bougainvilaea. It gave the impression of being turned away from the sun, as indeed the whole house was. A drained swimming-pool gaped at the far end.

I had been shown into the living-room by the maid. Grateful for the silence and coolness, I waited there. Time passed and I waited still. It was now long past the lunch-hour and I had begun to get very hungry. Nothing had been said about lunch when I had spoken on the phone from Gaborone to the doctor I had come to meet: he had said merely that he would be glad to see me if I should call. The usual zig-zag trail – a name given to me by someone who passed me on to someone else, who had then extended a kind invitation – had brought me there. Eventually I decided not to push my luck any further. I went to the kitchen and told the maid that I would be leaving – would she please say to the doctor that I had waited and was sorry not to have seen him?

She was a tall woman with a girl's figure and meek, lively eyes. She followed me beseechingly into the little yard behind the kitchen. 'But I have made lunch for two people,' she cried out, her concern for me beyond anything I expected or deserved. 'Where will you eat? Doctor said you would be here for lunch. You must not go.'

'Are you sure?'

'Sure-sure. I'll phone the doctor,' she went on with as much severity as her nature permitted, 'and you will listen to what he says.'

We went back into the house, she phoned the clinic, conducted a quick-fire conversation in Tswana, and turned to me in soft-spoken triumph: 'He says the same thing. Now you will stay.'

So I stayed. I learned that her name was Lebeni and that she had three children. When I asked her what her husband did, she answered bashfully, with a lowered head, 'I have no husba-a-and.' How did she manage, then? 'My boy-friend' (that word also offered

bashfully) '– he helps me.' Was he the father of the children? 'No –
not one of them.' 'Then it's kind of him to help you with them.'
'Very kind,' she agreed.

All this emerged because I had asked her if she had been working
in the mission house since leaving school. 'No, I've been out of
school for ten years now.' 'Ten years! But you look so young!'
Laughter; a shaking of the head; an upward, assessing glance, quick
but circumspect. 'I'm not saying it to flatter you,' I assured her,
quite truthfully. It was not just her face and figure and neatly
plaited hair that made her appear so youthful, but the smoothness
of her skin, the grace of her movements, the shy softness of her
voice. The compliment pleased her, but she was determined to put
me right, precisely. She gave me the date of her birth. 'So you can
see I am now thirty-one years old.'

Then Dr McArthur came in: surgeon, missionary, pilot, director
of the Flying Mission, parent (with his wife – herself a midwife) of
'a fine family' of no less than seven adopted Batswana. 'Well, some
of them are grown-up now – two are studying in England; one is a
lorry-driver and lives in this neighbourhood; one is a nurse.' He
was a weighty man, in his mid-fifties, I would guess; large-headed,
moustached, bespectacled, with black eyebrows and silver hair
receding from a widow's peak; dressed in an impeccable pale-green
safari suit. It was plain that he was fatigued after his long morning
at the clinic, where he had been acting as locum for an absent
colleague. A single nervous gesture of his shoulder and facial
muscles contrasted with the quiet assurance of his manner, the soft
self-confidence of Scottish-accented speech. 'My only connection
with Scotland is that I spent my childhood in Perth; then I lived in
London and trained at King's College.'

He said a brief grace before we began to eat what turned out to
be a delicious stew of beef and vegetables prepared by Lebeni. Over
the meal I learned that the Flying Mission had five Cessna planes at
its disposal – four based in Gaborone, one in Maun. It tried to
cover as much of the country as it could: a difficult task, given its
size and emptiness. The services it provided were both medical and
missionary. Dr McArthur and his colleagues flew about the same

number of hours for medical and 'mercy' reasons as on missionary flights. The medical side of their activities received funding from the Botswana government and overseas aid organizations. In the 'old days' he and a colleague had piloted the planes, as well as doing the doctoring once they had landed; now they had the 'luxury' of being piloted to their destinations. The pilots, however, were not hired commercially; they too were members of the mission. 'We are all missionaries. We all have our tasks.'

He spoke quietly, matter-of-factly, impersonally, as if the two sides of the work of the mission, the medical and the religious, were indistinguishable from each other; each necessitated the other, in his eyes, if either were to be done. Later I was to discover that the motto of the Flying Mission was simply *Go Preach Heal*, with not so much as a conjunction between any of its three imperatives.

As for my presence – he was moderately interested in my reasons for coming to Botswana; also in my report on Kuruman and how I had found Butler and Wing (both of whom he knew); not at all interested in hearing about the most recently built of the glistening splendours of Mmbatho. But he did express some astonishment at the size of the International School there, and even more at the size of the fees it charged. He spoke with such feeling on the subject that I wondered if he and his wife had thought of sending one or more of their adopted children there and had been forced to change their minds.

After the main course there was a fruit salad followed by coffee. Time for me to go. He promised to send me some literature on the activities of the mission. I thanked him and Lebeni for their hospitality and gave her a tip which she accepted with a curtsey and the traditional gesture of thanks: one hand graciously supporting from below the arm and outstretched hand that receives the money. (The implication being: your gift is so weighty it cannot be carried by my unaided arm.) Outside, the sun was still at it, full-tilt, unabashed, staring balefully at flimsy-looking dust and ragged thorn bushes, termite heaps, one-roomed stores of brick and iron, waving urchins and wandering goats, smoke rising into an immense sky from who knew what and who knew where, huts of mud and thatch scattered at random alongside the road, or hundreds of yards from it, or yet further afield. No fences anywhere, except for the little one of mud or branches around each cluster of huts. And a man asleep under a thorn tree, with his head reposing comfortably on the flank of a giant black bull, also asleep.

And the emptiness beyond.

That always: the emptiness beyond.

Again and again in the diary I kept while I was in Botswana I find entries like the one just above describing the brief drive from Molepolole back to Gaborone. There was something hypnotic and inexorable about the repetitiveness of the country's topography and vegetation; as well as what could be seen of its scant people and their flocks. Here, baldly enough, is another such entry, made after my first, much longer drive up the main road – the only road – running from south to north.

The railway line is never more than a few hundred yards to the right. It comes into view and is lost again as the weedlike growth of scrub determines. Scaly black trunks, skinny black branches, invisible leaves, thorns – it is all a tangle, a raggedness, a formless repetition; thicker than anything I saw in the northern Cape, yet somehow more barren too. You would not believe there could be so many thorn bushes and termite heaps and so few people; that the sky could be so vacant; the road so empty, aside from the occasional truck; the sun so lordly and solitary, undisputed king of nothing.

A sign by the roadside reads: *The Tropic of Capricorn 25° South* and the trees suddenly become taller and produce genuine leaves too, some turning brown, as if for the autumn. Mopanes, I would guess, with iron-hard, scorched-looking trunks as their trade-mark. But there is barely time to marvel that a tropical species should appear so precisely in what has officially been declared a tropical region, when they disappear. The interminable thorn resumes, with tufts of low, pale grass between. The grass by the roadside waves in obsequious salutation every time a truck passes; it ignores my lightweight car. No attempts at cultivation anywhere; no one to make the attempts. Litter and trodden places around the occasional roadside store, with a bus-stop and squatting would-be passengers attached.

In irregular alternation the landscape provokes first claustrophobia, then agoraphobia. Claustrophobia because it is so flat and the scrub is so thick you see only a short distance into it on either side. It hems you in; it gives you plenty of sky and no horizon at all, which is bewildering and disconcerting. Agoraphobia because whenever a rare, slight rise elevates you a few feet, and you do have a chance to see further, to see more, all you get is a view of exactly the same scrub as ever – only from a distance.

Now three donkeys walk in single file in the middle of the road, with an air of the utmost purposefulness, as if determined to get to their destination before nightfall (Palapye? Shoshong? Even Francistown?). Ditto the inevitable solitary footslogger who raises his head despairingly as I pass. A sign: *Disease Control Barrier*, the barrier consisting of a gate across the road, a cattle grid, a uniformed man with a clipboard in the doorway of a small building, and another man, not in uniform, his friend, fan, helper, sitting in the sand outside. Again a sign: *Another Contract Completed by Goldstein Civil Engineering Ltd* with a double-track going off at right angles and no trace to be seen of the completed work, whatever it may be. So to my tally of Jewish traces along the route I can add, in this remote place, Goldstein the civil engineer.

Some termite heaps rise eight feet high, with a bend in the funnel at the very top; other are lingam-like; some fatter, curved like Mr Punch's hat, or Mr Punch's nose; others look like nothing more than outsize heaps of animal or human dung, deposited in dung-like fashion anywhere on the surface of the veld. All are the same grey, grey, grey. The new 'in' shade for decorators of office blocks: termite-heap grey.

At last – purplish, mist-footed in the afternoon sunlight – the Shoshong Hills. Elsewhere you might think little of them; here, after the horizon-deprived plain you have been driving over, their appearance is dramatic enough. The highest of them is heavily serrated across the top, as if battlemented; others are domino-shaped; some appear to be reclining on their elbows and showing their bosoms. Now the serrated one, sideways on, has mysteriously transformed itself into a cone, with another cone behind it. In those hills is the town of Shoshong, Khama's town once, where the hunters and travellers from the south either turned left across the desert, or continued straight north, over this almost-desert, this ordinary dearth.

More hills that way; more flatness ahead; the sun at a sharper angle now, spreading a dry ruddiness everywhere.

CHAPTER FIFTEEN

☆

A Short Chapter on David Livingstone

David Livingstone is much the most famous of the medical missionaries who lived and worked in southern and central Africa during the nineteenth century. However, it was not because of his success either as a missionary or as a medical man that he became one of the most celebrated of all Victorians: a hero and exemplary figure whose emaciated remains were brought back to Britain from Africa to lie in state before being interred in Westminster Abbey. It was his second career as an explorer, and as a writer and lecturer about his explorations, that made a legend of him. His appeal to those who knew nothing of Africa was derived not only from the vast extent of the regions he mapped for the first time, but also from his habit of disappearing into them for years on end, before reappearing in equally dramatic fashion in some unexpected corner of the continent. That was why his name suffered the indignity, too, of passing into the language in the form of an unintendedly comic catch-phrase. ('Dr Livingstone, I presume?') For this he had to thank his fellow-explorer, Henry Stanley, who had been paid to find him after the alarm raised by the longest of all his absences, and who greeted him in these terms when the two men finally met at Ujiji, on the shores of Lake Tanganyika, in 1871.

Their meeting took place twenty years after Livingstone had abandoned his life as a missionary; and a full six years after he had again vanished from the view of everyone other than his African guides and porters, the tribesmen he encountered, and the occasional Arab trader or slaver. All the journeys he undertook, once several ambitious, preliminary forays through the Kalahari Desert were behind him, were of prodigious length. No hardship or danger, either in prospect or reality, ever deterred him; nor did any obligation to wife, children, fellow-missionaries, would-be travelling companions, or the sponsors of his later journeys. The photographs taken of him suggest something of his indomitability and truculence: qualities that can be inferred as much from the setting of his head and neck on his shoulders as from his heavy black moustache, swarthy skin, and boulder-like features. The ten-year-old boy who in Blantyre, Scotland, had worked as a mill-hand from six in the morning to eight at night, and had then studied Latin until the small hours, so that he might fulfil his ambition of one day becoming a doctor, was not to be overborne in later life by anyone or anything – other than his own irascibilities, suspicions and depressions (which his quasi-Calvinistic faith seems to have made more intense rather than relieved). Certainly he believed that he was always doing God's work on his journeys; he was helping to stamp out the slave trade and to bring in its place the blessings of what he called 'Christianity and Commerce'. But he was prepared to do the Lord's work only on his own terms; and he despised those who attempted to instruct him or to control his movements or failed to pursue to the letter the orders he erratically threw out at them.

As a missionary he was in fact not just a failure but a cause of failure in others. In his seven years in and near what is now Botswana, from 1844 to 1851, he succeeded in converting just one man, Sechele, the chief of the Kwena tribe, to the faith he preached. His advocacy of hare-brained schemes of his own devising later sent other brave missionaries and their wives and children to die of fever or thirst on the banks of the Chobe River, the sands of the Kalahari Desert, and the highlands of southern Malawi. Intolerant of opposition from any source, he was also extremely jealous of his own reputation, and systematically denied other European travellers any share of credit for the 'discoveries' he claimed – the Victoria Falls being probably the most spectacular of these.* Even the regard

---

* It tells one something about Livingstone's attitude to the continent that it was only to the Falls, as he himself points out, that he ever 'affixed' an English name. Compare this with John Campbell's procedure, described on pp. 89–90 above.

he increasingly felt for the Africans he lived and worked with, and the warmth of the affection he came to have for them, are to some extent vitiated by the fact that he was never in danger of having to think of *them* as his social or professional superiors. He could therefore afford his generosity to them.

All that said, any reader of the biographies of which he is the subject, and above all any reader of Livingstone's books, private journals, letters, and papers, is bound to come away astonished by the physical power and intellectual energy of the man. That he was a great adventurer and seeker after knowledge, courageous to the point of obsession, and well beyond it, is evident enough. What is less well known is that he was also a remarkable writer, both in the more formal style of *Missionary Travels* and the later *Narrative of an Expedition to the Zambesi and its Tributaries* (1865), and in his much more unguarded family letters and private journals. In my opinion he is the finest writer of English prose ever to have dealt with southern African scenes and themes.

For seven years, from one more or less chance-chosen spot or another, Livingstone looked over the bleak, dusty, thorn-ridden landscapes of Botswana, or lumbered across them in his wagons, sometimes accompanied by his wife and infants, sometimes not. He quarrelled fiercely with his fellow-missionaries; preached unavailingly to the unconverted and never-to-be-converted; tried to teach their children to read and write; fathered five children of his own on his dejected wife Mary (and buried one of them); raised vegetables, did whatever gunsmithing (and, it seems, whatever gunrunning) he could for the locals; doctored them; studied their language; argued about the nature of the Almighty with the indispensable but constantly backsliding Sechele; and never ceased fretting over the best direction his future should take.

No doubt those Botswanan years, with all their failures and frustrations, contributed more than he could ever have imagined to the fanatical resolve that was afterwards to carry him through the journeys that lay ahead – the length of the Kalahari yet again, then relentlessly north-west to Luanda on the Atlantic coast, then eastwards across the breadth of the continent to arrive at the Indian Ocean; followed by a protracted and tormented series of forays up, down, and around the hitherto unmapped river and lake-systems of Zimbabwe, Mozambique, Malawi, Zambia, and Tanzania, in a misguided search for (among other things) the sources of the Nile. He died in 1873, near Lake Bangweulu, in Zambia. His African bearers packed his body with salt and carried it back to Bagamoyo, near Zanzibar, on the east coast of the continent, where they delivered it to the British authorities. The journey took them over five months to make, and cost the lives of ten more members of the party.

The last of his homes in Botswana – the last home of any kind he was ever to know – was at a place called Kolobeng, to which he had persuaded Sechele to move with his people. The site is not marked on any of the modern maps I looked at, and though it is only about twenty miles south-west of Gaborone, I would never have been able to find it had I not had a companion, Stewart, who knew the district and agreed to make this journey with me. Nothing is visible from the road to tell you that you have come to the right place: no huts, no houses, no roadside sign. Only when you have left the road at the new bridge over the Kolobeng River, and walked about a hundred yards up the stony, red-soil slope, with still higher slopes to the south and east looking down on you, do you come to the remains of the Livingstone house. All that is to be seen, behind a broken wire fence and a battered enamel sign, is a few rows of boulders hardly more than a couple of hand-spans high. About twenty yards above these are the even rougher remains of what might have been a stable or workshop. Clusters of other rounded, half-buried boulders lying about the slope tease the eye with their resemblance to orders and arrangements made by men; then another look tells you that the ramps, terraces, stepped pathways, and broken foundations which you think you see are phantoms merely, illusions, the work of your own imagination.

Of the huts of the people to whom Livingstone preached there is not the faintest trace. They had not been built to last. Abandoning them must have come fairly easily to their builders, who had moved to Kolobeng from Chonwane at Livingstone's urging, and who then moved further north once he had turned his back on them. Today, too, all over Botswana, alongside the new ones being erected to replace them, abandoned huts of traditional design and materials can be seen going through the elaborately varied stages of their decay. First the thatch loses its firmness of outline; then it sags; then it thins like the hair on an ageing man's head; then it gapes open to reveal a lattice-like cranium of curved roof-poles below. Time passes and these poles too fall away; and the circular mud walls, open to the sky, erode from the top downwards, until only stumps are left. When they are gone nothing remains. The poles are devoured by termites, the mud and grass return wholly to the soil from which they came.

In an early passage in his *Missionary Travels*, Livingstone gloomily remarked that he had found himself living in a land where 'the very rocks are illiterate'. Standing in front of the exiguous ruins of his house, I felt that I knew better than before what he had meant by this sombre phrase. Apart from a small group of men working on the bridge over the Kolobeng River, my guide and I were alone. No houses or huts were to be seen in any direction. Only in the north, where the country was more open and plateau-like, a haze of smoke and the small shapes within it suggested that people were out there. Of the stones around me, some Livingstone had picked up with his hands and ranged in rows to shelter himself and his wife and children; they had defended him (meagrely) against the cold of winter nights and the savage heat of summer days. Yet how hard it was to distinguish them from all the other boulders, scattered at random in the straggling thorn scrub and on the bare red carapace of soil, which had no human associations and had never been assimilated to any human purpose.

However, it is not only the ravages of time that have reduced Livingstone's house to nothing more than fragments. In 1852, while he was away on a journey to Cape Town, the Colonial Office made yet another of its spasmodic renunciations of interest in everything that went on to the north of the Cape Colony's borders. On hearing this welcome news, a commando of Boers from the Transvaal at once set out to crush Sechele and his people. They destroyed the Kwena settlement which had moved some miles upstream after Livingstone's departure with his family; they also killed many people, kidnapped some sixty children (to serve as 'apprentices'), and drove off about a thousand head of cattle. However it was more than the prospect of loot that had sent the Boers out on this expedition. They had come to punish Sechele for turning to a British missionary for protection; and also for failing to carry out the curt command they had issued to him two years previously, when he had been told 'to stop all English travellers and traders proceeding to the North'.

At some stage in the running battle that ensued, the empty Livingstone house was sacked. In his later writings he blamed the Boers; the Boers blamed Sechele's people; the truth is probably that both parties broke into it. (The enamel sign at the site follows the Livingstone line in putting all the blame on the Boers.) By the time he heard of the destruction of the house, Livingstone was on his way north from Cape Town, where he had gone to despatch his wife and children 'home' to Britain. He never returned to Kolobeng. He had had no intention of doing so, anyway, for in effect he had given up on Sechele's people, and on the rest of the Tswana too. 'Dry bones' he called them, which would never fulfil the word of the prophet and come to life. By now his mind had turned irrevocably towards the task of exploring the interior. However, both in his polemical writings and his *Missionary Travels* he used the sacking of his house and the plundering of the native settlement to blacken indelibly the reputation of the Boers in the eyes of the British public. Among other things, he accused them of deliberately destroying his stock of Bibles. He also wrote, though not for general consumption, that he felt

quite grumpy when I think of a big fat Boeress lying on my sofa and drinking coffee out of my wife's coffeepot. Ugh! I suppose King Pretorius [the leader of the Boer commando] will write his despatches on my wife's writing desk.

*

Livingstone had acquired a true missionary hatred of the Boers shortly after arriving in Cape Town, and the longer he lived among the blacks the more anti-Boer he became.

These white thieves will find imitators among the blacks; and though now the boers think a Caffre's blood as the same value as that of a baboon, the time may not be distant when their own will be counted as cheap. When that day arrives, we may be spared to say, the outbreak is neither 'unjust nor unprovoked'.

There are many such formal anti-Boer anathemas in his writings; they are reinforced by offhand references in his letters and journals to Boers 'embrued in human blood'; to Boers 'being similar in character to those in Newgate [prison]'; to Boers 'roaring out' their 'hypocritical prayers'; to 'dilly-dallying potbellied predikants'. He even declares the Boers to be incapable of living in a 'febrile region' because, he reports with undisguised pleasure, the fever 'cuts down the fat people first, and Boers in general are stout'.

Not that he spared the blacks, the Tswana especially, the lash of his pen.

While [Sechele] was away from his town[,] Pillanie, another Bakwain chief, came to fight him, and finding nobody in his town but old men, women, and children, of course like a valiant Bechwana murders the most of these, burns the town, and seizes all the cattle . . . [He is now] inflated by having acted so valiantly against the helpless women and children – I do not speak in irony, the murder of a child is in the eyes of a Motchuana a very brave deed, and they are not ashamed to boast of it afterwards . . . The Lord is punishing the people of this land and making them a scourge to one another.

If a Morolong [a member of another of the Tswana tribes] kills a khoodoo he breaks out into a loud wail, 'Oh, I have killed my father, what shall I do, yo yo yo yo.' If asked why they do so, 'It is our custom, we saw our forefathers do so & we do the same.' They laugh at it. Have not the smallest devotional feeling, unless spitting on the ground when they see the animal after which their tribe is named can be denominated such an emotion.

As for that 'sorry set', his fellow-missionaries – there was, he wrote, 'no more Christian affection between most if not all the "brethren" & me than between my riding-ox and his grandmother'. Even the Jews managed to draw his fire, though it is hard to think of a more remote target for him, in the circumstances. Making mock at one point of Sechele's European clothing (adopted partly to please Livingstone), he writes to a friend: 'You would be amused to see his royal highness . . . [in] an old red coat and a few other duds the which if sold to a Jew in London would not realize 5/-.'* At another point, complaining in his private journal of the mendacity, greed, stinginess, and filthiness invariably to be found among the Boers, he casually throws in the remark that they remind him more of the Jews than of any other people he has ever met. (A left and a right, as we might call it today.)

The members of his family, too, got it in the neck from time to time. Married to Moffat's daughter, he favoured his father-in-law's much-admired volume, *Missionary Labours and Scenes in Southern Africa*, with three epithets so insulting that some later hand heavily obliterated them. When his sister Janet copied a few verses into one of her letters, a furious Livingstone responded with half-a-dozen lines of contemptuous and slightly lewd doggerel of his own. Six months later, his anger still not abated, he went back to the subject.

No more of your poetry if you please, nay I command it; and if you again venture to fill up a letter with such everlasting nonsense, blethers strung up in rhyme, instead of what ought to be in it, you may expect a bull fulminated against your person.

He also pointed out to her that his 'magnificent' letters were 'perfect newspapers in size', while hers were mere 'ladies notes'; and, from the depths of Botswana, he repeatedly instructed her and the other members of the family on the importance of keeping their bowels open.

The finest writer of English prose to have dealt with southern African scenes? Well, in order to admire Livingstone as a writer it is not necessary to find him an especially likeable person, or to trust

* i.e. five shillings.

his judgement, or to believe everything he says. What one has to do is acknowledge that his powers of expression lent themselves not only to the ambiguous pleasures of vituperation but also (and often enough at the same time) to candour, curiosity, patience, exactness of observation, amusement, nonchalance, an amazing capacity for self-scrutiny in the midst of sufferings and deprivations which would have silenced any other person.

Consider, for example, his famous description of the experience of being mauled by a lion:

Growling horribly he shook me as a terrier dog does a rat. The shock produced a stupor similar to that which seems to be felt by a mouse after the first gripe of the cat. It produced a sort of dreaminess, in which there was no sense of pain or feeling of terror, though I was quite conscious of all that was happening. It was like what patients partially under the influence of chloroform describe, who see all the operation but feel not the knife. The shake annihilated all fear and allowed no sense of horror in looking round at the beast.

Or his account of the death of his baby daughter:

Never concieved [sic] before how fast a little one can twine round the affections. She was just six weeks old ... I have not the smallest doubt that she is saved by the one whom she could not know. She is home now, yet it was like tearing out one's bowels to see her in the embrace of the King of Terrors ... She had very fine blue eyes.

Or consider the metaphoric power which enabled him to say of a proclamation by the British forbidding slavery in the Transvaal: 'As good as bolting the castle gate with a boiled carrot.' Of a prominent figure in Cape Colonial politics: 'His nose is bent round as if it were disgusted with itself.' Of a newly-married couple: 'May they be a mutual blessing and never cat-and-dogify.' Of the thorns on an acacia: 'Most ... are bent backwards like fish hooks, but there are like wise a goodly array of straight ones pointing in every direction, ready to do mischief both ways and all villainously sharp and strong.' Of scavenger beetles pushing balls of dung, 'Keeping their heads down they push with their hind legs, as if a boy should roll a snowball with his feet, while standing on his crown.' Of a fellow-missionary: 'At present the shape he has is something between a sack of meal and a tar-bucket.' Of a tree-frog, 'about half-an-inch long': '[it] leaped on a grassy leaf, and began a tune as loud as that of many birds, and very sweet; it surprised me to hear so much music out of so small a musician.' Of a species of large red ant: 'On man they insert their sharp curved mandibles and then with six legs push their bodies round so as to force the points by lever power . . . We put ashes on the defiant hordes. They retire to enjoy the fruits of their raid, and come out fresh another day.' Of himself in a high fever: 'Ideas flow through the mind with great rapidity and vividness, in groups of two and threes: if I look at any piece of wood, the bark seems covered over with figures and faces of men, and they remain, though I look away and turn to the same spot again.'

Such an anthology could be extended almost indefinitely, from all phases of his career. The last three quotations are in fact taken from the journal he kept on his final, fatal journey. ('I saw myself lying dead on the way to Ujiji, and all the letters I expected there useless.') In their speed and spontaneity passages like these seem to me comparable with what we might expect to find in the work of the greatest of writers – in Dickens, say, or D.H. Lawrence.

Of Kolobeng, where, according to one of Livingstone's letters, lions 'walk around the house at night', where hyenas 'abound exceedingly', where buffaloes, zebras and elephants 'have left their traces' – of Kolobeng he also wrote that one day it would perhaps contain 'only marks of the pleasant haunts of men'. That prophecy has hardly been fulfilled. The animals have all gone, true; but so have the people. On the other hand a new tarred road now runs past the ruins of his house. It is a fine road, one of the best I travelled on in Botswana, though also one of the most heavily disfigured with litter. For some reason it seemed to specialize in plastic bags. They lay in the verges; they thrashed and struggled to free themselves from thorn bushes; they puffed themselves out like balloons and rolled along briefly in the wake of the car; they even tried to block its passage with hopeless kamikaze tactics.

The road had been built to cut the journey-time from Gaborone to the recently opened diamond mine at Jwaneng. One wonders what Livingstone would have made of it. Would he have thought of it as a pleasant haunt of men? As a victory for Christianity and Commerce?

CHAPTER SIXTEEN

☆

Cattle Stations and Subject Peoples –
Corruption in High and Low Places – Africa
at Last – My Putative Business Partner –
Lost by Day, Lost by Night

Stewart, my companion on the journey to the ruins of Livingstone's house, came from Mochudi, a town to the north of Gaborone. He had originally trained as a teacher and worked as one for several years, before taking up a job as a youth worker with a charitable organization funded from abroad. To qualify for the post he had been sent on a year-long training course in Zambia, and had also spent some time in South Africa and Zimbabwe. Now he, his wife, and baby son were about to leave for Aberdeen, where his employers were sponsoring him to take a three-year degree course in social administration. The prospect excited and alarmed him: what he was most nervous about, he said, was the cold weather in Scotland.

He had a surprisingly deep, rasping voice for a man with such a slight frame and so small a face; his voice did more to give him an air of authority than the beard and moustache he had tried to cultivate, without much success. Usually he kept his eyes lowered modestly, but their movements were sharp enough whenever he looked up. His white shirt was too big for him and the arms that stuck out of the holes of his rolled-up sleeves were as thin as a boy's. When he relaxed he had a habit of whistling quietly over a stiff, straight lower lip, African-style – a style I was never able to emulate as a boy, though I had spent many hours trying to learn the trick of it.

His parents, he told me, had been 'just farmers'. Neither of them was still alive. His older brother had inherited their cattle; he had inherited their house in Mochudi. He and his wife now owned seventeen head of cattle of their own: some of them they had saved up to buy; some she had 'brought with her' – a phrase I took to refer to her dowry or bride-wealth (*bogadi*). The cattle were suffering greatly in the drought, he said; it was terrible to see the condition they were in. Shouldn't he have sent some of them away for slaughter, then? 'That is one thing we don't like even to consider, if we can help it. They are our cattle; we must keep them as long as we can.' Where did he graze them? Who looked after them? From his answers I gathered that certain other Tswana institutions were flourishing: one among them being that of maintaining 'cattle posts' at a distance from the centres of population. 'If I find some water in the bush, then I can put my cattle there; nobody will mind, so long as it's not right next to someone else's post. I don't even have to tell the Land Commissioner.' And the local chief? 'He won't care, if we go far enough into the bush.' And who would be herding the cattle, at such a distance? 'There are some men we pay every month to do it; we give them some rations also.' What kind of men? He did not answer directly. 'People who have always done that kind of work.'

In other words they were either Bushmen or members of the Kgalagadi tribe. (The word 'Kalahari' is actually a corrupted form of the tribal name.) These were the peoples whom the Tswana had found living in this part of Africa when they first migrated into it, and whom they subjugated and have dominated ever since. Until fairly recently the two groups had been held in a state resembling slavery – 'an abject form of servitude' is how one sympathetic black historian describes it – and they remain still a subordinate caste, assigned especially by their masters to the tasks of cattle-herding and domestic labour.

So if the majority in Botswana are poor (which they are indeed), what word describes those who are fated to be their servants? Or, to put the question more generally: where is there a beginning or an end to the domination and dispossession of human groups by other groups better armed and organized?

＊

Stewart himself was relatively well-to-do: he owned a three-roomed house, a petrol-driven 1.6 h.p. generator to supply it with electricity, a car, a television set. His wife worked as a primary school teacher, which she would not have been able to do if they had not also had a servant who came in every day. They watched the usual mixture of CNN, BOP TV, and South African stations; Botswana itself was without a service and the Zimbabwe signal was 'too weak'. They did not yet have a video recorder but he hoped they would be able to bring one back with them from Scotland.

Having admitted to his anxiety about the cold in Scotland, he went on to reveal other worries about the forthcoming move. Most of them referred to his wife; so much so that I began to suspect he was foisting on her, in husbandly fashion, his own misgivings about the big change ahead. What would she *do* in Aberdeen, where they knew nobody and where she would be confined to the house by their child? Also, her English was not so 'strong' as his. He was anxious too about her health. Ever since she had had the baby she had suffered from some kind of trouble 'inside' and the doctors at the hospital here had not been able to help her. Would she have to pay for medical treatment in Scotland? I gave a reassuring answer (correctly, I hope) on that score; and then dissipated the effect by warning him of the incomprehensibility of Aberdonian English. He whistled softly for a while, staring out of the window, then asked another question.

What did I think was the biggest difference between Botswana and Britain?

It was my turn to look with more than just a driver's eye out of the window of the car. The Mokoro Small General Store, which in truth could hardly have been smaller than it was; the eternal thorn scrub casting shadows on the nakedness beneath; a broken trailer-truck, heavily loaded, its back axle snapped like a stick, with a boulder propping it up in lieu; goats scurrying across the road ahead, as busy and as black as ants, and hardly larger than ants at the distance we were from them; Gaborone more distant still, approaching by way of a scatter of dwellings, telephone poles, the usual auto-wreckers' yard.

More people in Britain, I suggested. Bigger cities and many more of them. Taller buildings. Double-storeyed houses. More roads and streets – all of them tarred. More greenness. More rain. More money. More goods. More newspapers. English spoken everywhere.

It was hopeless. I wanted to say also: more *thickness*. But as I would have had to explain not only to him but to myself too what I meant by that, and as each item in the catalogue had seemed to depress him more than the last, I desisted. We drove on in silence.

Even in 'Bophuthatswana' – created precisely in order to swindle a people out of their rights – a notional multi-party system was in operation. There, and in the other countries I visited, the courts operated by and large in accordance with the rules they themselves laid down. In all of them oppositional journals were published and circulated, however modestly, and were allowed to put forward their programmes and argue for change. Everywhere I went ordinary people were ready to say aloud (to a visitor, at any rate) what they thought of their rulers.

Like most people in most countries they thought poorly of them. The difference – certainly in Bop, in Botswana, in Zimbabwe, in Zambia – was that they gave just one reason for the contempt they felt. It was as if all other complaints were trivial in comparison. 'They are only interested in money.' 'They are thieves.' 'They are robbers.' 'They are all crooks.' 'They want to be rich, so they go into politics.' 'They take even more for themselves than the white people did.' 'They only know how to cheat.' 'Money, land, cattle, shops, they just grab everything they can get.'

In South Africa things were more complicated, because of the revolutionary changes under way – the novelty of the social arrangements everyone was being forced to adjust to, the hope and dread of what might lie ahead, the killings. But in South Africa too I heard many complaints about the corruption of the Afrikaner Nationalists who had been in power for so long, and about the leaders of the African National Congress whose turn was coming soon. 'Oh, they're not yet the bosses, and just look at them already . . .' As for the rulers of the expiring 'homeland' republics (for example, Bop) – their names invariably produced a truly biblical hissing and wagging of the head.

That the whites in the black-ruled states cursed the venality of their new rulers, and made elaborate jokes about it, came as no surprise. Especially as some of them plainly took a perverse satisfaction in seeing their worst predictions about black rule confirmed. ('This is what you get when you try to do business in a fucking third-world kaffir state – if you'll pardon my language,' said a stertorous, chain-smoking, thick-haired businessman in an office in Masvingo, Zimbabwe, tremulous with anger as he spoke, the expulsion of his breath on the 'f's' in 'fucking' and 'kaffir' sending ash from the ashtray on his desk flying into my face.) For the blacks, however, no such satisfactions were available. They saw their rulers as parasites twice over: once on the white-owned and white-managed businesses on which their countries largely depended; secondly, and even more painfully, on themselves.

Yet even more depressing than the words they used was the hopelessness of their tone. They spoke tiredly, cynically, without any expectation of a change for the better taking place, either as a result of their words or anyone else's. Nor did they appear to believe that any conceivable replacement at the top would make a difference. They spoke of the greed and dishonesty of their rulers as they did of the drought: it was another phenomenon beyond human control or remedy.

In a desolate area just outside Palapye one morning I saw several Herero women going about their business in multi-layered, full-length, full-skirted dresses, all sapphire and scarlet, white and aquamarine, with great turbans above. (I had seen the garb just once before, in Walvis Bay, Namibia. It looks something like that worn by the White Queen in Tenniel's illustrations to *Alice Through the Looking-Glass*.) What were women in such outfits doing there? The answer is that they were descended from the Hereros in Namibia, who had risen in rebellion against their newly-acquired German masters almost a hundred years ago. To punish them, von

Trotha, the general sent out from Germany to remedy matters, gave explicit orders that the entire people be destroyed. The forebears of those women in Palapye had struggled in handfuls across the Kalahari Desert to find refuge in Bechuanaland. There a small group of them had chosen to remain ever since – keeping itself distinct from all others and remaining loyal, too, to the mode of dress by which its womenfolk identify themselves.

How and where had they acquired so colourful a garb? The answer, ironically enough, is that it was given to them by the missionaries of the Rhenish Mission Society, who had penetrated the Namibian coast fifty years before a 'final solution' of the 'Herero problem' had been attempted.

The traditional Tswana 'households', each with its cluster of three or four round huts connected by a hard-trodden courtyard and surrounded by a winding wall of sunbaked *dagga* or other material, owed nothing to alien inventions, or interventions. Provided you chose your angle of vision carefully enough, in some places – even in the bigger settlements – you could see only what someone standing there a thousand years before would have seen. It was as if time suddenly became transparent to your gaze, for as long as you stood there. The thorn trees; the thatched roofs buried among them, all shaped like coolie hats (only steeper); the palisades of thorn or mud winding about each group of huts; the cultivated plots and brushwood kraals for cattle and goats nearby – all were wholly and immemorially African. Africa as it had once been and in part still is.

No less African was the fact that when for the first time I went uninvited into a traditional household, I found myself promptly being urged by the son of the place to invest in a 'kombi' with him. The kombi is a minibus used in the cities, and between them, as a shared (jitney) taxi. They are found all over southern Africa: crowded to the gunwales, going like hell, Afro-pop blaring from their stereo cassettes, their drivers simultaneously steering, giving change to passengers, and signalling with their third and fourth hands to people on the roadside. In my experience (three rides in all) getting into a kombi is a way of investing your life, instead of a mere sum of money, with somebody who may make off with it.

Anyway, this man's proposition was as follows. I should put up the money for the vehicle; he would drive it; we would share the takings. He had a dark, long-nosed, violent face; he was dressed in the inevitable knitwear shirt and pair of shorts; his legs terminated in a pair of bare feet and ten thumb-thick toes. 'Joh'burg–Gabs [Gaborone], Gabs–Joh'burg,' he said, waving his hand next to his ear with a circular motion, miming the journeys this hypothetical kombi of ours would make. 'Nissan, Honda, Isuzu . . .' he chanted, now generously offering me my own choice of models we could go for. A ghetto-blaster, as big and shiny as the grille of a gangster's car, was parked beside him. Surprisingly, it was silent. Perhaps he was saving the batteries. Some yards away, in the doorway of one of the huts, his mother was plaiting an item of the basketware traditional to the district. She was using coils of a pale green, reedlike grass, which had previously been prepared for her. An array of baskets – some open, some flagon-shaped – along the top of the wall of the palisade had emboldened me to come into this particular courtyard, which joined together three huts.

It was quite late in the afternoon; late enough for the sun to have become enlarged and bloody-looking. Several children stared at me in astonishment; a naked, dusty infant toiled on all fours about the floor; two women sat on kitchen chairs, each with an infant in her lap. While I lingered, ostensibly examining the baskets on the wall, another woman came out of a hut, carrying a bucket of water in one hand and a small tin tub in the other. She poured the water into the tub, went inside to fetch a kettle of hot water (it had been heated, I saw, on a primus stove), and poured that too into the tub. After testing the temperature of the water she picked up the baby and put it into the tub. I suddenly felt quite cold, as if I had not been conscious before of the breeze that was blowing, or of the sun going down. The baby yelled, the mother washed it rapidly, talking to it in amused fashion, while the others looked on; then, squatting down, she dried it with her apron on her lap, and put a tiny vest on it. And now? If she put it on the mud floor of the hut or courtyard it would instantly become as dirty as before. Who could be surprised that hut-dwellers like these had shown again and again how ready they were to exchange them for the permanence and convenience of the unsightly, cement-floored, iron-roofed (or asbestos-roofed) breeze-block boxes which also littered the veld round about?

Sitting in her doorway, the old lady went on plaiting with deft fingers, hardly looking at what she was doing: indeed, she hardly seemed to look at anything. Neither she nor any of the others made any effort to talk me into buying the wares on offer, though a muttered command from one of the watching matrons had sent a child to bring yet more baskets for me to see. Eventually I made my choice, paid, and departed.

Gaborone is a small-scale, purpose-built capital, and had the amenities of one. Some of the smaller places like Palapye and Lobatsi, Mahalapye and Francistown, had effectively been called into their present shape by the railway line, and still bear the mark of it in their layout. Desultory and banal they may be, but their buildings make a low commercial sense in their relationship to one another. I felt I could understand them.

But the older Tswana settlements – 'households', breeze-block boxes, iron-faced stores, schools, new government buildings, and all – were so centreless, shapeless, planless, irregular, and yet so much like one another, I hardly knew what to call them. Towns? Villages? Collections? Scatters? Sprawls? Attempts? Failures?

They produced in me something of the bewilderment I had felt in a place and a country that could hardly have been more different. In this thinly populated, poverty-stricken land I was reminded, improbably, of driving for the first time down El Camino Real, south of San Francisco, where each supposed 'city' ran unbrokenly into the next; connected only by the road itself, with its drive-ins, used-car lots, giant advertising signs and incessant, rushing traffic.

Yet on Camino Real suburbs to the right and left of the road were at least ranged on either side of *streets*, and those streets met one another at *corners*. Here in Botswana the habitations, traditional or otherwise, were ranged on either side of nothing, or of a meandering, lapsing double-track at best (the main road excepted). Indeed they were not ranged at all, but stood about in no visible relation to one another, or to the large empty spaces between them, or to anything else; they just appeared wherever they happened to be as inscrutably, it seemed to me, as the rocks and termite-heaps and thorn bushes. On the map, Kanye and Molepolole, Shoshong and Serowe, look like towns, they pretend to be towns, they figure there as thick round dots or blobs of a perfectly recognizable kind; but when you drive through them it is hard not to wish that some other symbol could be used to represent them. A question-mark, perhaps?

And at night?

One evening I drove out of Gaborone in a direction I had not taken before. I did this out of curiosity partly; but also because I had seen an advertisement in the paper for a motel some miles out of town which was much cheaper than the 'lodge' I was staying in. Within five minutes I knew I had gone wrong. I passed a fenced-off area filled with electrical transformers and tall, ungainly, demi-human pylons, above which high-intensity lamps gave off a gaseous glare and a perpetual crackle and hiss, like an ill-tuned radio, vastly magnified – and found myself on an unlit, unmade road. Clearly no motel, not even the cheapest, lay this way.

I went on, somehow drawn forward by the strength and purity of my headlights cutting into the pure darkness. How long I continued – a mile, several miles – I could not say. Then something else began to draw me on; or rather made it impossible for me to stop. Silent, ghostly figures had begun to appear on the fringes of my vision, on both sides, where the edges of the road imperceptibly merged with the veld. I could not be mistaken about their presence, or their numbers. Who were they? What were they doing? What sort of place was this, where so many people thronged the roadside – all of them difficult to see because of the darkness of their skins – and where there were no lights, no buildings, no vehicles other than my own? Not a sound came from them. Some waited for me to pass, shapes of arms and shoulders showing momentarily and going back into nothing; others silently and unpredictably flitted across the road; others drifted away like wraiths into the vacancy that lay around them.

Then, quite suddenly, as if a filter had been lifted from my eyes, I saw huts, habitations, little places, scattered across the flat earth. There were hundreds of them: non-existent a moment before, unmistakable now. With smaller or wider spaces between them, all were lightless, only just distinguishable from the night enveloping them. If I had been nervous before, I was now really afraid – terrified of hitting someone and finding myself at the mercy of a mob; or of being compelled to stop by criminals; either way, of coming under a hail of stones with worse to follow. No white person coming from South Africa and finding himself alone at night in an area like this could feel otherwise. And I felt another fear which seems more trivial now, and harder to explain, but was no less intense then. I was afraid of being lost among the huts, many of which were actually smaller in size than my car, of being unable to distinguish what might be roadway from what could be somebody's kitchen, back door, front door. Not to speak of ditches, random fences, potholes, outhouses. It was the dream-fear of entrapment, of being caught in a maze.

So I stuck to the track I was on. Only (after how long?) when I could see that the wraiths had been left long behind, together with the settlement or shantytown or whatever it was, did I stop, turn the car to face the way I had come, and switch off the headlights.

Strangely, the extinction of their glare did not plunge me into blindness. Most of what I was looking at was still impenetrable, yet immediately I was able to make out faint, squarish patches of light. Discreetly gleaming – gold, yellow, red – one after another they showed themselves, occupying different places and as it were different dimensions in the darkness. It was like seeing an abstract composition assembling itself before my eyes. It came from all the sources of light which the car's beam had prevented me from seeing before. Candles, oil-lamps, braziers, tiny fires were showing themselves through doors or windows, or gaps where doors and windows should have been, or through chinks in rickety structures whose outlines I could only guess at.

As I sat there two thoughts contended and merged in my mind. Talk about 'empowerment'! *This*, not what I had twice experienced in town for an hour or two, is a real power-failure, a denial of power, an experience of powerlessness. And then: if this is where you come from, how do you get out of it? How do you read, study, get to grips with a world which takes its access to power for granted; which is indignant and scornful, as I had been in Gaborone, when the lifts stop and the phones don't work? How limited our imaginations are! Because I had always taken for granted the availability of light after dark, and had gone without it only when I wished to, I had never really tried to consider what it is like to be deprived of it every night – and especially when others have it; I had never thought of the kind of effort such a deprivation imposes on you, what a sense of exclusion it enforces, how it limits the possibilities open to you, how it even denies you your privacy (for if you do not share with others whatever source of light is available, there is only the darkness for you). No wonder that those who do 'make it' from areas like this so often appear exhausted even before their careers have begun: schoolteachers and officials and sales-women interested in nothing other than keeping their jobs, deferring to their bosses, avoiding thought, playing it safe.

Of course I had known from childhood that most dwelling-places in southern Africa are without electricity; just as they are without mains drainage or piped water. That was the way in which the difference between how 'we' lived and 'they' lived had always defined itself. Yet most black townships in South Africa are il-luminated, gulag fashion, by clusters of skyscraper-high lights, looking down on them like a god that is determined never to let the people below forget his presence.

Not here. Here all was hidden, guesswork, shrouded. With only the lights from those distant pylons, Gaborone somewhere behind them, like an ironical stain on to the horizon.

☆

Maun: 1

It was in Maun, Botswana, that, after following the ivory trail for so long, I met the keeper of the electronic elephant.

Strictly speaking I had no business to be there. It is a long way from the Great North Road. But excuses were easy to come by. I had a special interest in David Livingstone, whose first long journey of exploration had been across the Kalahari Desert to Lake Ngami, south of Maun and the Okavango swamps. Rhodes, too, whose eye roved everywhere, had not failed to notice the possibilities of the area. Finally, I felt it would be a shame to be in Botswana and *not* visit the Okavango, which is the country's major international tourist attraction.

All that said, what really drove me there was the tedious prospect of a long weekend on my own in Gaborone.

The trip did not turn out quite as I had expected. My plan had been to fly to Maun and to make onward arrangements from there. It would be easy, I was told, to join one of the many touring parties which fly in little planes from Maun into the swamps, where camps of varying degrees of luxury or sparseness await them. In retrospect I should have been warned by the fact that I got on the Air Botswana flight only because there was a cancellation immediately ahead of me. But the travelling I had so far done had made me complacent. I had not seen a single tourist since setting out on my first journey from Kimberley to Griquatown. The people at the Taung Sun Hotel and Casino may have been taking their leisure, but they could hardly have been described as tourists. I had forgotten what it was like to be back in the thick of things.

That last phrase is a joke, as readers will probably have surmised. Botswana is one of the earth's emptier places. Covering an area

about that of France and England combined, it has a total population of about a million people. Almost all of them live on the
narrow eastern plateau – in effect, along the line of the road to the
north. For want of rainfall, everything else is virtually uninhabited.
In the extreme west, in Ghanzi province, on the border with
Namibia, there are cattle-grazing lands owned by the descendants
of some of the hardiest of the trek-Boers. (Can you guess who sent
them there? Yes: Rhodes again.) In the north, around the Okavango
swamps, live a relatively minor branch of the Tswana called –
confusingly to a Western eye and ear – the Tawana. Groups of
Bushmen survive here and there. Newly-opened mines are scattered
about in various localities, most of them at a considerable distance
from one another.

And then, gathered in and around the swamps, are the members
of a species even more nomadic in its habits than the Bushmen, and
much more newly-arrived: the tourists.

This is the way of tourism nowadays. Distance and difficulty of
access are no longer the issue. You can fly to Maun in a biggish plane
and into the swamps in a tiny one. Your linen and food and chilled
white wine will be flown with you. True, it is necessary that certain
conditions be met if the promoters are to pull off a trick like this over
and over again, season after season. If the place is really distant and
difficult to get to, and hence inherently expensive, there must be locals
living nearby who are ready to work for a pittance. Otherwise it cannot
be done profitably. There must also be a cadre of incomparably better-
paid, efficient, organized, English-speaking people to run the show:
pilots, doctors, guides, managers, inspectors, engineers. In other
words, whites. Without them investors will not put up the capital; and
middle-class tourists from America and Europe will not feel safe.

So one can understand why the Okavango swamps have been so
much in demand over the last many years. They are a wonder: even
I could see that, though the nearest I got to them was to look down
from a little plane at a height of about five hundred feet. And they
are really pretty close to South Africa, where trained, efficient,
organized, English-speaking whites abound.

*

I arrived in Maun soon after midday on Friday. Tens of toy-planes waited on parade in the little airport. Around the tarmac were the shacks of the various tour operators. I went from one to the other looking for someone to take me into the swamps. The problem was that I had to leave by Monday afternoon, because of arrangements made previously. It now took me about twenty minutes to discover that none of the companies could do what I wanted. The tours that fitted my timetable were full; the tours on which there were vacancies would bring me back only in the middle of the week.

The people who had been on the plane with me had already disappeared, along with their bags, cameras, sun-hats, canvas money-belts, Walkmen. Some had gone straight into small planes which took off like startled wasps; others, whose planes would be leaving later, were already eating and drinking in a half-covered, cement-floored space behind the Duck Inn, about twenty-five yards from the airport's unconvincing fence. Then, near the gate, I saw a van with the name of a nearby hotel/rest-camp painted on its door panels. Salvation. Later in the afternoon, having secured a room, I returned to the airport in the company of a young Austrian whom I had met at lunch. *Faute de mieux*, we persuaded a caricaturally laid-back Canadian pilot, dressed for the task in T-shirt, tiny shorts, and plastic flip-flops, to fly us over the swamps for an hour or two (in return for a hefty fee, naturally). His plane was parked on some roughish ground nearby. Never before had I been obliged to push on to the tarmac the plane in which I was about to fly. While we were trundling it along I asked the pilot where he had worked before coming to Maun. 'Saskatchewan,' he replied. What had he flown there? 'Indians, mostly.'

Those ninety minutes in the air made up my entire Okavango experience. I enjoyed them greatly. The landscape around Maun is one of sand and more sand; a few shrubs; the occasional ploughed field and cluster of thatched huts; many solitary, marooned thorn trees at distances from one another, each endowed with a sufficiently deep root to reach beneath the sand to underground water. Little enough to look at, but a cause for gratitude nevertheless. For behind Maun, almost all the way back to Gaborone, there is virtually nothing, the hardiest stretches of scrub and shrub having been scorched away by two years of a drought savage even by Kalahari standards. You would not think, as you fly over it, that there could be degrees of desolation in so devastating a spaciousness; but there are. Nor would you think that there might be a call for so many decorators' shades of grey. Among them are corpse-grey, VDU-grey, cream-grey, semen-grey (with the same faint shine to it), transparent grey, ordinary or sock-grey. Worst of all are the Makgadigadi salt flats, which lie across the terrain for God knows how many miles, like a decaying jellyfish on the shore, at once shrivelling and spreading, going out in rivulets (only dry), sundered from itself in places by other bits of matter. Then the greys finally begin to yield to a pinkish colour, powder blue, brick, and the first clusters of huts appear, like children's playthings put out on a huge carpet, and signs of faint, blackish scrub here and there, waterless river-beds like furrows made by a stick dragged through the ground, with a thin ridge of ashen trees on both sides. Gaborone now is only ten or twenty minutes away.

That is the view south-east of Maun. Go west from Maun and almost at once you are looking into a world of water. It begins mildly, with pools in the sand like those left on the shore by a retreating tide; then it turns into English parkland, with lakes here and there, and greenish stretches, and trees in thicker clusters. A little tribe of warthogs, unglamorous and endearing, are the sole living things to be seen; they bend their front legs back and kneel humbly as they root about for their fodder. English parkland gives way to English wetland – almost Norfolk Broads-like in appearance, but uncultivated, unmarked, with great stretches of standing water and rivers winding this way and that, and clumps of islands, themselves clumpy with thorn and tall, skinny palms. More animals appear: restless springbok raising silvery splashings from their hooves wherever they go, wildebeest, buffalo, giraffes in disdainful pairs, kudu, impala, three roan antelope ('Very rare!' shouts the hairy-legged pilot, banking steeply around and around them, in the fashion of a small boy with a toy aeroplane in his hand), a pair of

elephants back to back, like bookends. Then more water. And
more. What growth there is now comes directly out of the water,
so that you can hardly tell where the islands begin or end. The
animals are gone. There is papyrus everywhere. The prevailing
colours are buff and reddish; with bits of blue where the water
reflects the sky. This is a place for wading birds and the occasional
small party of tourists being poled along in a dugout. The whole
mass of water and reeds meanders away west and north, mirroring
the sky, chased across by the fly-black shadow of the plane we are
flying in.

The grand stupidity of it all! Water here; unutterable aridity
there. Why? Because in effect this is where a system of rivers rising
in Angola, of which the Okavango is the chief, meets the sand of
the Kalahari; and is baffled by it. There is nowhere for the water to
go. The swamps are the result. Every year they are replenished by
the flooding of the whole system; indeed, I was told in Maun that
the annual floods were only two weeks away, more or less, and if I
waited long enough I would see the little town engirdled. Maun is
about as far east as the mass of floodwater manages to get, in all
but the wettest years; from there a trickle of it, the Botlele River,
goes on as far as the salt flats, which it moistens for a few weeks at
the end of every season; the rest retreats to the swamps, which are
never dry and never take the same shape year after year. Not far to
the north runs the Zambesi River, which rises near the Atlantic but
proceeds to make its way across the breadth of the continent before
finally discharging itself into the Indian Ocean. The Okavango
begins in much the same fashion, and from near the same sources.
Then it takes a fatal loop south and is trapped.

Inevitably people have put forward plans (since the 1920s, in
fact) to do something about it. They want to pump water from the
swamps and pipe it eastwards for mining, agricultural, and
industrial purposes. No doubt some such plan will be put into
operation eventually, over the protests of conservationist and tourist
interests. The case of the latter is strengthened by the fact that the
swamps are nowadays smaller than they used to be – difficult
though it is to believe that, even after seeing just a corner of them.

The proof is to be found in Lake Ngami, south of Maun, which was once shallow but large, and is now permanently dry.

I really do not know where my own sympathies lie. There is something offensive to reason about all that water and all that desert lying side by side, like a married couple unable to converse with one another, even in bed.

He was small, slight, middle-aged; his skin was very dark and deeply wrinkled; on his upper lip was a moustache so brief and thin it was hard to know the purpose it was intended to serve. He had a round head with a tight covering of curls faintly tinted, as if with a dusting of flour, by the approach of age. He wore a short-sleeved cream Aertex shirt, with black piping down the front and around the breast-pocket; brown, creased trousers; trainers with no brand-name pretensions. In his hand he held a rolled-up newspaper which, I later discovered, was a three-week-old copy of the *Bulawayo Chronicle*, and from which he was not to be separated. He was evidently shy of sitting on the lawn at the back of the hotel, with the holidaymaking whites and the younger, more self-confident local blacks who came in for a drink or meal. So he had chosen to ensconce himself on a low brick wall in the shade of the brick-built, thatched-over entrance to the grounds. (It looked almost like an Africanized version of the lych-gate in an English country church.) Opposite him, on the other side of the gate, capaciously disposed over a kitchen chair, sat a security guard. What initially struck me about the pair of them was that they were exchanging not a word. I asked the newspaper-bearer if there was a chemist shop nearby and he pointed in the direction I would have to go. Then he offered to go with me. As a result we got into conversation and never made it to the chemist shop.

Like me, he was an unwilling, temporary resident of Maun, though in a much more thoroughgoing and protracted way. He had already been there for three weeks and thought he would have to stay for another six. Then he added without much hope, 'Maybe not so long.' His name was John. He was from Zimbabwe, from Harare. He worked for a transport firm – a big firm. His boss was very rich. He owned another trucking business in South Africa; in Harare the company had two hundred trucks. (Then: 'Maybe not so many. Maybe a hundred and fifty.') John had worked for them for twenty-four years. (This figure he did not qualify.) Before independence, during the war, since independence, now also. That was why he was here.

You see, he'd brought this electronic elephant down from Harare. It was to be fixed here in Maun. Then it would go back to Harare.

He spoke very softly; so softly I sometimes had difficulty in hearing what he was saying. Also his voice would occasionally drop away in mid-word – hun'ra 'n fifty; elepha'; Tswan peop'. At first I thought it was no more than a bad habit; later I realized his low tones were also those of low spirits and loneliness; his unfinished words a symptom of the sense of superfluity that oppressed him. He knew nobody in Maun, except for the people who were supposed to be fixing up the elephant. He could not speak a word of Tswana – his language was Shona – and the black people here didn't like it when he spoke English to them. He was just a truck-driver; so they think he must speak Tswana. As for the white people in the hotel – 'Tchah!' The gesture he made as he brought out this syllable was an angry one; but the anger was all self-dismissive, directed against himself. Why should they want to have anything to do with him? Why should they bother?

Also the boss here with the elepha' . . . he was making trouble over his Pee Dees. When this other boss from Harare lef' him here, he fix' up with the hotel to pay for his room. OK. But the Pee Dees, the people in Maun must pay. That's what he said. All ri'. First week Pee Dees, fine. (One thumb goes up in the air.) Second week Pee Dees, fine. (The other thumb goes up.) Now, Fri' night, third week finish – no Pee Dees. Now they say, 'Oh, maybe Pee Dees Monday.' (Thumbs drop, hands drop, bloodshot eyes look despairingly into mine.)

Only then did I understand that he was talking about his *per diem* payments. Thank God for a classical education. Silent, he was now consoling himself by patting softly his springy, greying, turf-like hair. He did it with a cupped hand from front to back – pat, pat, pat – and then from back to front – pat, pat, pat.

And the electronic elephant?

'Rubbish!' he said fiercely, his voice dropping lower than ever as he brought out the word. 'Such rubbish you won't b'lee' ... Nobody want such a rubbish thing! It b'long to a film company. I think a film company. Or maybe amuse-park. It move like this –'

In the late afternoon light, watched with bountiful scorn by the security guard on the other side of the gate, he extended his arms, put his hands together at nose height, approximately, and moved them from left to right and up and down, in trunk-like fashion, with swaying head-movements to match.

'And like this –' Now his hands were held high over his head, and he stamped his feet up and down.

The performance came to an end. 'For two years already, it bust! Broke! Dead! So they bring it here.'

'Who's fixing it?'

'I don't know what they call ... Young people. I think, Americans.'

'And when it's fixed, what's going to happen to it?'

'Maybe it go to safari park. Maybe they make films. Maybe children play with it.'

'Where's it kept?'

He pointed in the general direction of the declining sun. The only semblance of life out there was the silhouette of a pair of grazing donkeys, at a distance.

'It still standing on the truck – they work there because it so *heavy*!' Challenging me not to believe him, his voice practically vanishing with the importance of what he had to say: 'More than two tons.'

'*Two tons?* What's it made of?'

He counted off the ingredients with his fingers. 'Plastic, foam-rubb', fibreglass. Metal. Springs. Wire. They take out the electronics, then they put them in, then they take them out. I try to help them. Why not? I got nothing else of work here.'

When I expressed astonishment that sandy little Maun, with only its airport to boast of by way of public amenities, should be the best place for carrying out electronic repairs on anything, even an elephant, he shrugged. 'They say it must come here.' Then, for the first time, he laughed: softly enough, but putting his head back and showing the dark gaps between his teeth. 'Four veecel, travel fifteen hundra' kays for rubbish – a plastic elepha' ... don' even know how to work. And the road from Nata! No tar, only dust, sand, corrugate ... First gear!' – he exclaimed, using his newspaper as an imaginary gear-lever and even now spitting the recollected dust out of his mouth.

'Why four vehicles?'

'The peop' it b'long to, they say they must come with me. In three cars they come, they stay one day, then they go home. Also they pay custom at the border.'

'Why should they pay customs if you're going to take it back?'

'Deposit.'

This mention of money, indirect though it was, reminded him once more of his own situation. The animation that had come into him during the conversation departed. It did so visibly, in stages – from face, neck, shoulders.

'Now it Saturday. Tomorrow Sunday. Nothing to do.' He blew sadly into the end of his rolled-up newspaper, as if into a musicless flute. 'No Pee Dees.'

Later that night we had a couple of glasses of beer together, at the open-air bar behind the hotel. He was married, he told me, and had eight children. One of them was the headmaster of a school near what used to be called Enkeldoorn. That was the district where he, John, had his farm – eight hectares of ground, plus two owned by his wife. He owned seven head of cattle; his wife, four. She was the farmer; he didn't take from her any of the money she made; she had to decide what to do with it – keep it, spend it, or give it to the children. But there would be no money from the farm this year. ('This the worst drought *never*! Since 1947 we have not had such a one.') Luckily he had his job and brought back his pay every month. Usually he didn't drive the trucks, but supervise' the yard, check' the veecel, check' the loads, check' the roster. They'd asked him to do this job because it was a special one. They'd told him he'd be home in two weeks. And now, look.

At that point we were interrupted by a white who'd been sitting with two black men at a table on the other side of the rough lawn. He had been talking non-stop throughout, in a high, quacking voice: London inflections roughened by the time he had spent in southern Africa; *non sequiturs* flying like missiles through the air. 'I was digging up the stuff with my bare hands ... I said to your Minister of Shit Wagons or whatever he's called, You do this to me and we'll see who gets fucked up first ... Power-steering ... I was drinking for ten days, non-stop ... I went to Israel, they had one of those machines there, at the Dead Sea, and I worked on it for six months ...' Now, arriving at the counter to refill his glass, he fell on me. 'Another human being! No more jabber-jabber, eh! With our darkie friends!' I gestured warningly towards John, to show him that I too had a darkie friend. He was not put off. 'Oh, he looks like a good sort,' he said generously. John lowered his head as if to put it right inside his glass. Close up, the newcomer was plump, and quite young, and crazed with unhappiness. His freckled skin was tight to splitting over his cheeks; his large, flat blue eyes roved everywhere; his voice had no modulations – it could shout and quack only. The buttons of his shirt were undone and so was the belt of his khaki trousers. For a few minutes he shouted at me in much the same fashion as he had done at his previous companions; then in mid-phrase he got up suddenly, defensively, clutching his glass – 'OK, OK,' he said. 'You got business deals? Good luck. I'm not interfering.' And off he went – peremptorily, and yet like a stray dog – to another group.

It took many minutes, and many small pattings of his hand back and forth on his own head, before John plucked up the nerve to start talking again. He then got on to the *chimerenga*: the war between the last white government of Rhodesia and the guerilla movements which, after eight years of fighting in the bush, had brought a black-ruled Zimbabwe into existence in 1980. He'd been twice 'in trouble' during the war, he told me. They used to travel in convoys in those days, with 'the soldiers' (by which he meant the government forces) in front, behind, in the middle. Once the truck just in front of him was blown right off its axles by a land-mine. 'P'tchoo-o-o! Even the chassis upsi' down! Pieces fly everywhere! My win'-screen smash! Engine rip' –!' (Gestures to match.) 'And me? A little scratch here . . .' (Gently strokes, with one finger, the back of his left hand.) Then the soldiers opened fire into the bush, just shooting everywhere, to try and hit the guerillas (pronounced 'jewrillas'). He ran into the cab of another truck, behind.

The other time was at the end of the war when the UN forces were already in the country. He drove some British journalists in a car they had hired to a place where the soldiers were on one side and 'the jewrillas' on the other, with just a narrow space between them for the UN. Then the journalists said he must drive into no-man's-land and he said no. So the journalists said they would go and he got out of the car and they started down the road. 'Next thing – ka-ka-ka-ka-ka!' (Machine-gun miming.) 'Both sides! Only the UN don't shoot. They don't know where to shoot best.' (Laughs.) 'So the journalists turn round and rush back – rush! – rush! – right past me, and I still by the road like this.' (Holds up a solitary finger.) 'No car. No nothing. Only shooting.' Then, in the tone of one being reluctantly fair to them: 'After, when the shooting stop, they come back and look for me. "John, you still alive?" Tchee! Heh! Still alive!'

Now, he assured me, Zimbabwe was peaceful. The only problem was that too many people from Malawi and Mozambique and Angola were coming in. Also there were too many people in the country who were lazy and wouldn't work.

Even under pressure from me he would not admit that there could be a genuine problem of unemployment in the country.

'If it wasn't for the lazy people and the foreigners, everyone would have a job.'

The following morning John went at my request to ask the boss of the electronic elephant repair team if I could pay it a visit. (Since it was a Saturday, he had told me, they would not be working on

it.) The boss lived 'the other side Maun'. He went off carrying his
newspaper with him like a baton. His flat-footed walk, I noticed,
was the most assertive thing about him. A great deal of activity
took place at the knees, and none at all at the ankles. He simply
flung his feet away as if never expecting to have a use for them
again.

While waiting for him to return I sat on a deckchair in the sun
for a while; then went into my room to work. Soon there came a
knock on the door, followed by a familiar coo of 'Housekeeping . . .'

The owner of the voice was an elderly, even grandmotherly,
woman eager to earn a few extra pula by providing this solitary
male traveller with a few special extra services. (What kind of the
latter in return for how many of the former I do not know, for we
never got to talking terms.) She had made her first approach quite
gently, the previous evening, by coming just that much too close to
me on entering the room and handing me an extra towel – which I
had not requested. In return, I sternly asked why she had not
flushed the lavatory before letting me into the room for the first
time. I doubt if she understood me. The only answer vouchsafed
was a slow, mesmeric sliding of the lid over her left eye, before she
made her way out of the room – reluctantly, backwards. Later,
returning with an extra piece of soap, also unasked for, she took
stronger measures. She came straight at me and nudged her shoulder
into the hollow of mine, with a look of hopeful enquiry.

Given our age (mine quite as much as hers); her wordlessness
(for she seemed to have no English other than that cry of
'Housekeeping . . .'); her toothlessness; her extreme gauntness (to
which only afterwards did I ascribe another, possibly sinister meaning); the fact that I had been a-jangle with sleeplessness for nights
past (which I could not blame her for not knowing) – given all this,
the whole thing was so preposterous I could not even laugh at it.
Even irritation was precluded, let alone lust.

This morning there was to be no messing about. Since I had
shown myself so slow to understand what was on offer, she stood
at the door and went rapidly through a series of gross gestures,

accompanied by more winking. Still I did not respond. Her departure this time was as wordless as ever, but there was also something final about it. She had made her last throw. When John returned it was to tell me that he had successfully accomplished his mission. The two of us set out at once. My lady-friend was now flicking casually with a cloth at one of the pillars holding up the roof of the covered walkway outside. She smiled at me in a straightforward, uninjured manner. Perhaps she had concluded that John was more to my taste.

Before us is a gate and wire fence enclosing about an acre of Maun sand – grey, leached-looking sand, dream-like in its thickness and uniformity. I can feel on my face the heat coming off it. Three corrugated iron buildings are stuck in the middle of the enclosure. Two of them, like small hangars, are fairly new; the other is an aged lean-to, its open side facing the gate. Inside it are bundles of thatching reeds heaped in piles; it also contains a few sacks of straw swept out of a stable, though no animal, electronic or otherwise, is in evidence anywhere. Just outside the lean-to, but still in its shade, sits an old woman clad in an ankle-length assemblage of rags. She is eating mealie meal porridge out of a tin pot, scooping it up and moulding it with her fingers into little balls which she slides from below into her mouth. Near her, also on the ground, a man as old as she is lies asleep on some sacks. The three sheds take up perhaps ten per cent of the space. Its farther fence is made of reeds strung loosely together. A battered pick-up truck stands under one of the thorn trees.

We go around the corner of one of the sheds. Parked there is the flat-bed truck which John has driven a thousand miles from Harare, much of it over dust, sand, corrugate . . . It too stands under a thorn tree; some extra shade is given by a canopy extending from the nearest shed. Another old man sits on the ground, his back against the trunk of the tree. His ancient shins, as sapless and black as thorn-branches, are exposed. He no more moves at our approach than does the elephant.

It is a full-grown, full-size affair, as big as any elephant bull I

have ever seen: wide wrinkled flanks, a spinal ridge you could walk
along, a trunk to put out fires with, ears as big as palm-leaves,
tusks swooping down before curving up and narrowing to a point.
It has no legs; instead it is mounted on a squat, rusty, wheeled
bogie which itself sits on the bed of the truck. The creature's sides
are painted grey and are furrowed in realistic fashion, even if they
do come to an abrupt end where its legs should be. Its back and
shoulders are pitted all over with white, as if bespattered by birds.
Closer inspection reveals that this is because white plaster shows
through wherever the paintwork has been chipped. The plaster is
applied over wire netting, some of which has broken and come
away. 'Ach! It stand in the rain, anything, for two years,' says
John, noticing the direction of my gaze. Inside the cavity of plaster-
and-netting is a seat of some kind, hardly more than a wooden
cross-piece on a wooden upright, with a horizontal steering wheel
and an upright metal gear-lever in front of it. A pair of pedals, also
made of wood, are set at an angle below; two-by-four planks,
carrying electric cables in different colours, are attached to them.
Most of the cables hang over the side of the truck and disappear
into a little, locked caravan, a generator presumably, standing a
few yards away. Others lie on the floor of the truck. Various joints
and cog-wheels are linked to the pedals, wheel, and gear-lever, to
produce movement in different directions.

So much for the electronics! So much for my fantasy of some
secret group of American computer experts holed-up in Maun!

'That where the driver sit,' John explains helpfully, pointing at
the wooden seat. 'He make it go like this –' and again he launches
into his trunk-up, trunk-down routine, hands clasped, head wagging
sideways, legs rising and falling. Only this time he adds ear-flapping
effects by cupping his hands behind his ears and pushing them
forward and back.

'And the legs?'

Silently John points to four large, rusting springs standing upright
on the sand next to the shed. Each is about two foot high and
about six inches in diameter.

Walking around the creature, touching it, prodding it, I discover its trunk and ears (the latter shredding at the tips) to be made of rubber and its tusks of a roughened, ivory-coloured plastic; its eyes are half-spheres of smooth brown and black plastic, rather like the cheap paperweights you buy in souvenir shops. Trunk and ears are affixed to the torso by a binding of fibreglass which is itself unravelling into a greenish wool or candyfloss. On a table under the tree is an enamel tray full of a brownish substance hardening into the consistency of rubber. That, John tells me, is 'to mend the ears'.

Once more I go to the back of elephant and peer up its arse, or where its arse would have been if it had had one. The same sad, rusty collection of metal pipes, wires, and wood again meets my eye; but I see now that the steering-wheel has the words 'Massey-Harris' stamped into it. So it has been taken from an old tractor. Obviously when the elephant is in action some unfortunate person has to sit on the wooden seat, enclosed in that stifling shell, and operate the whole contraption with help from the generator. I can hardly bear to think how hot it must get in there, even on a day like this, ostensibly in the middle of winter.

'This isn't *electronic*,' I say to John, and I hear the note of disappointment in my own voice. 'It's just electrical. If it's anything.'

'Yes, I think it just electrical,' John says mournfully from behind his newspaper, abashed by the error he has made.

During this time the old man at the foot of the thorn tree has been regarding us without moving or speaking. One might have thought him blind and paralysed; but the movement of his blue-rimmed eyes, and the stick lying in the sand at his feet, show that he is neither.

'Well, it's a wonderful elephant, anyway,' I say to John, after a long silence.

'If it work, maybe, one day,' he answers, still deprecating, still abashed. 'I think maybe in six weeks he'll work again. Then – tchah! – home!'

Our departure no more registers with the old man than our arrival had done. When we reach the gate I look back. Now that I know what I am looking for I can just make out, above the roof of the lean-to, a shred of the elephant's ear and a reproachful gleam from one of its great brown eyes.

What was it that Livingstone had written? 'The chace of the elephant is the best test of courage the country affords.'

Absolutely.

A few months later I met at a party in London the editorial director of a large publishing house, who asked me what I was working on. I told him briefly about this book. He listened attentively. When I had done he asked, with a frowning brow and an air of more-than-compassionate, indeed suffering, earnestness, 'Would you say that your book is about the Soul of Africa?'

It was as if the electronic elephant's eye was looking directly at me.

'Yes,' I answered.

That night in Maun I had a meal with a tall, gleaming, golden-haired, mid-thirties American. I would have put him down as a champion tennis-player – a champion something, anyway – he was so slender and athletic-looking, so tensely composed in manner. It turned out that he was the vice-president of one of the biggest (and most expensive) of the American safari companies.

He was carrying with him a paperback entitled *The Road Less Travelled*. Having heard what his occupation was, I naturally took it to be a book about the wildernesses through which his company guides its customers. But I had got that wrong too. It turned out to be a book on pop psychology.

Registering my surprise, he said apologetically, 'Oh, I read all sorts of things.'

He had been in game reserves in Kenya, Tanzania, Zimbabwe, Natal, and the Tuli Block. When I asked him how he had got around he answered, with a diffident lowering of his head, 'Private plane.' He was due to go into the swamps the next morning. 'Inspecting the properties?' I said ironically, and he responded without irony, 'We don't own them. But we've got to check out what the people on the ground are doing.'

It soon became apparent that he was thoroughly homesick. He had been away from home (in Texas) for four weeks; now he was going to have two days in the swamps, then back to Gaborone, then straight to Houston. 'I was supposed to spend a few days in our office in London – but uh-uh – I sent them a fax from Joh'burg, nothing doing. I want to see my two boys again. They're three and four, and they can't understand why their daddy has been gone for so long. My one boy, the older one, he's a bearer of grudges and I *know* he's going to take a long time to forgive me.'

There was something engaging about the unabashed intensity with which he brought this out. Of his wife he did not speak. I fully expected his hand to dive into the pocket of his safari suit and pull out a wallet with his boys' pictures. But after a fiddle or two at the button to his jacket pocket, he restrained himself.

Ten per cent of Botswana's income, he told me with some pride, was derived from the tourist trade; the rest came from mining, beef, and donations from friendly governments. ('Botswana is the State Department's favourite African country. It's kind of democratic and its economics aren't as futile as the rest.') Tourism in Botswana meant exclusively trips into the game parks and the sale of hunting licences. His firm organized ordinary parties, photographic parties, hunting expeditions. The Botswana government also freely issued, to locals only, what they called 'people's licences', which the recipients immediately sold on to foreigners. In effect it was a black market in hunting licences. It was illegal but it went on all the time.

He did not tell me whether his company dabbled in this market. But he did say that he had been hunting once or twice only and hadn't cared for it. He didn't think he would ever do it again. Nor did he know when he would again come this way. What he wanted most was to get home.

And he gave me a wry, boyish smile: this acutely homesick man who was making large sums of money by sending other people on the 'exotic' vacations they craved.

CHAPTER EIGHTEEN

☆

Maun: 2

Sunday. Still in Maun, but gratefully so now, missing the swamps and my putative fellow-campers not at all. John the Zimbabwean has gone to watch a football game. The American has left on one of his trips to inspect the facilities enjoyed by his customers. Parked at the side of the road is a four-wheel-drive vehicle. (A friend had warned me beforehand: 'Maun? All four-wheel-drives and three-legged dogs.') On its door panels is a round white badge with a picture of a Bushman in silhouette gazing up at a flat-topped camelthorn tree and two eland. It is his distinctive physique and the bow and quiver of arrows at his back that indicate the group to which he belongs. Below is an inscription in brown lettering: *Jerry and Jana Lacey: Ministries Inc. – Missionary and Evangelistic Outreach.*

Alongside is another car with a bumper-sticker reading JESUS IS REAL – LUKE 24:39. (Subsequently I looked up this verse in the Gideon Bible in my room. *See my hands and my feet*, says Jesus to his disciples, appearing to them for the second time after the crucifixion: *that is I myself; handle me, and see; for a spirit has not flesh and bones as you see that I have.*)

Suddenly I hear singing from a nearby hall and understand better why these vehicles are parked side by side in the road.

There must be about fifty people in the hall: a low, white-plastered building with the inevitable iron roof above and a verandah running the length of one side. A bed of zinnias and a slope of lawn lie in front of it. The double doors towards the back of the building are open; so I can slip inside easily and remain unnoticed, at least for a few minutes. At the end of the row I have joined is a sun-scorched, bare-armed white couple, in their thirties.

They are clearly American – she in casual cotton dress and he in khaki trousers. (Jerry and Jana, I am willing to bet.) More surprisingly, in the middle of the throng stand an immaculately turned out Indian couple. He wears a green safari suit and she a green and gold sari. A thick, glossy plait hangs down the middle of her back. Their son of about eight or ten years old stands next to them, in shorts, sandals, and a bright shirt. Everyone else in the room is African: women mostly, of all ages, smartly dressed in Sabbath gear. Hats included. The men are in dark suits; the children sparklingly clean. One boy wears a Bart Simpson sweatshirt. At the lectern a young woman is leading the singing. Her dress is pink and is elaborately frilled and collared; she has a hat of matching colour. A pull-down screen hangs on the wall behind her; the other walls are decorated with large, framed photos of rhino, hippo, buck, etc. She rattles the tambourine in her hand and from time to time bangs it on the side of the lectern. I will soon learn that she is not a local, for the man standing (and dancing) beside her will reveal himself to be her translator, who has the task of giving the Tswana version of her sermon, sentence by sentence.

At the moment they are singing over and over again a simple, repetitive verse in English –

> Take me, O take me, to the Lord
> Holy, O holy, is the Lord
> Jesus, O Jesus, Jesus is the Lord

– singing with such gusto, with such effortlessly improvised variations and contrapuntal effects, with such a vibrant accompaniment not only from the tambourine but from feet and hands beating out their rhythmic variations that you would think it impossible not to be caught up by the excitement and exhilaration of it all.

Then I look again at the Indian boy. He is not excited or exhilarated. Not in the least. Plainly he is humiliated by his presence there, and by that of his parents. He and I are the only people in the room who are not singing, clapping, swaying, twisting, taking little steps backwards and forwards, letting hands and arms fly out in supplication. Instead, with jaw set, he squirms, looks down, looks at the slow revolutions of the four-bladed fans hanging from the ceiling, cranes his neck to glance out through the open windows. And now, even while I am watching him, or because I am watching him, he has found another source of shame; one from which he cannot keep his eyes. It is me. He knows at once that I am a spectator merely, looking at these people – himself included! – out of nothing more than curiosity. Others in the congregation who have by now spotted me are more naive than he is; they smile and beckon me forward, they extend their hands towards me even while clapping them together, they make motions of friendship towards me with their shoulders.

But not the youngster. He knows. He would kill me if he could, for witnessing the whole performance, and himself in the middle of it. How much of his shame, I wonder, is racial? How much intellectual? How much social? His parents are not just the only Indians there; to judge from their clothes they are also far better off than anyone else in the room.

The moment the hymn ends a clamour rises from the entire congregation to the ceiling, to those indifferently turning fans: no words, certainly no words that sound to me like Tswana, let alone English. Yet the utterance is made of more than mere cries and sobs. They are speaking in tongues. It is like the noises babies make before they actually begin to speak, but are already practising to do so; it has the rhythmic and tonal resources of speech, but is babble none the less. Babble with an entirely adult urgency of appeal, even of despair. Eyes closed, their hands fly in all directions. Only the Indian boy's eyes, and mine, remain open and our mouths closed; our hands are still. He watches me to make sure of it.

The babble dies down. Another, slower hymn begins.

> I need you, how I need you
> Every hour I need you
> Take me now my Saviour
> Let me come to you.

It is sung in a more subdued manner, with fewer variations and solo cantillations; perhaps for that reason it sounds even more heartfelt, if possible, than the previous hymn. There is no speaking in tongues when it comes to an end. Everyone sits down. The preacher immediately launches herself into her sermon.

'We are here for a very important reason.' That is her opening sentence. It is duly translated by her companion. Other sentences follow as steadily as her pauses for translation permit. 'Nothing is more important than our immortal souls. We must think every day how we can save them. The Lord gives us one chance, one chance only, here on this earth to do it. So we must make sure to be delivered from sin and that our souls find their way to him. For that we have to ask his pardon for our many sins. What a heavy thing that is to ask for, and how much he must love us if he is ready to give it . . .'

She leans low over the lectern to make her points; the congregation responds with random cries of 'Amen' and 'Hallelujah'; the translator furrows his brow, punches the air with his fist, his deep voice rising and falling in a musical miming and contrast with hers. Every time he finishes his version of what she has said, she herself cries out, 'Amen!' The Indian couple strain side by side towards the speaker, drinking in every word, the father chiming in with 'Come to me!' and 'Hallelujah!'.

The little boy twitches. He blows out his cheeks in irritation and shuts his eyes. I slip out sideways.

The new shopping precinct, some yards off the main road, is just stuck like everything else on the sand: Triple A Hairdressing (closed); Meet 'n Eat (open); Root's Pies and Pastry (closed); Gunn's Camps (open); a spanking new, slate-fronted Barclays Bank (closed); a Standard Chartered Bank around the corner (closed). Inside Meet 'n Eat are thinly stocked shelves of tinned foods behind one counter and cigarettes behind another. A glass-fronted refrigerator has roast chicken parts wrapped in cling-wrap; fried fish the same; some sandwiches. Stuck on the wall near the door is a handwritten notice advertising three video recorders for sale at 'giveaway prices'; also another notice announcing a disco at a place called Masedo.

The Barclays Bank is distinctively 'African', not to say
Botswanan, in style: that is, its roof tiles culminate more or less in a
hut-like point. Even more ostentatiously would-be African, also
brand new, with a roof that comes down in tent-like fashion almost
to the ground, is the National Development Bank. Every few
minutes a car passes along the road, travelling fast, making a
surprising amount of noise. Each time this happens a cockerel on
the other side of the road bestirs itself to crow in vain competition.
Inside Gunn's Camps sits a barefooted, heavily bearded, heavily
accented Austrian in shirtsleeves and shorts.

That he is Austrian is just about the first thing he tells me about
himself. He has been reading a thick paperback novel, one of those
with embossed gold lettering on the cover. He puts it down to talk
to me, keeping his plump index finger between the pages to mark
his place. 'Dere's no business today,' he says. 'But – you know –
dere's not a lot to do in Maun on Sunday. So I mide as well come
and sid here. At least here I have de air-conditioning.' And a little
later, after I have told him my sad story about how I had not found
anybody to take me into the swamps in the time available to me: 'Why
you din' come and see me yesterday? We had a helicopter going out to
[name inaudible, incomprehensible] in de swamp – we coulda fix you
up easy.' In return I let him know that I had met a compatriot of his
(who has since gone back on the bus to Francistown).

Across the road is a traditional 'household' or *segotlo* (a word I
had at last learned, amid much giggling, from the stewardess in the
plane that brought me here): three or four circular mud-and-dung
huts with thatched conical roofs, the inevitable courtyard of beaten
earth connecting them, the whole surrounded by a chest-high fence
of bamboo-like reeds. That makes the ninth different fencing material I have seen used for this purpose, around just such households,
since arriving in Botswana: the others being mud (*dagga*), stone,
weedy hedgeplant, breeze block, cactus, thorn-tree branches, thorn-
tree trunks, ordinary mesh fencing. Behind the huts lurks the
indignant cock I had heard from across the road. The huts are also
the home, apparently, of a goat tethered to a tree right next to the
road; so close to it, in fact, that he appears to be in danger from

every passing vehicle. His coat is black and his ears are brown and he has white patches on the upper part of his rear legs. He also has the usual black, pillar-box slit in his yellow eye; hard callouses on his knees; sunken flanks; an anxious air; no beard to speak of.

While he and I are looking at one another, a blue-shirted, khaki-shorted young man emerges eagerly from one of the huts. His bare thighs shine in the sunlight. 'You want to buy this one?'

I retreat hastily. Now I realize why the goat is tethered so perilously close to the road. It is to tempt the passer-by.

What are 'hypothecated cattle'? That is one of the things, or services, that the Standard Chartered Bank advertises its readiness to deal in or arrange for. Could the goat I have just been inspecting be 'hypothecated' too?

The local policeman has sought shelter at the nearby Shell filling station. In Hartswater, in South Africa, about a thousand miles to the south-east, also on a Sunday afternoon as hot as this one, I had seen exactly the same thing: a policeman with nothing to do squatting in the shade of a petrol pump. That man had been a Cape Coloured; this one is a Tswana. Of the two the latter has the better deal, for the attendant at this pump is of the female sex: obtrusively so, in her tight blue overalls. One sees the logic of the policemen's taking up this position. They are watching the traffic, and therefore doing their duty; they are in the shade; there is the likelihood of conversation with the pump attendant as well as with whatever passing drivers happen to stop to fill up their vehicles.

The football field is an oblong area of grey sand, nothing else. There is no grass anywhere on its surface; no lines are visible either. Presumably they are just scraped into the sand by a stick beforehand and then obliterated in the course of play. There are goal posts (without netting) at either end, and a fence running around the whole place. At the only gate stands a man with a plastic bag in his hand. 'Two bucks!' he shouts jovially at me, his words carrying with them a strong smell of beer. 'Only two bucks to watch!' (I have heard the word 'bucks' used for both rands in South Africa and pula here in Botswana; people like using it because

they think it sounds so cosmopolitan, so worldly, so American.)
Several spectators, John among them, are saving their two bucks by
standing at the fence and peering through it at the players, at a distance
of about fifty yards. About the same number of spectators have paid
the entrance fee, or have sufficient influence with the gateman to have
got in for nothing, and are privileged to stand on the touchline. A few
cars are parked on the touchline too. The heat is unendurable; I can
hardly contemplate standing in the open with the sun on the back of
my neck for fifteen minutes, let alone for whatever is left of this soccer
match. On the other hand it seems pointless to remain at the fence and
watch a cloud of dust shift back and forth across the field, which is all
that can be seen from there. When I explain my dilemma to the
gateman he graciously lets me in for fifty cents. Even from the
touchline it is difficult to make out anything within the large, excited
pall of dust containing the players. From this travelling obscurity
emerge many cries and the shrill whistling of the referee (himself
invisible), as well as occasional glimpses of players in yellow shirts and
blue ones. My guess that I would be able to take fifteen minutes of it is
soon proved much too optimistic: after five minutes I begin to be
afraid of what will happen to me if I stand in the sun for much longer.
But in this fearsome heat the play continues unabated.

No doubt Botswana will be entering a team into the African
section of the World Cup; no doubt overweight men will be flying
about the country at the taxpayers' expense, to places like this one
too, investigating the talent available. And who can say what they
might find? For all I can tell some youngster who will one day be
worth hundreds of thousands or even millions of pounds in the
European football market may be running himself exhausted at this
very minute, before my unseeing eyes. It has happened to
Zimbabweans, Ghanaians, Cameroonians. Why not Botswanans?

A four-wheel-drive Toyota comes to a halt at the side of the
road, to let the driver take a quick look at the game. On the back
bumper are two stickers: YOU CAN'T TAKE IT WITH YOU
BUT YOU CAN HOLD IT FOR A WHILE, and I WOULD
LOOK GOOD ON YOU.

*

Now I am joined by a companion: Ellen, a straw-hatted young woman from the United States, who strides along in a long blue cotton dress, her body thin above the waist, and broad (and swinging freely) below it. She has a plain, friendly face, pointed at the nose and chin, beaded with sweat droplets here and there. Her dark glasses are not over her eyes, nor are they pushed up into her hair; they are worn above the wide brim of her straw boater, as if it has eyes of its own that have to be protected from the glare. She is one of several Peace Corps workers I have met since coming here. Her job is to teach English at a junior school nearby. She has just been to Meet 'n Eat and is carrying home the dinner, wrapped in greaseproof paper, which she will be eating later. She is the first white person I have seen on my perambulation this afternoon; and I cannot help thinking that in a black area in Johannesburg or Kimberley or indeed anywhere in South Africa we would never be out walking as casually as we are here. Not that 'security' is not a big preoccupation here too; but there is a difference. A great difference. Ellen is from Chicago, she is a graduate of Loyola University. Yes, she is – well, she *was* – a Catholic. She went to Loyola because she wished to make her parents happy, and because she thought it was a good school, not because she wanted a Catholic education. But she'd enjoyed some of the compulsory theology courses she had done there. And what do her parents think about her being in Botswana? 'They're not too thrilled.' For herself she thought it was great, though she'd be glad to get home when her two-year stretch was up. She shared a house with two other American girls, one a teacher, the other a nurse. 'We have a pretty good time, I guess.'

Our footfalls are silent. The dust we tread on is as fine as flour. All of it is the same grey, sucked-out colour. Imagine how heavy and unappetizing would be a cake made out of it! There is nothing but such dust, it seems, for a hundred miles around. Every isolated tree that grows in Maun comes out of it. Everything that is built stands on it. It flies into the air behind every set of moving tyres. It shrouds the football players. It drifts everywhere, as fine as smoke.

The road turns to the airport, which is the direction I wish to take: Ellen indicates that she is going straight ahead. A cordial, perfunctory parting. Swing of skirt, swing of hips – swing-swing – off she goes with indomitable, long strides.

Well, long strides for such a short-legged woman.

On the corner is Le Bistro, with gabled ends and wooden ornamentation in modern, cottagey style: a Californian kind of structure, largely catering for Californians, I suspect.

There is no one at the airport. Having had to abandon my fantasy of another sundowner flight over the swamps, I must now resist the temptation to go and pay a secret, solitary visit to the electronic elephant. One of the things drawing me back is that I have no recollection of its tail.

That way obsession lies. Better to keep on walking.

The police station has several tin boats, to which outboard motors can presumably be attached, piled up in a yard across the road from the imposing and fiercely fenced-off headquarters building. The boats look utterly incongruous in this ashen landscape, but no doubt when the water comes down the river there will be a use for them. At the moment there is no water at all in the river: it is nothing more than a long, pale depression curving around one side of the settlement. To reach it you have to cross a kind of *vlei* which must itself fill up at the right time of year: even now it is grassier and greener than anything else to be seen here.

A little further: The Boat Inspection and Treatment Centre. (Nothing less.) Also a Labour Office, a Veterinary Station, a Prisons Department (complete with sealed, silent prison of modest size), a school or two. Maun does not live for the tourist trade alone. The prison shows not the slightest sign of life: no guards are to be seen in the grounds; no visitors have come this Sunday.

The air, laden with its dust, has gone quite still now. Over on the left is the river bank and *vlei*, and a bank of reeds beginning to merge into the darkness. From them suddenly comes a great noise of ducks, as if they know the water is coming. (Ten days away, say optimists; twenty, others.)

The sunset is all scarlet and black, nothing else. The scarlet: a ferocious, flat, single-coloured band across the entire western horizon. The black: everything outlined against it. Each blade in a fence of razor wire is distinct; so is the last branch and leaf and thorn of every tree. The lines of roofs and overhead wires have the finality of things painted.

When I look away, look down, all I can see of the roadway ahead of me is that it is paved with scarlet and black stripes, a half-dozen of them, lying parallel to one another, moving ahead of me as I move.

My final Maun encounter took place at the airport, the following day, just before I left. It was with a woman who had come to say goodbye to her two children, who were about to leave on the same plane for their schools in South Africa. The boy was to go to Michaelhouse, a school of which I had heard; the girl to St Anne's, a name new to me. They were both already dressed in school uniform: grey flannels or grey skirt, white shirt, ties. The mother was heartbroken to see them go; the children tense at what lay ahead of them. The terminal building, the size of a small bungalow, somehow contained a passport and customs room as well as a waiting-room for the rest of the passengers. Into the former the children were duly shepherded, well ahead of everyone else; for some reason they were not permitted to go through customs at Gaborone, their next stop. There they would be put on to a plane to Johannesburg; then they would change to another plane to Durban, where a school coach would pick them up and take them the last fifty miles to their schools.

'A long day,' their mother said. Once they had vanished behind the closed door of the passport room, she stationed herself outside the building, to give them a final wave as they walked to the plane. She was one of those fair-haired, fair-skinned women whom one sees quite often in South Africa: endowed at birth with a delicate 'English' complexion and punished by the sun for her temerity ever since. Her skin was not so much wrinkled as shrunken, sucked dry, peaked, pouched, with drifts of freckles under her eyes and only the ghosts of lips left to her. And yet, with all this, some softness and distinction remaining. And a pair of unquenchably youthful blue eyes.

She stood at the sagging fence, handbag clasped in front of her.

Her husband worked for the Anglo-American Corporation, she told me, at a place that sounded like Okwaxade (the x gutturalized, not clicked). It was about a hundred kays south of Maun. He was a geologist. The Corporation was investigating a 'seam of copper' there. Some of the 'intersections' were very promising; others much less so; so nobody knew yet if anything would come of it. There were about fifteen expatriate staff on the site, almost all of them from South Africa, like herself and her husband, and some wives. 'And local labour, of course.' She and the children had flown up from there in the morning – 'The road is impossible –' and then with an ironic flicker of her faint lips – 'and the Corporation is very good to us.' She and her husband planned to fly down to Pietermaritzburg in four weeks' time for the children's half-term break. Then it would be only another five weeks to wait until the end of term.

'I hate seeing them go. I'd much rather have them at home. They don't like it either, though they do their best. You saw them doing their best, didn't you? They were trying, weren't they?'

Some minutes later the children appeared on the tarmac, on their way to the plane along with a few others from the customs room. She waved until they had gone out of sight, and they did the same. Then the rest of us were called; not by loudspeaker but by word of mouth merely. When I looked back I saw that she had not yet left the place she had assumed. She was obviously waiting until the plane had taken off. I too was favoured with a shy wave.

So: for her, back to Okwaxade (if that was what it was called); for me, back to Gaborone and the road to the north; for her children the comics they dived into immediately the plane took off.

Incidentally, I had seen John at lunchtime, just before going to the airport. He was sitting on the ground, in the shade, outside the takeaway section of Le Bistro. He was eating a hot-dog and had a large bottle of Coke to wash it down. He looked more cheerful than at any time during the weekend. He was back at work, which he much preferred; and, he told me, he had been given the Pee Dees owing to him.

'Maybe four weeks – gone!'

It was the most optimistic guess he had yet made.

PART THREE

☆

Zimbabwe

CHAPTER NINETEEN

☆

The Kingdom of Monomatapa – Great Zimbabwe – The Plaza Kinema and Other Fantastications – Asbestos Again

One of the items in the National Archive housed in Harare, the capital of the Republic of Zimbabwe, is *A Geographical Historie of Africa* published in 1600. The book is supposedly written by one John Leo – as unlikely a name, in this context, as one could hope to find – who is described as 'A More [i.e. Moor] borne in Granada and brought up in Barbarie' and whose work is said to have been 'translated and collected by John Pory, lately of Gonevill and Caius College Cambridge'. Among the marvels referred to in the book is a building in the kingdom of Monomatapa with 'a mightie wall of five and twenty spannes thicke, which the people ascribe to the workmanship of the divvel'.

By the time *A Geographical Historie* appeared, the Portuguese had been active on the east coast of Mozambique and in the interior of what is now Zimbabwe for something like a century. Compared with the reports they were sending back about the country, then vaguely designated Monomatapa, the tale by 'John Leo' about a wall of diabolical workmanship was almost restrained.

For example:

In all the Regions, or the greatest part thereof, are many Mines of Gold . . . It is pain of death for any Moore which discovers a Mine to take away any, besides his goods forfeited to the King . . . This severitie is used to keep the Mines from the knowledge of the Portugals, lest covetous desire thereof might cause them to take away their Countrey. It is found in poulder like sand; in graines like beades; in pieces some smooth as they were melted, others branched with snags, others mixed so with Earth, that the Earth being well washed from them, they remayne like Honiecombe . . .

The words are those of the Dominican priest João dos Santos, who arrived in Mozambique from Lisbon in 1586, and whose book on the wonders of the territory, *Ethiopia Oriental*, was published in 1609. Eighty years later another sagacious English geographer by the name of John Ogilby published a volume entitled *Africa: Being an Acurate Description of the Land of the Negroes, Guinee, Aethiopia and the Abyssines*. A copy of this too is kept at the National Archive. When it comes to describing the marvels of Monomotapa, Ogilby elaborates happily on the work of his predecessors.

The Palace of the Emperor covers a vast extent, having four Eminent Gates, and very many large Chambers, and other convenient Apartments . . . within hung with Cotton Hangings of divers colours, wrought with Gold and richly embossed; and also overlaid with Tin gilt, or, as others say, cover'd over with Plates of Gold, and adorn'd with Ivory Candlesticks fastened with Silver Chains: The Chairs gilt and painted with several Colours: The four chiefest Gates of the Court richly Embossed, and well-defended by Life-Guards of the Emperor, whom they call Sequender . . .

The Kingdom hath the benefit of a temperate Air, and enrich'd with luxurious Villages . . . [and] Provision of Cattel and Fruits sufficient to store both themselves and Neighbours; nor is it destitute of pleasant Woods, stor'd with variety of Fruit-Trees and Sugar-Canes that grow without Planting . . . The greatest Wealth of the Country consists in Oxen and Cowes with them more highly esteemed than Gold or Silver. They have no Horses nor other Beasts of Carriage beside Elephants which flock together by whole Herds in the Woods.

All this plus 'certain War-like Women, like the ancient Amazons [who] do possess a Peculiar Territory, appointed for them by the King'.

In 1725 *The Complete Geographer* by Herman Moll declared the 'dominions' of Monomotapa to be certainly 'the richest of the world in gold':

No mines affording such quantities of that precious metal as those of Musapa, and Manichica, and Batua, in the first of which has been [seen] a Lump of Pure Gold worth 12000 Ducats and another 400000 ... The Emperor's palace [is] of wood ... all is gilt or covered with Plates of Gold, so are the Chairs and other Moveables, except the Candlesticks which are made of Ivory hanging by Silver Chains and his Plates and Dishes of Porcelain.

One notes both the plagiarism and elaboration of the earlier 'Acurate Description': the chairs, plates of gold, and chained ivory candlesticks recur, along with wilder (and yet purportedly more exact) claims about the treasures in the possession of the emperor.

By comparison with these writers, Rhodes's estimation of what lay at this end of the road to the north reads, at first sight, prosaically enough.

It would be advisable at once to enter into such arrangements with the chief of the Matabele as would preserve the only road that is left to us ... [Mashonaland] has been frequently traversed by reliable explorers and is known to have pastoral resources and mineral wealth such as do not exist in any portion of Africa south of the Zambesi ... [and to be endowed with] exceedingly rich auriferous indications as shown by the old Portuguese records ...

Rhodes was right about the pastoral resources of Zimbabwe. But like many others he was wrong about those 'auriferous indications'. The country's production of gold over the last century and more has been insignificant in comparison with that of South Africa. Just a year after Rhodes had written the words quoted above, the largest goldfields the world has known were discovered on the Witwatersrand, where Johannesburg and its satellite cities now stand.

So what was all the fuss about? Whence these rumours about a kingdom in central Africa (Monomatapa) ruled by great emperors and endowed with immense wealth and a highly developed social system? Perhaps the most direct answer to that question is to be found in the buildings of Great Zimbabwe, which lie at a distance of about fifteen miles from the small town of Masvingo (formerly Fort Victoria). Smaller structures of a similar kind are to be found in several other parts of the country, but none is comparable in size or elaboration or fame with Great Zimbabwe; in fact nothing like it exists anywhere in Africa south of the Sahara.

As many readers will know, the site contains the ruins of two major stone edifices, with minor buildings in an even more dilapidated state connecting them. On the plain is an elliptical 'Enclosure' several hundred feet in circumference; on the cliff overlooking it an 'Acropolis'. The widest of the walls surrounding the Enclosure are about fifteen feet across at their base and rise to a height of thirty feet; scattered about within these are a variety of platforms, standing stones, internal walls, passageways, and a conical tower which is the highest structure in the place. All are made of stone blocks, brick-like in shape and size, of a slatey-blue colour; no mortar is used to bind them together. The top of one section of the outer walling is decorated with a chevron pattern. The walls on the Acropolis merge with the natural granite formations of the cliff-top and extend over several acres; they give a commanding view of the surrounding bush and its hills. Different origins and purposes have been assigned to the entire complex by some sober historians and many credulous optimists and greedy rogues. Even today, or especially today, it surprises me that South Africa's legions of white hippies have not made more of the magical powers which such a site, spreading over its open land and guarded by its frowning cliff, might be supposed to possess.

The story now agreed by historians and archaeologists runs as follows. Over several centuries from about 1100 A.D. onwards there existed in the region a preliterate, monarchical society with a degree of wealth and social organization sufficient to erect buildings like these, to mine gold, and, with the help of Arab middlemen, to trade over great distances. Or rather, several such societies developed in the area, in succession to and in rivalry with one another. Both the rulers and the populace of these societies were black, indigenous, and Shona-speaking, and their descendants make up much the largest single language-group in present-day

Zimbabwe. In later years the various kingdoms came to grief. All that was left of the kingdoms of Zimbabwe, Mutapa, and Rozwi were the heavily overgrown remains of stone buildings (fortresses? temples? walled cities?) and boasts, rumours, conjectures, bogus historical records.

Of the tales told about Monomatapa none was more influential than the claim that it was the biblical kingdom of Ophir – the Queen of Sheba's homeland.* This fantasy, apparently first espoused by those 'covetous Portugals', had something of the effect that the legend of El Dorado ('The Golden One') had on the Spaniards in South America. It was to have a long life, too, as Rhodes's solemn remark about the 'old Portuguese records' shows. 'Delusions,' a historian of the territory has written, 'can shape history as potently as realities. The lure of Ophir drew adventurers, explorers, invaders to Rhodesia over many centuries, and indeed led directly to the creation of the modern state.' *To Ophir Direct* was the title of a book by M. Broderick published in London in 1864 – seven years, it should be noted, before the first whites coming from the south stumbled on Great Zimbabwe. (Broderick had in mind the ruins and gold-workings at Tati, many miles to the south-west.) 'So the question of ancient Ophir is at last settled,' declared Richard Babb flatly, in his *The Gold Fields of Southern Africa and How to Reach Them* (1876), after the find had been announced.

It is not surprising, then, that the first whites to make their way into the region from the south should have wasted no time in pillaging Great Zimbabwe itself and the lesser structures to be found elsewhere. (The Portuguese had not had such a free hand in the matter, since in their day the buildings had been occupied.) Nor were such acts of vandalism the work of independent freebooters

---

* 'And King Solomon made a navy of ships in Ezion-geber, which is beside Eloth, on the shore of the Red Sea, in the land of Edom ... And they came to Ophir, and fetched from thence gold, four hundred and twenty talents, and brought it to King Solomon. And when the queen of Sheba heard of the fame of Solomon concerning the name of the Lord, she came to prove him with hard questions ...' (1 Kings 9:26–28–1 Kings 10:1.)

merely. Before the turn of the century, The Rhodesia Ancient Ruins Company Limited had been set up and formally been given a monopoly of the right to ransack the eponymous ruins. The brother of an English peer, one of Rhodes's chief rivals and collaborators in London, was on its board. No gold of any significance was found; many artefacts were carried away; much damage was done to the fabric of the buildings.

If the treasure-hunters went away disappointed, so did almost all the excited prospectors who entered the territory with the Pioneer Column in 1890, under the aegis of Rhodes's British South Africa Company (the Charter Company). Nevertheless, with hindsight we can see that the myth of Zimbabwe-as-Ophir was to be extremely useful to the incoming colonists. It made their conquest of the country virtually a missionary act, a reclamation for Christendom of a quasi-biblical region that had fallen into the hand of the infidel. It proved also that the local people's title to the land was worthless, since the whites were convinced that the cattle-herding, hut-dwelling Shonas could never have been the builders of Great Zimbabwe. They were nothing more than a race of degenerate squatters who had somehow displaced the white, or whitish, race come from afar to do the job – if not Solomon's ancient, temple-building Hebrews, as some thought, then the Phoenicians; and if not them, then the Arabs; and if not them, then a people wholly lost to history. Look at the remarks of Theodore Bent in his book, *The Ruined Cities of Mashonaland* – quoted on p. 156 above – about the 'highly civilized' people who had left as their monument 'the gigantic remains at Zimbabwe' and who had occupied the land 'in far distant ages like a garrison in the midst of an enemy's country'.

He might as well have written it out: *Just like us!*

The truth is that many whites in southern Africa would far rather have believed Great Zimbabwe to have been the work of the 'divvel', as John Leo had put it in 1602, than that of the Shona whom they first dispossessed, then despised.

Each age has its own myths and its own methods of perpetuating them. I cannot guess how many hours of my boyhood were spent in the Plaza Kinema (spelt thus) in Kimberley, watching weekly serials and full-length movies about the 'Africa' of Hollywood – of which the Tarzan films were merely a sub-species. In almost all of them the intrepid white hero and heroine, clad in obligatory pith helmets and jodhpurs, would come on a 'lost' or 'buried' city in the jungle, a maze of stone walls, arches, holes, cliffs, idols, roots, creepers. The sight of it rearing out of the forest always terrified the gang of half-naked black porters accompanying the party: shrieking and jabbering, they would throw down their bundles and flee, leaving the hero and heroine on their own – he with his revolver in his hand, she with a pair of binoculars bobbing on her bosom. Unseen drums would begin to beat; the eyes of one of the idols would glow and move, revealing the couple to be under observation from hostile tribesmen; a capering witch-doctor would emerge to seize her; a stone trapdoor would open and close; not a trace would be left to show her companion where she had gone. The lost city had engulfed her as mysteriously as it had itself been engulfed by the jungle.

Of course everything came right in the end. A bullet from the hero's revolver would put paid to the witch-doctor, who would writhe about in his feathers for a while and die. Or he might fall into his own personal snake-pit or sacrificial fire. Then it was the turn of the hostile tribesmen to jabber and run away. A bad white man would be unmasked as the figure behind the hostility of the natives. (There was always such a white man in these pictures, often enough an unsuspected member of the hero's party. His motive was invariably revealed to be a base greed for riches – diamonds or gold, of all things.) A brave, loyal black man (there was always such a figure, too) would die affectingly. The hero and heroine, their porters reassembled behind them, would set out for the coast and civilization once again, leaving the ruined city to its ancient calm. I would emerge into the banal daylight of the Kimberley market square. On one side was the dwarfish, crenellated clock-tower of the high court buildings; in the middle were the Doric columns and tin roof of the town hall; on the right Louverdis's café. This was the Africa I knew. Anything less jungle-like and romantic it would have been hard to imagine.

Who can tell how much the pictures I watched in the Plaza actually owed to Great Zimbabwe and the legends it had engendered? Many 'lost cities' had been uncovered by white explorers in South-East Asia and Latin America during the latter half of the nineteenth century and the early years of the twentieth: why should Hollywood not import a few of them into Africa too? But no one who browses in the romantic-sensational literature connected with Great Zimbabwe can doubt that it played a significant part in making such fictions and such films plausible and attractive – there being no structure like it on the continent, and none whose discovery had roused so much curiosity and comment.

Not that the process of legend-making has since stopped, or that it will ever do so, or that it will lose its creeper-like power to entwine itself with reality, and disrupt it, and re-work it into new forms. When I returned to Zimbabwe for the first time after the war of independence, I went on an outing on horseback, with a professional guide, to view game near the Victoria Falls. On the dominating hill of the area was the burnt-out hulk of a tourist hotel which had been mortared and set on fire by guerillas operating across the river from Zambia. In due course we rode up to this ruin. It was deserted, apart from a few marauding warthogs. A strange feature of the roofless walls was that they were half-covered by squares of brown plastic, all with 'African-style' (Bushman-style, if anything) motifs in white stamped on their outer face: little stick-men and animals, dots in patterns, wavy lines. Many of the panels had fallen on the ground and lay in heaps, curling in on themselves; most were still stuck to the walls or in the process of slipping down from them. It was obvious that the whole job had been carried out, shoddily enough, after the building had been shelled and abandoned. What was it all about, I asked. Oh, said my guide, it had been done by some movie company. They'd come out to make a jungle picture about white hunters and black tribesmen and stuff like that. Some of the big scenes had been shot here. Roger Moore was the star. She couldn't remember the name of the picture. Could it have been one of the James Bonds?

I did not know. But I doubted it was a James Bond.

On the present visit I returned to the site. The bombed-out-hotel-become-lost-city-in-the-jungle had disappeared. In its place was a monstrously large, brand-new hotel, the only building in the neighbourhood truly destructive of the view when you look upstream, westward of the Falls. I dare say that that Roger Moore movie is sometimes available to guests through the in-house video system.*

To return to the real, the original, Great Zimbabwe. In his *A Tourist in Africa* (1963) Evelyn Waugh finally dismisses the Enclosure, despite all he admits to be impressive and enigmatic about it, as the 'Wrong Shape': the wrong shape especially for any conceivable act of worship. For my part, I have to confess that when I wrote an article about it many years ago for an American magazine, I devoted a paragraph or two to saying how sinister I had found it. This, I claimed, was because of the circularity of the Enclosure's walls and passageways, and the fact that you can never see very far once you are inside them. Being heavily under the influence of D.H. Lawrence at the time, I declared the structure to be serpentine, feminine, secretive, conspiratorial, and several other such adjectives.

To which on this visit my wife, herself Zimbabwean-born, made a belated but forthright reply. '*They* [her fellow-whites] always used to sneer at the Africans for not being able to draw straight lines. So how could they have doubted that the Africans built all this? There isn't a straight line in the place!'

These remarks were unlikely to endear her either to black or white in the 'new Zimbabwe'. But I could hardly deny the logic behind them. If everything a people has ever built out of reeds or

---

* See Chapter 21 below for the 'story behind the story' of *King Solomon's Mines* by Rider Haggard. The Sun City leisure and gambling complex north of Johannesburg has recently been enlarged by the indefatigable Mr Sol Kerzner to include a vast, purpose-built 'Lost-City'.

dagga or wood is circular in form – every hut, every kraal, every storage-place for grain – then why, once they have become rich and powerful enough to build fortresses and temples of stone, should they not carry on in the same style? And what is it that gives a twenty-two-year-old apprentice-writer from South Africa the right to declare the end result 'sinister', of all things?

So that settled that. Still, I soon had reason to revert to my original intuition about the place. We had hardly returned to the hotel from our first visit to the Enclosure when I was stricken with a stomach complaint. It kept me in bed most of the time we were there. It was not quite as virulent as the one which had laid M. low in Taung, but it was effective enough. Lying in my bed, or starting up to go to the bathroom and returning from it without having finished what I had gone there to do, I was haunted by a recollection of a passage from the Bible which (I was convinced) had an application to my illness. From time to time, whenever I felt well enough, I turned once again to the copy of the Bible provided by the Gideons, to see if I could find the verses mocking my half-fevered memory.

I came across a couple of 'possibles' (*And Joseph made haste; for his bowels did yearn* – Genesis 43:30; and, even better, *His meat in his bowels is turned . . . He hath swallowed down riches, and he shall vomit them up again* – Job 20:14–15). Yet I knew neither of these to be the passage I was looking for. They were too direct, somehow. The passage I wanted was both more subtle and more painfully accurate as to what was going on inside me.

It was not until I returned to England that I suddenly remembered what I had been looking for. True, the text needed a bit of amending; but I had not been mistaken about its applicability.

There are three things that are never satisfied, yea, four things say not, It is enough: The grave; and the barren womb; the earth that is not filled with water; and the fire . . . Proverbs 30:15–16.

Yea, five things say not, It is enough: the diarrhoetic bowel also.

On our last visit to the Enclosure, we were accompanied by Jane, a young Englishwoman whom we had met by chance in Masvingo. Stubby, dusty, bowed down by her back-pack, she was an intrepid, matter-of-fact creature, kitted out appropriately in every detail, from jeans and boots below to cropped hair, snub face, and doggedly tilted head above. She came from Nottinghamshire, where she worked as a secretary; she and her boy-friend had spent several months hitch-hiking from England across Europe and down Africa as far as Cape Town; then he had had to fly back to England because of the death of his father; now she was doing the reverse journey on her own, hitch-hiking still. She obviously did not see anything remarkable in this undertaking (though she admitted that she might 'cheat' by flying north from Nairobi, since the Sudan was closed because of the civil war, and conditions in Zaire were so hopeless it was impossible to cross). Anyway, she now had the first twelve hundred miles of the return journey behind her. She had spent the previous night at the South African–Zimbabwe border, sharing the cab of a lorry with its driver, because she had been held up by the queues there; her present plan was to spend the night at a camp-site near Great Zimbabwe and to make it to Harare the next day.

There was one other party of tourists, about a dozen of them, in the Enclosure that afternoon – young Italians who were zealously disobeying the notices posted up that requested visitors not to climb the walls. This so that they could photograph each other from improbable, comic angles. As we were leaving, a solitary, barefoot boy who had been longingly watching them jumped up in front of M. 'Please photo me, madam,' he politely requested her. He wore the standard garb of the Zimbabwean urchin: shorts too big for him, tattered shirt. But she could not oblige as none of us was carrying a camera. Eastwards there stretched some acres of excavated walls; further still were extensive tilted sheets of granite, wonderfully warm underfoot, on which were scattered the mud-and-thatch huts of an African 'village'. Presumably they had been constructed to give visitors an idea of how most of the inhabitants had lived at the time of Great Zimbabwe's efflorescence. The huts were empty, except for one which had three boys sitting outside it. Immediately we appeared they began beating on traditional drums of wood and hide. We drew nearer. In the darkness of the hut's interior sat an elderly African healer or *nganga*, cross-legged on a reed mat. ('Witch-doctor', in old-style, colonial parlance.) Around his head he wore fur; around his neck beads; around his ankles seed pods; around his loins a skirt of animal-skin. Spread in front of him were the tools of his trade: bundles of twigs and herbs, knuckle bones, stones of special shape and colour; bits of dried entrail; small, unidentifiable bottles of liquid or powdered *muti*.

His features were impossible to make out in the gloom but his gestures of welcome were unmistakable; so was his diviner's eye for the tourist trade. While we hesitated another small party of white tourists (South Africans, to judge from their accents) appeared and promptly entered the hut. The drumming ceased. The South Africans – there were enough of them to fill the hut – sat down docilely in front of the healer. He produced a *mbira* (a hand-held thumb-piano) and began playing on it, while chanting repetitively in Shona. A third party of visitors, a group of middle-class Africans, was now drawn to the hut by the music. They stood with us on the outside looking in, displaying in equal parts curiosity, pleasure, and embarrassment at what was afoot. When the healer began catechizing the people in front of him (in English), his voice and theirs were unfortunately too low for me to hear what they were saying. But I was struck with the earnestness of everyone involved, white and black alike. It was obvious that some serious healing would shortly be taking place.

By the time we returned to the Enclosure the sun was setting. A solitary monkey sat on one of the walls, silhouetted like a sentinel. I wondered and still wonder why the stones of Great Zimbabwe should in that light have been so strongly blue in colour – as blue as the eyes of a blue-eyed person – when the inside of the granite one sees in such profusion in Zimbabwe is always brown, creamy, black, every shade of grey; but never blue. Never. It is as if the builders' stones have been able to take *into* themselves something of the distinctively African haze and hue of distance.

Jane could not afford to stay at an hotel; she was anxious to reach before sunset a camp site she had heard about on Lake Kyle nearby. So we drove her down a tarred road that wound for miles

through the bush. It was empty but for the occasional woman
walking indomitably into the dusk, always with a great bundle on
her head. The first two camp sites we passed were deserted: hardly
surprisingly, for Lake Kyle had been turned by the drought into a
vast bowl of dried-out clay. We saw just two stretches of water in it
– positively puddle-like, they were, compared with the dimensions
of the meandering valley which the lake is supposed to fill. From
time to time we passed jetties stuck into space, some thirty feet
above the tormented-looking earth that should have been deep
under water. The whole thing was like a mutilation, not a lake.

Eventually we found a site which appeared to be slightly
inhabited; at any rate an electric light was burning in one of the
small buildings near the gate and a couple of cars were parked
under trees. We waited until Jane came out to collect her pack and
assure us that everything was OK.

We had passengers on the way back too. We picked up two
young women who were walking the many miles to the main road
to Masvingo. One of them said that her name was Amnitzia; then
she spelled it out to make it easier for us to pronounce.

What did it mean?

Modest laughter: 'Trouble.'

'Is that what your mother thought about you?'

'It actually means "Troubled".'

'You are Troubled?'

'Yes, that is what it means.'

'And is that how you feel?'

Amnitzia (bringing hand to bosom): 'Deep in myself here, it is.'

D.J. (like some oily, compassionate 'counsellor'): 'I think we all
feel troubled sometimes.'

Amnitzia's friend (hitherto silent, suddenly moved to speak up
loudly and firmly): 'I don't.'

M. and I, having parted in Mafikeng, had met up again in Harare;
from there we had flown straight down to Masvingo. A consequence
of having made this arrangement was that we would be compelled
for a while to follow the road to the north in a circuitous, not to

say arsy-versy, fashion. This did not bother me, since here in Zimbabwe the road no longer marched directly towards it unattainable end.

Masvingo (Fort Victoria) had been the first halt made by the Pioneer column after it had come up from Bechuanaland and ascended on to the central plateau of present-day Zimbabwe. For M., rather more importantly, it was also the site of her earliest memories. She had lived there between her second and seventh years, when her father had been headmaster of the local school and warden of its hostel. So she had some visits to pay – not to people, for she knew no one who would have remembered her or her parents being there, but to places in the town and outside it.

The hostel was still standing: a handsome building with tall windows, an arched entrance, and two pedimented gables at either end, under the inevitable iron roof. It was little changed from her memories of it. Its grounds were all bare sand interspersed with trees, apart from a patch of green grass around a leaking tap. That little patch had once been a favourite place of hers, for the playing of her solitary games. Then it had been forgotten; or so she would have supposed. Now, seeing it again, rediscovering it, the grass still drawing its sustenance from the same leaking standpipe, still stuck in the earth at the same angle, she was overwhelmed by the intensity of the memories it released in her after so many decades. Whole and unsullied those memories were, distorted not at all by the strains, the manipulations, the anecdotalizing, to which we inevitably subject all the memories we are conscious of preserving.

As I am doing here, writing this book.

Masvingo has some other modestly handsome buildings: among them the conical towers of the fort originally built by the Pioneers; the government offices nearby; and the old hotel (now housing a little museum). But it is a bleak-looking place, on the whole, and I doubt we would have spent the time we did in it if M. had not a special reason for doing so.

Then we set out for Bulawayo, Zimbabwe's second city, which I knew to be of special importance to the story I am trying to tell.

The same went for the city's hinterland to the north and south. *En route* we passed many mines bearing names of the kind invariably attached to such places: Fred Mine, Epoch Mine, Echo Mine, Marvel Mine, Nil Desperandum. The veld was wearing its sullen drought-garb of black, pale brown, and black again. The river-beds had not a drop of water in them: only boulders. The most vivid colour everywhere was that of the sunlight itself, which had a curiously hot, buttery yellowness to it; something I think of as distinctive to Zimbabwe. It is as much a texture as a hue, and I have seen it nowhere else.

Right on top of the town of Zvishavani we came to much the biggest mine of all. It is an asbestos mine, though you would not know this when you drive up to it, for it has no sign to give it a name or declare its ownership. We were not fooled, however, since we have friends who come from Zvishavani. Above ground, the plant consists of a single, sealed, oblong building about ten storeys high, made from top to bottom of identical steel sections clamped together. There is not a window, not an aperture of any kind in it. Behind this forbidding structure is a great heap of tailings on which conveyors are constantly at work; in front of it an incomprehensible notice:

ITEMS NOT PERMITTED TO PASS THROUGH SECURITY GATES:
CARDBOARD CIGARETTE BOXES
MATCHES AND MATCHBOXES
NEWSPAPERS NONTECHNICAL PERIODICALS ETC
PLASTIC OR PLASTIC WRAPPED SANDWICHES SWEETS ETC
MEALIE COBS SUGAR CANE UNSHELLED COCONUTS ETC
ANY DISPOSABLE CONTAINER
PLASTIC MILK/LACTO PACKETS
ANY OTHER ITEM DEEMED AS A CONTAMINANT

Unlike the asbestos mines in South Africa, this one was working full-tilt. Needless to say, my car was 'deemed as a contaminant' and we were not allowed by the security guards to pass through the gates. Before they told me (quite politely) to clear off, I had the chance of seeing dusty workers in overalls and helmets from one shift knocking off; and others, less dusty, going through the gates to begin their stint.

Zimbabwe is a strange place. Two of the items of export most crucial to its economy – asbestos and tobacco – are poisons. Both products are also used openly, flagrantly, patriotically, in every corner of the country. In Bulawayo someone told me that the exports of asbestos go mostly to 'various Third World places'. After a pause, and with a slight smile, he added, 'The same is true of the tobacco, actually.' Another pause. No smile. A slight air of defiance. 'Anyway, Zimbabwe asbestos is the white variety, not the blue, like you get in the Cape. It's much less harmful to people.'

☆

Some Universal Rules – The Ndebele Road Northward – Inyati – Robert Moffat's Last Appearance

Not only were the Shona unworthy inheritors, in the eyes of the British colonists, of the mysteries and splendours of Great Zimbabwe; they were not even masters of the territories they occupied. In effect those in the southern and central regions of the country were vassals and tributaries of a more powerful and warlike tribe to the west, the Ndebele (Matabele). And how ancient, how well founded, was the claim of the Ndebele to the land and to their hegemony over the Shona? Was it any better than that of the white newcomers? Hardly. The Ndebele were also new arrivals, interlopers from the south, who had conquered their country just a few decades before Rhodes's Pioneers took it over.

This litany of claim and counter-claim was always of great importance to the white Rhodesians. From the moment of the Pioneers' arrival (in 1890) to the final extinction of 'Rhodesia' itself (in 1980), they recited it to each other and to visitors from abroad. Even today one can still hear it being intoned by some 'Old Rhodies' – a term applied to those whites who continue to live in Zimbabwe but hanker incessantly after the days when they ran the show and both Shona and Ndebele acknowledged their supremacy. It is not that they believe anyone will attend to their claims now or will give back to them the position they once held; the litany has become an act of mourning rather than an assertion of right.

Listening to them, and to representatives of the various other tribes I met at different places on this journey, I was sometimes driven to wish that tablets of bronze – or asbestos – bearing the following message could be placed along every national, ethnic, and tribal border in the world, and at every crossroads where mixed communities are temporarily living at peace:

NO GROUP'S CLAIM TO THE TERRITORY IT INHABITS IS MORALLY SUPERIOR TO ANY OTHER'S

EVERY GROUP ON EARTH WILL BELIEVE ITSELF TO BE AN EXCEPTION TO THIS RULE

NO GROUP THAT HAS LOST A PIECE OF TERRITORY IT ONCE HELD, AND IS STILL CONSCIOUS OF ITSELF AS A GROUP, WILL EVER GIVE UP ITS CLAIM TO WHAT HAS BEEN LOST

HOW DO YOU MAKE SENSE OF THIS?

DON'T TRY

Today's victors in Zimbabwe, anyway, are the Shona, who have become its politically dominant group. (Economically speaking, they have yet to displace the greatly shrunken number of whites who remain. Before independence 250,000 whites lived in the country; the figure now is barely a quarter of that.) In earlier years the Shona-speaking peoples were despised by Ndebele and white settler alike: an attitude the members of neither group can now afford to adopt. The Shona have achieved their position by outbreeding the Ndebele; by showing a greater ardour for education than their rivals; and by realizing that the power of modern weaponry would ultimately enable a larger group to defeat a smaller, provided the disproportion in numbers was great enough. All they had to do was to get the guns – which in the 1970s the Soviet Union, then at the height of its own era of colonial pretension, was happy to supply – and thereafter to hold on, to keep on fighting. Together with the Ndebele, the seven or eight million of them would sooner or later grind down the obduracy of a quarter of a million whites: especially if the latter were to be abandoned (as they were in due course) by the 'home' government in London, by the Portuguese in

Mozambique, and by the Afrikaner government in Pretoria. Then they would have the chance to deal with the Ndebele too.

Which, in the first few years after independence, they did. With a vengeance. And with the help of a cadre of instructors from communist North Korea.

During the earlier years of the nineteenth century the Ndebele had succeeded in hacking out their own northbound road from South Africa. Hailing originally from Natal on the east coast of South Africa, they had been nothing more than a minor Zulu clan, subordinate to the tyrant Chaka. In the 1820s Chaka was in the process of uniting various scattered groups into what soon became a scourge to his black neighbours and the most formidable indigenous power Boer or Briton ever confronted in southern Africa. Mzilikazi, chief of the Ndebele, fell out with Chaka over the division of spoils after a raid; whereupon, sensibly enough, he took to his heels. Making off in a north-westerly direction, he carried with him a few hundred warriors and the tactics, weaponry, social organization, and military ethos developed by Chaka. The members of this fugitive but ferocious group first tried to make themselves secure in the Magaliesberg mountains, near where Johannesburg now stands; from there they were driven further west by the Boers; later they clashed with the Griquas. Slowly, gathering strength as they went, driving their stolen cattle ahead of them and absorbing into their own people more and more of the women and children they captured (from the Tswana especially, whom they pushed deeper towards the Kalahari Desert), the Ndebele made their way north. In the last stages of their journey they travelled more or less along the line of what later became the missionary road. Finally they crossed the Limpopo River, settled in the south-western corner of Zimbabwe, near the present-day city of Bulawayo, subjugated the Shona and kept them subjugated, constantly threatened the northernmost groups of Tswana (Khama the Good among them – hence his especial display of Goodness when the British missionaries arrived), successfully repelled another Boer assault, and settled down to the life of inter-mittent agriculture and intensive cattle-raiding that suited them best.

While still in the Transvaal, Mzilikazi had twice been visited by Robert Moffat; as a result he had formed a deep yet impenetrable attachment to the missionary. Unlike Khama, Mzilikazi showed no inclination whatever to listen to missionary preachings, or to permit any of his people to do so, but he greatly valued Moffat's visits and treated him with courtesy and affection. Once he and his people had established themselves in the Bulawayo district, Moffat visited them again. In all he went there three times. The first journey (in 1854) was a holiday of sorts, taken after he had completed his labours on the Tswana translation of the Bible. He also carried with him supplies for his son-in-law, David Livingstone, many hundreds of miles away on the westbound leg of his first trans-African journey. (More than a year later the depot of supplies was duly found by Livingstone, by then on his way eastwards.) I suspect that the timing of the visit also had something to do with a successful embassy the Boers of the Transvaal had sent to Mzilikazi the previous year, though no mention of this motive is made either in Moffat's *Journals* or in the biographies of him or Mary Moffat that I have read.* His second journey (in 1857) was made in order to ask the chief's permission for missionaries to work among the Ndebele – which request Mzilikazi, with many misgivings, agreed to. Two years later, Moffat came yet again, this time to help his son John Smith Moffat, John's wife Emily, and two other missionaries and their wives found the station.

Every missionary group sent to southern Africa by the London Missionary Society had to endure much hardship and disappointment. The members of the various groups often made things worse by quarrelling among themselves. The mission to the Ndebele set new records for hopelessness in both these respects. Established in 1859 at a place called Inyati, about forty miles to the north-east of Bulawayo, the mission could boast twenty-eight years later of

* On the way to Bulawayo Moffat passed the time by reading *Uncle Tom's Cabin*. It moved him to tears – 'bleered een', as he puts it. 'It makes one melancholy – the inevitable evils of the lot of man ... The horrors of slavery are awful beyond description. Poor afflicted Africa!' (*The Matabele Journals*).

having made a total of two converts.* Isolated, gnawed by a sense of failure, their morals and sensibilities constantly outraged by the ferocity of Ndebele customs and the indifference of the Ndebele to the message brought to them, the three missionaries and the two wives who survived fell out among themselves to an unprecedented degree. A scholarly argument about how best to reduce the Ndebele language to written form seems to have generated particularly violent animosities among them. Eventually they stopped speaking to each other. Living in cottages a stone's throw apart, in a valley carefully chosen for them by Mzilikazi precisely because of its isolation from the mass of the Ndebele people, with their nearest fellow-missionaries two or three weeks away by ox-wagon, the members of the group took to communicating with one another by letter only. ('We think we may be excused if we express our contempt for such an imputation.' 'I must tell you candidly that some of your letters are most insulting.') They also went to the trouble of making copies of the lengthy reproaches they exchanged, which they sent back to the head office in London, so that the officials there would be able to appreciate how justified each of them was in his complaints against the others.†

M. and I were taken to Inyati by a direct descendant of one of the

---

* The figure is given in Northcutt's biography. However, the French Protestant missionary François Coillard wrote in 1878 that *not one* (his italics) convert had yet been made. (Letter reprinted in his book, *On the Threshold of Central Africa*, 1897.) On this subject the letters of the Inyati missionaries themselves have their own dismal eloquence: 'How satisfying and encouraging would it be to see even one converted! That longed-for and promised blessing has been delayed,' wrote the Reverend Thomas Thomas, three years after his arrival (23 September 1862). A year later (3 August 1863) William Sykes complained that his sermons were greeted by such congregations as he could muster with a philistine shout of 'Give us porridge!'. Eight years later (15 May 1870) John Scott Moffat exclaimed pathetically – and bathetically – to his superiors, 'What a smouldering heap of dust and ashes must our African missions appear to you, engaged as you are in fanning the splendid conflagration in Madagascar.'

† The only copy of this internal (or internecine) correspondence that has survived is in the British Library. In *The Rulers of Rhodesia* (1968), Oliver Ransford suggests that 'perhaps . . . the others were deliberately destroyed'. The sentences quoted in the text are from Ransford's book; those in the previous footnote are taken from the LMS archive.

original founders of the station. We travelled there in a bronze-coloured Mercedes. Once the outskirts of Bulawayo were behind us we encountered little enough traffic, apart from an occasional overloaded bus that threw up thick dust interspersed with sharp stones as it careened along. Where the people crammed into the buses had come from was a mystery, since scarcely a habitation was to be seen. The blank flatness and emptiness of the terrain and its copious supplies of thorn scrub were reminiscent of Botswana, rather than of the spectacularly varied landscapes of Zimbabwe. At intervals along the road were some defunct gold mines, once quite large operations obviously, now depopulated, watched over only by two or three bored-looking guards with many acres of barbed-wire to patrol. Behind the wire – what treasures remained for them to protect? Tailings from the mine, rusting machinery, overhead cables, clusters of iron-roofed cottages of the kind to be seen on such sites all over southern Africa. Intended as living quarters for the lucky white staff, not the black, their roofs wincing and winking in the sunlight, they were about twelve feet high, and equipped with splintered windows, a garden of scratches in the sand, and something broken nearby. A car, it might be, or a set of bed-springs. The barracks for the blacks, in long rows, were at the back.

Opposite the gate to each of these mines was a store huddled behind its Coca-Cola sign and iron-barred windows: evidently still open, after a fashion. Who ran such stores, I asked. 'Oh, blacks – now,' came the answer. 'In the old days it was different. They all used to be owned by whites. When I was a young man, working as a commercial traveller – on the road, you know – I'd go and have a cup of tea with —' And he pointed at the particular shop we were passing, and said a name with all the intimacy of those bygone years; even with an odd, wholly unconscious confidence that it would be meaningful to me.

Jimmy Macpherson, it might have been. Roddy Campbell. Something Scottish, anyway.

The name went out of my mind immediately; but not the tone of driver's voice. He was a thickset man in his fifties; his hair, still

dark, was brushed back smoothly, close to his head; his skin too
was smooth, though it had been burned by the sun to the colour of
varnished pine. For all the weight and sombreness that middle age
had imposed on his face, you could still see in it the lineaments of
the boy he must once have been: he had a boy's wide brow and
warily ingenuous eyes. He was generous of his time and effort with
us, partly because it came naturally to him to be so, and also
because he was eager to share with us the pride he felt in his
ancestry. (He had a full generation's advantage, in terms of descent,
over those 'aristocrats' who went back as far as the Pioneer
column, merely.) Not only was he knowledgeable about the ramify-
ing inbreedings and outbreedings of the original missionaries'
descendants; it soon transpired that he knew a good deal about the
history of the mission itself. It was from him, for instance, that I
first heard of the exchanges of letters between the missionaries after
they had fallen out with one another.

In some ways, though, his intimate connections with the country,
the generations in it which he could trace behind him, made more
acute his incredulity that it was no longer 'his'; no longer 'ours'. It
was twelve years since the Republic of Zimbabwe had come into
existence, longer still since the whites had effectively lost the ten-
year war they had fought to maintain their position. But he was
like a man who that very morning, on getting out of bed, had seen
the sun rise in the west or water suddenly begin to flow uphill. Had
it really happened? Would it do it again tomorrow? How could
such things take place?

'When *they* took over, it was as if we'd been suddenly moved to
a foreign country,' a cousin of M.'s had said to us a few days
before. 'That's how we live now. We just had to get used to it.
There was nothing else we could do.'

The trouble was that she and her husband had been born in this
'foreign country'; they had lived in it with a village-like feeling of
intimacy and familiarity (their community being so small) and the
self-assurance of a master-race (the blacks apparently being so
submissive, and so little educated in the skills and technologies of
which the whites were convinced they would always be sole posses-

sors). The landscapes around them were exactly as they had been
before; they lived in the same house and held down the same jobs.
But everything was changed, vitiated: their community dismembered;
their monopoly of privilege lost; upstart strangers in charge, who
had to be treated with caution and politeness if you wanted to keep
out of trouble.

Where had it all gone wrong? Whose fault was it?

'The African,' our present guide had said flatly, before setting out to
drive us to Inyati, 'has never done a thing for Africa. Whatever you
see here is the white man's doing. They didn't have the wheel, they
couldn't write, they had nothing.'

'They have no *culture*,' his wife chimed in. As if to prove the
point she showed me a document written and privately printed in
the 1890s by one of her husband's missionary forebears. Half-
memoir, half-sermon, it stated roundly that 'in his natural state . . .
the adult Matabele seeks only to settle down to a life of inactivity,
laziness, and uselessness'. Fortunately, it went on, without any
irony, the coming of the whites had brought about great changes,
since 'the natives are now free to work for the white man and to
wear clothes'.

The author of that document had obviously had no problems in
drafting and publicizing his views. His descendants, on the other
hand, could express theirs only in private. That same morning, as it
happened, I had come across a contemporary document from the
other side: a report by a journalist named Pikirayi Deketete in the
Sunday Mail, which had a bearing on these topics. It was headlined
ZIMBABWEAN CULTURE AS YET NOT VISIBLE. In it
the author made the following complaint:

Twelve years after independence Zimbabwe does not have a clear national
culture as the grip of Westernization increases its hold. Even after all these
years, the country's legislative assembly, the courts, education, and economy
still remain Westernized with no clear thrust to promote the country's culture
. . . The teaching in schools is conducted in the English medium with
emphasis being put on speaking 'like the English' without a trace of
vernacular. Children of middle and upper-class Zimbabweans attend creches
which emphasize on [*sic*] the English medium. These parents also converse

with their children in English at home, further alienating them from their mother languages and cultural values and norms.

Deketete did not make any proposals in his article as to how this process could be reversed; nor, apart from mentioning dancing, music, and Zimbabwean achievements in soapstone sculpture, did he manage to suggest what a 'clear national culture' might look like. (He nowhere remarked on the fact that his article was itself written in English.) He did, however, correctly in my view, cite as yet another example of 'Westernization' the hideous national memorial at Heroes' Acre, in Harare, which was designed and constructed in shamelessly Stalinist style by President Mugabe's North Korean allies.

Of Heroes' Acre, more later. For the moment here we are at Inyati, the site of yet another mission station. Another cemetery. More graves in the sand. IN REMEMBRANCE OF ANNE, THE BELOVED WIFE OF THE REV. THOMAS THOMAS, MISSIONARY TO THE MATABELE. SHE DIED AT INYATI JUNE 16TH 1862 AGED 16 YEARS. SHE IS NOT DEAD BUT SLEEPETH. ALSO OF ANNE MARY, DAUGHTER OF THE ABOVE, WHO DIED JUNE 7TH 1862 AGED TWO MONTHS. In my room in Bulawayo, I know, there is a transcription into one of my notebooks of the letter in which the Reverend Thomas Thomas had informed the Society's directors of his wife's death. I had copied out the letter in London because it had touched me, not because I had then expected to see her gravestone. 'When treading the verge of Jordan,' he wrote, 'though conscious her dissolution was at hand, she was calm, and even cheerful.'

Of Jordan's waters there is no sign where she lies. The reddish soil of the cemetery and of the denuded acres around it could hardly be more parched. Even compared with what I have seen elsewhere of the effects of the two-year drought, Inyati looks especially desolate: wholly in thrall to the tyrant in the sky, that global Chaka or Mzilikazi gazing steadily down on us. There is scarcely a blade of grass to be seen; the trees, not all of them thorn by any means, have gone black and brittle or have lost their bark entirely and turned into scarred, greyish ghosts of themselves.

Yet the place is as calm as the Reverend Thomas Thomas would have wished it to be; it is even unexpectedly cheerful, after a fashion. Seated in the shade just outside the battered brick wall that runs around the cemetery is a group of four elderly men. Apparently they are engaged in repairing the wall and cutting down one of the trees that threaten to topple a section of it. They are pleased to see us and engage in an animated conversation in Ndebele with our guide – who in this company and in that language suddenly reveals an affability and fluency hitherto hidden from us. It is as if only now, standing on the ground in which the bones of several of his ancestors lie (SACRED TO THE MEMORY OF THE REV. W. SYKES OF THE LONDON MISSIONARY SOCIETY, BORN IN MIRFIELD YORKSHIRE MARCH 13TH 1829, DIED AT INYATI JULY 22ND 1897, WHO LABOURED FOR TWENTY-NINE YEARS AS A PIONEER MISSIONARY AMONG THE MATABELE. 'HE WENT FORTH AS A SOWER TO SOW') – it is only now, speaking to the workmen and translating their words for us, that his relationship with the country, his sharing of it with them, appears to be a source of strength and comfort rather than of bewilderment and anger.

One of the workmen wears a ceremonially tattered, bright red boiler suit; another has passed pieces of string through holes in the brim on both sides of an ancient felt hat, and then tied the strings tightly under his chin, thus pulling the brim over his ears, as if in a mad parody of a Victorian bonnet. Within it a two-toothed smile and a beard of little white whorls can be seen. The others smile too; they tell him how long it is since they have last seen any rain; they say that they are doing the work for 'the government'; they say also that nobody ever comes to visit the cemetery. Then one adds, 'Except sometimes for burying.' The thought of this exception arouses much mirth among them, as if, their age notwithstanding, they have secured a permanent immunity from such a thing ever happening to themselves.

On the other side of the wall, indiscriminately scattered in the hot, red sand, are graves of all kinds and of a variety of dates. A whole team of tiny Sykeses from the earliest years of the settlement. The recent, gleaming tombstone of a black pastor, Mzingaye Dube, dead in his mid-thirties. A flaking monumental column, surmounted by a cross, erected to the memory of four members of the Matabeleland Mounted Police 'murdered by natives in March 1896 in this district'. Most of the graves, though, are marked not by names but by the broken utensils put on them, in the traditional Ndebele manner, to serve the departed soul on the other side: tin wash-basins, clay pots, mugs, aluminium pans, a carved knobkierie. Yet further down the slope are the barely discernible remains of the original mission houses and church, each marked by a bronze tablet set in a stone plinth. One of them reads 'Brighton Cottage: Occupied by John and Emily Smith Moffat.'

Even at a distance we can hear the chipping noises and the soft conversation of the old men, who have now gone back to their work on the cemetery wall.

Strictly speaking, Inyati was the terminus of the missionary road as such: the road which had been pioneered northwards from Griquatown by the emissaries of the London Missionary Society, and which remained peculiarly in their charge for the next eighty years or so. (At one time Mzilikazi would allow no white to enter his territories who did not approach through Kuruman – that is, through the good offices of his friend Moffat.) Of course the Society's and many other missionaries of different denominations went further north still, beyond Inyati, and eventually spread their stations all over Zimbabwe and Zambia. But they did so under different conditions, circumstances, and auspices from before. The greatest difference was that previously, as the members of the Society had come up the missionary road, they had tried to defend the peoples they were evangelizing against the advancing colonists – against the Boers especially, but often enough against the Cape Colonial government too; not to mention their resistance to Rhodes's takeover bid for the whole of Bechuanaland. It was not that the missionaries were anti-imperialist. Anything but. Their complaint was that the imperial government was all too ready to leave everything to be sorted out by the white men on the spot; people who, in missionary eyes, had nothing in mind but the grabbing of land and the dispossession and enslavement of the native peoples.

But here in Inyati an open alliance between the interests of the local missionaries and the colonizers finally declared itself. There was nothing new in the fact that the presence of the mission made it much easier for other whites – hunters, traders, prospectors, concession-seekers, crooks, and con men – to enter the country. The difference here was that the missionaries actively schemed and openly propagandized for the destruction of the Ndebele kingdom at the hands of the colonists. John Smith Moffat, having left the service of the Society and entered that of the administration of Bechuanaland, virtually became one of Rhodes's agents in his dealings with Mzilikazi's heir. Another still-serving missionary was a crucial go-between in the negotiations which led to the vital concession of mining rights to Rhodes and his friends – a concession from which the occupation of the entire country inevitably followed. Another missionary hailed the subsequent granting of the royal charter to the British South Africa Company 'as a God-sent deliverer'. 'Indeed,' he went on, 'it is not difficult to see the hand of God in this whole business, and we are devoutly thankful for the turn events are taking.' Yet another 'remarked with satisfaction that God was about to "speak in a very different manner" to the Matabele than his LMS emissaries had been constrained to adopt'.

Why so great a difference here? The reason is plain. It is to be found in the power of the Ndebele. Their contempt for the missionaries' message. The fear that they inspired in their subject peoples. As the historian from whom I have taken the above quotations puts it: 'In Matabeleland it was total missionary failure which led to the vision of the Chartered Company as an instrument of God to crush the Matabele and provide missionary access to a haughty warrior nation.'

After a further quarter-mile of dust and thorn, interspersed by a

shed-like church, some teachers' houses, and a hostel or two, we
came to Inyati school. Low and shed-like too, the school buildings
were placed around a quadrangle adorned with jacaranda trees. In
the middle of the quad a Zimbabwean flag drooped from a flagstaff,
as if the heat were too much for it.

No one was to be seen. The place was silent. We sat in the car,
uncertain what to do next. Then a door in one of the buildings
opened. Out of it came a man dressed in a dark suit. He was
carrying a white plastic bag and had a piece of paper pinned to the
lapel of his jacket. He was followed by another, also suited, also
labelled, carrying an identical plastic bag. Then another, and
another, and another. Five of them, ten, fifteen – some talking,
most silent, all male, all uninterested in us. They went around a
corner and disappeared. The sound of their voices vanished. They
had come and gone like a hallucination. I got out of the car to see
what had happened to them, at which point yet another man,
identically accoutred to all the others, came through the open door.
He said, 'You look for –?'

Printed on his plastic bag, in letters of black and red, were the
words, 'Zimbabwe National Census'.

A few minutes later we were sitting in as dusty and cluttered an
office as I have been in. Everything in it had a beaten-about look:
the chairs we sat on, the splintered shelves piled with books (also
splintered, spineless, coverless), the desk laden with stacks of paper,
the bare floorboards under our feet. A wooden armorial shield,
buckled by the heat, leaned against a wall; it bore several smaller,
tarnished shields of silver-gilt with names and dates engraved on
them. For some reason a number of sewing machines were pushed
into a corner on the floor. Perhaps they had been brought there to
prevent them being stolen during the vacation.

Opposite us, behind his desk, sat the headmaster of the school: a
large man, with a headmaster's high shoulders, big head, big hands,
and deep voice. What he lacked, though, and was conscious of
lacking, was an adequate command of English. It was impossible to
listen to him and not to think what a blessing and a curse the
language was to people like himself, or like Mr Diketete of the

Sunday Mail, who were struggling to assert themselves as masters in their own country. They could not do without English. It opened up the world to them. But it also made it hard of access. Look at the schoolchildren who had to learn subjects like mathematics and biology in a tongue that was foreign both to them and their teachers – as if those subjects were not hard enough anyway! And where did this leave the languages which were immemorially theirs, yet whose written tradition went no further back than the Inyati mission itself?

The headmaster explained that we had seen the end of a 'training seminar' for census-takers; the group would be assembling again in the afternoon for a further session. The national census was due to take place in ten days' time; so many teachers had volunteered to become census-takers that the school holidays had been extended by two weeks to enable the count to proceed.* He also told us that though the school had been started by the missionaries 'many years ago', it had been taken over by the government after independence. 'I work for the Education Department.' Still, he was gratifyingly impressed to hear of our guide's connection with the founders of the mission and the school. So impressed, in fact, that he promptly invited him to attend a prize-giving during the coming term. The visitor politely accepted the invitation, though I doubt he had any intention of again going over that road for the sake of a school prize-giving.

Above the door there hung a small, cracked reproduction of the famous Baxter print of Robert Moffat as a young man. Beardless, waistcoated, cravatted, half-smiling, he stood with one hand holding his hat and the other at his midriff, rocks in the foreground, nameless trees behind him, and some all-purpose, naked savages in

---

* Later, in Harare, M. and I filled in the census forms we were given. The distribution and collection of forms appeared to have been carried out efficiently. Some of the questions asked of her, in particular, had a grim, Third World note of realism to them – for example, 'Have you ever given birth? If yes, number of children born alive? How many boys are still alive? How many girls are still alive? How many boys have died? How many girls have died? State age at first live birth. Was it male or female? Is the child still alive?'

distinctly un-African headgear sitting around a fire and gesticulating at more of their own kind in the distance. Still further back, huts, goats, hills. I made some remark about the picture, assuming that the headmaster would know who it portrayed. But he did not. It had been hanging there when he had come to the school, he said, and no one had ever told him anything about it. He had often wondered why it was there, who 'it did show'.

So I broke the news to him that it was a portrait of Robert Moffat, Mzilikazi's friend, the man who had been given the ground here at Inyati to establish the mission and its school.

'Him?' the headmaster exclaimed, hand to jaw, looking up at the picture. 'I have a picture of that important man in my office?'

He opened one of the many exercise books lying about on his desk, flattened it along the margin with a thumbnail, and wrote in pencil on the top of the page: 'Picture of Robert Moffat.'

Indeed, I had come to the end of the road.

☆

CHAPTER TWENTY-ONE

Rhodes's End and Lobengula's – The Matopos Hills – The Destruction of the Ndebele – King Solomon's Mines – The Bulawayo Club

Many roads, I found, ended in or near Bulawayo. It was impossible for me to visit the remains of one of the kraals of Lobengula, Mzilikazi's son, last king of the Ndebele, and not feel that a road had ended there. (Even if Lobengula's death came later, beyond the Shangani River, in flight from pursuing imperial and colonial troops.) The same applied to the grandiose spot in the Matopos Hills which Rhodes selected for the site of his own grave. And what of the moment when, wandering into a waste space behind the Bulawayo Museum, I suddenly found myself on level terms with the humiliated, de-plinthed statue of Rhodes that had once dominated the city's main thoroughfare?

Now it stood amid heaps of rubble and gardening equipment. It faced from a yard away the equally stranded, disproportionate figure of Charles Coghlan, the long-forgotten first Prime Minister of Rhodesia. Like Rhodes, Coghlan had emerged from Kimberley and then gone north. The two of them, cast in bronze and designed to be looked at from below, now gazed at one another with the loathing we feel only for those who have witnessed our humiliation.

Later, in Harare, I was to find yet another jacked-down, de-sacralized statue of Rhodes. This one had been put behind the National Archive, in a discreet if slightly less ignominious position than the effigy behind the Bulawayo Museum. Previously it had stood at the very centre of the city's central square – known then as Cecil Square (what else?), now dubbed African Unity Square (what else?). No longer gazing north, the statue looks instead at a nearby brick wall, like a chastised schoolchild.

Here is what two of the greatest writers of his time had to say about Rhodes. First, Mark Twain in *More Tramps Abroad*, which was published in 1898, four years before Rhodes's death:

I know quite well that whether Mr Rhodes is the lofty and worshipful patriot and statesman that multitudes believe him to be, or Satan come again, as the rest of the world account him, he is still the most imposing figure in the British Empire outside England. When he stands on the Cape of Good Hope his shadow falls on the Zambesi. He is the only colonial in the British dominions whose goings and comings are chronicled and discussed under all the globe's meridians, and whose speeches, unclipped, are cabled from the end of the earth; and he is the only unroyal outsider whose arrival in London can compete for attention with an eclipse . . .

What is the secret of his formidable supremacy? One says it is his prodigious wealth – whose drippings in salaries and in other ways support multitudes and make them his interested and loyal vassals; another says it is his personal magnetism and his persuasive tongue, and that these hypnotize and make happy slaves of all that drift within the circle of their influence; another says it is his majestic ideas, his vast schemes for the territorial aggrandisement of England, his patriotic and unselfish ambition to spread her beneficent protection and her just rule over the pagan wastes of Africa and make luminous the African darkness with the glory of her name; and another says that he wants it for his own, and that the belief that he will get it and let his friends in on the ground floor is *the* secret that rivets so many eyes upon him and keeps him in the zenith where the view is unobstructed . . .

He raids and robs and slays and enslaves the Matabele, and gets worlds of Charter-Christian applause for it . . . He has done everything he could think of to pull himself down to the ground; yet there he stands, to this day, upon his dizzy summit under the dome of the sky, an apparent permanency, the marvel of the time, the mystery of the age . . .

I admire him, I frankly confess it; and when his time comes I shall buy a piece of the rope for a keepsake.

Actually Rhodes died of heart-failure. Rudyard Kipling was his house-guest in Cape Town at the time, and he immediately wrote a poem, 'The Burial', to be read at the funeral in the Matopos Hills. It is the Matopos that he refers to below as 'The granite of the ancient North':

> It is his will that he look forth
>   Across the world he won –
> The granite of the ancient North –
>   Great spaces washed with sun.
> There shall he patient take his seat
>   (As when the Death he dared),
> And there await a people's feet
>   In the paths that he prepared.
>
> There, till the vision he foresaw
>   Splendid and whole arise,
> And unimagined Empires draw
>   To council 'neath his skies,
> The immense and brooding Spirit still
>   Shall quicken and control.
> Living he was the land, and dead,
>   His soul shall be her soul!*

The round boulders poised on the granite slope look as if they have been left there in the middle of an unimaginable game – the marbles or bowls of a race of giants. Some of the boulders are as big as rooms, others hardly smaller; all are so casually disposed you feel you could roll them downhill with a single push of your hand. They are mostly a brownish-orange in hue, or seem so at first. Then the light shifts or you look at the rock more closely, and you see its innumerable lichen-tinted shades: ochre-reds that fade to rust and russet; dark greens turning black; pale greens as delicate as water; blues like the veins in a woman's arm.

---

* Kipling and Rhodes became friends during the last decade of the century. Of Kipling Rhodes wrote – in the dishevelled, how's-that-again style characteristic of him – '[He] has done more than any other since Disraeli to show the world that the British race is sound at the core and that rust or dry rot are strangers to it.'

The site is known by a version of the name which Rhodes himself gave it. He called it 'View of the World', which has since been contracted to 'World's View'. His grave is sunk into the granite at the highest point of the immense slope. The plaque on it states simply: 'Here lie the remains of Cecil John Rhodes.' Another sunken grave nearby contains the body of Leander Starr Jameson, he of the Jameson Raid, among much else, and always, even in death, Rhodes's sidekick.* The third grave in the group is that of Charles Coghlan, the very man with whom Rhodes shares his degraded vigil in the backyard of the Bulawayo museum. Finally there is a pale, squared-off, pedimented stone box standing some twenty feet high (here, where all surfaces are curved and irregular) in which the members of the Shangani Patrol are buried: thirty-five white soldiers cut off and killed while trying to capture the doomed Lobengula. It has martial bas-reliefs in bronze on all four sides and is quite as ugly, in its heroic-imperial fashion, as any of the Korean–Stalinist extravagances of Heroes' Acre, Harare.

'World's View' is the highest spot for many miles around. Only the horizon limits the view in all directions; and even it, even at sunset, is faint with distance. Everywhere you look down on the unique Matopos landscape, itself composed of granite formations so crowded on one another, so crazily elaborate and variegated, so full of prankish, delicate, imposing touches, that it is hard not to feel two mutually incompatible responses warring in your breast as you try to take it in. First: these effects *cannot* be accidental. Second: no mind could have conceived them, not even God's, before they had come into existence.

Entire hillsides of granite are sloughing off their skins, peeling in onion-skin layer after layer – if you can imagine onion-skin that is twenty inches thick, composed of solid stone, and stretching for hundreds of feet across. Granite pillars and buttresses emerge to balance on their heads and shoulders boulders of every shape and size, as if awaiting your applause at the triumphant conclusion of

---

* See page 181. The raiders set out from Pitsani, on the missionary road.

an incomprehensible juggling trick. Granite balls lie at such acute angles on such smooth slopes that you think the movement of your car in the valley below or the tread of your foot above will send them rumbling and crashing down into the valleys. Whale-coloured sheets of granite are pierced with circular 'breathing-holes' twenty feet deep and almost as much in width – why then do not jets of water and vapour shoot out of them at intervals? On the very edge of cliff-tops, boulders shaped to each other like grapes in a bunch cluster together; or they nest in such rounded, comfortable contiguity they could be the toes of a foot or the bodies of lovers in a bed; or they lie apart, barely touching, showing their rounded tops like eggs in a clutch; or they assemble themselves into Rorschach reminiscences of vultures, lions' heads, a madonna nursing her child. So much cracking, splitting, layering, rolling, halting, sundering apart and blundering together is evident everywhere, so much change and upheaval is plainly in mid-process, so many circus-like tumblings and balletic balancings of immense weights still wait to be completed, that you cannot believe, as you drive or walk through the landscape, that you will not actually see it shifting before you: something is bound to topple, plunge, send other boulders flying, splinter where it lies or stands. Nor can you believe, when you lie in bed at night, that you will not hear the dynamite explosions that must accompany such events.

But all is motionless. Not a sound is heard. Ever.

I asked an African who had lived in the Matopos all his life if he had heard even once the detonation of a rock splitting, of a layer being shed, of a great boulder tumbling from one of the crests. No, he said; never. Had anyone else told him that he had heard it happening? No, he said; never.

It has taken place a million times – you see the evidence of it everywhere; it is going to happen again – you see that too; the rock is in such a state of tumult. But it is a tumult not to be measured in days or nights or human lifetimes. Or even in the lifetimes of the giant trees (wild fig, paper bark, msasa, kaffirboom, and many others) and the thick creepers with which the rocks are festooned, and amid which birds constantly flicker.

No one who has visited the area will be surprised that the Bushmen chose to fill some of the Matopos caves with their vivid, enigmatic paintings; or that the area was holy to the Shona people, too, who lived there before the Ndebele came, and that they believed it to be the residence of a high god, the Mwari, who spoke through oracles to his priests. Nor can it come as a surprise that the Ndebele adopted elements of the cult when they arrived; and that it was in a cave in the Matopos that their first king, Mzilikazi, was buried. In due course Rhodes decided that he should follow suit, when his turn came. (He liked things 'big and simple', he had said: 'barbaric if you like'.) All its other historical and mythological associations aside, he knew that in the Matopos he had performed the single most courageous action of his life, in going unarmed into the hills, along with a small number of companions, to meet and make peace with the leaders of the Ndebele people after the disastrous failure of their uprising in 1896. That is the 'Death he dared' which Kipling refers to in his funeral poem.

In choosing World's View as the site of his grave, Rhodes clearly intended it also to become a place of pilgrimage. ('And there await a people's feet/ In the paths that he prepared.') He has had his wish, in a manner of speaking. Much the most assiduous pilgrims are the African women who sit half a mile below the slope, their wares spread out for sale on the ground in front of them: beadwork, basketware, clay pots, knobkieries, wooden bowls and spoons, seed necklaces. In the evenings they pack up their goods and trek with them back to the stricken 'communal lands' outside the boundaries of the Matopos National Park, where they have their homes. Some walk, carrying their bundles on their heads, and often enough babies on their backs; others arrange their parcels on the carriers and cross-bars of bicycles and set out, lampless, along sandy tracks that appear to be lowering themselves deeper and deeper into the darkness with every moment that passes.

And cars? Customers? Pilgrims in the ordinary sense? Well, sometimes there are one or two cars in the car-park, sometimes as many as three or four, often none at all. The optimism of those women vendors – so many of them for so little traffic – astonishes me. But their optimism is as nothing compared with that of the tiny, half-naked children whom you see in the communal lands: lands dusty-grey in hue; trodden to powder by the feet of the populace and the hooves of skeletal cattle and goats; riven with *dongas* and littered with rocks; marked out here and there in squares for crops that have failed to grow. (The drought again; always the drought! As if the people here would not be poor beyond depiction even if the rains had come this year and the last!) The huts scattered everywhere are of the same grey colour as the dust – and how strange it is, after Botswana, to see each hut stand nakedly by itself, yards from its neighbours, instead of being grouped in cosy familial clusters of threes and fours, behind an encircling wall.

No sooner does the sound of a car engine become audible, as it crawls in first gear along the seamed slough of a road, than out of this or that hut there bursts a little creature clutching in its hand some single item: a string of beads, a wooden spoon, a two-inch head sculpted in clay. It races as fast as its skinny legs can carry it towards the road, hoping to get there before the car does, so that it might hold out at arm's length this twopenny item. In one of the afternoons we spent travelling and halting along such a road, we saw exactly one other car passing by: so how much trade can they hope to conduct, even if they get to the road before the vehicle has passed? But there they go, rags of clothes whipping behind them, dust rising in silent puffs from bare feet; and there they remain, left behind, baubles clutched in uplifted fists.

To tell the truth, when you see this sight over and over again, it begins to fill you (me) with a kind of rage. It is the combination of desperation and futility, of nonsensical hope and frantic effort, that is so infuriating. You feel like sticking your head out of the car window and shouting at them: 'How can you *do* it? For God's sake, how can you be so *stupid*? Can't you *see* it's a waste of time?'

A few more questions: directed not at them, but at everyone, myself included. Has the extreme poverty of the people around the

Matopos been alleviated or aggravated by the proclamation of the area as a national park? Were they better off before they were driven from the lands they had occupied inside the park borders? (I was shown traces of their villages, now destroyed, and of their ploughed fields, now merely blond grass and sallow bush. Yet the grass was so much taller than anything to be seen outside; it was almost as I remembered the grass in Zimbabwe had once been: man-high, at least.) Has the use of the land for holiday and sightseeing purposes, almost entirely by a straggle of white tourists, actually put more in the pockets and stomachs of the local people than they would otherwise have had? If they had not been dispossessed, what would have become of the game the visitor sees there (water buck, wildebeest, hyrax, impala, sable, duiker, reed buck, bush buck, sessebe, and many other varieties); and the birds (hornbills, kingfishers, bulbuls, black eagles, rock kestrels); and the trees?

And what might have been the condition of the country if the whites, from the earliest days of their implantment, had not taken over for their sole possession such preposterously large swathes of the Africans' lands? (Well over half its total area went into their hands, though they never numbered more than four per cent of the population.) Or if the whites had not come at all –?

Lobengula succeeded in 1870 to the headship of the Ndebele. Some historians say that he was reluctant to take on the burden of the office. If so, even in his worst forebodings he could never have imagined just how troubled his reign was to be, and in what despair and humiliation it would end. In *A Tourist in Africa*, Evelyn Waugh describes him as a 'figure from Shakespearean rather than classical drama; Lear, Macbeth, Richard II'. 'Contemporary accounts of the last decade of Lobengula's life,' he adds, 'make shameful reading.'

The shame Waugh speaks of was not Lobengula's but that of the white concession-seekers and government agents who came to Bulawayo in the 1880s. They fawned on him, lied to him, cheated him, conspired against him, plied him with drink and morphine

(Jameson's speciality), confused him with verbal and legal niceties that had little meaning to him and no moral meaning whatever to themselves; they ignored his messages when he pleaded for peace and killed the messengers who were carrying them; finally, having secured most of the lands he ruled over, they set out to destroy him and to reduce his nation to servitude. All this while constantly assuring him that they had no designs whatever on his people, his territory, or his throne. All this in spite of the fact that not one of his white visitors ever came to harm while they were in his care, and that he repeatedly endangered his own position in the tribe by protecting them from the anger of his warriors.

The sequence of events is complicated in detail but straightforward in momentum. From the early 1880s Rhodes had intermittently turned his eye towards the territories beyond the Limpopo River. Others had done more: they had gone there to hunt, to scratch under the soil, to bring back exaggerated reports of the country's mineral wealth. What eventually provoked Rhodes into action, and made the British government look in a more kindly fashion on his efforts than they might otherwise have done, was the combination of German acquisitiveness in the west, Portuguese restiveness in the east (they were now actively trying to resuscitate their ancient claims to 'Monomotapa'), and an attempt by the Boers of the Transvaal to expand directly northwards, across the Limpopo River. As against all the other concession-seekers badgering Lobengula, Rhodes had on his side the wealth and status given to him by the De Beers Corporation. He also had the more or less wholehearted cooperation of key British officials on the spot, the administrator of the Bechuanaland Protectorate and the Governor of the Cape Colony included. (Both of them were later to be well rewarded financially for their pains.) In 1889 Rhodes wrung a concession from Lobengula – for mining rights only – which was more effectively worded than any other of the prospecting concessions already granted. Then he went to London and used this document to procure a royal charter which enabled his newly-floated Charter Company to claim the territories for its own and to do virtually anything it pleased within them.*

In 1890 the members of the Pioneer column assembled in
Mafikeng and set out on their long march northwards. Jameson
went with them as Rhodes's personal representative. Because they
did not dare to confront Lobengula and his warriors directly, they
followed the missionary road only as far as Tati, and then veered
east. A new road was hacked out through difficult country. When
it reached the relative safety of Mashonaland the column turned
northwards once more. A fort was built at Masvingo, as we have
already seen, and then another at the point where Harare (formerly
Salisbury) now stands. The flag was raised and 'God Save the
Queen' was sung. Before dispersing, each Pioneer received a grant
of 3,000 acres of land and fifteen gold claims. The Shona had
offered no resistance at any stage. They may well have been pleased
to see the heavy yoke of Ndebele dominance removed from them. If
so, their pleasure did not last long.

After the ceremonial dispersal of the column several bands of
armed men kept on marching – not north now, but eastwards.
They were pursuing Rhodes's ambition of seizing from the
Portuguese a port on the Indian Ocean. Each of his several efforts
in this direction was frustrated by the authorities in London, who
had their own balance-of-power reasons for keeping the Portuguese
sweet. Three years later, when it had become pretty clear that no
new Kimberleys or Witwatersrands were to be found in
Mashonaland, the settlers turned westwards and launched the
assault on Bulawayo and the Ndebele people which many of them
had long been itching to make. ('The sooner the brush is over, the
better,' Jameson had written, well before the formation of the
Pioneer column had been mooted.) They were assisted in this
attack by some newly-recruited volunteers and a column of imperial
troops. The Ndebele were mown down by rifle fire and Maxim
guns. Lobengula set his kraal on fire and fled northwards, with a

---

* Neither the British government nor the shareholders were told that the concession
was owned not by the Charter Company itself but by yet another semi-secret group
consisting of Rhodes and a few of his cronies and ex-rivals.

mounted force in pursuit. Some reports say he died of smallpox, which was then raging almost as murderously through his kingdom as the armies of the invaders. Others say that once he knew that the fate of a captive, at best, was all that awaited him, he committed suicide by taking poison. It has also been said that he died simply of a broken heart.

The site of his grave is not known. Even the bag of gold sovereigns he sent to the commander of the pursuing troops with the stark message, 'Take this and go back. I am conquered' – even that was stolen by the first two soldiers to get their hands on it and never seen again.

The colonists who took part in this campaign were rewarded more generously than those who had marched to Fort Salisbury. Each was given twenty gold claims apiece, a 6,000-acre farm, and a *pro rata* share of all cattle 'loot[ed]'. (The word 'loot' was used in the contract offered to volunteers by the Company.) Now the country was well and truly 'pacified'; or so it was believed. In 1896, however, the Ndebele launched the first sustained campaign against a colonial authority to take place anywhere in Africa. They were encouraged by the failure of the Jameson Raid in the Transvaal – Jameson now being in jail and Rhodes himself having been forced to resign the premiership of the Cape Colony. The uprising was as savage as Ndebele history would lead one to imagine; it was put down with a corresponding mercilessness.

To everyone's astonishment, the downtrodden, docile Shona then rose up in a similar rebellion. The ferocity with which it was suppressed owed something to the colonists' anger at Shona 'ingratitude'. This time the country stayed pacified, in effect, for eighty years.

A common joke to be found in writings about Africa during the nineteenth century is the story of a meeting with a 'king' who turns out to be a naked drunkard in a mud hut; with a 'queen' who begs the writer for a cigarette; with a 'prince' who takes employment as a porter or cook; with a 'great chief' who appears in a pair of cast-off boots too big for him. And so on.

Lobengula is seldom made the butt of such jokes. There is some dispute about whether his expression was 'cruel' or 'benignant'; disgusted references are made to the huge quantities of meat he ate and his manner of eating it, as well as the amounts of beer he drank; complaints are constantly aired about his capacity for temporizing – 'wasting time', as his petitioners put it. (Since they were petitioning for his country, no less, and he knew it, and knew also the power behind them to be ultimately much greater than his own, temporizing was the wisest policy he could follow.) The squalor of his kraal comes in for some scornful comment. A tone of horror enters the visitors' accounts when they describe the cruelties they witnessed in the royal kraal: flayings, stonings, the murder of entire families that had fallen into the king's disfavour, less-than-lethal tortures inflicted in moments of random displeasure. (Cut off the lips, nose, and forehead of someone who had unwittingly drunk the king's beer; brand the mouth of a herdboy who had not answered the king's questions satisfactorily.) It would be pointless to try to palliate the fact that Lobengula was as ruthless in dealing with his people, and with their enemies and tributaries, as any leader of the Ndebele had to be, if he was to survive. At the same time it is plain that many of the white newcomers had a strong interest in depicting Lobengula's reign, and Ndebele life in general, in the most lurid possible terms, since it justified what they were intending to do, or hoping to do, or had already done to him and to his people as a whole.

All of which makes it the more remarkable that so many of the references to him in the writings of the time are admiring, appreciative, respectful, and (not just out of fear) even awe-struck. Some of the writers suggest that he was both too honourable and too mild a man to cope with the situation in which he found himself. 'He was not sufficiently civilized to break his word,' Ellerton Fry, the photographer to the Pioneer Column, wrote sardonically, 'and not savage enough to force his people into submission.' J.S. Moffat, the ex-missionary who had played a double role in the negotiations that led to the granting of the concession, and thus to the destruction of the kingdom, said of him after his death, 'He was a gentleman in his way; and he was foully sinned against by Jameson and his gang.' Robert Thompson, a negotiator on Rhodes's behalf, wrote that he was 'every inch a king'. Sir Sydney Shippard, administrator of the Bechuanaland Protectorate, and (against stiff competition) one of the most unscrupulous of Lobengula's enemies, described him as having 'a most majestic appearance'.* J. Cooper-Chadwick, an unsuccessful concession-chaser, complained that his 'features exhibit great cunning and cruelty'; but then added: 'When he smiles the expression completely changes and makes his face appear pleasant and good-tempered.' The French explorer Lionel Décle said of him that he was the most imposing monarch he had ever seen, 'with the exception of Tsar Alexander'. The startlingly precocious, happy-go-lucky Frank Johnson – who at the age of twenty-three contracted with Rhodes to deliver the Pioneer Column to Fort Salisbury for a fee of £87,500, a grant of 80,000 acres, and 240 gold claims; and who even before the Column set out had proposed a raid on Bulawayo either to kill Lobengula or to take him hostage – wrote in his autobiography:

He was an enormous but majestic figure of a man, with his waxed head-ring and plume of crane's feathers. Naked apart from some skins hanging from his waist he yet retained a regal appearance . . . He possessed a native shrewdness and abilities of no common order. He had force of character and was a good judge of his fellow-men. He realized, I think, the great difficulties that faced his people by the penetration of the white man, and did his best to prolong their independent existence, which he knew must one day end. It was not an easy task, for his warriors were full of warlike desires against the white men and it required great skill and tact to restrain them.

*

* A letter of Shippard's gives the flavour of his contribution to the proceedings: '[I]t would offer me sincere and lasting satisfaction if I could see the Matabele . . . cut down by our rifles and machine guns like a cornfield by a reaping machine.' Shippard also used his power as representative of the crown in Bechuanaland to hold up a letter from Lobengula to the Queen which expressly repudiated Rhodes's interpretation of the concession he had gained. Thus Shippard, a friend of Rhodes from their time together in Kimberley, made sure that the proclamation of the Charter would not be delayed. His reward came not only in seeing the Ndebele 'cut down', as he had hoped, but also in later being nominated to the board of directors of the Charter Company.

Some of the qualities Johnson refers to come out clearly in Lobengula's own recorded utterances.

To the youthful Johnson, when he first came looking for a concession: 'But there is no gold in my country ... I cannot understand this digging for gold. There is no place in my heart where you can dig for gold.'

To his warriors, who pressed him to allow them to kill all the white claimants at one blow: 'You want to drive me into the lion's mouth.'

To Queen Victoria in a letter (via a scribe): 'The white people are troubling me much about gold. If the Queen hears that I have given away the whole country, it is not so.' (This is the message which Shippard delayed, lest it affect the granting of the Charter to Rhodes.)

To Jameson, after the Charter had been granted and the British government had thereby set its seal of approval on the drive northwards: 'Before it was only Rhodes [in your mouth]; now it is always the Queen and Rhodes.'

In a letter to the commanders of the Pioneer column assembling on the border: 'Had the king done any fault? Had any white men been killed or the white men lost anything they were looking for?'

To Queen Victoria in a letter after the colonists' march on his capital had begun: 'Your Majesty, what I want to know from you is if people can be bought at any price ... Your Majesty, what I want to know from you is: Why do your people kill me? ... I have called all white men living at or near Bulawayo to hear my words, showing clearly that I am not hiding anything from them when writing to Your Majesty.'

To his followers shortly before his death: '[T]he white men will never catch me. I will throw myself over a height. Now you will find what real trouble is. You will have to pull and shove wagons; but under me you never did this kind of thing ... Now you be joyful because here are your future rulers.'

Two things about Lobengula still remain to be said. First, there is the question of his relationship with Rider Haggard's most

famous novel, *King Solomon's Mines*.* Lobengula was in fact
not the direct heir to the unhappy throne he occupied. His brother
Kulumani (or Kurumane) – who had been named after the mission
station, as a delicate tribute to Robert Moffat – had precedence
over him. But Kulumani never succeeded to the headship of the
tribe. One version of the story says that he was killed by his father,
Mzilikazi. Another that he fled to Natal to escape this fate. Another
that after his father's death he set out to dislodge Lobengula, but
lost heart and turned back either at Shoshong, in Botswana, or in
the Matopos.

In Haggard's novel the noble and ultimately successful pretender
to the throne (who had had to flee for his life to Natal) is called
Ignosi. The evil upstart who occupies the throne, Twala, is eventually killed by a 'yellow-haired' Englishman, Sir Henry Curtis. The
throne at issue is that of Kukuanaland, a country full of Ophir-like
resonances. Known in the distant past to the Portuguese, it is
endowed with the mines of the title, a twin pair of mountains
called 'Sheba's Breasts', and (much to my purpose here, though
quite unlike the real thing) a paved road to the north, Solomon's
Great Road, lined with 'Egyptian' statuary.

Haggard wrote the novel in 1885, five years before the Pioneer
column set out on its march. Even then, though, he must have
known that perhaps the most fanciful thing about his story was its
notion that the white men who had entered Kukuanaland, and
come back from it with a haul of diamonds, would thereafter
chivalrously leave it alone. Or that those who did not respect its
isolation would be compelled by the heroic Ignosi to do so.

No other white man shall cross the mountains . . . I will see no traders with
their guns and rum. My people shall fight with the spear, and drink water,
like their forefathers before them. I will have no praying-men to put the fear
of death into men's hearts, to stir them up against the king, and make a path
for the white men who follow to run on. If a white man comes to my gates I
will send him back; if a hundred come I will push them back; if an army

* Translated into Ndebele in 1977, under the title *Imigodi ye Nkosi u Solomon*.

comes, I will make war on them with all my strength, and they shall not
prevail against me. None shall ever come for the shining stones; no, not an
army . . .

So much for Haggard and *King Solomon's Mines*. The second
fact or fancy about Lobengula that I feel obliged to pass on is this.
Since visiting the remains of his kraal at 'Old Bulawayo' – a few
broken walls of stone, stone circles on the ground where huts had
once stood, nothing else – I have read in a newspaper that a
'Lobengula Theme Park' is to be built on the site.

In Bulawayo we took up quarters amid the colonial-baronial
splendours of the Bulawayo Club: itself a kind of Cecil Rhodes
Theme Park, dedicated to a celebration of the pioneering virtues
and the unassailable superiority of the British race. Rhodes's statue,
now banished to the backyard of the museum, used to stand on a
great sandstone plinth just a few yards from the club's front door.
The first thing you see in its vestibule is his bust, larger than life-
size. On the first-floor landing he is represented in oils. In the
committee-room hangs a pastelly portrait of him as a young miner
in Kimberley, shovel in hand, the whole thing dwindling away
unconvincingly towards his feet and the blade of the shovel. A
brass plaque states that it was donated by the Rhodes family. He is
to be found, once more in oils, in an ante-chamber leading to the
main dining-room, next to large portraits of a youthful King
George VI and his consort. The coffee-room contains some
photographs of him, along with one of his brother, Colonel Frank
Rhodes.

The other photos on the walls are chiefly of many amazing
moustaches (like waterfalls, like two-headed spears, like swept-
back, swept-up buffalo horns), as well as slouch hats, beards, high
white collars, swords, guns, Sam Browne belts, and bemedalled
chests. With names and faces attached. Plus Winston Churchill and
various royals. Of Lobengula the only memento, on one of the
landings, is an enlarged sketch-map of 'Umvutcha Kraal Where
Lobengula Signed the Concession Giving his Mineral Rights to

Rhodes on Oct. 30th 1888'. Elsewhere animal heads on plaques and elephant's-foot waste-baskets abound.

We had entrée to the club by virtue of the three generations of my wife's family who had been prominent members. The last of them had arranged for us to stay there. It is a fine building, adorned outside with white pillars in clusters, a red-dyed, cement-floored verandah kept in a high state of polish, and the hooped Italianate arches of the subcontinent's best colonial-style architecture. Inside you find panelling in sombre African woods, tall doorways and windows with a Cape Dutch swerve to their tops, wide staircases that split into two at each half-landing before uniting again at the next floor. There is also a (dry) Italian fountain in a colonnaded courtyard at the centre of the building. The dining-room, in deep salmon-pink and white, boasts a coffered ceiling and pillars that stand on wooden bases three feet high; its sideboards are laden with silver tureens and epergnes to be handled only by weightlifters on steroids.

At five on weekday afternoons the long bar on the ground floor fills up, and for the next hour numbers of Bulawayo business and professional men down several stiff drinks apiece and roar at one another; then they make their way home in their BMWs and Hondas. A mausoleum-like stillness at once returns. Two or three tables out of thirty may be occupied at dinner; a subsidiary dining-room, presided over by the cherubically Jewish features of Sir Alfred Beit, is deserted; so are the reading-room, the coffee-room, and the library – which contains collected editions in full leather of all the Victorian worthies, six shelves of bound copies of *Punch*, and a large case devoted solely to books on cricket. In the half-darkness the white jacket of the occasional servitor stands out sharply. The two members who live there permanently, both ancient, go to bed early.

A wealthy businessman I know, of whom we saw a fair amount while we were in the city, was not a member of the club and disapproved of my using its facilities. His reason was that until fairly recently (twenty years ago, perhaps), it had barred Jews from becoming members. He had since been invited several times to join, but his pride as a Jew would not permit it. That Asians, Africans, and Coloureds had been barred went without saying. Since independence a few members of these groups have been enrolled. Women are permitted as guests, but they cannot join the club.

It was an appropriate place, therefore, for me to think about the relationship between Rhodes and certain Jews (very close indeed); and the relations between Rhodes's admirers and the Jews in general (as distant and hostile as the former could make it). All this was familiar to me from my youth in Kimberley, where jingoistic sentiment and a virulent social anti-Semitism had gone hand in hand. Here we had a club which was like a shrine to Rhodes; with a side-chapel in it to Alfred Beit. Yet it had kept out the latter's 'co-racials' – on principle, as it were.* Beit was not Rhodes's closest friend; but he was his closest and most trusted collaborator and adviser. Without Beit's aid he would never have been able to pull off several of his most important deals; it was through Beit, too, that he made contact with the Rothschilds, who backed him first in amalgamating the Kimberley mines and then in the flotation of the Charter Company. In return, in the fourth of the six wills he drew up, Rhodes left his estate to Lord Rothschild, on condition that the money be used to set up a society devoted to the expansion of the empire. 'In considering question [of the nature of this society],' he instructed the most eminent Jew in Britain, in telegraphic fashion, 'suggest take Constitution Jesuits if obtainable and insert English Empire for Roman Catholic Religion.'

In drawing up the articles of association of the De Beers Corporation, Rhodes conferred the title of 'life governor' on both Beit and Barney Barnato, another Jew. (He also prudently insisted that the company should have the right to acquire and administer territories, raise armed forces, and build railways.) After his death, Sir David Harris, a nephew of Barnato, became chairman. He was succeeded in due course by Ernest Oppenheimer, also a Jew. Yet during the

* I can hardly say 'co-religionists', since Thomas Pakenham in *The Scramble for Africa* (1991) says that Beit was baptized as a Lutheran. Everyone usually writes about him simply as a 'German (or Hamburg) Jew'.

early years of my childhood it was universally known in Kimberley
that in no circumstances would the company employ Jews.

Thus the local directors of De Beers and the members of the
Bulawayo Club had zealously and happily done their best to keep
faith with the racial and imperial doctrines, as they understood
them, of their founder:

For the furtherance of the British Empire, for the bringing of the whole
civilized world under British rule, for the recovery of the United States, for
the making of the Anglo-Saxon race into one Empire. What a dream! But yet
it is probable! It is possible!

CHAPTER TWENTY-TWO

☆

Some Zimbabwean Voices

Spring-hares have the habit of dunging in one special area outside their warrens. They all do it there, even the young ones. When you get a new puppy, therefore, the thing to do is to collect some dung from a spring-hare and make the puppy eat it. Then it won't do its messes in the house any more. It will have become house-trained at once . . .

If a witch puts the egg of a crocodile behind the hut of an enemy, then the hut will be struck by lightning. The people inside will be killed. This is because there are two kinds of lightning: 'natural lightning' and 'magic lightning'. Natural lightning falls in the fields or the forest and does no harm; magic lightning is brought by witches and it kills people (or their cattle). It can also be made to fall on crops and set them alight . . .

Sometimes 'the fairies' snatch children away and they are never seen again. In a village nearby, two children, a brother and a sister, were taken by the fairies. They had gone to the river to fetch water and did not come back. The parents and everyone in the village looked for them; the police were called and they came with dogs; no scent or trace of them could be found. Two years went by before the father went to a healer and asked for help. The healer told him the name of the man, an enemy of his in the next village, who had made the fairies take the children. Three days later they found the little girl wandering by herself in the rocks by the river. She could not speak; so the healer took a knife and cut the girl's tongue where it had been knotted, and she was able to speak again. But she could say nothing about where she had been or what had happened to her while she was gone. Of that she had no memory. Nor could she say where her brother was. The healer could do nothing more with her. The little boy was never seen again.

And the man who had asked the fairies to take the child?

He died.

Do you mean, he was killed?

I mean that he died . . .

There was another man in a village down the road – we would be passing it soon – who kept a baboon in his hut. He kept it in a cupboard. No one knew that it was there, not even his wife and children. His plan had been to use the baboon to give him a power over other people. He wanted it to be his servant. To do things for him. It was an old male baboon, very big and strong. It could talk to him and he could talk to it. But not long after he had brought it into his hut, he started to behave like a madman. A sick person. Sometimes he would shout and scream and run into the bush; he attacked his wife and children and tried to kill them. So they left him and went back to the wife's village. The other people there could see that he was dangerous; but they knew nothing about what he was keeping in the hut.

Then someone saw him walking with the baboon at night. They were holding hands. Then they realized he was doing witchcraft. They told the family about it, and a relative brought a famous healer, a very expensive one, to the village. He had a boy with him. He told them to take the man away, and he made the boy stand outside the hut all night, so that no one could come near it. Early in the morning he went into the hut by himself. Soon terrible noises came from it, screams and shouts and big bangs. But the boy would not let anyone come near. Then the healer came out of the hut, carrying the baboon. It was dead. He threw it on the ground and said, 'You can go into the hut now.'

When they went inside they saw that everything was smashed in pieces, the cupboard also. Then he said, 'Now bring the man here.' The man came and he admitted everything: how he had kept the baboon in the cupboard, and tried to get power from it. But instead of him getting power from the baboon, the baboon got power over him. He had to do whatever the baboon told him. That was why he had behaved so strangely. The baboon was his master. Afterwards the healer made them burn the hut down, and everything in it, with the baboon in the middle of the blaze. The fire burned until nothing was left. Ever since then the man has been well again, and his wife and his children have come back. They have built themselves a new hut . . .

If we stop there, just a little further, and get out, and walk across the veld, past those huts – no one will mind – we will come to the place where the hut used to stand. Look, there it is, the circle in the ground where the hut had stood, how white it is, and look (stirring the ground with a stick) – ashes. Nothing else. The man now lives in that hut over there.

The newly-built hut was circular, made of mud and thatch, like almost all the others. It was windowless. Its door of variegated, battered planks was closed by a piece of wire twisted around a nail in the wall. Other grey huts were scattered across the plain; some of them, unusually, were square rather than round. A few had abstract, wavy patterns etched into their walls, made with a comb-like instrument. In the distance rose a granite-littered slope; nearer the road, in the direction we had come from, trees and granite boulders appeared to be grappling fiercely for space, as if the stone were as alive as the trees. No fences were to be seen anywhere, not even around the little patches where crops (in a better, wetter year) would have been growing. No one was about; no one looked at us as we examined the remains of the baboon-man's hut. From the next group of huts, perhaps five hundred yards away, we could hear voices and the sound of goat-bells. The sun shone on the hillside and its boulders, but not where we stood. Everything was still. A single cyclist appeared around the next bend in the broken track we had been driving along. Effortfully, slowly, he drew level, turned his head in our direction, had a good look, then concentrated once more on the hard task ahead of him.

M. said to our companion on the drive, 'Those are strange stories you've been telling us.'

He answered without taking offence, but evidently standing on his dignity: 'They are not stories. They are the truth.'

I said, 'How could the man's wife and children not have known about the baboon in the cupboard? Look how small the hut was.'

'The baboon was cleverer than they were. It would keep quiet when they were there. Everyone saw the baboon after it was dead, and the man made a confession of what he'd been doing. He knew it was there.'

'Well, he was crazy. You said so yourself. I think that what happened was that the healer brought a dead baboon with him in his bag, and pretended to fight it, and then dragged it out of the hut.'

'The man has not been sick ever since.'

'Probably it was a great relief to him to see the baboon lying there. He had something to blame for what had gone wrong.'

'Yes,' he said, quite unperturbed by my scepticism. 'It was a relief. Now it could not rule over him any more.'

He was a tall, sparsely bearded man of middle height; his cheeks were sunken and the bones beneath his eyes correspondingly prominent; he carried his head upright and his shoulders back; his khaki clothing was threadbare but neat; his voice was deep and soft, and his manner grave; he had a good if slightly pedantic command of English, with an especial fondness for ready-made, formal phrases ('rest assured', 'well accustomed', 'tried our patience', and so forth). His manner and phraseology contrasted oddly with the wildness of the tales we heard from him. But we saw another side of his character when we passed a cow mooing pitiably by the roadside, milk dripping from its udder as it waited to be relieved of its load. The whites in the jeep said, 'Poor thing! It must be in agony!' He spoke even more passionately; but it was to express something quite different. 'What a waste!' he exclaimed, with an anguish that revealed how intimate he was with the hunger in the village from which he came. 'What a waste!'

He had been a despatch-clerk for a firm in town for some years; then he had gone home to teach in the local school; now he was looking for something else, something better paid, if only he could get it. When the children in his school were naughty he used 'the stick'. They had to learn what was right and what was wrong.

Among the questions he asked of me (what was my profession, how long had I been in Zimbabwe, what did I think of it) were several about the European Community. What was my own 'national status' now? Did I have a European or a British passport? Could I work anywhere in Europe? Was the European parliament in Strasbourg a real parliament – did it 'have authority' over the parliament of each member-country? Or was it just a place for politicians to go to and draw their salaries? Were the politicians in Europe thieves like the ones in Zimbabwe?

Then he made the only joke that passed his thinly fringed lips; it took him some time to work it out; but he got it in the end. They called it poli*tics*, he said, because the politicians were nothing more than ticks: they sucked the blood of the people until they were fat and the people were thin.

There were several postcards on display at the counter. The one I liked most was a picture of a soapstone sculpture entitled. 'The Witch and His Mate'. The winged, beaked witch stood to one side, leaning over a container which was something like a bathtub, or a sarcophagus, or an elongated womb. Inside it lay the mate: a strangely complacent creature, much more youthful in appearance than the witch, smiling upwards.

I bought half-a-dozen copies of the card to send to people to whom I had promised to write. The woman behind the cash-register, all straightened hair and dark red lipstick, counted out the number of cards and told me the sum I should pay. While I was digging in my pocket for the cash she said, 'You are buying a lot of this card.'

'Yes,' I said. 'I like it.'

'You like witches?'

'No, but I like the card.'

'You believe in them?'

'No, I don't. Do you?'

'Oh no,' she said scornfully, giving me my change.

She put the cards in an envelope; as she was about to hand it to me a look of caution came on her face. 'I don't know,' she said. 'I

think I don't believe in them.' I was conscious of her eyes following me as I walked away. It would have been difficult to say, at
that moment, which she thought the more sinister: the cards or the
man who had chosen to buy them.

She was American: cotton-frocked, small-faced, small-bodied,
small-voiced; so youthful in appearance, in fact, that I wondered if
she had not been anorexic at one time or another. Her hair was
done in two pigtails. The pale freckles on her cheeks were like tiny,
vague clouds; once you had noticed them it seemed almost surprising not to see them slowly on the move. On her pigeon-sized,
pigeon-soft breast there hung a large wooden cross, varnished
brown. Her manner of speech was intense, with an involuntary,
tremulous closing of her eyelids that showed the strain she went
through in bringing out her words. But having got herself going,
she kept at it, pausing from time to time to look not at her
interlocutor but at some point immediately in front of her nose.

   She and another young American woman had come to Zimbabwe
to do 'internships' for their Masters degree in public health. They
were at different colleges in the Middle West. They were both
interested in AIDS; that was one of the reasons why they had
chosen to come to Africa. They would be staying in Masvingo for
about a week, sharing a room in a dormitory of the new Technical
College. (And what a desolate place the College was, more
building-site than anything else, all turned-up earth and four brick
buildings behind a chain-link fence, on the edge of the unlovely
little town.) Then they would be going some place else; she wasn't
sure where. Their work consisted of helping to 'construct and
monitor public health intervention programmes'. Her own special
interest (eyelids working with even more intensity than usual) was
in 'awareness and education'. Having produced the last phrase, she
added pre-emptively: 'Yes, I know that giving people information is
not the same thing as changing their behaviour.'

   Anyway, before they could disseminate information they had to
acquire it – which they were doing chiefly by going into the bars at
night and talking to the 'sex-workers' and finding out about their

'practices', and asking them to identify their 'clients', whom they would also try to interview. Barmen and waiters were also often useful sources of information. In Zimbabwe the clients were on the whole very reluctant to use condoms. ('They don't like it, it's inconvenient, it stops them having babies.' 'Babies? From the sex-workers?' 'Well, that's what they say. Also they tell you, "Everybody's got to die some day."') Free condoms were available at health clinics, as well as from barmen and waiters – a Scandinavian charity had put up the money for their distribution – but there were relatively few takers. The government also had an active policy of trying to reach the women through music and drama: all women, not just sex-workers.

Did she and her friend have anyone to protect them when they went into the bars at night? 'Well, we go with the local health-workers. So far we've had no trouble.'

Forty-one per cent of mothers reporting to the maternity clinic at Masvingo had been found to be HIV positive. The rate in Masvingo was high even by national standards. Twenty-five per cent of the HIV mothers produced children who were HIV positive. Another twenty-five per cent of the children later got infected through breast-milk. No, it would not be better if the HIV mothers did not breast-feed their babies. Then even more of the babies would die because of polluted water and unsterilized equipment.

'It's very hard to change people's behaviour. That's just one of the things that make the work so depressing. But it would be even more depressing if we did nothing. You've got to have hope.'

I was suddenly, if belatedly, moved to ask: 'Are you a member of a religious order?'

'No,' she answered, eyelids fluttering vigorously. 'But I am very devout.'

Sister Lucy was unquestionably a member of a religious order: she was a Roman Catholic nun who had been educated at a Loreto Convent somewhere in Zimbabwe. She wore a grey-blue habit, a white veil, a silver cross. Stoutly built, bespectacled and motherly in appearance, calm in manner, she spoke unassumingly but firmly, like the good housekeeper she evidently was.

She had appeared while we were inspecting the church at the Serima Mission, about fifty miles north of Masvingo. Lost among tracts of (literally) pulverized communal lands, and the crazy shanties scattered across them, the church is something of a showplace – even if it was obviously one that was seldom visited. Coming up the driveway, lined in hopefully Italian style with two rows of struggling, plucky cypresses, we had seen not a soul. The only sound that greeted us at the church was the drawling disputation of a few hens scratching in the gravel outside. But it was not long before three boys arrived: one in a tracksuit, one in blue jersey and jeans, and one in a flowered shirt and spectacles. Their ages ranged from about twenty years to twelve: they solemnly introduced themselves as 'Brother Paul', 'Brother Mathias', 'Brother William'. They gave us to understand that they bore these titles because they were studying at a seminary near Harare. They were back in Serima, they said, because it was now the school holidays.

They did not know anything about the history of the church, but one of them pointed out the priest's house to the right of it; and the convent – a small, gauzed, iron-roofed cottage – on the left. Secretively, proudly, pleased at passing on this bit of scandal, he said to me, 'One of the nuns is leaving today.' 'Leaving?' 'Yes, going for good. She won't come back.' From their expressions I could see that to them the nun's departure was a source of glee and apprehension. I feared that we had arrived on a day of crisis in what was obviously a minuscule community.

How many nuns were there, I asked.

Again a furtive flicker of pleasure crossed his face. 'From tonight, two.'

Then Sister Lucy joined us, and the boys promptly disappeared. If we had indeed arrived at Serima in the middle of a crisis, she showed no sign of it. She took us around the church, pointing out items of special interest in it. An elegantly bare concrete structure, it was designed by a Swiss German priest, Father Groeber, who had used local woods for its interior and local craftsmen and artists to decorate it. Its most striking feature was the many wooden columns holding up the roof; each column carved in totem-pole fashion, with one devotional face or figure supporting the next, all the way up to the reed-matted ceiling. Their faces and gestures were stylized but expressive, with strong foreheads and noses. (Sister Lucy said flatly, 'I don't like their lips.') The altarpiece consisted of carvings of Old Testament characters below and New Testament characters above, identified by name as well as by the actions they were performing. Then there was the roof itself, which fanned out in two wings from a point just above the altar, as if a single beat would see the whole building airborne. Zimbabwe's one major, indigenous art-form is that of soapstone carving; and it was not surprising to hear that some of its most gifted practitioners had discovered their gifts while working in wood at Serima, or had been trained by some of those whom the late Father Groeber had himself trained.

Having opened the sacristy where several 'spare' carvings were kept, as well as the Nativity figures for the Christmas crib, Sister Lucy guided us around the quite elaborate garden of the priest's house – terrace, fishpond, a hedge of Crown of Thorns – and complained about what the drought had done to it. But as for what the drought had done to the people –!

'Come,' she said, and from outside opened a door let into the wall of the church. 'This is my store-room. This is where I keep the mealie meal and soya beans.' There was a single hessian bag of each item in the corner, and a little spillage of both on the concrete floor. 'The soya beans,' she explained, 'are for the beggars. I have to give them away. The mealie meal I try to keep for selling, so I'll have money to buy more. But this is all we've got for the rest of the month. So now I wonder how we are going to manage.'

Later she fed us on tea and home-made ginger biscuits in the priest's house. (He was at a mission hospital further to the north, resting after a heart attack.) The room she had taken us into was bare but neat, its most prominent furnishings being a wooden cross, a framed coloured photograph of the Pope, and a large radio. No TV. She had been born in Swaziland, she said; her father was a Swazi and her mother 'a Kimberley Xhosa'. This last designation being new to me, I asked her what it meant. 'Well,' she said patiently, as if talking to a particularly slow-witted child, 'she was born in Kimberley and she was a Xhosa.' Both her parents were now dead. Her father, an Anglican, had come to Rhodesia and had taught at a mission station whose name I did not catch. Her brother was in the Salvation Army, and his son was soon to be ordained as a Roman Catholic priest. 'Did you ever have religious arguments in your family?' I asked. Again she spoke patiently. 'Not at all. Never. Why should we do such a thing? We had too much respect for each other.'

She too, it transpired, had a health problem. It was arthritis. She put her hands out with their swollen finger joints. 'When we do our office in the mornings, and it's cold, I have to put my hands in my sleeves, like this' – and she demonstrated how. When I asked if I could give her something for her stores, she answered me simply, 'That would be a great help.' So we did a calculation about the cost of three bags of mealie meal which, she said, would more or less see her through until the end of the month, and some notes exchanged hands.

The sun was declining as we came outside. The boys were now trying, in a distinctly half-hearted manner, to pump up a flat tyre on the mission pick-up van. Perhaps it was being made ready to carry away the absconding nun. On seeing us they wandered off in the direction of the little school, beyond the convent, only to return immediately Sister Lucy had shaken hands with us and gone back into the house.

Did I have a pencil and paper, Brother Paul wanted to know. I produced a notebook and a pencil. Each of them wrote his name inside the back cover. Brother Paul said, 'Now you'll be able to send us papers and magazines from England.'

'What sort of papers and magazines?'

'Any sort.'

Back in Bulawayo once again, we visit a family connection of my wife's. She is a lady in her nineties: immaculately dressed; silver hair carefully coiffed; tartan rug over her legs; at her side an elegant walking-stick. From her accent you would judge that she had left some superior Edinburgh drawing-room just the day before; not an inflection in it reveals that she has spent the past eighty years in the tiny colonial communities of Namibia, first, and then Zimbabwe. She lives in a cottage on the large estate which her husband (quasi-husband, actually) developed on the outskirts of the city. He is now dead; she is childless. But she does have a plentiful supply of small, white, curly-haired dogs. They too are beautifully washed and coiffed. While we are talking to her, the cousin who has brought us to the house has apparently had the chance of inspecting her dogs' dishes out in the yard. Now, coming into the room, he says teasingly to her, 'With what you spend on steak in a single day for those dogs, you could a feed a black family for a week.'

The old lady turns her remarkably clear blue eyes in his direction. 'Now why on earth should I want to do *that*?' she asks.

The same evening, quite by chance, we pick up her temporary day-nurse, as she is walking back to the main road at the end of her shift. Her name is Sitibele – which, she tells us, means 'You bring happiness'. She has to walk two miles to get to the main road; once there, had we not come on her, she would have waited for a bus ('maybe one hour, maybe two') to take her the eight miles to the centre of town. From there a further eight-mile journey by another bus will take her home. For the second bus, she says, she would not have to wait so long, 'unless there are big queues'.

Dressed in a nurse's starched white uniform, she is tall, slender, large-headed, youthful in appearance. She has a winning smile. This is how things stand with her. She is the mother of three boys aged respectively seven years, three years, and ten months. Their names are Prince, Ishmael, and Albert. Prince goes to school, for which she pays Zim $20 a term. Included in this sum are pencils and writing materials as well as his lessons. The lessons are all in English, though he does study the Ndebele language too. His favourite subject is English. 'He loves reading, he picks up any newspaper or magazine in the holidays and will try to read it. Also if he can get hold of books.' While she is at work the children are left with her sisters aged fourteen and ten. (It is the school holidays.)

Her mother used to help her with the children but she 'passed away' four years ago. 'She was a young woman – forty-eight. She died because she was so ill. It was cancer.' So now Sitibele provides not only for her own children, but also for her brothers and sisters, including two unemployed brothers in their early twenties. 'I am the first-born, so I have to do it.' Her brothers had been employed until six months ago, and then the work stopped. 'No, the work went on,' she corrects herself, 'but they were not needed in it.' Since then they have had no job. They go to 'the industries' and ask for work but there is nothing for them. 'Sometimes I buy vegetables from people out of town and then my brothers try to sell them in the street. But I am the only one who brings in money, and with the bread and the mealies going up so much I don't know what I am going to do.'

There is nothing whining or complaining in her voice; so far from trying to exploit this account of her circumstances, she reveals it only in response to direct questioning. She makes no reference at any point to either her own father or the father(s) of her children. She wishes us well when we drop her at the second bus-stop. Fortunately a bus is waiting and the queue is short.

Tony was wearing a long-sleeved white shirt and loose scarlet trousers cuffed at the ankles. His hair was carefully barbered to wave down the back of his neck. His frame was slight, his features boyish, his expression changeable. He was in charge of the cooking and worked extremely hard at it. Even under the strain of bringing everything to table in the right order, at the right time, and at the right temperature, his manner to his African helper remained courteous, even subdued. Some of the dishes pleased him; others not. Only when he was satisfied that everyone else was satisfied did he sit down at the dinner-table.

Speaking rather shyly at first, he proceeded to tell us tales of such wealth and splendour in the back of beyond that we began to feel positively sorry for the other very rich people we had met on our journey. He told us about his family's tea, coffee, and tobacco estates (in Malawi), their cattle ranches and groves of macadamia

nuts (in Zambia), their vineyards and house in Siena (yes, Italy).
Then about the journey around the world he had recently made.
About a brother who had just left on a ten-day honeymoon to Rio.
About a pregnant sister living in South Kensington, London, who,
as she had not been well recently, was visited every two or three
weeks by her mother from Malawi. About the cars owned by his
father: the three Rolls-Royces (details of models, colours, and years
of manufacture eagerly supplied); the Bentley (details ditto); the
Jaguar (ditto); the Austin Princess (ditto); several four-wheel-drives;
and various boats on Lake Malawi.

There was also the old family house, built in the nineteenth
century, standing at the end of a one-mile drive lined with mango
trees, and all locked up now and under tight surveillance, because
of the silver, furniture, and tapestries inside, as well as the
Stradivarius in a glass case. (His parents had moved to a smaller
house a few kays away.) The game ranch, too, was closed now, as
the government had insisted that the land be given back to 'the
people'. So it had gone to – 'you know – what do they call them?' –
with a bewildered flap of the hands – 'oh yes – the lepers, that's it,
the lepers . . . Before my father turned it over he had a church built
for them of Kamba glitter-stone, and he gave them the glass to
make the stained-glass windows. They've done it very nicely actually, telling the story of Jesus all in African terms – quite crude, you
know, but very pretty. The thing I don't like about the church is
that the stone is pinkish.'

On the other hand, on hearing about the decor of the dining-
room of the Bulawayo Club, his immediate response was, '*Salmon
pink?* I'd better go and join at once.'

His ideal in life, he confessed, was to have an open 1927 MG
(exact details of colour, tyres, and horsepower supplied) and to
take his 'beloved' for a picnic. With a hamper at the back and all
the cutlery and glassware; and he to be wearing the right 1920s
clothing – blazer, flannels, straw boater, goggles too.

'The only time I tried it, though, it was an utter disaster. The
motor burnt out. That was the end of my love life.'

After brooding on this for a while he cheered himself up by

telling of another ambition he was nurturing. He was going to advertise for holidaymakers to come to Malawi to enjoy 'the Complete Karen Blixen Experience'. 'Everything . . . Meeting them at the airport in the Austin Princess. Wearing one of those jackets with two rows of buttons down the front. And one of those stiff caps. And white gloves. Putting them up in the big house. Taking them on picnics in the bush.

'What do you think? Do you think it would work? I think it might.'

CHAPTER TWENTY-THREE

☆

The Victoria Falls – Another Foray into Botswana – Across the Zambesi into Zambia – Some Zambian Voices

If I had thought of the Okavango swamps as a 'tourist land', what should the Victoria Falls be called? Here, two hundred and fifty miles north-west of Bulawayo, the tourists were present not in scores or fifties, but in thousands. Dressed in bright windcheaters and anoraks, shorts and safari hats, sandals and trainers, their bodies slung about with cameras and camcorders and money-belts, their sweatshirts announcing the previous locales to which they had travelled – Nepal and M'Vatn, Dodd Golf Course (wherever that may be) and Beach Heaven (the same), Kenya Giraffe Lodge and Yosemite Park – they wandered up and down the length of the falls. Most were young; some middle-aged; a few old, with bare, sinewy, veiny legs. It would be hard to say which countries were best represented among them; my guess would be that Italians and Australians outstripped the rest, for some reason. But all Western Europe and North America had contributed to the throng; not to mention the contingents from South Africa.

Only the Japanese were missing. As if to make up for this, Japanese products abounded. Some of the young men shut out the roar of the falls by keeping their Sony or Panasonic Walkmen firmly clamped into their earholes, as they did the obligatory walk through the narrow strip of rain-forest (spray-forest, to be more precise), from Livingstone's statue on the western side to Danger Point in the east. The last-named is a kind of isthmus jutting into sheer space, beyond which it is impossible to go. There they watched the whitewater rafters assembling for their voyage down the second gorge below the falls: tiny figures, at the bottom of a naked abyss. For those who sought entertainments less adventurous than rafting the rapids, a 'Flight of Angels' was available in the monoplanes almost always circling overhead; and for the less adventurous still there was the evening 'Booze Cruise' on the Zambesi River. Also on offer were gambling, swimming, game-viewing, as well as visits to the crocodile farm, the snake park, the handcraft markets, and the 'traditional village' which promised A SPECTACULAR DISPLAY OF CIRCUMCISION RITUALS, MYSTERIOUS N'YOU DANCING, VIBRANT WAR DANCING, SPIRIT COSTUMES, A LEGEND REVEALED. BOOK NOW, ENQUIRIES ETC AT OFFICE. And then there were the falls as well.

Still, I do not want to give the wrong impression. The little town is an agreeable one; and even if the falls are not a place for the solitary contemplation of nature at its most tumultuous, they have remained unobstructed by clutter, mess, stupid intrusions. The site is big enough to swallow much bigger numbers of people than those now visiting it; and there is nothing in its vicinity like the grotesque funfair that surrounds the Niagara Falls. (As a spectacle, anyway, the Victoria Falls are more splendid and terrible in every respect.) In most places you are not prevented from going to the very edge of the mile-long chasm and looking – as if across the width of a street – at the stretch of water opposite hurling itself into its hundred-yard drop. Or rather, you see it hurling itself towards you, as if of set purpose, even as it twists, arches, and plunges down, sending its spray everywhere.* The torrents are many shades of green and black; they are adorned with white layers

* 'From this cloud rushed up a great jet of vapour exactly like steam, and it mounted 200 or 300 feet high; there condensing, it changed its hue to that of dark smoke, and came back in a constant shower which soon wetted us to the skin. This shower falls chiefly on the opposite side of the fissure and, a few yards back from the lip, there stands a hedge of evergreen trees whose leaves are always wet. A number of little rills run back into the gulf; but as they flow down the steep wall there, the column of vapour, in its ascent, licks them up clean off the rock, and away they mount again. They are constantly running down, but never reach the bottom.' – David Livingstone, *Missionary Travels*.

of foam as delicate as the down on a bird's chest, yet constantly in violent agitation and alteration. If you stare long enough at them, and then slowly lift your gaze above the lip of the cataract, you see the whole commotion seeming to rise too – going straight up, with a steady movement, ascending to a level impossible to fix, for it is itself as illusory as the upward drift you are watching.

Perhaps the strangest thing about the falls, though, is also the most obvious; the feature on which it seems most childlike to remark. It is that they *never stop*. They go on all the time. They always have and always will. They are not an entertainment put on for our benefit (though we may try to turn them into one). Not even the sea, which ebbs and flows, which is sometimes stormy and sometimes calm, can compete with their savage incessancy. If we try to picture eternity we usually find ourselves thinking of stillness; or if not of stillness, then of unending repetition, as with the sea. The falls present us with an eternity of a different kind: one of never-diminishing violence, urgency, uproar. I confess that after my first sight of them (not on this visit), the memory came back almost like that of a trauma when I was hundreds of miles away. The tumult started again every time I closed my eyes.

The Victoria Falls Hotel, the oldest in the vicinity, is built on a series of terraces and courtyards. All day tour parties are brought in, disperse to their rooms with their baggage, return to sit on the terraces and look at the view, start out on the hike down to the falls, return once more to eat and drink in large amounts. All day other parties assemble, again with their baggage, and throng together in the foyer, before being loaded into the buses that take them to the airport or on to the next stop on their overland tours. Everyone there has just come, or is about to go, or is attending to those who are coming or going. In other words, either you are earning money or spending it: no other activities are possible.

Having breakfast on the terrace one morning – a breakfast distracted by the gambolling of monkeys overhead and practically underfoot – I noticed a man sitting by himself in the corner. He had no drink or food in front of him, so he at least could not have been accused of being there to spend money. Or to earn it, as far as, I could see. He was thickset, middle-aged, neatly dressed in a cream shirt and khaki trousers; his colourless hair was brushed back from a red, coarse-skinned, emphysemic face; his manner was watchful, unrelaxed, solitary, strikingly different from that of the holiday-makers around him. He was smoking non-stop, sucking in the smoke as if to drag it down to the heels of his canvas shoes, exhaling it in swathes, knocking the ash off the end of his cigarette with nervous frequency, lighting another immediately after stubbing the last. His half-closed eyes, brown in colour, were never still. For a moment I wondered if he was one of the hotel detectives, then decided he was not. He looked too shabby – not so much in his clothing as in his face and manner; too ill at ease.

I saw him several times later that day, always seated, always on his own. He did not even have a newspaper to help him pass the time; just his cigarettes. Late in the afternoon I came on him in the lounge above the main terrace. He was sitting with his back to the view. When I got up to go he approached me. Suddenly it was clear to me that he knew I had been looking at him earlier. He had taken as much note of me as I of him. I felt as if I had been found out: the watcher, watched. Outdone.

Standing close to me, speaking softly, he told me his story. He had come up by train from South Africa a few days before. On the journey his money had been stolen from him.

The camp site he was living in charged $25 per night. He already owed the charge for two nights. He had been trying to phone his daughter in Durban to ask her to telegraph him some money, but the telegraph office wouldn't be open until Monday morning. (This was on a Friday afternoon.)

'I really hate doing this,' he said; and in some way it was true – the only truthful thing he had said so far. He hated me for being his prey, the one he had finally chosen for this approach. I could see it in the darting of his eyes, in the deeper wrinkling of his coarsely furrowed brow. 'If you could give me something to keep me going – anything – whatever you can –'

Then: 'I know what you must be thinking. But I'm desperate.'

He stood even closer to me than before, anxious that no one else in the room should overhear what he was saying. He made no gesture or movement of any kind. Only his eyes flickered towards me, over my shoulder, towards me, over the other shoulder.

'I'm already two nights behind,' he repeated. 'I have to do something.'

Wondering at his nerve in choosing this place for his panhandling, ashamed for him and ashamed of myself too, for taking what seemed the easier way, I put my hand into my pocket and brought out two Zim $10 bills. His hand closed over them and he sidled off instantly, saying, 'Very kind, that's very kind of you.' Now that the money was in his grasp, a slight infusion of gentility or self-regard had suddenly entered his voice.

Barely fifteen minutes later, M. and I were standing in front of the hotel waiting for the arrival of a taxi-driver; we had arranged with him earlier that he should take us to the nearest Botswana border post, about fifty miles away. While standing there, I saw the panhandler with two $10 bills in his hand – *my* $10 bills – talking *sotto voce* to a young member of the hotel staff. The youth was shaking his head and backing away. The man pursued him, holding out the money. The other pushed his arm away. But he was not to be deterred. He came closer. With a sudden movement he stuck the notes into the boy's shirt pocket. I could see that the latter was weakening; he took the notes out of his pocket, but did it half-heartedly; the man had retreated and wouldn't let him return them.

'Well – maybe – I see what I can do,' the youngster eventually said, breaking away. The man leaned forward, just long enough to put a few more words in his ear. 'All right – just wait here –'

With an oddly sly and shamefaced expression the boy went into the foyer of the hotel. Unfortunately our taxi-driver turned up before he came back. I could only conclude either that the older man would soon be smoking something stronger than tobacco with my $20; or, judging from the youngster's expression, and from the distaste with which he had undertaken the task, that some more intimate form of satisfaction was being arranged for him.

*

Travelling briefly in the northernmost strip of Botswana, along the Chobe River, we met a Rhodesian-born Afrikaner, by the name of van Niekerk, who told me how awful the 'bladdy Tswana' were and how much he longed to be 'back in Zim', working with the Ndebele again. They were a wonderful lot of people, he said. He went on passionately, 'I tell you, one Ndebele in my eyes is worth ten of the crap you find here. I'd go back to Zimbabwe tomorrow, if I could.' When I asked him why he did not do so, if he felt so strongly about it, he fell silent. Eventually he said: 'I can't go back. It's because of what went on during the war. I was in – in a special unit – and we . . . well, you know . . . some things happened. They mean I just can't go back. Never.'

With his dark past, and his dark pinings for Zimbabwe, van Niekerk was one of the mere handful among the people I met who so much as mentioned the war that had brought about the end of white rule in the country. The whites avoided speaking of it, I thought, because they had lost; the blacks because they had won. Today both sides are agreed that relations between the races in Zimbabwe are remarkably good-tempered, especially compared with how things then were in South Africa. This notwithstanding the fact that there is virtually no social mixing between black and white outside tiny academic, clerical, and 'overseas aid' circles; and that crime remains a pressing preoccupation for all. (Even the ticket-collector on the overnight train that brought us from Bulawayo to Victoria Falls had been accompanied everywhere by his bodyguard.) It is easy to understand why so many whites who fled to South Africa during the war, and after it, should now be making enquiries about doing what van Niekerk could only dream of.

Incidentally, while in Botswana I saw the only groups of real elephants – as against that solitary electronic one in Maun – to which I came close on this journey. As ever, I was struck by how shabby and imposing they are, and with what ponderousness and delicacy they move. One moment they are stepping softly over obstacles, touching at things in front of them with their tenderly swaying trunks; the next, they are tearing down branches and stuffing them whole into their slack, triangular mouths. Everything about their appearance is paradoxical and self-contradictory. Their baggy skins, droopy behinds, and disproportionately small tails make them look as vulnerable as old men; their heads and ears, tusks and tree-like limbs, as dangerous as battle-tanks.

The town of Victoria Falls is handy not only for the northernmost strip of Botswana, but also for the southern regions of Zambia. Originally Rhodes had intended the railway to the north to run through Harare (Salisbury). It was only after the discovery of coal in western Zimbabwe that the line was diverted in a north-westerly direction from Bulawayo. That is why the bridge carrying the railway crosses the Zambesi in such spectacular fashion just below the falls.

Physically, getting into Zambia is easy – you can simply walk over the bridge. Bureaucratically it is more complicated: there are the usual customs and passport queues to negotiate. That done, getting to Livingstone, the nearest Zambian town, which is about twelve miles away, also turns out to be easy enough. No taxis wait at the curio-sellers' stalls above the viewing-point on that side of the border; but when a rattletrap car pulls up and I ask the driver if he will take us to Livingstone he is more than willing to do so – once a price has been agreed. He explains that he's just got to see someone here, then we have ah cool drink, then we go. Sure. Fine. OK.

His name is Roy. He has a mate with him, Jonas, a scrap of a chap dressed in scraps, who nurses a car-battery on his lap and whose role in life appears to be to nod in agreement to everything Roy says. Roy himself is pretty skinny too, sturdy only in comparison with Jonas, and vaguely Rasta in appearance, though without dreadlocks and woolly hat. His expression is scowling and self-absorbed, his eye cloudy, his speech blurred, his gestures expansively unpredictable. After an exchange between the two of them they go off, Roy with a swagger, Jonas stumbling behind him, bent almost double by the weight of the battery. They are making for the huts behind the trees.

Some time later they return. Jonas, free of his burden, is as upright as he will ever get. Now for the cool drink. Ja. OK. No problem.

By the time we have finished the drink and are ready to get into the car, I have discovered that everything of which Roy speaks takes place in a darkly unchanging world; one trapped and paralysed in a present tense from which his consciousness never emerges. I have also learned that he sticks an all-purpose sound – not 'a', not 'the', but something like a small, throaty 'hah' or 'ah' – before most nouns, singular or plural. The same sound serves also for 'to'.

OK. So this is how AIDS spreads, according to Roy, though he is careful to say, 'I don' know how it go with Europeans like you – this is how it go here with us.' How it goes with them has everything to do with women and their pregnancies, abortions, and miscarriages. Men have nothing to do with it, except as victims. If he, Roy, sleeps with his wife when she is more than two months pregnant, then she will have a miscarriage ('certain') and the AIDS will come. 'Then me too – finish!' If the 'hotel-girls' get pregnant, and go into the bush to 'make it come down' (with a pulling, downward gesture of both hands between his legs), and then come back into the bars to 'speak with some men – you know – make ah business' – then the men will get AIDS also.

If so, I ask, what is to be done about it? Roy shrugs. 'Maybe kill ah hotel-girls.'

It isn't only AIDS, according to him, that goes about its business differently with each race. Outside town there is a textile factory which used to be run for its South African owners by 'ah big, fat Afrikaner called Myburgh'. After Myburgh's departure they brought in as manager 'ah black African man married with ah Russian woman'. At first all went well. Then not so well. 'Soon he become confuse in his mind. He is confuse mentally. To go in ah hospital do nothing for him – he try it, he see it, he learn for good he must go ah African doctor. Ah white wife don't help him nothing with this. What he got is African sickness. The *nganga* make ah medicines for him, he drink it, now he better already. Hundred per cent OK.'

On the left we pass a place called the Zambian Cultural Centre. It consists of some lemon-coloured rondavels behind a lemon-coloured wall. Roy has a story to tell about that place too. In the Centre not long ago there had been two traditional dancers, both men. 'They dancing all ah time, day and night. One dancer, they choose him ah go ah London, he dance there in ah concert. The other one, he also want ah go ah London. He want ah go *bad*. So the one they choose for London, he walking near ah river one day and ah crocodile take him. Yeh, by ah leg. He shout and ah women come running and screaming and ah crocodile let him go. They take him ah hospital and straight away – amputate – leg gone.'

Enthusiastically Roy bangs the side of one hand against the steering-wheel, chopper-fashion: 'Like that.'

Then the tale resumes. 'You see, ah other man – he witch him so he won' go ah London. With one leg? Dancing? No way! So when he come out, on ah crutches, he go ahnother witch and soon-soon – other man – he *dead*! Gone! Puukh! Finish!'

How had it been done? Roy knows exactly. 'They take ah bone like from here' – digging at his forearm – 'or from here' – with a poke at his thigh – 'and they scrape it empty inside, so it ah special gun. Then they put in ah medicines, like ah bullet. Then it don' matter *where* you are – if you in England, anywhere, and they here in Zambia, and they put in ah bullet, point ah gun right way – fire! – puukh! – you finish!'

Later he tells us why the black people are so poor in Zambia. It is because the whites have left the country. In Zimbabwe things are better: lots of white men stayed there after independence. But here in Zambia, according to Roy, all you have is 'Indian, Indian, Indian'. Doctors, teachers, shopmen who own all the shops and won't buy anything from ah black man like himself: 'Not even ah chicken or ah egg – nothing!' He came from a province called Mungo (?), where things were a little better; they still had some white people there. 'Not like here. In Livingstone? Just Indian, Indian, Indian,' he says yet again, the word gaining velocity and ferocity with each repetition. And to show the depth of his feeling on the subject he turns his head aside and spits through the open window.

*

It is true that all the shops in Livingstone appear to be owned by Indians. All, too, are permanently enclosed in thick steel mesh and have large, knobkieried, semi-uniformed guards at the door. Most have another similarly armed guard inside. When not at their counters, the shopkeepers ensconce themselves in raised, pulpit-like mini-forts behind their cash-registers.

The trouble is that the guards are guarding nothing. At least that is how it strikes a visitor fresh from Zimbabwe – itself a country tormented by drought, by debt, by under-investment, unemployment, and exhausted foreign exchange reserves. The chemist shop has a particularly wretched appearance: inches of dusty shelf-space lie blankly between each jar of Vaseline, packet of sanitary towels, tin of powdered milk. (A notice about AIDS is stuck on one of the walls: above an amateurishly printed picture of a girl in school uniform is the legend *Say NO to Sex*; beneath it the pathetic plea, *Be A Responsible Girl*.) The food shops are in hardly better shape. On offer in this shop are a few cabbages, oranges, and carrots, some cans of fish and open sacks of rice and mealie meal, with tin scoops buried in them. (No wonder we have seen so many women trekking on foot across the border into Zimbabwe, in order to buy their permitted two loaves of bread and two kilos of flour.) Next door a single ghetto-blaster and a couple of transistors occupy a particularly heavily fortified window. Across the road another barricaded display consists of a dress and a few T-shirts suspended from a pole.

Seated on a throne behind her cash-register is a pale-faced, long-necked woman in a dark-green paisley dress, who is evidently delighted to have a white, middle-class, middle-aged couple to talk to. She is endowed with the delicate features and dramatic eyebrows of a classical Indian miniature. The slender hands too. The entire community in Livingstone, she tells us, is composed of Gujeratis. The only Indians in the district who are not originally from Gujerat, or whose parents are not from there, are 'the expatriates'. She was born in Lusaka, the capital of Zambia, but came down to Livingstone after her marriage. The expatriates are mostly doctors, engineers, teachers, and what sounds like counsellors – lawyers perhaps. And the permanent residents? 'We are only minding the shops.' How does she find things? 'No complaints,' she answers gallantly, in that picked-clean shop of hers, from behind her fortified cash-register. 'Making a living.' Her guard stands behind her left shoulder, not attending, perhaps not understanding, prodding list-lessly at the end of his nose with the rounded end of his stick.

The shop across the road is run by a man with plump, fierce cheeks, a hooked nose, and hair cut short and bristling up above his forehead. He too is caged at a height above his raised cash-register. From there he gazes about him in authoritative fashion, like a commander on the bridge of his ship. His father, a grey-haired man with a submissive air, lays on the table next to him several bundles of kwacha notes. Each bundle is neatly held together by a paper-clip. The denominations are inflation-high and the bundles thick enough to put the paper-clips under considerable strain. For the moment the man ignores them. From his accent I judge that he too is locally born. 'We feel quite safe here,' he says. 'They won't bother us' – 'they' being the black Zambians: the two or three ill-clad customers in his shop, the millions of them outside, the pair with cudgels guarding him. He goes on gloweringly: 'This is a peaceful country. One reason we feel safe here is that Zambia got its independence with no bloodshed. We didn't have a war like they had in Zimbabwe. Look, they chucked out President Kaunda in the last election without fighting, no trouble.'

When I ask him if he had voted in the election, his expression grows even angrier than before. 'No, I took my family to England.' Obviously this decision to leave the country at what might have been a time of crisis has to be explained or excused, after what has gone before. 'We all go to England sometimes,' he says. 'We've all got family there. In India too. Also we go to South Africa for holidays or if we need hospital treatment or something like that. They have first-class medical services there, cheaper than in England.'

Then he excuses himself and begins counting the bundles of notes his father has put in front of him. The old man gives us several enthusiastic nods as we leave the shop. Outside, almost everything in the main street is in a barely comprehensible state of disarray and disrepair. A tall building of concrete and of blue plastic panels, once a block of flats evidently, stands there like a ruined man, a drunkard or a hobo: windows smashed, blinds hanging out, balconies with railings gone, balconies gone entirely, internal ceilings down, stairways blocked. Yet it is clearly still inhabited. Only the offices of the district council, the banks, the tourist department, and the Zambian State Insurance Company appear to be in reasonable condition. And the echoing Livingstone Museum, which contains many dusty exhibits of an educational kind, including some mementoes of Livingstone himself, and an excellent plaster model of the Victoria Falls and the gorges around it. While we are wandering about the building, a female starveling, about six years of age, on her own apparently, with a minute head and calves I could have encircled between finger and thumb, attaches herself to M. and follows her everywhere, before finally plucking up the courage to take her by the hand. But not a word does she say. Off the main street the largest and best-kept building to be seen is the V.K. NAIK HINDU HALL.

We are taken back to the border in a drifting wreck of a car called the Fun Taxi. A thirty-year-old Standard, a model which has disappeared not just from British roads but from the British memory, it has doors that do not close, a shattered windscreen, a gear-lever afflicted with palsy, no instruments at all – only wires hanging out of holes in the dashboard, a steering-column kept in cylindrical shape because it is literally lashed together by twine. The camberless surface of the road (potholed in the middle, with bite-shaped portions taken out of its sides) looks no better on the way out than it had on the way in. Our time in Zambia is over – almost.

First, though, I try to get as close as I can to the falls on the Zambian side. My reward is a view of them in profile, extraordinarily unlike that of the apocalyptic, mile-long series of cataracts that can be seen frontally from Zimbabwe. Here the whole thing is reduced to a succession of vertical, whispering, feather-like Japanese plumes, whose bottom it is impossible to see and whose colours are white and delicate shades of grey only.

While taking in this view I am joined by a group of Indians. My final Zambian–Indian conversation therefore has for its backdrop a spectacle that makes everything we say or do seem absurdly inadequate. Only gods or giants or creatures with the innocence of animals would know how to ignore it entirely. The group consists of man and wife, grandfather and grandmother, several children who are driving the mother to distraction by their antics near the precipitous edges – so much so that she and her husband take them away after only a minute or two – and a plump, bald gentleman in saffron robes. They are accompanied by a thickset African, who is the first to start talking to me. He carries a set of car keys in his hand, like a badge of office, but his build and demeanour, and his bright red shirt and tight black trousers, give him the unmistakable look of a bodyguard. He complains bitterly to me about the state of the roads. The strip of road I have just traversed in the Fun Taxi is, he claims, one of the best in Zambia. 'All the way from Lusaka I'm like this,' he says, and puts his two hands together in front of him, hunches up his shoulders, and makes violent shuddering and steering-wheel motions to the left and right.

The grandmother is wearing a sari; grandpa a lightweight business suit; the other man has a cardigan over his saffron robes and sandals on his feet. He carries an aluminium cane in his right hand. His skin is pale, the colour of weak-tea-with-milk; it darkens to something like purple under his eyes. Having been deferentially introduced to me under the title of swami, he feels impelled to explain himself. 'I am a devotee,' he says, inclining his head slightly. 'I have come to Zambia to teach. I have been teaching in Kitwe, Ndola, Lusaka, and now in Livingstone. Soon I am returning to India, to New Delhi. I am a professor at — College' – uttering a name I cannot catch. Then he sizes me up, in kindly enough fashion, with black eyes and a brow that is somehow smooth between its horizontal wrinkles. The top of his head is smooth too; it gleams in the spray-diffused sunlight, which comes to us from somewhere behind the whispering falls.

'You are a professional gentleman?' he asks.

I cannot resist telling him that I too am a professor, in London. The coincidence delights him so much that he at once invites me to visit his college in New Delhi and do some teaching there. I would be welcome to stay in his house while I am in Delhi. I can stay there as long as I wish.

Only then does he think to ask what my subject might be.

'English literature is a wonderful literature for reading and teaching,' he says generously, after I have told him.

We stand side by side, gazing at the falls, and at the haze-filled gorges which zig-zag away to the east for many miles – each one having served its time as the line of the cataract, before being superseded by another gorge upstream. In all the brittle dryness of the tangled plain, with these fissures slashed through it, no movement is to be seen. I explain to the swami my understanding of why the gorges have changed direction again and again over the aeons – an understanding derived mostly from the model I had studied in the Livingstone Museum – and he listens attentively. When I am finished he makes another connoisseur-like response. 'That is a very satisfactory explanation. It is the best I have heard.'

Later, while we are slowly walking up the path, the grandfather and grandmother tell me that the swami had come out to Zambia at the invitation of their son, who is a businessman in Lusaka. He has been staying with them, except when travelling and teaching elsewhere in the country. Now they are all having a little holiday before his return to Delhi next week. He is a very fine man, grandmother says, a wonderful man. Grandfather evidently feels that this cannot convey their companion's special qualities. He draws me aside with a touch on the arm and comes to a halt. I do too. For some reason the noise of the falls is louder up here than it was when we were nearer to them. He stands to one side of me. His expression grows more solemn. He leans closer and his voice deepens for greater emphasis. 'He is a *double M.A.*'

Our Zambian visit is not quite finished, however. First, a brief historical note. Then an account of an episode on the Zambia –

Zimbabwe border. I leave it to the reader to make the connection between the two.

Once 'Southern Rhodesia' had been secured, Rhodes turned his attention to bringing under the Company's control the territory north of the Zambesi River ('Northern Rhodesia': now Zambia). Climatically and agriculturally it was not nearly as attractive to white settlers as the lands to the south; nor was it believed to contain legendary reserves of gold. Still, it was indispensable to his vision of an all-British overland route to the Mediterranean; he was also anxious to get to the Katanga copperfields before Leopold II of Belgium managed to do so. He was even more anxious to have the Charter Company, not the British government, administer the territory.

Here again he was thwarted; or rather, he managed to thwart himself. Just as the Jameson Raid finally put paid to his hope of securing Bechuanaland for the Charter Company, so too did it wrest the trans-Zambesian territory from his grasp. The imperial goverment was too embarrassed by the raid – or by its failure, to be more precise – to allow yet another tract of the continent to pass into his safekeeping. Subsequently, various schemes to federate the two territories were mooted; one such scheme was even put into operation for a few years in the 1950s. But the severance between the countries was never to be undone. 'Northern Rhodesia' may have borne Rhodes's name until it became the Republic of Zambia in 1964; but he himself never set foot in it.

Ahead of us in the queue in the Zimbabwe customs office, on our return journey, is a man in late middle-age carrying a Zambian passport. He wears a threadbare shirt, a pair of black trousers, and black leather shoes almost crushed out of existence. Everything about him, even his attempt at a moustache somehow, reveals him to be both poor and worried. He holds a rolled-up jacket under his arm. By contrast, the customs officer dealing with him, the only one on duty, is unusually dapper: long-sleeved white shirt buttoned at the wrists; red and white striped tie; dark-blue trousers of a stationmaster's hue. The setting looks unworthy of him. The cement floor is gritty underfoot. The plywood counter has a top brought to a high polish by generations of sweating outstretched arms. The walls are smudged by the heads and hands of people long since gone over the border. Notices written in felt-tip pen are stuck with scotch tape on the walls, which are also decorated with many other dirt-edged pieces of scotch tape marking the sites where similar notices used to hang.

Something is going on between the official and the would-be entrant to Zimbabwe. Neither looks at the other. The official's voice is loud; the man replies in a despondent mutter. With a jerk of the head he is finally summoned to come around the counter. The two of them disappear through a door to the side. They remain behind it for five minutes, ten, fifteen, while the queue behind us builds into a crowd, and many hands reach past us, to the side of us, above us, holding up their passports and customs forms, as if in supplication to what theologians call the *deus absconditus*: the hidden or absent god. Twenty minutes now. When the god finally emerges, his victim in tow, the latter is more dejected than ever. Only a lifetime's training in humiliation and disappointment is keeping him from tears. The official seats himself, puts a wad of Zimbabwe dollar bills on the counter, reaches for a pad, and proceeds, with much finesse, to stick three pieces of ancient carbon paper between its uppermost leaves. So four copies will be made of this document, which is headed 'Receipt for Forfeiture or Seizure of Currency'. One is white, one yellow, one pink, one buff. (The last of them, as I was shortly to see, so faint as to be wholly illegible). He then counts the notes in front of him, and divides the wad into two heaps. One contains Zim $150 – £15, say, or US $22. The other amounts to Zim $110 (£11). He then says, 'You know the maximum sum you are permitted to bring into Zimbabwe is Zim $150?' Nod. 'You know it is an offence to deal in Zimbabwe currency?' Nod, followed by a choked, unfinished plea, 'It was just for a friend. He asked me . . .'

The man's name, passport number, and length of intended stay in Zimbabwe are inscribed on the form. So is the excess sum ($110) he has had in his possession. The pile of notes containing that amount is then locked away in a strong-box, with much rattling of key and chain before and after. The dangerous currency smuggler, caught at his tricks, blinks slowly, as if his lids are made of flame. Or his eyes of sand.

There then follows a series of questions, the answers to which are carefully written down. The average income per head in Zambia, remember, is something like US $220 a year; and this man, to judge from his appearance, manner, and the beggarly sum he has been trying to get across the border, is rather worse-off than most of his compatriots in the crowded room.

What is your profession? (Farmer.)

What is your business address? (Plot 12, Sapetla Lands.)

What is your personal address? (P.O. Box . . .)

What will be your address in Zimbabwe? (A pause, while he wonders whether he will be getting his acquaintances or family in Zimbabwe into trouble. Finally an address in Hwange is half-heartedly offered.)

You understand why this currency has been taken from you? (Yes.)

Will you now read this form? (The farmer-smuggler reads it slowly, one cracked finger moving along the line.)

Is the information on it correct? (Yes.)

The form is then painstakingly signed by the man, and the top copy is ripped off and given to him as a keepsake. The wad of Zim $150 he is entitled to take across the border is pushed across the counter to him and instantly disappears into his wrapped-up jacket. Some minutes later, still on the Zambian side of the border, I see him sitting on the edge of the verandah outside the office. His feet are in the gutter. Two or three shawled women, none of them young, are standing around him. He is obviously trying to explain to them what has happened inside, but is hardly able to produce audible sounds, so great is his shock at what he has been through and at the sum of money he has lost. You would not think that a skin so dark could assume so grey-green a hue. Automatically, repeatedly, he unfolds the paper given to him, as if to show it to them, and then folds it again.

What it was in him or about him that had roused the official's suspicion, not to say sadism, I do not know. Nor have I any idea of what took place between the two of them behind that closed door.

Before leaving Victoria Falls, M. and I pay a last visit to the bronze effigy of Livingstone which broods over the Devil's Cataract on the western side of the falls. It shows him wearing the peaked cap, complete with flap over the back of his neck, that appears in so many Victorian engravings. He stands upright, in mid-stride, staring directly ahead. Over his shoulder is slung a case to carry his binoculars; in one hand he holds a Bible. The words 'Holy Bible' are impressed into its spine, so that the onlooker will not mistake it for a diary or medical textbook or best-selling novel. An index finger marks his place between its pages. His gaze is directed towards the falls. At his feet is a small garden of aloes.

A plaque set among the aloes explains that the statue was erected in 1935: 'to the memory of their distinguished countryman through the united efforts of the Caledonian Societies in the Union of South Africa and the Rhodesias'. M. has a dim memory of hearing from her parents that her grandfather, himself a Scot and at that time a minister in the colonial cabinet, had made a speech at the unveiling of the statue. Another plaque informs us that in 1955 the statue was re-dedicated in the presence of 'the Governor General of the Federation of the Rhodesias and Nyasaland', when 'men and women of all races dedicated themselves and their country to carry on the high Christian aims and ideals which inspired David Livingstone in his mission here'. A few years later this Federation, a half-hearted, misbegotten, late-imperial invention, had ceased to exist. Zambia and Malawi (Nyasaland) went their own way. The bloody birth of Zimbabwe lay ahead.

CHAPTER TWENTY-FOUR

☆

Scrambling for Africa – The Many Forms
of Power – Harare Parades – Heroes' Acre
– Generations Coming and Going

The town of Livingstone in Zambia was the furthest north I went. It had been clear to me for some time that my pursuit of the road to the north, begun in Kimberley, would have to end in Zimbabwe. As I saw it, and see it still, it was there that the political and strategic concept of the road to the north at once achieved its fulfilment and expired. Like a salmon, it spawned there and died. Once the Ndebele had been crushed and their territory occupied, all the advantages that could be got out of this route from the Cape were secure. The Boers had been outflanked and contained; the blacks in Zimbabwe and to the south of it subdued; the trade-route further into the interior made safe; British missionaries given an unassailable position of advantage in east-central Africa.

Quite an achievement. The peoples of the subcontinent still live with its consequences. But as for the larger intentions the chief projectors of the route had propagandized for and half-believed in – a single British colony and a British railway stretching from the Cape to Cairo, the brushing aside of all other Europeans who might stand in the way, the natives chastely clad in English cottons, working for English masters, and attending church services everywhere – no, these fantasies had in turn been outflanked and overwhelmed by historical forces which those who had come up the road had helped to put in motion, and had themselves been helped by, but which were now well beyond their control.

To put it briskly: the aims and deeds of the missionaries and empire-builders, freebooters and traders, had been overtaken by the larger 'Scramble for Africa' then reaching its height among the European powers. During the 1880s a political process or fever, if you like – had begun to affect not only the powers long established in Africa, like the British and Portuguese, but also the French, Germans, Italians, and most spectacularly of all, the Belgians in the person of King Leopold II, whose megalomaniac and secretive scheming almost matched that of Rhodes himself. Expeditions bearing flags, 'treaties', charters – and guns to enforce the treaties and keep the flags flying – were entering the continent by a variety of routes from the east, west, and north. Even the most reluctant and parsimonious of European governments felt compelled to try to forestall the ascendancy which they feared neighbours and rivals would gain by seizing the vast territories that had been mapped in the preceding decades. Unless *we* do it, the argument went, *they* will get their hands on the treasures known to lie under some of these lands, and the even greater treasures still awaiting discovery. To *them*, not *us*, will also go the prestige and moral credit enjoyed only by those who rule over great imperial possessions.

In terms of this struggle, it was apparent that only so much could be done by commanding the road to the north from the Cape. By 1890 other questions in other areas of Africa were demanding attention. Would the copper resources of Katanga go to the Belgians or to Britain? Would King Leopold, having grabbed Katanga, be agreeable to permitting British interests to retain a strip of land through which they could keep open communications to Uganda? (In effect a notional continuation, never to be realized, of the road.) Who had endowed Carl Peters of the German Exploration Society with the magnificent title of 'High Commissioner for Kilimanjaro'? Was the whole of Uganda worth the island of Heligoland in the Baltic Sea? Who would seize and control the waters of the Upper Nile – General Kitchener's British troops marching down from Egypt or General Marchand's advancing from the French territory of Gabon?

And so forth. The road from the Cape could never be more than contributory to the outcome of the conflicts that lay ahead, whether

you looked further north or turned your gaze southwards once
more, where a major war between Briton and Boer over the
goldfields of the Witwatersrand was drawing ever closer. Among
all these developments, one minor event seems to me of remarkable
symbolic significance, though I have never seen it commented on in
such terms. When Cecil Rhodes entered Rhodesia for the first time
– the vast and beautiful territory which already bore his name
(unofficially), and which was owned by a company wholly of his
own creation – he did not do so via his road to the north. For
more than fifteen years he had schemed and politicked to gain
control of the route, blackmailed, bribed, and gone to war for it.
Now he found it easier and quicker to come into Rhodesia from
Beira, via the east coast, through the selfsame Portuguese territory
which just the year before he had tried and failed to snatch for his
Company.

This version of the Great North Road was *fait accompli*.
Northern and Southern Rhodesia would not have been able to
survive without it. Yet it had also become just one mode of access
among many others to the interior of Africa.

Once upon a time, not all that long ago, it was plain to most
people in Europe that the process of lording it over alien, resentful,
impoverished peoples of a different colour was good both for those
who did it and for those to whom it was done.

That it was good for them – those 'sullen, new-caught peoples,
half devil and half child', as Kipling described them – was self-
evident, even if they themselves were too stupid to realize it. It
brought them Christianity, medicine, discipline, training, trousers,
centralized government. In return, so to speak, it helped to avert
from the European nations the dangers of overpopulation supposedly threatening their racial 'stock'; it also provided them with an
invaluable Darwinian test of national 'fitness'. And all at a profit,
too. All as a way of winning exclusive markets for your own
products, cheap agricultural imports, and monopoly supplies of
strategic and precious minerals.

And now? Now, it seems, the industrialized or industrializing nations are confident they can have access to all the minerals and raw materials they need without actually going to the trouble of planting their flags right on top of them; let alone of burdening themselves with administering territories and peoples distant from their own. Let the natives do it, as best they can! Those who have nothing but raw materials to sell will in the end have to offer their stuff at prices which they will only rarely be able to rig. They cannot even mine it, pump it, grow it, without the technology and the capital of those who will buy it from them. If any rigging is to be done it is the buyers not the sellers who have the upper hand.

Much the same goes for markets. What is the point of having a closed market for your products when the people inside it are penniless? Better by far to woo people living in the wealthier, or at least the economically expanding, regions of the world. They are the ones with money to spend; the impoverished rest can be relied on to follow their example with as much zeal as their pinched purses allow.

So who now needs full-blown, old-fashioned empires on which the sun never sets? To whom nowadays does it not come naturally to abominate imperialism? Or to put such questions in quite another way: When was Japan, say, the more powerful country – when it was ravaging half a continent in the course of establishing what it called its 'Asian Co-Prosperity Sphere'; or today, when there is no corner of the world where Japanese goods are not sought, bought, sold, bartered for, and stolen, whenever the opportunity arises?

The truth is that power of any kind is almost as little under the control of those who possess it as it is of those who do not. Again and again on this journey I found myself being forced to conceive of power as being rather like water – by which I mean that it cannot choose whether or not to flow downhill: it must seek whatever outlets it can find and then proceed to inundate levels lower than its own. It cannot *be* power if it does not do so. This is true of it in all its forms – technical, military, political, organizational, intellectual; true also of all the changing modes of manifesting itself which historical circumstances permit or encourage.

Those circumstances being of course the record of past manifestations of power. The alphabet and the Bible, Chaka's regiments and those of Queen Victoria, sextants and ideologies, among them.

Like most capital cities in Africa, Harare is a mixture of a few high-rise buildings and innumerable no-rise ones. It has some broad avenues and a central square or two. To the north are expensively sprawling, well-guarded suburbs; to the south rundown, cheaper versions of the same; elsewhere an incomparably vaster population is crammed into what are politely called the 'high-density areas'. For truly high high-density I have never seen anything, not even in Soweto, near Johannesburg, as crowded as Mbare, close to the centre of town. Nothing there was more than head-high; the roadways or pathways were so aswarm as to be virtually hidden by bodies.

Because more construction goes on in Harare than in the rest of Zimbabwe put together, it now has fewer buildings worth looking at than Bulawayo, the country's second city, which retains a fair scattering of Edwardian and Victorian survivals. On the other hand Harare is the more climatically and topographically favoured of the two: it gets more rain; it has more trees and grass; some of its suburbs slope a little, this way and that – which is more than can be said of any of Bulawayo's. And it does have one brief row of buildings, along Herbert Chitepo Avenue (formerly Rhodes Avenue), representative of an architectural style to be found from Cape Town to Nairobi – and further afield, in Australia too for instance. White or cream walls, heavily incised; pedimented windows; rusticated stone on the ground floor; ornamental pillars rising from the first floor up; red-tiled or orange-tiled roofs above (though red-painted corrugated iron will do, if needs be): those are the hallmarks. Something vaguely Roman about it all (for obvious reasons); something vaguely tropical; something definitely ponderous (signifying financial and constitutional solidity). Excellent for government offices, banks, building societies, school hostels, subsidiary De Beers buildings, and law courts.

*

In Harare we attended more by accident than design various public functions of a sort we would not have gone to elsewhere. We heard two choirs singing songs in praise of Breast-Feeding, and put some money in the collection boxes that were being rattled to advance the cause. We went to the prize-giving of the Zimbabwe Wild Life Conservancy Photographic Competition: an all-white affair, with the exception of one youthful Indian photographer and the small party accompanying the deputy minister who gave the prizes away. We watched the Environment 2000 ceremonial march through the city, led by a bicycle (presumably because of its environmental soundness) bedecked with grass and posters, followed by the police band in dark-green uniforms with silver stripes; by a troupe of all-female traditional dancers in black and white two-piece outfits, with bands of seed-pods attached to their shins and ankles, who jigged industriously; and the Girl Guides in blue bringing up the rear.

In the city's central park we listened to an open-air concert of African xylophone music, apparently as part of the Harare International Book Fair. When the music stopped several feminist poems were read by one of the few white women present, who brandished her dyed head of thick red hair like a weapon throughout the performance. The poems were listened to attentively by the women in the audience and derisively by the men, especially those on the outskirts of the crowd. One poem with the refrain 'For I am a woman!' at the end of every verse was greeted with especially loud snorts of contempt. By chance, too, we found ourselves at a fund-raising event in M.'s former high school, where we watched disco-dancing and saw a fashion parade by the senior girls. They wore self-designed dresses and strutted up and down an improvised catwalk with all the approved swayings, turnings, divestings, display-ings. The audience consisted entirely of African girls in green tunics and blazers – not one of whom would have been allowed on the premises in M.'s day – who greeted every costume and gyration with wholehearted shrieking and clapping.

The last public spectacle we witnessed, wholly involuntarily, was the passing through the streets of the armed convoy that carries

Comrade President Mugabe from one place to another. It is terrifying to be at the wheel of a car and to see it bearing down on you at high speed: headlights blazing; sirens howling; lorry-loads of troops with AK 47s sticking out sideways; limousines crammed with civilian bodyguards, and the one with tinted glass windows in which the great man invisibly sits; then still more of the same, guns now pointing behind.

It is forbidden, on pain of death, for anyone in sight of this cavalcade to move until it is well past; and should you think that I have thrown in 'on pain of death' as a rhetorical flourish – well, I advise you to have another think before you choose to visit Harare. People have been shot for being insufficiently immobile in sight of it; during our present visit (though not while we were in Harare) a motorist who did not slam his brakes on quickly enough had his car deliberately rammed and split in two. He subsequently died, poor man, without even knowing that President Mugabe had not been anywhere near the scene, and that the convoy which had killed him had merely been *rehearsing* for some forthcoming function.

When I had last visited Harare, four years before, the fantasy that it was the capital city of an important member of a global socialist and revolutionary bloc was cultivated at every turn. I mentioned earlier that all official discourse in Zimbabwe used to divide the world into two categories: the good people in the socialist countries ('comrades'), and the evil remainder. In much the same way, the streets were placarded with large road-signs pointing to the embassies of comradely countries that really mattered – THE EMBASSY OF THE PEOPLE'S REPUBLIC OF LIBYA JAMHARIYA; THE EMBASSY OF THE PEOPLE'S REPUBLIC OF CZECHO-SLOVAKIA; THE EMBASSY OF THE PALESTINE LIBERA-TION ORGANISATION and so forth – while the diplomatic presence of the United States, France, Italy, and Britain went unadvertised. As for the building which housed the South African consular offices, outside of which there stretched day after day much the longest queue to be seen anywhere in town (for visas, I discovered later) – that went without so much as a little brass plate.

A dozen rose-bushes in a little garden-bed were almost hidden behind the notice declaring them to be A GIFT FROM THE PEOPLE OF THE SOCIALIST REPUBLIC OF BULGARIA TO THE PEAS- ANTS AND WORKERS OF THE REPUBLIC OF ZIMBABWE; while major benefactions from the West went unadorned. Expressions of socialist solidarity and of confidence in the pre-ordained victory of Marxism world-wide abounded in the speeches of politicians, especially when welcoming the right sort of visitors from abroad.

Even then it was patent that it was all a sham. One did not need to wait for the subsequent collapse of the 'world socialist system' to realize it. A walk through the city, a journey by car around its outskirts, were sufficient. Every bit of investment coming into the country, every major item of economic aid it was receiving, was from the despised, corrupt, decadent West (Japan and Taiwan included); whereas the contribution of the socialist world consisted of nothing but AK-47s.* As for the 'leading cadres' of this revolutionary regime, it was plain that the only Comrades to whom they paid more than lip-service were Comrade Mercedes and Comrade BMW, Comrade Sony and Comrade Hitachi.

And today? Since the collapse of the socialist bloc? Well, at the most recent congress of his party, the Zimbabwe African National Union (Patriotic Front), Comrade President Mugabe was pleased to announce that he had received 'fraternal greetings' from North Korea and Cuba; but even he knows that the game is up. (Nothing like fraternal greetings from *them* to make a president feel insecure.) So he has fallen back on another kind of demagoguery, and has taken to stoking up anti-white sentiment. A particular target of his hostility has been the so-called 'commercial farmers' – i.e. the white farmers who are heirs to those acres seized when the settlers

---

* The war against the last white government of Rhodesia could never have been fought without the military equipment supplied by the former Soviet Union. Western countries maintained a series of inefficacious economic sanctions against that government, which had disowned its ties to Britain and had been disowned by it. But no Western state ever considered supplying the guerillas with weapons.

occupied the country a hundred years ago, and who still own immense tracts of land and farm them on a capital-intensive basis.

That there is fierce land-hunger in Zimbabwe, and that any leader would have to respond to the pressure from below for a more equitable distribution of pastoral and arable farmland, is indisputable. But does this particular leader have to go about it by telling his followers that the white farmers are 'as greedy as Jews'?

Apparently he does.

Here is an entire shelf in a Harare bookshop devoted to volumes put out by Progress Publishers Moscow, some of them printed as late as 1988, barely two years before the great collapse. They strike almost as distant an echo in my breast as the leather-bound volumes of *The Boy's Own Paper* in which, half a century ago, I used to immerse myself in the Kimberley Public Library. The biggest and thickest of the books is entitled *Zionism: Enemy of Peace and Progress* – an unsurprising title in itself, perhaps, given the former Soviet Union's inveterate enmity towards the State of Israel. Then I look inside the covers and see that this book is Volume *Five* of an entire series with that same title, and the stench of anti-Semitic obsession at once wafts off its ill-printed pages. So I put it back in place, wondering if Comrade President Mugabe has all five volumes of the series on his own shelves, and look at the other works on offer.

What Is Scientific Communism?, *What Is Labour?*, *What Is Revolution?*, *What Is the Transition Period?* (an especially gripping read, that one, no doubt). Then my own favourite among them all: *What is the World Socialist System?* Nearby, among much else, stand Lenin's *Works* in eight volumes; Engels' *The Peasant Question in France and Germany*; a translation into Shona of *The Three Sources and Three Component Parts of Marxism*; and, finally, *Mathematics for Marxists*.

After that, there was only one place to go: Heroes' Acre, the official site celebrating the war of independence and the establishment of the Republic of Zimbabwe.

The name of the site had led me to suppose that some of the twenty thousand guerillas who had died during the war, fighting in the two liberation movements, Zanu and Zapu (the one Shona, the other Ndebele), would be buried there. I was wrong. The only people at rest in Heroes' Acre, so far as I could see, are cabinet ministers and party officials – all but one of them deceased after Zimbabwe had become independent. The exception, who is described on his gravestone as a guerilla commander, was killed in a road accident during the war; in what circumstances we are not told. The most elaborately decorated grave is that of Sally Mugabe, the president's wife, a Ghanaian by origin, who had died just a few months before. Standing over it was a six-foot, heart-shaped wreath of white plastic flowers and ribbons, with the pink tinsel initials 'SFM' entwined within.

The graves are laid in a semi-circle half-way up a hill, with plenty of space for more to come. On its summit is a lofty pylon-like structure; below is a podium overlooking a group of thirty-foot-high upright figures in red stone. Male and female, bedraped in a flag, they clutch automatic weapons and rocket-launchers, and gaze towards the horizon. They look about as much like African guerillas as you might expect talentless, Soviet-trained, North Korean sculptors to produce. Below them are swathes of wide, semi-circular steps, flanked with brick walls at a slant. On the walls are terracotta tableaux showing North Korean-type white policemen setting dogs on same-type blacks, more such blacks at meetings addressed by shirt-sleeved comrades, blacks taking up arms, attacking white settlers, triumphing, marching bravely into the future under the flag of Zimbabwe, with President Mugabe, out of scale but complete with lapels, necktie, and spectacles, towering in profile over them. End of story.

In fact the journey I had made came to an end in a strangely studious calm, since I passed a good part of my time in Harare at the National Archive, a well-run and well-endowed institution set among sunny, terraced gardens and frequented by scholarly folk of all ages. M. and I also spent time with her relations who live in the city. One of them is a bachelor, a businessman, who gave us the freedom of his house for as long as we were there; the other an agronomist who had recently resigned from a position in the Zimbabwe forestry department, so despairing had he become of the nepotism and inefficiency he encountered at every turn. The agronomist is married to a film-maker, and they have a nine-year-old son who is the most fluent white-skinned speaker of any of the indigenous languages (Shona, in his case) I have ever met. I have known many white people who could speak a Bantu language more or less convincingly; but never one whom African bystanders stare at with astonishment, as they do when they overhear this boy in casual conversation with other speakers of Shona. In fact, his parents tell us, with an amused mixture of pride and dismay, his Shona is probably better than his English.

Knowing that her grandmother is buried in Harare, M. goes to the trouble of finding out where. At her instigation, the members of the family gather one morning to visit the grave. The Shona-speaking youngster is also a member of the party, and is much impressed by the solemnity of visiting the grave of his great-great-grandmother. The cemetery, an all-white, 'colonial' affair, perhaps the oldest in the city, is still carefully tended. It is bounded on three sides by main roads vibrating with traffic. The African verger finds the plot-number of the grave in his battered old index-file and leads us to it without hesitation, in the Scottish Presbyterian section. A plain stone cross is inscribed with the name 'Mary Struthers', who is declared in letters quite as large to be 'Wife of R.D. Gilchrist'. Her children are not mentioned, nor are the dates of her birth and death. M. tells us that in all probability this is the first family visit to the grave to be made since her grandmother's death in the flu epidemic of 1919. Her mother, who nearly died at the same time, never went there and never spoke of it. Nor did her uncle. Her grandfather is buried in British Columbia, Canada, where he retired after a second marriage.

The great-great-grandson of Mary and R.D. Gilchrist, struggling with imponderables, says, 'It doesn't matter *when* anybody died. It was just as sad for them in those days.'

Nearby lie many other deceased Scottish Presbyterians. On one of the stones a particularly harrowing story is inscribed: it tells of a fifteen-year-old girl who was attacked by 'an unknown assailant near this place', and whom 'the Lord in His mercy took before she was forced to surrender that which was more precious to her than life itself'. Not far away is the Jewish section of the cemetery. I have not read of any Jews who were members of the Pioneer column; but evidently there were several who did not lag more than a few months behind. Among other markers, side by side, are two little ones for 'Child Cohen (1901)' and 'Child Levy (1902)'.

Beyond the tallest of the crosses, angels, and broken columns, rise some trees; taller and further off still loom the cooling-towers of a power station.

One day, while sitting in the National Archive in Harare, I found that instead of perusing the volumes which had been brought to me, I was writing in my notebook about the last evening I had spent in Mafikeng. Even in its unfinished state – or because of its unfinished state – the diary entry I made that morning seems as good a passage as any with which to end.

Sunset: dusty pink, dusty silver, dusty rose, all glowing more intense as the sky darkens and deepens to mauve. Outlined against it, silhouettes of trees: thorn, karreeboom, eucalyptus. And a single cypress in front or behind a house I cannot see. Each shape intimate and unmistakable; found in this conjunction only in the northern Cape, nowhere else. I could be on the outskirts of Vryburg, or Kuruman, or Kimberley. The sun resigning from it everywhere with the same sad flourish; the surface of the veld and its abject stalks of grass invisible already, gone into the dark.

How sounds carry across a flat country! A passing train fills the entire hemisphere overhead. A car engine is audible for minutes on end, every change of gear like the beginning of a different chapter in a book. Unseen Africans talking somewhere in the veld, their voices as musical and meaningless to me as the sound of running water.

Thorn trees, flat-topped, wide-branching, bristle into the dark. Gum trees stand bedraggled, like ill-dressed women embarrassed by their own height. Colours behind them now drained away, but for a last bloody streak. The smell of dust in the air; and now the smell of frying fish; and all of it for ever.

Additional References

☆

CHAPTER ONE

(*page* 28) The description of the measures adopted against the smuggling of diamonds out of the De Beers compounds is taken from *Matabele Thompson: His Autobiography and the Story of Rhodesia*, ed. Nancy Rouillard (1936).

CHAPTER TWO

(*page* 33) With a few exceptions noted in the appropriate places, quotations from letters by missionaries of the London Missionary Society on this page and on all succeeding pages are from the archive of the Council for World Missions, deposited in the Library of the School of Oriental and African Studies, University of London. Individual letters are referred to by date rather than by box and folder number.

CHAPTER THREE

(*page* 67) The report of the Civil Commissioner for Namaqualand is taken from *The Cape Coloured People: 1652–1937*, by J.S. Marais (1957).

CHAPTER FOUR

(*page* 77) An account of the 'summit meeting' at Nooitgedacht appears in *The Road to the North: South Africa 1852–1886*, by J.A. Agar-Hamilton (1938). It is mentioned also in *Kimberley: Turbulent City*, by Brian Roberts (1976).

CHAPTER FIVE

(*page* 91) The 'memorial' drawn up by the missionaries who met at Dikgatlhong appears in *Robert Moffat: Pioneer in Africa*, by Cecil Northcutt (1961). The destruction of the community at Dikgatlhong is mentioned in *The Colonisation of the Southern Tswana: 1870–1900*, by Kevin Shillington (1985).

CHAPTER SEVEN

(*page* 112) *Voyage to Cochin-China: to which is Annexed an Account of a Journey to the Residence of the Chief of the Booshuana*, by John Barrow (1806). (Reprinted in *South African Explorers*, ed. Eric Axelson (1954).)

(*page* 117) All quotations from Robert and Mary Moffat's letters are taken from *The Lives of Robert and Mary Moffat*, by John Scott Moffat (1886). Some of the passages appear also in Northcutt, op. cit. *Beloved Partner: Mary Moffat of Kuruman*, by Mora Dickson (1976), is based on Mary's letters and gives the reader a good idea of her epistolary style.

(*page* 118) *The Matabele Journals of Robert Moffat 1829–1860*, 2 vols., ed. J.P.R. Wallis (1954).

(*page* 126) Livingstone's description of the '*English path*' is taken from *David Livingstone's South African Papers*, ed. I. Schapera (1974).

CHAPTER NINE

(*page* 144) 'The Journey', in *Collected Poems*, by Yvor Winters (1952).

CHAPTER TEN

(*page* 156) *The Ruined Cities of Mashonaland*, by J. Theodore Bent (1892).

(*page* 157) On Hartley, Viljoen, and Jacobs: *To the Banks of the Zambesi*, by B.V. Bulpin (1954).

(*page* 158) (footnote) *David Livingstone: Family Letters*, 2 vols., ed. I. Schapera (1959).

(*page* 165) (footnote) Rhodes on 'the Kafir parson': *The Founder: Cecil Rhodes and the Pursuit of Power*, by Robert I. Rotberg (1988).

CHAPTER ELEVEN

(*pages* 170–73) 'Stellaland' and 'Goshen' make an appearance in many histories of the region. I have relied chiefly on Agar-Hamilton, op. cit.; Shillington, op. cit., and *The Bechuanaland Protectorate*, by A. Sillery (1952).

(*page* 180) A description of 'The Black Watch' appears in *Mafeking: A Victorian Legend*, by Brian Gardner (1966). This is also my source for the numbers of black and Coloured fatalities during the siege. *Baden-Powell*, by T.J. Jeal (1991), strenuously defends its subject against the charge made by both Gardner and Pakenham in *The Boer War* (cited on page 155) that Baden-Powell deliberately allowed large numbers of the black inhabitants of the town to starve to death.

CHAPTER TWELVE

(*pages* 191–2) Quotations from Rhodes on Bechuanaland and 'the road' are taken successively from *Rhodes*, by Sarah Gertrude Millin (1933); *The Scramble for Southern Africa 1877–1895*, by D.M. Schreuder (1980); *Cecil Rhodes: The Colossus of Southern Africa*, by J.G. Lockhart and C.M. Woodhouse (1963); and Rotberg, op. cit.

(*page* 192) Rhodes on 'humiliation': Rotberg, op. cit.

(*page* 192) For the protocol defining Bechuanaland's borders: *A History of Ngamiland: 1750 to 1906*, by Thomas Tlou (1983).

CHAPTER THIRTEEN

(*page* 204) On Seretse Khama's education: *Tshekedi*, by Mary Benson (1958).

(*page* 205) On the road from Francistown to Okavango: *Kalahari Sands*, by Frank Debenham (1952).

(*pages* 205–6) On the crimes and punishment of Phinehas McIntosh: *The Flogging of Phinehas McIntosh*, by Michael Crowder (1988).

CHAPTER FIFTEEN

The personal diaries, letters, and papers written by Livingstone during his time in southern Africa are best read in the editions produced by I. Schapera: *David Livingstone: Family Letters*, op. cit.; *David Livingstone's South African Papers*, op. cit.; and *Livingstone's Private Journals 1851–53*, 2 vols. (1960). It is from these, from Livingstone's *Missionary Travels*, and from *The Last Journals of David Livingstone in Central Africa: From 1865 to his Death*, ed. H. Waller, 2 vols. (1874), that all quotations in this chapter have been taken. I am indebted also to two relatively recent biographies: *David Livingstone*, by T.J. Jeal (1973), and *David Livingstone: The Dark Interior*, by Oliver Ransford (1978), both of which bring us closer to the man than his Victorian hagiographers would have wished. *Mackenzie's Grave*, by Owen Chadwick (1959), which deals with the disastrous mission to the Shire Highlands in Malawi – an enterprise which was inspired by Livingstone and more or less abandoned to its fate by him – is also a revealing piece of work.

CHAPTER SIXTEEN

(*page* 235) On the position, historically speaking, of the Bushmen and the Kgalagadi: *A History of Northern Botswana*, by J. Mutero Chirenje (1977).

(*pages* 238–9) On the attempt to wipe out the Hereros of Namibia: *The Scramble for Africa*, by Thomas Pakenham (1991), and *History of Southern Africa*, by Kevin Shillington (1991).

CHAPTER NINETEEN

(*page* 276) Rhodes on the 'rich auriferous indications' of Mashonaland: Rotberg, op. cit.

(*page* 278) On the importance of the 'lure of Ophir' to the history of the region: *A History of Rhodesia*, by Robert Blake (1977).

CHAPTER TWENTY

(*page* 301) The quotations from the missionaries on the impending destruction of the Ndebele people, and the remark about the 'total missionary failure' that had led to these utterances, are taken from *Prelude to Imperialism*, by H.A.C. Cairns (1965).

CHAPTER TWENTY-ONE

(*page* 307) (footnote) Rhodes on Kipling and Disraeli: *The Strange Ride of Rudyard Kipling*, by Angus Wilson (1977).

(*pages* 316–17) The descriptions of Lobengula by Fry and Moffat are taken from *Rhodes and Rhodesia: The White Conquest of Zimbabwe: 1884–1902*, by Arthur Keppel-Jones (1983); that by Thompson from Rouillard (ed.), op. cit; the others from *The Passing of the Black Kings*, by A.M. Hole (1928). Johnson's summing-up of Lobengula's character and political situation appears in his autobiography, *Great Days* (1940). So do the details of his fee for delivering the Pioneer column to its destination. In that volume Johnson implies that he simply forgot about the grant of land the Company owed him. 'Perhaps,' he writes jocosely, fifty years after the event, 'it may still be waiting for me!'

(*page* 317) (footnote) Shippard's letter is quoted in Rotberg, op. cit.

(*page* 318) The first quotation in this section is from Johnson, op. cit.; the penultimate one from Millin, op. cit.; the others are from Keppel-Jones, op. cit.

(*page* 319) Versions of Kulumani's life can be found in Agar-Hamilton, op. cit.; Keppel-Jones, op. cit.; *Path of Blood*, by Peter Becker (1966); *Bulawayo: The Historic Battleground of Rhodesia*, by Oliver Ransford (1968).

(*page* 322) The terms of Rhodes's (fourth) will: Rotberg, op. cit.

(*page* 323) Rhodes on Empire and the Anglo-Saxon race: Rotberg, op. cit.

CHAPTER TWENTY-FOUR

(*page* 358) The quotation is from Kipling's poem, 'The White Man's Burden'.